INVISIBLE INSTITUTIONALISMS

Taking its cue from theoretical and ideological calls to challenge globalisation as a dynamic of homogenisation – and resistance – as led from, and directed against, the Global North, this volume asks: what can we see when we shift the lens beyond a North–South binary?

Based on empirical studies of 'frontier-zones' of legal globalisation in India, Pakistan and Latin America, the book adopts an original format. Framed as a relational dialogue between newer as well as more prominent scholars within the field, from various cores through to postcolonial academic peripheries, it questions structural variables in the shadows of legal globalisation and how we as scholars build a space for critique.

Invisible Institutionalisms

Collective Reflections on the Shadows of Legal Globalisation

Edited by
Swethaa S Ballakrishnen
and
Sara Dezalay

• HART •
OXFORD • LONDON • NEW YORK • NEW DELHI • SYDNEY

HART PUBLISHING

Bloomsbury Publishing Plc

Kemp House, Chawley Park, Cumnor Hill, Oxford, OX2 9PH, UK

1385 Broadway, New York, NY 10018, USA

29 Earlsfort Terrace, Dublin 2, Ireland

HART PUBLISHING, the Hart/Stag logo, BLOOMSBURY and the Diana logo are trademarks of Bloomsbury Publishing Plc

First published in Great Britain 2021

A catalogue record for this book is available from the British Library.

Library of Congress Cataloging-in-Publication data

Names: Ballakrishnen, Swethaa S., editor. | Dezalay, Sara, editor.

Title: Invisible institutionalisms : collective reflections on the shadows of legal globalisation / edited by Swethaa S. Ballakrishnen and Sara Dezalay.

Description: Oxford, UK ; New York, NY : Hart Publishing, an imprint of Bloomsbury Publishing, 2021. | Includes bibliographical references and index.

Identifiers: LCCN 2020038503 (print) | LCCN 2020038504 (ebook) | ISBN 9781509930210 (hardback) | ISBN 9781509943128 (paperback) | ISBN 9781509930227 (Epub) | ISBN 9781509930234 (epdf)

Subjects: LCSH: Law and globalization. | Law—International unification. | New institutionalism (Social sciences)

Classification: LCC KZ1268 .I58 2020 (print) | LCC KZ1268 (ebook) | DDC 340/.115—dc23

LC record available at https://lccn.loc.gov/2020038503

LC ebook record available at https://lccn.loc.gov/2020038504

ISBN: HB: 978-1-50993-021-0
ePDF: 978-1-50993-023-4
ePub: 978-1-50993-022-7

Typeset by Compuscript Ltd, Shannon

To BG and DBW
who first invited us to the table.

FOREWORD

Where the Wild Things Are: India as Legal Education

MARC GALANTER

Toward the end of my first year of law school, the United States Supreme Court decided *Brown v Board of Education*,[1] holding racially segregated schools to be unconstitutional. I can recall my exhilaration and feeling of validation that the law, which had disappointingly seemed so dedicated to maintaining existing patterns of privilege and so resistant to the wider sweep of justice, did indeed have a core that was benign and progressive and, I imagined, a capacity to transform society closer to democratic ideals.

A few years later I envisioned going to India, a place about which I knew very little. I was drawn by Jawaharlal Nehru's *The Discovery of India*[2] and especially engaged by Heinrich Zimmer's *Philosophies of India*.[3] At the same time, one of the things that attracted my interest was the struggle to abolish untouchability, which I naively assumed was closely analogous to the struggle for civil rights in the United States. My picture of that struggle was enlarged by reading Morroe Berger's *Equality by Statute*,[4] parts of Emerson and Haber's massive *Political and Civil Rights in the United States*[5] and C. Vann Woodward's *The Strange Career of Jim Crow*.[6] Looking for material about comparable developments in India in a downtown Chicago bookstore, I chanced on a copy of Dr Ambedkar's *What Congress and Gandhi have done to the Untouchables*[7] which raised the suspicion that notwithstanding the parallels, the Indian situation might be profoundly different.

[1] *Brown v Board of Education*, 347 US 483 (1954).

[2] Jawaharlal Nehru, *The Discovery of India* (New York, John Day, 1946).

[3] Heinrich Zimmer, *Philosophies of India*, Joseph Campbell (ed) (New York, Meridian Books, 1957).

[4] Morroe Berger, *Equality by Statute: Legal Controls over Group Discrimination* (New York, Columbia University Press, 1952).

[5] Thomas I Emerson and David Haber, *Political and Civil Rights in the United States* (2 vols) (Buffalo CO, Dennis & Co, 1952).

[6] Comer Vann Woodward, *The Strange Career of Jim Crow* (New York, Oxford University Press, 1955).

[7] BR Ambedkar, *What Congress and Gandhi have done to the Untouchables* (Bombay, Thacker & Co Ltd, 1945).

A year after graduating from law school, I went off to India on a Fulbright scholarship; the topic of my project was the abolition of untouchability, which I imagined would resemble the civil rights drama playing out in the United States. I encountered a world vastly different than my training had led me to expect or equipped me to deal with. Immersion in another culture is a celebrated but not painless method for exposing our presuppositions and showing us that familiar arrangements are problematic rather than the way things are supposed to be. I had not been a student of India, but a law student and before that a philosophy student. My only venture outside the United States had been a brief trip to Canada. India provided a profound cultural shock both generally and specifically to my newly acquired legal persona. The spectacular display of familiar elements arrayed in dramatically different ways was especially well suited to expose the contingency of my picture of what law was like.

That picture, I should emphasise, was not the product of extensive experience with the American or any other legal system. It was the picture I had acquired in the course of going to law school – an elaborated and detailed version of the hazier picture I grew up with as a mid-twentieth century, middle-class, white American. That picture itself was fractured: on the one hand I worried about conservative forces limiting reform and perpetuating injustice; on the other hand, the law seemed a benign but clumsy presence that gradually, with some slippage and friction, might nudge behaviour in the surrounding society toward alignment with its principles of freedom, equality and fraternity. Particular segments of this behaviour might, I imagined, be deliberately modified by appropriate alterations of legal rules. Hence law could be used to re-design and improve social arrangements; it could guide and monitor the transformation of social life.

In the late 1950s, at the very time of my exposure to India, two Harvard law professors assembled an influential set of teaching materials that depicted the American legal system as a 'Great Pyramid of Legal Order',[8] a benign but balky instrument for improving social institutions, filtering out old inefficiencies and injustices. Hart and Sacks provided a picture of the normal shape of legal reality – a picture that proved sufficiently resilient to withstand dislodgement by ordinary experience of counter-instances. I didn't encounter the Hart-Sacks materials until a few years after my first stay in India. But when I did it was with a sense of recognition that I had emerged from law school with a similar view of American law as a basically benign hierarchic order, tightly articulated to the surrounding society, and possessed of an internal dynamic of evolutionary improvement.

[8] Henry M Hart and Albert M Sacks, *The Legal Process: Basic Problems in the Making and Application of Law* (mimeographed, 1957), published in book form in 1994, edited by William N Eskridge and Philip P Frickey. On the setting and influence of these materials, see Charles L Barzun, 'The Forgotten Foundations of Hart and Sacks' (2013) 99(1) *Virginia Law Review* 1.

Then came India! To one not socialised to screen out its challenges and contradictions, India presented a series of lessons that undermined my expectations of consonance and correspondence between society and its legal order. To a naïve and curious student, India proffered instead a set of bewildering and discomfiting possibilities. To summarise in propositional form – with an assist from hindsight – the encounter with India suggested that:

- A legal system might flourish and become deeply rooted although dissonant with central cultural values;
- A legal system may be internally disparate, embodying discordant norms and institutionalising conflicting practices at different levels and in different agencies;
- The divergence of legal norm and social practice is not transient and exceptional, but normal and institutionalised;
- Deliberate legal changes do not routinely produce the effects that their proponents seek or avow; and the effects they do produce are in some measure (sometimes in large measure), unanticipated;
- The effects of legal regulation depend not only on the conduct of legal authorities but equally on the consumers or users of the law and their differential capacity to use or resist the law;
- Law as a system of symbols diverges from, and obscures, the law as a system of operative controls.

That is a rather abstract catalogue of my second legal education. It didn't take place in an instant. But while it was happening the experience was something like that of the young lawyer in a story that I heard when I first travelled around India, observing lawyers and courts.

> A fresh junior lawyer was dispatched by his senior in Calcutta to argue his first case in a remote district town. At the hearing, after a long argument, the young lawyer prevailed. He was elated and immediately proceeded to the telegraph office and wired his senior 'Justice is done.' Exhausted, he retired to his hotel and fell into a deep sleep. He was rudely awakened by a pounding on the door. It was a messenger with a return telegram, which he tore open hastily to find a message 'Appeal at once.'

Having cherished this as a characteristically Indian story – full of cynical wisdom about the disjunction of law and justice – I was bemused when some years later I heard it told in America as a story about American lawyers. Many years after that, when I was researching jokes about lawyers, I discovered that it was originally an American story that had been around from the early twentieth century.[9]

[9] The joke is discussed in M Galanter, *Lowering the Bar: Lawyer Jokes and Legal Culture* (Madison WI, University of Wisconson Press, 2005), at pp 233–36.

This reflected the larger realisation that much of what I once thought peculiar to India turned out to be pertinent when I looked closer to home and discovered that, as in India, law here in the US is a realm in which we find wild and unexpected things wandering through the movie set of the Great Pyramid.

The contributions to this unusual book reveal surprising journeys and unexpected discoveries that upend our naïve expectations of the directionality of scholarly inquiry and the shape of scholarly careers.

Madison, WI
July 2020

ACKNOWLEDGEMENTS

Every book is a sum of gratitude. This one perhaps more than others, which is why a separate acknowledgment section feels restrictive. For one, this book reflects conversations over many years and has been shaped and formed (aptly) by more invisible actors than we can name on a page. Further, the structure of this book is predicated on reflexive recall, so attributions of gratitude form much of its substance, certainly well beyond this section. Still, there are several debts that call for explicit, visible mention. We hope to do them justice here.

Our deepest gratitude is to the contributors who trusted the format to keep talking with us and each other, not always knowing what we meant when we asked them to go on a journey or offered them carte blanche. We had ideas of the many books this could have been, but it is *this* one because of their trusting our prompts at different stages and the fairly ambiguous demands we made on them.

For trusting this ambitious project to actually *be* a book, we thank Ulrike Schultz and Sinead Moloney who introduced us to Kate Whetter at Hart and gave us a chance to pitch this project. From almost the first instant we mentioned it to her, Kate was sold on the idea. Kate's early enthusiasm and confidence in the project helped us soldier on when we were still in two minds about whether we had the makings of a book (an unease we unpack in the *Introduction*), and the anonymous reviewers she solicited gave us important early feedback that structured its tone and trajectory. If Kate's conviction (and Hart's contract) helped institutionalise the commitments to and from authors, it was Joanne Choulerton, Rosamund Jubber, Rosemarie Mearns, Emma Platt, and Linda Staniford who offered structure to the processes that would actually produce it. Ros and Rosie were crucial to helping us seamlessly coordinate the many moving pieces of the editorial process over the years. Linda and Jo were key to ensuring the drafts became proofs, and it was Emma who made the book have a presence beyond these internal processes. For lending us the most perfect image that would hold this book, we thank Gail Tarantino. Gail's image and her statement offer an important meta-theme for this project and we are grateful for both her generosity and the work's many synergies. For working with Gail and bringing this image to life as a cover, we thank Ben Anslow.

As we lay out in the book, the Law and Society Association was central to our ability to have the meetings that produced the many conversations within this book. Many thanks to the administration at LSA – and in particular, to Penelope Andrews, Steve Boutcher, Heather Haley, Melissa King, Kris Monty, Kim Lane Scheppele, and Megan Warren – for making these meetings possible and to the International Research Collaborative (IRC) that funded some of our participants' travel to them. Greg Shaffer and Terry Halliday's collaborative research network (CRN 36) was a network home for our IRC over the years, and comments from those who attended these sessions were crucial to shaping this book, including as a resource for culling the final contributors who would eventually make its contents. For these many earlier conversations, collaborations, and iterations of what eventually became this book project, we thank Rick Abel, Mohsin Alam, Bernadette Atuahene, Anurima Banerji, Binyamin Blum, Kim Chanbonpin, Agnes Chong, John Comaroff, Josephine Dawuni, Rohit De, Jean-Phillipe Dequen, Ronit Dinovitzer, Klaas Eller, Manuel Gomez, Priya Gupta, Terry Halliday, Sandile Hlatshwayo, Y-Vonne Hutchinson, Aniruddha Jairam, Ron Levi, Pavan Mamidi, Amaya Marin, Nancy Reichman, Nicholas Robinson, Cesar Rosado, Rupali Samuel, Susan Silbey, Carole Silver, Julia Stephens, Joyce Sterling, and Peer Zumbansen.

In addition to these LSA meetings and conversations, we are grateful to other fora where parts of this book were discussed, presented, and workshopped at different stages. Our deepest gratitude goes to Yves Dezalay, whose relentless passion and feedback we relied on as we built this project over the years. Special thanks to colleagues and commentators who read parts of the manuscript at the Harvard Institute for Global Law and Policy 2020 Workshop at the Graduate Institute in Geneva, and at the 2019 Spring and 2020 Summer Intellectual Life Workshops at the UCI School of Law. At the IGLP workshop, the writing group convened by Charlie Peevers and Filipe Calvao offered important reader perspective that allowed us to position this book's introduction. Many thanks to Rabiat Akande, Jessika Eichler, Cynthia Farid, Yang Liu, Miriam Matinda, Reeju Ray, and Dinesha Samararatne for thoughtful comments during the workshop, and to Deval Desai, Preeti Narayan, Rose Parfitt, and Oishik Sircar during conversations after. At UCI Law, Sameer Ashar and Carrie Menkel-Meadow offered respondent comments at a faculty workshop that helped us make crucial final edits before the book went to press. Comments and reactions from Vic Fleischer, David Kaye Stephen Lee, Carroll Seron, Greg Shaffer, and Ann Southworth were really helpful in clarifying pitch and import at different stages of writing and conception.

This book's *long table* framing was an extension of the *Transnational Feminism Long Table* at NYU Abu Dhabi co-hosted with Fawzi Afzal Khan, and May Al Dabbagh's *Making Space Workshop* (with Pato Hebert) was crucial to 'making space' for this idea to emerge and take shape. This book's approach also built on discussions about epistemology beyond a North-South binary in the framework of a 2016 workshop at the Cluster of Excellence *The Formation of Normative Orders* at Goethe Universität, Frankfurt. Our gratitude goes to Stefan Kadelbach for hosting the event, to Romain Bertrand for walking us through his own intellectual journey of building history on an equal footing with globalisation's so-called undersides, as well as Keith Breckenridge, Isabel Feichtner, Jeremy Gould, Jonathan Klaaren, Heinz Klug, Jay Krishnan, Sol Picciotto, Peter Rosenblum and Ute Röschenthaller for their insights. Our project also found a home at Cardiff University, particularly at its *Law and Global Justice Centre*, and we are thankful to David Boucher, Branwen Gruffydd Jones, John Harrington and Ambreena Manji. For creative extensions that came from these projects, we thank Eman Abdelhadi, Uma Chakravarti, Hazem Harb, Ayesha Omer, Tina Orlandini, Nighat Said Khan, Adrianne Koteen, and Deepak Unnikrishnan.

For helping us think through important logics and debates at different stages of writing this manuscript, including reading drafts and responding to pitches of our argument, we are grateful for conversations with and comments from Meghaa Ballakrishnen, Berenice Cleeve, Rabie Kadri, Veena Ganesh, Bryon Fong, Peter Goodrich, Chaumtoli Huq, Raya Lakova, and Alex Streim. For research and editing assistance, we are grateful for the keen reading of Bella Furth, the administrative handling of Laura Castillo and Diana Pangan, and to the librarians at the University of California Irvine School of Law, especially to Jessica Pierucci who helped source many of the comparative materials, and to Dianna Sahhar and Jeff Latta who made sure we had the all of the academic resources we needed.

For a book about networks and recursive ties, it is fitting to end this section on the bonds that tie us whole and together. Our families have always been at our core, and they form the very visible orienting logics that bind us to our deepest selves, to each other, and to this book. Across continents, time-zones, and parallel lives, our constants have stayed the same and at the root of our strengths. For feeding us and nourishing us before we knew how to sit at any tables, we thank Amma, Appa, Berenice, and Yves. For bringing us to *this* table together and building families of choice with us over the years, we thank (and dedicate this book to) Bryant and David. For giving us reasons to laugh and roll our eyes, for being the grandest things we have yet done with our lives, and for being our most optimistic hope of future table conversations, Elena and Magi have our hearts' deepest, brightest pieces.

Swethaa S Ballakrishnen
Irvine, California
[Madras, India]

Sara Dezalay
Paris, France
[Cardiff, Wales]
August 2020

CONTENTS

LIST OF CONTRIBUTORS

Swethaa S Ballakrishnen is an Assistant Professor of Law (and, by courtesy, of Sociology, Asian American Studies, and Criminology, Law and Society) at the University of California, Irvine. Employing a range of socio-legal methods, their research investigates the intersections between law, globalisation and stratification from a global south, feminist perspective. Ballakrishnen's first monograph, Accidental Feminism, was published by Princeton University Press in 2021; and their research has appeared in, among other journals, the Law and Society Review, Law and Social Inquiry, Feminist Legal Studies, International Journal of the Legal Profession, and Canadian Review of Sociology. In addition to their affiliations at UC Irvine, Ballakrishnen is affiliated faculty at the Harvard Law School Center on the Legal Profession, and on the elected board of trustees of both the ISA Research Committee on Sociology of Law, as well as the Law and Society Association.

Shamnad Basheer (14 May 1976 – c 8 August 2019) was an Indian legal scholar and founder of the blog *SpicyIP*. He was also the founder of IDIA, a trust which works on making legal education accessible for underprivileged students. Basheer was a Ministry of Human Resource Development Chaired Professor of Intellectual Property Law at the WBNUJS, Kolkata, and the Frank H Marks Visiting Associate Professor of Intellectual Property Law at the George Washington University Law School, and a research associate at the Oxford Intellectual Property Research Centre (OIPRC). In 2014 he was awarded the Infosys Prize in Humantities. He founded several initiatives such as SpicyIP, IDIA, P-PIL and Lex Biosis. Basheer intervened in the landmark *Novartis* case, filed a number of other public interest litigations and took the initiative to bring about changes in the IPR regime in India.

Kate Bedford is an interdisciplinary scholar with a background in political economy, development, socio-legal studies, and gender/sexuality studies. Her first monograph (*Developing Partnerships: Gender, Sexuality and the Reformed World Bank* (University of Minnesota Press, 2009) explored the World Bank's gender and development lending in Latin America. She is involved in a new project exploring the consequences of the turn to law within gender and development. Kate is also interested in gambling. In 2008 she began a project on the gendered political economy of gambling regulation, using commercial and non-commercial bingo to think in new ways about the regulation of everyday speculation. In 2019 she published *Bingo Capitalism: The Law and Political Economy of Everyday Gambling* (Oxford University Press).

Rachel Brulé is Assistant Professor of Global Development Policy at Boston University's Frederick S Pardee School of Global Studies. Her research expertise spans political economy, development, gender, representation, and migration. She combines careful causal identification with innovative theory-building to test the impact of changing political institutions on substantive equality in society, the economy, and politics. Her articles are published and forthcoming in the *Journal of Politics*, the *Journal of Development Economics*, and *Asian Survey*, and her first book, *Women, Power, and Property: The Paradox of Gender Equality Laws in India*, will be published by Cambridge University Press in summer 2020.

Eve Darian-Smith is Professor and Chair of Global and International Studies at the University of California, Irvine. Trained as a lawyer, historian, and anthropologist, she is interested in postcolonialism, legal pluralism, global governance, authoritarianism and sociolegal theory. Her first book *Bridging Divides: The Channel Tunnel and English Legal Identity in the New Europe* (University of California Press, 1998) won the Law & Society Association Herbert Jacob Book Prize. A more recent book, *Laws and Societies in Global Contexts* (Cambridge University Press, 2013), won the Kevin Boyle Book Award. She is a co-editor of a book series 'Global and Insurgent Legalities' with Duke University Press, and is on the editorial boards of leading socio-legal journals such as *Social & Legal Studies* and *Canadian Journal of Law and Society*. She has also been an associate editor of the *Law & Society Review* and *American Ethnologist*.

Fabio de Sa e Silva is Assistant Professor of International Studies and the Wick Cary Professor of Brazilian Studies at the University of Oklahoma. He is also an affiliated fellow at Harvard Law School's Center on the Legal Profession. He studies the social organisation and the political impact of law and justice in Brazil and comparatively.

Sara Dezalay is a Senior Lecturer in law and international relations at the Cardiff School of Law and Politics. Anchored in political sociology, her research focuses on the roles played by lawyers in international non-governmental markets for peace-building and conflict resolution; international dispute settlement mechanisms; and state transformations in the African South. In this last aspect of her work, she is pursuing a field-building strategy to reinvigorate debates on the position of Africa in globalization. She has edited and co-edited four cross-cutting special issues for the Journal of Law and Society, Actes de la recherche en sciences sociales, and Politique africaine. Published in English, French, and German, her research has appeared in, among other journals, Actes de la recherche en sciences sociales, Cultures & Conflits, Critique internationale, International Criminal Law Review, International journal of the legal profession, International Journal of Socio-Economics, Journal of Law and Society, Law and Contemporary Problems. Parallel to her position at the Cardiff School of Law and Politics, she is a Visiting Fellow at King's College London, Associate researcher at the Institut des Mondes Africains in Paris and elected member of the editorial board of Actes de la recherche en sciences sociales. Since August 2020, she is also associate judge (appointed by the UNHCR) at the French national court for asylum rights.

Yves Dezalay is a Directeur de recherches emeritus at the CNRS (Centre National de la Recherche Scientifique). He was trained and worked closely for 20 years with Pierre Bourdieu at the Centre de Sociologie Européenne (CSE) a research institution affiliated with the Ecole des Hautes en Sciences Sociales (EHESS.) and Paris 1 Sorbonne. He has also been an affiliated scholar of the American Bar Foundation. For most of his professional life, his main topic of interest has been the internationalisation of the legal field in relation with other professional fields of expertise. He has published 12 books, including 8 in collaboration with Bryant Garth, with whom he has worked closely for 30 years. Main titles: *Dealing in virtue: International Commercial Arbitration and the Emergence of an International Legal Order* (University of Chicago Press, 1996); *The Internationalization of Palace Wars: Lawyers, Economists and the Contest for Latin American States* (University of Chicago Press, 2002); *Asian Legal Revivals: Lawyers-Compradors and Colonial Strategies in the Reshaping of Asian States* (University of Chicago Press, 2010) and *Law as reproduction and revolution: an interconnected history of the internationalisation of national legal hierarchies* (University of California Press, forthcoming 2021). In 2009, he was awarded the International Scholar Prize by the Law & Society Association.

Marc Galanter is the John and Rylla Bosshard Professor Emeritus of Law and South Asian Studies at the University of Wisconsin – Madison and formerly LSE Centennial Professor at the London School of Economics and Political Science. A leading figure in the empirical study of the legal system, he has been editor of the Law & Society Review, President of the Law and Society Association, Chair of the International Commission on Folk Law and Legal Pluralism, a Guggenheim Fellow, and a Fellow of the Center for Advanced Study in the Behavioral Sciences. Much of his early work was on India and he is recognized as a leading American student/scholar of the Indian legal system. Galanter is an Honorary Professor of the National Law School of India, served as advisor to the Ford Foundation on legal services and human rights programs in India, and was retained as an expert by the government of India in the litigation arising from the Bhopal disaster. He is also the author of a number of highly regarded and seminal studies of litigation and disputing in the United States including *Why the 'Haves' Come Out Ahead: Speculations on the Limits of Legal Change*, one of the most-cited articles in the legal literature and the *Tournament of Lawyers* (with Paley, 1991), widely viewed as the most robust explanation of the growth and transformation of large law firms.

Bryant Garth is Distinguished Professor Emeritus at the University California-Irvine School of Law, where he began in 2012, and Director Emeritus and Affiliated Research Professor at the American Bar Foundation. His scholarship focuses on the legal profession, the sociology of law, globalisation, and legal education. He is a graduate of Yale (BA 1972), Stanford Law School (JD 1975) and the European University Institute in Florence (PhD 1979). He began his career working with Mauro Cappelletti on the Florence Access to Justice Project, which resulted in five published volumes (1977–79). He has been Dean at Indiana University School of Law – Bloomington and at Southwestern Law School – Los Angeles, and Director of the American Bar Foundation. He served as co-editor of the *Journal of Legal Education* from 2011–14. He is also on the Executive Coordinating Committee of the 'After the J.D.' project, the first longitudinal study of the US legal profession, and the Board of the NALP Foundation; and he chairs the Advisory Committee of the Law School Survey of Student Engagement.

Yugank Goyal is a curious person, who likes to observe his surroundings and then pen it under some important theory he learned in books and schools. He has written in some pretty good journals in vocabulary that (only) academics would comprehend, and travelled to fancy places to talk about what common people would often already know. He has studied here and there, but he truly learns from his experiences, and connecting with people. Few things he does are useful, however. His pupils admire his teaching (at OP Jindal Global University, India). He once prepared the *Gazetteer* of Karnal (a north Indian town), writing real life (theory-less) stories of a city and its people. More recently, he is helping build a school in Tumariya Ghat, an impoverished village in western Uttar Pradesh in India (if anyone wants to donate, please get in touch with him at ygoyal@jgu.edu.in.

Rahela Khorakiwala is a lawyer by training, having completed her law degree in India and her LLM at New York University School of Law. Rahela has worked as a legal consultant with the Ministry of Foreign Affairs in New Delhi and the World Bank in Kabul. She has completed the integrated MPhil/PhD from Jawaharlal Nehru University, New Delhi, where she did an ethnographic study of the colonial courts of India, studying them as a legal anthropologist. After completing a postdoctoral fellowship at the Max Planck Institute in Frankfurt, Rahela has most recently published her first book titled *From the Colonial to the Contemporary: Images, Iconography, Memories, and Performances of Law in India's High Courts* (Hart Publishing, 2019). Rahela has eight publications to her credit, including peer-reviewed contributions to the *Indian Law Review* and the *Asian Journal of Law and Society*. Her research has an extensive outreach as she has presented her work at several conferences across the world.

Maryam S Khan is a Research Fellow at the Institute of Development and Economic Alternatives (IDEAS) in Lahore, Pakistan, and presently an SJD candidate at the University of Wisconsin-Madison Law School. Maryam's published works and ongoing research interests focus on themes of socio-legal studies in post-colonial South Asia, including comparative constitutionalism, federalism and ethnicity-based politics, politics and sociology of the legal bar and the judiciary, institutional design of the court system, law and social movements, and law, development and globalisation.

Kalpana Kannabiran, feminist sociologist, legal scholar and rights advocate, is currently Professor and Director, Council for Social Development, Hyderabad, an ICSSR institute. She was part of the founding faculty of NALSAR University of Law where she taught sociology and law for a decade, 1999–2009, and is co-founder of Asmita Resource Centre for Women set up in 1991, where she has led the legal services and outreach programme. Recipient of the Amartya Sen Award for Distinguished Social Scientists 2012 in the field of law, her work has focused on understanding the social foundations of non-discrimination, structural violence, and questions of constitutionalism and social justice in India – with a specific focus on gender, sexual minorities, caste, *adivasi*/indigenous rights and disability rights.

Stefan Kroll is Senior Researcher at the Leibniz Peace Research Institute Frankfurt and the scientific coordinator of the Leibniz Research Alliance 'Crises in a globalised world'. Trained in social sciences, Kroll studies norms in international relations, informality in law and international politics as well as the politics and history of international law.

Carrie Menkel-Meadow is Distinguished Professor of Law (and Political Science) at the University of California, Irvine and AB Chettle Professor of Law, Dispute Resolution and Civil Procedure, Emerita at Georgetown University. She is the author of over 15 books and 200 articles on dispute resolution, the legal profession, feminist legal theory, legal education, socio-legal studies, globalisation and international law, and law and popular culture. She has been active in socio-legal studies for over 40 years and was awarded the American Bar Foundation's award for Outstanding Scholar in 2018 and the American Bar Association's (first ever) Award for Distinguished Scholarship and Contributions to the field in Dispute Resolution in 2011. She has taught in over 25 countries and is also a professional mediator and arbitrator.

Usha Natarajan is Associate Professor of International Law and Associate Director of the Center for Migration and Refugee Studies at the American University in Cairo. She uses post-colonial and Third World approaches to international law to explore the interrelation between development, environment, conflict, and migration. She is currently visiting Columbia University as Edward W Said Fellow. Natarajan leads several international research projects on law, environment, and migration. She received the 2016 IUCN Environmental Law Award for pioneering new approaches to law and the environment. Natarajan is a founding editor of the *TWAIL Review* and executive editor of the *African Yearbook of International Law*. Prior to joining the American University in Cairo, she worked with UNDP, UNESCO and the World Bank on law reform programmes in Asia.

Jules Naudet is an associate research professor (French title: CNRS Research Fellow) at the Centre d'Etudes de l'Inde et de l'Asie du Sud (EHESS), Paris. He is co-editor-in-chief of *La Vie des Idées/Books and Ideas* (an open-access online journal published by the Collège de France) as well as the Co-editor, along with Surinder Jodhka, of the book series 'Exploring India's Elite'. Naudet is the author of *Stepping into the Elite* (Oxford University Press, 2018), a comparative approach of the experience of upward social mobility in India, in France, and in the United States of America. He has furthered his approach of India's social stratifications through several quantitative articles published in the *South Asia Multidisciplinary Academic Journal (SAMAJ)* and in the *Socio-Economic Review*. He now dedicates his research to an ethnographic study of the role of sociability in power and wealth dynamics, doing fieldwork both in Paris and in New Delhi.

Andrés Palacios Lleras is a Colombian lawyer who specialises on competition law issues. He holds a BA in law from Universidad de Los Andes, an LLM degree from Harvard Law School, and a PhD from University College London. He is currently working with the Colombian transportation authority to improve the enforcement of the applicable regulation. He has published several academic articles about competition law in Latin America and is currently working on a book on this same subject.

Gitanjali Prasad currently leads advocacy efforts at iProbono, an organisation providing legal support to grassroots organisations for access to justice ends. Before this she worked at the Centre for Equity Studies (CES), a non-profit organisation in New Delhi, first as a researcher, primarily on empirical studies on exclusion in access to legal justice and on a project focused on urban rental housing discrimination in India, in addition to developing resources on social justice education. She later led the Delhi HAUSLA programme team at CES, which runs interventions on access to health and citizenship rights with and for the homeless community. Gitanjali majored in psychology at Wesleyan University in Connecticut for her undergraduate studies, and received a Masters at the Tata Institute of Social Sciences in Mumbai, where she specialised in Dalit and Tribal Social Work. Her Masters research submission was an ethnographic project on incarcerated women living with mental illness at the Tihar Jail complex in Delhi. During the course of research on the criminal justice system at CES, she enrolled in a bachelor of laws programme, which she completed in 2019.

Suryapratim Roy is Assistant Professor of Law, Trinity College Dublin. He works on Environmental Law and Legal Theory. He is the convenor of the Constitutional Governance and Social Change Research Group at Trinity.

Danish Sheikh is a PhD Candidate at the Melbourne Law School and a member of the Institute for International Law and the Humanities. His research is located at the intersections of law, literature and performance, drawing upon his work as an activist lawyer and theatre practitioner. He has law degrees from NALSAR University of Law, Hyderabad and the University of Michigan, Ann Arbor, which he attended on a Grotius Fellowship. His writing has been cited by the Supreme Court of India in 2018, shortlisted for the Jan Michalski Award in 2017 and won the Publishing Next Award in the same year.

Gail Tarantino, cover artist: Thinking of ways to interpret language and its myriad of meaning have been an ongoing thread in daily creative pursuits. Creating short narratives, translations and the distillation of language are a reoccurring fascination.

Ricocheting between painting, drawing & photography, ideas coalesce. Work can be viewed at *Fouladi Projects*, SFMOMA's Artist Gallery in San Francisco and *Uprise Art* in NYC.

David M Trubek is Voss-Bascom Professor of Law and Dean of International Studies Emeritus at the University of Wisconsin-Madison and a Senior Research Fellow at the Harvard Law School. He has written extensively on international and comparative law as well as other topics in legal studies and has published articles and books on the role of law in development, human rights, European integration, the changing role of the legal profession, and the impact of globalisation on legal systems and social protection schemes. He has also made contributions in critical legal theory, the sociology of law, and civil procedure.

Amy S Weissenbach is a PhD student in sociology at Columbia University. She completed an MPhil in History and Philosophy of Science at Cambridge University in 2019 and a BA in English Literature at Stanford University in 2017. Between 2015 and 2018, she also studied synthetic biology, worked as a research assistant in biosecurity, and participated in and contributed to an international genetic engineering competition.

David B Wilkins is the Lester Kissel Professor of Law, Vice Dean for Global Initiatives on the Legal Profession, and Faculty Director of the Center on the Legal Profession at Harvard Law School. He is also a Fellow of the Harvard University Edmond J Safra Foundation Center for Ethics, an International Research Fellow of the Oxford Centre on Professional Service Firms at the Said School of Business, a Senior Research Fellow of the Centre for Professional Service Firms at the Cass Business School, and a Senior Research Fellow of the American Bar Foundation. Professor Wilkins has written over 80 articles on the legal profession in leading scholarly journals and the popular press, and is the co-author or editor of five books, including *Diversity in Practice: Race, Class, and Gender in the Legal Profession and Professional Careers* (Cambridge University Press, 2016), and volumes on India (2017); Brazil (2018); and China (forthcoming 2021), published by Cambridge University Press, as part of the *Project on Globalization, Lawyers, and Emerging Economies* that he founded and directs. Professor Wilkins holds honorary degrees from Roger Williams University (2017) and Stockholm University (2012). In 2012, Professor Wilkins was elected to the American Academy of Arts and Sciences, and in 2014 he was selected as a Corresponding Member of the Spanish Royal Academy of Doctors.

Christopher Williams, a native from Chicago, received his undergraduate degree in Sociology from the University of Missouri. Afterwards he attended the University of California-Irvine school of law where he received his JD. Currently Chris is a graduate Neubauer Fellow in the Department of Sociology at the University of Chicago. His research interests are grounded in highlighting interlocking oppressions that disproportionately impact vulnerable populations. These interests motivate Christopher in thinking of praxis that transforms and eradicates the systemic oppression that vulnerable populations experience.

Introduction

Law, Globalisation and the Shadows *of Legal Globalisation*

SWETHAA S BALLAKRISHNEN AND SARA DEZALAY

This book emerged from a chance encounter – to the extent encounters can happen by chance in such a structured setting – at the 2013 annual meeting of the Law and Society Association (LSA). We were introduced to each other by giants in the field of law and society, who had independently decided that we had *things to say to each other*. On the face of it, this introduction made self-evident sense. We were then junior scholars – one in grad school at Stanford, the other starting a research fellowship at the Goethe Universität in Frankfurt. We were both researching themes broadly related to law and globalisation. Despite the very different institutions and geographies of our respective training – in India and the United States for the one, and in Europe and Canada for the other – we shared a common stock of words and concepts. Particularly, we had both been trained to *walk the talk* of legal globalisation studies across our empirical sites (the transformation of legal professions in India, and across Africa under the pull of globalisation, respectively) by using available templates to trace processes of diffusion, domination and resistance. We also had a similar perception of the deliberations involved to enter the academic market: as young scholars staking our claims in these established micro-fields, we were acutely aware of the tension of pitching marketable stories to the right audience.

We realised this introduction meant we were not just saying the things our interlocutors expected us to say to each other, we were also saying them in expected ways. Over the course of the evening, we would discover the layer of connectedness that has buttressed the production of this book – not the fact that we both were studying things in common. Rather, that in that study, in that process, we found ourselves as empathetic navigators. Yet, between stories of research and writing, trips and findings, we also found ourselves engaging in a self-reflexive process that would eventually become the backbone of this volume.

Our first interrogation revolved around the repertoire of words that we seemingly shared to study our respective empirical fields. We could not help but notice how we were speaking in code, and how that code was both useful and insular. In particular, we wondered about the weight of the lenses we used to see the worlds around us. At first, it was just about what those words meant, about the process of meaning-making, about how we were using words that were meant to be bridging difference but instead just going further into our own silos. We wondered as we spoke alike and apart about these concepts – What were the contours of worlds without shared language, worlds that depended on the meaning-making processes of those listening? Who were we talking to? Was 'talking to' what made our contribution relevant? What about all of our unwritten, unanalysed, under-theorised thoughts? Were they less important for having been had without structure, for not having been had within the confines of an existing conversation, for not, as we were trained to do (and as we now train *our* students to do) 'furthering the discipline'? As interdisciplinary researchers across law, sociology, international relations and area studies steeped in what felt like a relatable training, we wondered if we were even speaking *to* each other, not only due to our very different empirical foci but because of our very different trajectories, as a South Asian Tamil based in California, as a French-Irish woman who had moved between Florence (Italy), Toronto, Frankfurt and, later on, to Cardiff.

We also acutely, though uncomfortably, felt the limits of the lenses we used to study our respective empirical material. Our training and interests had steered us towards long-tested sites of law and society scholarship, focused on patterns of legal globalisation: *peripheries* and how those sites proved elastic, vulnerable or resilient to legal transfers, predominantly from the United States. But our respective empirical foci seemed to resist in unexpected ways these mainstream US templates of the sociology of legal professions. There were, in the one case, *female* lawyers at elite corporate law firms in India who were deeply embedded in a US-driven corporate legal globalisation, but not simply as *comprodoras*. Legal globalisation looked the same but with an unexpected twist, as it had fostered a niche of gender equality that would otherwise remain invisible without a gendered focus.[1] In the other case, resistance to mainstream scripts was both more obvious though not less problematic: Africa was simply a foil for (Western) conceptions about legal evolution. When not obliterated to the point of oblivion, African lawyers were either missionaries of the rule of law, or mercenaries of neo-colonialism. Legal globalisation appeared therefore Janus-faced: either *hyper-intensified* as at once politics *through* law and *against* law; or *unscripted* with legal professions deemed to be in their infancy requiring at once translation, mutation, conversion, catch-up.[2] We also wondered whether what we observed could be theorised as something different than mere exceptions or anomalies in relation to the orthodoxy of legal globalisation scripts. In particular, was the ongoing surge of populism in Europe and the United States challenging not only the policies and institutions of globalisation,

[1] SS Ballakrishnen, 'Just Like Global Firms: Unintended Gender Parity and Speculative Isomorphism in India's Elite Professions' (2019) 53(1) *Law & Society Review* 108–40.

[2] S Dezalay, 'Lawyers in Africa, Brokers of the State, Intermediaries of Globalization: A Case Study of the "Africa" Bar in Paris' (2018) 25(2) *Indiana Journal of Global Legal Studies* 639–69.

but also what we even think of as the global? Similarly, was the prominence taken by China (and increasingly, other emerging countries) questioning the position of the United States as unrivalled hegemon and therefore legal globalisation as a top-down, North–South diffusion process? *Were these shifts and shoves changing what we had taken for granted in the field we had learnt to study from a certain kind of perspective?*

The last interrogation sparked by our initial conversations was perhaps the least articulate and the most arduous to confront. What about our own positionality – not only *qua* aspiring scholars, but also as individuals whose lenses and trajectories had been shaped by specific local cultures, privileges, and encounters with the global? How did it inform the words we used to interpret our empirical material; how did it shape the way we defined the parameters themselves of what we *saw* in our empirical sites? We both had a sense of originating from geographies defined as peripheries in relation to a core – the United States. Each of us had pursued intensely international trajectories – we both understood the international to be a core resource for young scholars, especially those from the periphery, and that we had a relatively privileged access to that resource. Each of us, in our own way, had steered away from what could be seen as known homes – defined as our familial, social, and cultural background, but also *qua* our gendered identities. Of course, we had our capital reserves and advantages – some visible, others less so – but there were markers of otherness too, that were similarly ambiguous in their relational visibility. We were struck by what these reserves could be used for (and on whose behalf), where they seemed to matter, and the places where they decidedly were still at the periphery no matter our strides and progress. We pondered about access and its interactional weight: What did it take for our voices to be heard; and what did it mean for our voices to be heard not only despite, but also because of, our inner contradictions? What did it take to speak the same language but in a way that allowed for and embraced this dissonance?

This, in retrospect, is perhaps how the conversations that make this book started and how we were geared toward the question at the core of this volume: *What are the politics at play that made some empirical sites and processes visible, and not others?*

Certainly, our interrogations did not emerge in an intellectual vacuum. They constituted the backbone of the field we were both seeking to enter. Studies of law and globalisation have matured over the past 30 years, since the first utterance of the tandem 'law and globalisation' in the late 1990s, and much earlier with the first Law and Development movement, out of a succession of empirically-grounded theoretical understandings of dynamics of legal exports and evolution. There have been, over the years, field-induced pushes to question, redefine, and expand the globalising ambitions of these theoretical canvasses: to account for the 'failure' of legal transplants in various empirical sites across the Global South[3] and tentatively

[3] D Trubek, and M Galanter, 'Scholars in Self-Estrangement: Some Reflections on the Crisis in Law and Development Studies in the United States' (1974) *Wisconsin Law Review* 1062.

to explain why some concepts seem to 'get lost in translation' within the law and society field itself.[4]

From the turn of the 2010s, there have also been powerful theoretical – and ideological – pulls to question anew the parameters of the field and the methodologies best equipped to deal with it.[5] These accounts have challenged globalisation as a dynamic whose forces of homogenisation – and resistance – are led from and directed against a diffuse conception of the Global North. Yet, these shoves seem to continuously fathom new layers of a theoretical scaffolding that remains built as a binary: between an amorphous 'global' North opposed to a not-less amorphous 'global' South; between domination/oppression versus emancipation; between top-down or bottom-up transfers from the Global North to the Global South, and vice versa.

We wanted to ask, instead, what happens when we de-centre and enlarge the gaze? How can we stop looking at postcolonial sites as sites of reinvention, accommodation, or de-phasing;[6] and not just categorise them in relation to global hegemonic forces or as failures that are doomed to de-couple;[7] or even as revivals[8] of pre-existing patterns of globalisation? What will (can) we see if we look at legal globalisation as a polycentric process, where legal evolutions, social change and political dynamics are not simply defined by mimicry and resistance from the *top down*, or the *bottom up*?

As we reflect further below, our questions – and imagination – have also been deeply shaped by scholarship that has powerfully questioned the invisibilisation of voices from the periphery, as subaltern, as minorities, as women, as bodies straddling the gender binary. These voices, however, have themselves been incorporated into epistemic binaries, as *alternative, critical* currents to mainstream episteme. *We wanted to ask instead*: *what is the power process at play, not only in the distribution of epistemic knowledge as mainstream versus critical, but also in the authorial voices that are being catalogued as such*? What is driving these authors to push against mainstream scripts? And how does the process transform them? Are they trailblazers bound to be celebrated by academic cores, eventually? Or is this a peripheral stance delineating a peripheral position? Further, how do their gendered, racial, ethnic and geopolitical identities matter? How does their social sense of belonging (or not) inform their academic course, and with it, their lenses?

[4] Y Dezalay and BG Garth, 'Lost in translation: on the failed encounter between Bourdieu and Law and Society scholarship and their respective Blindness' in G de Burca, C Kilpatrick and J Scott (eds), *Critical legal perspectives on global governance. Liber amicorum David M. Trubek* (Oxford, Hart Publishing, 2013).

[5] E Darian-Smith and PC McCarty, *The global turn: theories, research designs, and methods for global studies* (Berkeley CA, University of California Press, 2017).

[6] L Benton, *Law and Colonial Cultures: Legal Regimes in World History, 1400–1900* (Cambridge and New York, Cambridge University Press, 2002).

[7] JW Meyer and B Rowan, 'Institutionalized Organizations: Formal Structure as Myth and Ceremony' (1977) 83(2) *American Journal of Sociology* 340–63.

[8] Y Dezalay and BG Garth, *Asian Legal Revivals. Lawyers in the Shadow of Empire* (Chicago IL, University of Chicago Press, 2010).

In other words: what do power structures and their impact on agency do to academic trajectories and registers?

Our intent in confronting these questions was not to launch ourselves into the impossible task (which we saw as ideologically perilous) of uncovering the 'real' invisible lying beneath or beyond the *visible* of mainstream scripts about legal globalisation, or of unpacking the 'authentic voice' of the oppressed invisibilised by dominant doxas. Nor was it to build an additional theoretical layer about the process and outcomes of legal globalisation in an uncharted world. Rather, we sought to build this collection as a *methodological proposition*. We invited our contributors to partake in an open-ended discussion, defined within the parameters of a *collective reflection* on the (in)visible of legal globalization. In turn, we expected that the *reflexivity* of each is what would allow for the *dialogue of all*. As we recount below, we built this process as a way to confront *simultaneously* what we perceived as three layers at play in the politics of (in)visibility of legal globalisation: (in)visible institutionalism as academic (il)legitimacy; (in)visible institutionalism as knowledge ortho/heterodoxy; and (in)visible institutionalism as social belonging/dissonance. And it is in such processual unpacking that this book begins.

I. Law and Society: Finding and Making Communities

As we embarked on this project, we knew of – and were part of – large networks that were involved in questioning our epistemes on law and globalisation – foremost, of course, the LSA International Research Collaboratives (IRCs), the IGLP[9] forums, and others like the discussions on 'transnational law' fostered at King's College London in recent years. Looking for smaller, more intimate conversations modelled in that flair, we started the first curation of our conversation in the form of a panel at the 2014 Law and Society annual meeting with people who we thought were doing the work that we theorised about: ie thinking about globalisation as a lived process that questioned rather than mapped on existing frameworks of analysis. The prompt was simple. We asked people to think about ways in which projects they were working on already were embedded in latent and patent structures. We urged them to think about their project differently and asked them to surface for us the nuance that we would not naturally know to see. At that first meeting, we asked: *What can we see when we are looking?* Following that early conversation and the participation from the audience, we became committed as a group to keeping this discussion alive and reinvesting the discourse into subsequent panel discussions in 2015, 2016 and 2017. Testament to the success of our discussion, we received the status of IRC from the LSA and RCSL[10] in 2015 and benefited from funding for the 2017

[9] Harvard Law School Institute for Global Law and Policy.
[10] Research Committee on Sociology of Law.

LSA Annual meeting in Mexico City to fund the participation of colleagues from India who would otherwise not have been able to attend the LSA. In 2014 we also integrated our inquiry into a sub-group, set up with the late Wes Pue, *Lawyers and Legal Imperialism(s)* of the RCSL International Working Group for Comparative Studies of Legal Professions.[11]

We could have left these curated conversations to be an end in themselves. As a way of building community, as a way of having people reconsider their research alongside relational others.[12] But as the years went on, much as we loved the cumulating projects and perspectives, as much as our community of scholars grew, we still struggled with the structure. Saddled with our training and its expectations, we felt forced to ask what this exercise was a *case of*. Did we want to build another theory of globalisation and law? (NO). Did we think all the criss-cross conversations were building to an end? (Not necessarily). But we did seek to have some testament of these conversations, and in 2017 started to think about the possibility of a book project that would illustrate this meaning-making we had begun to do with each other.[13]

Alongside this crystallisation were other questions of structure and resistance, some obvious, others more latent. First, after all we had said about thwarting embedded structure, did we even need to write a book? (Was such writing the best way to in fact thwart structure?) If we did write a book, what would this book look like? How could we have a book that did the work in the world we wished to share? Was it going to be another edited volume of projects on globalisation? (Was being that a bad thing in itself?) Could we think beyond the structures of edited volumes and still remain a useful, worthy contribution? (What, then, was worth? Who did it need to be useful to?) Would there be interest in such a process? (Was lack of interest something we needed to consider? And, if so, whose?) What would an academic exercise that took such a journey feel like? What would its rewards be? (Should rewards matter? And would it have meaning without reward?) It was this dithering that led us to the *Long Table*, a structure we deliberate on below.

[11] See http://rcsl.iscte.pt/rcsl_wg_professions.htm.

[12] Although this question of building community often also brings up the logic of building consensus, this was *not* at the core of this project. Instead, from the start, we were interested in difference and seemingly abrupt mis-connections and miscommunications as method for understanding globalisation, law, and society. On conversation building that *does* promote consensus, more generally, see instead, LE Susskind, S McKearnen and J Thomas-Lamar, *The consensus building handbook: A comprehensive guide to reaching agreement* (Thousand Oaks CA, Sage Publications, 1999).

[13] We are grateful to two of our readers, Sameer Ashar and Carrie Menkel-Meadow, for their pinpointing a sense of multidimensionality (Ashar) and multigenerationality (Menkel-Meadow) at play in this project's process. Ashar, borrowing from Lucie White's lawyering collaborative strategies, offers that we go from doctrine to building frameworks of the visible, to then recreating frameworks anew; and Menkel-Meadow's review was that of an 'intellectual décollage' that used temporality to cut, tear away and rework an original image. We offer these as two of many ways in which this can be *seen* – as we suggest in the Conclusion to this volume, a sight that is central to us – and we hope that in the future and upon re-reading, it offers new and other ways to percolate or seep or drain, without a fixed plan in your receptions. On the three dimensions of lawyering, see LE White, 'Collaborative Lawyering in the Field? On Mapping the Paths from Rhetoric to Practice' (1994) 1 *Clinical Law Review* 157.

II. The *Long Table* – *Imagining* Non-Structured Synergies in a Formal Setting

The liminal nature of this project was experienced before it was inevitably structured into theory – a striking commoditisation of our trained frameworks. As we explain above, we were part of many LSA conversations, often not recognising the potential these conversations had for a book project (again, a crutch of our trainings), without thinking about what these conversations were a case of. Some of this resistance to conceptualising the exchange was inherent in our premise itself: How do you name a thing that was birthed on the premise of not needing to be named? We also actively resisted building another theory of globalisation. We rejected the idea that there needed to be another meta-theory, another full approach to how something was meant to be dissected. This book, like our initial conversation, started with the acknowledgment that enough serious thinkers, scholars, and activists – many of whom we have learnt from, many cited in this book, more than a few of whom have contributed to this book and personally shaped us – have thought thoroughly about globalisation. It was not another theory that we wished to propose, as much as a space for exchange about it. The inquiry that we concerned ourselves with over the years was reiterative: When people, sharing seemingly common lenses but from different disciplinary perspectives and social geographies, talk at and to each other, what could we gain?

A first framing of our exercise came organically in December 2017 when Ballakrishnen hosted with Fawzia Afzal-Khan, a Pakistani feminist and professor of English, a 'long table' on transnational feminisms at NYU Abu Dhabi. Tired of talks and conferences that reinforced hierarchy, the idea of the long table borrowed from emerging traditions in performance studies – and was inspired by Marleen Gorris's film *Antonia's Line*.[14] The 'long table' was a performance/discussion format stylised and adapted by Lois Weaver, first as a performance project that toured internationally (2009–2012), and subsequently as a structured, stylised, open-ended, non-hierarchical format for interactional participation and intellectual political commitment. The idea of the long table is to structure conversation as a dinner party where conversation is the 'only course.' There are hosts who invite the community but anyone sitting at the table is a guest and an active performer. The table starts with enough free chairs with the idea that to participate, one simply takes an empty seat, or, as the performance proceeds, requests an empty seat from a sitting member, in order to have a 'seat at the table'. The 'tablecloth' (running baking-paper over tables, in our case), 'napkins' (sticky notes) and 'cutlery'

[14] In *Antonia's Line*, the protagonist continually extends her dinner table to accommodate a growing community of outsiders and eccentrics until, finally, the table must be moved out of doors. The Long Table brings what might often be seen as 'outside' in – to a realm of conviviality – while showing how every-day, domestic things which might remain hidden can be brought out – into a realm of public ideas and discourse. See also *Split Britches*: http://www.split-britches.com/long-table/ (last accessed 11 July 2020).

(pens, pencils, markers) are all there for your use – for you to eat or share only what you feel like you might want to.

If all of this sounds ambiguous, it is because it is meant to be. With conversation as the central focus, it allows participants to take the exchange of ideas to go where it might organically, rather than structuring it within hierarchy and presumptive audience. The etiquette that the original set up offers, also acknowledges the possible discomfort inherent in conversations like this. As the instructions offer: 'There can be silence. There might be awkwardness. There could always be laughter. There is an end, but no conclusion.' This set up for organic knowledge-making that acknowledges its awkwardness appealed to us as a framework for what we were trying to do. It allowed us to see it as a conversation, prompting each participant to sit on an equal footing with others. It took on board that there were parts of the same conversation that might need public statement and others that might want quiet disclosure and experience. In doing so it offered us a way to think about the structure of our project, a space within which we could gain from its structurally queer leanings.

Several other performances have followed in the wake of this long table performance (eg, Silent Dinner, our own pedagogy in class[15]) and it felt useful to incorporate this into how we thought about this book. We decided that it would still be structured around the theme of law and globalisation – initial questions we were interested in and broadly beginning to settle into – but we were interested in the ways in which questions within it, some taken for granted, others unknown, could get dissected by different actors. We were interested in variations in training as well as positionality: What kinds of conversations might a political scientist working on gender in India have with an Indian queer theorist? How would a black law student in California, just learning this language about globalisation, encounter an established law and economics scholar writing about a relatively remote internal market in Uttar Pradesh? What could a TWAIL[16] scholar have to say about Colombian white-collar crime and regulation? We were not interested in these reflections as comments or reviews, as much as an illustrative exercise in noticing the points of friction and similarity across language and disciplinary syntax. What kinds of dissonance were these exchanges producing? How did it make the narrative more complex?

[15] Note that the *Long Table* follows in a long history of using conversation as method in other praxis that tries to subvert the ways in which hierarchies can be challenged. On 'dinner table' settings and 'round table' settings as methodology, more generally, see J Barnette, 'Performance and Community: Commentary and Case Studies ed. by Caoimhe McAvinchey' (2015) 25(1) *Theatre Topics* 99–100. On 'Phantom Conversations' as making space for reaction, see A Banfield, *The phantom table: Woolf, Fry, Russell and the epistemology of modernism* (Cambrigde, Cambridge University Press, 2007). Writing this in the middle of a global pandemic, we cannot help but think of the intimacies we are calling upon to be able to create these settings. We hope the future will have versions of these tables, but also that critical collaborations can find ways, especially as they bridge farther and farther categories, to do so with virtual connectedness as well.

[16] Third World Approaches to International Law.

This idea of speaking and writing across disciplines and language boundaries without visible agenda and with old (but novel due to unuse) tools of expression is not unique to this project. In fact, it has long been at the core of feminist methodology and praxis. Audre Lorde, for example, uses the logic of feeling and affect as an important method to think about knowledge production, when she talks about the work of poetry as 'not being a luxury'.[17] Feeling, Lorde argues, is not just the other, feeling and affect is a source of knowledge; it is a tool; it is a way of breathing new life into old ideas. What Lorde says about feeling is true about repeated human connection and meaning-making that comes from recursive and intentional conversation. Meanings change with repetition, they can intensify and differentiate, as Deleuze would argue.[18] But meanings are also *made* with repetition – the more we return to the places and words and ideas that hold value to us, the more value we can create from and with them. As Sara Ahmed reminds us, there are cultural politics to emotions; feelings are sticky and attach to objects and theories, not just people. In turn, they can have stickiness and circulation of their own – accumulating new kinds of affective values.[19] As a result, speaking back and forth without common words might be uncomfortable, incoherent even, but in those spaces what can first be experienced as oppression and othering could be also welcomed as 'new ways of seeing'.[20]

These spaces could also offer us new kinds of 'imagined communities'[21] that have the possibility for new scripts of mutual understanding and reflective consciousness. Feminist collaborative methods have been central not just to building networks of solidarity, but also as key agents in building theories beyond binaries.[22] In her work on collaboration and friendship across contexts, Richa Nagar reminds us that speaking across boundaries, sites, and spaces is only as important as speaking *of* the bonds and processes that produce them.[23] Conversations like these are common in the conceptions of queer and feminist phenomenologies[24] and are, in many ways, ends in themselves because they offer

[17] A Lorde, *Poetry is Not a Luxury* (Osnabrücke, Germany, Druck-& Verlagscooperative, 1993 [1977]): https://makinglearning.files.wordpress.com/2014/01/poetry-is-not-a-luxury-audre-lorde.pdf.

[18] G Deleuze, *Difference and Repetition* (New York, Columbia University Press, 1994).

[19] S Ahmed, *Cultural Politics of Emotion* (Edinburgh, Edinburgh University Press, 2014), 218.

[20] J Berger, *Ways of seeing* (London, Penguin, 2008 [1972]).

[21] B Anderson, *Imagined Communities*, revised edn (London, Verso, 2006 [1983]).

[22] K Kannabiran and P Swaminathan, *Re-Presenting Feminist Methodologies: Interdisciplinary Explorations* (New Delhi, Routledge India, 2017). On conceptualising location and the feminist upending of dominant narratives using conversational and third world epistemologies, see the work of Sandra Harding and especially this conversation: E Hirsh, GA Olson, and S Harding, 'Starting from Marginalized Lives: A Conversation with Sandra Harding' (1995) 15(2) *JAC* 193–225.

[23] R Nagar, *Muddying the waters: Coauthoring Feminisms Across Scholarship and Activism* (Champaign IL, University of Illinois Press, 2014) and R Nagar, Ö Aslan, NZ Hasan, O-S Rahemtullah, N Upadhyay, and B Uzun, 'Feminisms, collaborations, friendships: A conversation' (2016) 42(2) *Feminist Studies* 502–19.

[24] For example, See S Roy, 'The positive side of co-optation? Intersectionality: a conversation between Inderpal Grewal and Srila Roy' (2017) 19(2) *International Feminist Journal of Politics* 254–62.

the reader a range of emergent possibilities to derive from their ambiguity and orientation.[25] But beyond the reader, these exchanges can have impacts for actors too. As Nagar offers, feminists friendships afford spaces for 'radical vulnerability' while also allowing us to create 'messy terrains'[26] where meanings might get lost or misunderstood, but where conversations can – and do – produce important kinds of dialogue that can trigger different points of continuity and contrast for actors who are implicated in the exchange.

When we asked our collaborators to tell us how they saw their field – what about the field they felt was seen by them in particular ways because of their own identity – we were probing our comrades to be reflexive alongside us, but also vulnerable. At the same time, we had to contend with the reality that collaborative journeys are neither seamless nor linear. Still, even without producing 'everyday utopias',[27] they continue to infuse a certain kind of possibility in the conceptual life of exchange spaces, they require 'embodied translations', a concentrated effort to move beyond disciplinary silos and draining epistemologies to dream of new kinds of spaces and reaches.[28]

III. Setting the Conversation: Confronting the Risks of Ubiquity, *Babel* and the *Ruses* of an Imperial *Reason*

The *Long Table* analogy therefore provided a good frame for the discussion, as it allowed for a suspension (albeit temporary) of meaning-making. But such a setting could not be staged in a vacuum; nor could it be definite. The claim that Law and Society annual conferences could specifically lend themselves to apparently open-ended discussions needed, in itself, to be welcomed and critically explored. Since 2013 – and specifically after the LSA meeting in Mexico in 2017 – the geographical reach and demographic fabric of participation to LSA annual meetings have undergone a revolution. About half of the participants now come from non-US countries. Is this fostering a renewal of debates within the LSA, or is this apparent universalisation reflective of what Bourdieu and Wacquant called the ruses of imperialist reason,[29] blurring the power struggles at play under the guise of a happy Babel? The ubiquity of axioms about law and globalisation seemingly shared by US scholars, Europeans and a growing number of scholars from

[25] S Ahmed, *Queer phenomenology: Orientations, objects, others* (Durham NC, Duke University Press, 2006).

[26] Nagar at al (2016), n 23 above, at 516.

[27] D Cooper, *Everyday utopias: The conceptual life of promising spaces* (Durham NC, Duke University Press, 2014).

[28] B Pierre, N Petigny, R Nagar, and S Shakhsari, 'Performing Embodied Translations' (2019) 2(1) *Commoning Ethnography* 113–31.

[29] P Bourdieu and L Wacquant, 'Sur les ruses de la raison impérialiste' (1998) 121–122 *Actes de la recherche en sciences sociales* 109–118.

the Global South in this setting could give the illusion of a universal common sense about the empirical sites and processes seized by globalisation, and an equally universal common sense about the platforms and lenses of engagement, resistance and critique to these forces, flows, and even imaginations of modern globalisation.[30]

Over the years, some studies have explored the structuration of law and society as a scholastic field, with a few reflective critiques on its internal dynamics of expansion, specifically in the US, and the unequal distribution of collaborative efforts between law, and the social sciences.[31] Arguably, however, most critiques have been framed as a forward-looking and functionally informed dynamic driven by a process of constant reinvention of conceptual 'fixes' where earlier ones are seen to have failed. Specifically regarding the theme of legal globalisation, recent and exciting new theoretical scaffoldings have been developed to go beyond binaries between the national and the international, eg by looking into transnational legal orderings.[32] As of yet, however, there is no study that has systematically unpacked the reciprocal connections between the drivers of globalisation – legal, economic, social, cultural – in the Global North and the Global South, and within the South–South. Resulting theorising efforts therefore consistently reflect an apparently intractable opposition between globalisation 'from above,' and globalisation 'from below'.[33]

Because our own conversation was about the global in both its heuristic sense – *what is legal globalisation*? – and as an epistemic frame – *with what agency, to whom and with whom are we talking about legal globalisation*? – we needed to confront these issues, which we conceived as related to the translation of ideas across national scenes (or – rather – mis-translation) and the social conditions that partake in the production of knowledge, its circulation and legitimation. Both were essential to understand the possibility, and scope, for our *Long Table* to open a space of *critique* about legal globalisation.

The postcolonial critique in the social sciences, and to some extent in law (through the TWAIL scholarship and the IGLP forums of discussion, in particular), has amply underscored the embeddedness of knowledge in global structural patterns of inequality and domination and the entanglement of disciplines with the (ideological, economic, political) geographies of colonialism and empires.[34] Structural sociology scholars have also stressed that exploring the social conditions

[30] A Appadurai, *Modernity at Large: Cultural Dimensions of Globalization* (Minneapolis MN, University of Minnesota Press, 1996).

[31] BG Garth and J Sterling, 'From legal realism to law and society: reshaping law for the last stages of the social activist state' (1998) 32(2) *Law & Society Review* 409–72.

[32] TC Halliday and G Shaffer (eds), *Transnational Legal Orders* (Cambridge, Cambridge University Press 2015).

[33] B Rajagopal, *International Law from below. Development, Social movements, and Third World resistance* (Cambridge, Cambridge University Press 2005).

[34] G Steinmetz, *Sociology and Empire: The Imperial Entanglements of a Discipline* (Durham NC, Duke University Press, 2013). For a critique of expertise more generally, See R Grundmann, 'The Rightful Place of Expertise' (2018) 32(6) *Social Epistemology* 372–86.

for the production and international circulation of ideas[35] could account for the mis-translation of concepts within and across national fields, that is: to explain why some concepts, such as Bourdieu's core concepts of fields or habitus, find a limited echo in the US, but also why seemingly ubiquitous concepts are entrenched in national methodologies and struggles. This can also shed light on how hierarchies of domination are strengthened and reproduced through theorisation.[36]

These intersecting undercurrents were, albeit paradoxically, a strength for us, as they helped define the parameters of our discussion as a secure space. Whether our contributors, depending on their backgrounds, defined the Law and Society annual conferences as an additional, secondary platform to their legitimate spaces of (academic/activist) engagement, or as their main academic home, they found in this process a way to test and confront their lenses. But taking in these power processes at play was also a way to avoid what we saw as three traps: (a) that of *ubiquity* as the conceit – albeit veiled by the explicitness of not building a meta-theory – of 'uncovering' the invisible lying behind layers of theorisation; (b) that of the Babel of an apparently shared common language that would euphemise structures of domination within and across national fields of epistemic production that partake in the construction of legitimate lenses and their circulation; and (c) foremost, that of the activist stance of embracing the cause of counter-globalisation and emancipatory discourses without first ascertaining and acknowledging the structural position of these discourses in relation to mainstream scripts and institutions.[37]

By using the analogy of the *Long Table*, we followed the paths of other strains of critical scholarship to ask: what happens when we take concepts *out* of their legitimate realms of application, including in our case towards empirical sites that do not 'look' like law? With a focus predominantly on Indian sites, our book embraces the forceful postcolonial call[38] to de-provincialise globalisation scholarship and the push to see the South as more than a suppressed underside of the North.[39] It is also built as an invitation to shift the strain of legal globalisation that remains steered towards the South as an interconnected reversal 'from below' so as to question the position of these sites as 'peripheries'.

Taking the cue of critical socio-legal scholars,[40] our volume therefore asks: *How can we go beyond a North–South binary to understand legal evolution?* How can

[35] P Bourdieu, 'Les conditions sociales de la circulation internationale des idées' (2002) 145 *Actes de la recherche en sciences sociales* 3–8.

[36] Bourdieu and Wacquant (1998), n 29 above.

[37] This is not to suggest that curating these spaces is meant to necessarily reject the possibility of deployment. Rather than a dismissal of the empancipating positions of activists and their possibilities of knowledge production, it is to highlight the false dichotomy between critical thought and canon. The worlds we inhabit have determinate calls of action and our suggestion is not that it be euphemised with conversation; rather, it is that reflexive conversation is central to being able to act effectively at all.

[38] D Chakrabarty, *Provincializing Europe: Postcolonial though and Historical difference* (Princeton NJ, Princeton University Press, 2000).

[39] H Bhabha, *The Location of Culture* (London and New York, Routledge, 1994).

[40] J Comaroff and JL Comaroff, *Theory from the South. Or, How Europe is Evolving Toward Africa* (Abingdon, Paradigm Publishers, 2012).

we go beyond the focus on *transfers*, and more generally, on *encounters* between the Global North and the Global South to account for patterns of diffusion, transformation and resistance to legal globalisation? This interrogation builds on the paths opened by the Global History literature in the past couple of decades to trace legal globalisation as an iterative process of reciprocal – albeit asymmetrical – inter-connected histories between the imperial and the national, the international and the local, the past and the present,[41] and as a polycentric and haphazard process.[42] The threads opened by this scholarship underscore the tension between seeing legal evolution as a function of transplantation between the Global North and the Global South, and seeing it as a relational, dynamic and polycentric process produced by interconnected local histories. Nowhere is this tension riper than in postcolonial settings where studies predominantly look at receptor sites in isolation or build on the assumption of the Global North as a constant. What happens when we remove this yardstick? How do institutions emerge? Rather, how do we inspect their emergence?

By using these peripheral sites themselves as *petri dishes* for building theory, we sought to move from the power-laden imprinting / receiving / borrowing rhetoric and instead look at these sites of dubbed anomalies[43] and ironic globalisation processes[44] with the power to re-orient the way we understand and pursue these projects about interconnectedness and institutional emergence. Therefore, while using the term postcolonial as a definer of *empirical* sites, we also used it as a definer of forms of engagement, position-taking within the field. Most of this volume's contributors focus on postcolonial sites in their research – foremost India, as well as Pakistan and Latin America. But they are also themselves postcolonial *agents*: originating from and/or based in postcolonial sites, or in the US. They are all engaged in forms of displacement and unequal access to globalisation's mainstream scripts and marketplaces. Our own trajectories along with theirs could in themselves be sites of mimicry, resistance, resilience, innovation – or simply, chance encounters.[45] Indeed – not all trajectories go in a single direction, as Marc Galanter's Foreword to this book offers. In his words, the 'surprising journeys' and 'unexpected discoveries' that 'upend naïve expectations' of how we

[41] S Subrahmanyam, *Explorations in Connected History: From the Tagus to the Ganges* (Delhi, Oxford University Press, 2004).

[42] L Benton and L Ford, *Rage for Order. The British Empire and the Origins of International Law* (Cambridge MA, Harvard University Press, 2016).

[43] T Risse (ed), *Governance Without a State? Policies and Politics in Areas of Limited Statehood* (New York, Columbia University Press, 2011).

[44] Ballakrishnen (2019), n 1 above.

[45] Although we, and many of our authors, use chance in this book as a way of narrativising pasts, it is not meant to devalue in any way intentional action and choices, especially not in these times where calls to action are central to movement-making, resistance, and community building. Part of this book's contribution is to unearth what is less visible, what passes for chance, what might not be linear or paid attention to. But these choices of focus presume that action that is agentic will be more visible to and in other contexts. Theorising intention and accident more generally, see S Ballakrishnen, *Accidental Feminism* (Princeton NJ, Princeton University Press, 2021).

think of directionality in scholarship are necessarily accelerated and paused by personal stories and experience. In this sense, hierarchies of domination can trap actors, while also affording them new kinds of agency and perspective.

The question then arises, how do we go from there? Some authors have called for an epistemic levelling of the playing-field that would require observing and laying out, side by side, epistemic sources from the Global North and the Global South.[46] This is not something that we felt equipped, or entitled to do, even as a collective – for reasons that we unpack further in the Conclusion to this volume. Rather, we built our inquiry around the common denominators that defined us as a community. All of us have been shaped by our encounters with the global; each of us also identifies, to a certain extent, with law and society as a community of epistemic belonging. Hinged on the *Long Table*, as a process framed, as it were, by the Law and Society conferences as a venue, we opted for a two-fold strategy of *de-centring as distance-taking.*

IV. *Estrangement, Reflexivity* and *Refraction* with/from Peripheral Sites: The Theme of the *Long Table*

The first arm of this strategy is what the Comaroffs have framed as 'critical estrangement'[47] borrowing from Bertolt Brecht's concept of *Verfremdung*. We built this collection around a core group of six empirical chapters focused on sites in the peripheries of India, Pakistan, and Latin America. As we explain further below, all of these contributors are focused on empirical sites that seem to resist mainstream templates about legal globalisation, either because what they are looking at falls under the radar of legal globalisation scripts, or because the outcomes they are tracing look like not simply failed transfers but anomalies. We then invited another group of contributors to provide 'responses' to these empirical chapters. We did not prompt them to respond on the empirical material itself, but on how these empirical sites were interpreted and how this framing resonated with their own lenses. We were particularly interested in how a certain strain of research or inquiry reflected their own identity, agenda, and writing. 'Estrangement' could thereby be fostered through the dissonance of conceptual and disciplinary frames. Of course, as all our contributors identify with, in some broad sense – or at least know of – a kind of law and society scholarship, this was a limited form of estrangement. Yet, asking, for example, a sociologist of sciences to ponder on the question of 'innovation' when applied to the issue of informal economy in

[46] R Bertrand, *L'histoire à parts égales. Récits d'une rencontre, Orient-Occident, XVIe–XVIIe siècle* (Paris, Le Seuil, 2011).

[47] Comaroff and Comaroff (2012), n 40 above, 19–20.

India, or a TWAIL environmental scholar to respond to competition law regimes in Latin American settings could potentially disrupt entrenched scaffoldings of knowledge. This is what we sought from each 'course' between empirical chapters and their respondent(s). If authors were stalled, if they had crevices between their understandings and articulations, we did not see it as our role to course correct. Instead, it allowed us to lean further into this praxis of uncertainty and discomfort that we sought from the engagement. At the core of the kind of knowledge creation we sought was a usurping of knowledge itself, and its relationship to immediately shared language and meaning-making.

Secondly, we built this as a *collective* dialogue through a process of *relational reflexivity*. We borrowed the term from Bourdieu and built it as the thread of this collection. Reflexivity relates to what Bourdieu defined as a conscious comprehension of the self, that is: how agents attain knowledge of, and negotiate, various cultural fields, through an interrogation of three types of limitations (of social position, of field, and of the scholastic point of view) that are constitutive of knowledge itself.[48] Through an iterative process (building on our Law and Society annual panels and up to four iterations of each contribution in this book), we asked each contributor (be it of empirical chapters or response notes) to re-examine their original iteration by reflecting on their own platform of knowledge: what were the drivers that had shaped their lenses and how they understood processes of legal globalisation? The objective was not to replace one form of theoretical scaffolding with another, but rather to disrupt those lenses by channelling attention towards the structures that had contributed to shaping their lenses. We imagined that if we kept our questions open, there would be more room for yet unopened answers that we could not have imagined to cull from structure.

There are, however, obvious and deeply-rooted limitations to this exercise, which we reflect further on in the Conclusion to this volume. Biographies – especially auto-biographies – can easily lend themselves to biographical illusions. There is a natural tendency, even with the most minted scholars, to espouse the common sense of correlating an individual story with a longitudinal, linear – and by extension – logical succession of events and crossroads, with no referential other than that of the subject themselves.[49] At the same time, as Galanter's *Foreword* starts to set in place, this reiterative exercise may only be possible in retrospect – as a possibility, or an entitlement. Certainly, this self-reflective exercise involves vulnerability and an acceptance that what was could have easily not have been. Yet it also demands an in-depth understanding of the social, political, economic and family drivers of a given trajectory, as well as critical knowledge of the possibilities, and limits, of trajectories *qua* scholars within scholastic fields. By the same token, while the more junior scholars may have a more immediate

[48] P Bourdieu and LD Wacquant, *An Invitation to reflexive sociology* (Chicago IL, University of Chicago Press, 1992).

[49] P Bourdieu, 'L'illusion biographique' (1986) 62–63 *Actes de la recherche en sciences sociales* 69–72.

(and oftentimes painful) sense of the obstacles they face, they do not always enjoy the necessary distance to make sense of the structural embeddedness of these obstacles – and opportunities. Neither, by definition, did we.

Rather than confronting explicitly these limitations – and being, ourselves, limited by them – we embraced them as part of the process, by adding another layer of authorial voice to the dialogues between empirical chapters and response notes. We invited long-term members of the law and society field to lend their voices through what we dubbed 'refraction' notes. We prompted them to reflect on their own trajectories, as individuals and as scholars. Their reflective insights on their careers could be an entry-point to reconstruct the scaffolding of knowledge on legal globalisation as an iterative trail, so as to connect the paths these authors had used and opened in relation to their own mentors, competitors and audiences and the politics in which they were embedded, with a younger generation. Their position of authority also allowed them more distance – and with it, more freedom – to reflect on their past strategies, their possible errors, their more visible victories, and their chance encounters.

It is side by side, relationally, that these collated voices produce a collective reflection by looking at the interconnections between three-layered dynamics at play in the politics of (in)visible institutionalisms of legal globalisation: (in)visible institutionalism as academic (il)legitimacy; (in)visible institutionalism as knowledge ortho/heterodoxy; and (in)visible institutionalism as social belonging/dissonance. It is also relationally that they produce a space for critique by introducing the possibility of interconnectedness – between individual trajectories and the deployment of emergent and contending frames and concepts on legal globalisation.

V. The Six Courses | Jumping Points

The following **six** empirical chapters form the core of this collection. They are rooted in a range of disciplinary perspectives including legal history, anthropology, architectural iconography, sociology, politics, and economics. These six authors, just like the eight authors of the response notes, played a core role in the community we built for this project. All of them share a common interest for sites in the periphery where legal globalisation seems to produce anomalies.

In setting up these empirical chapters as primary points of reflection, our volume adds to a long theoretical tradition that uses law, legal process, and legal institutions as central nodes in unpacking globalisation processes. Each of these empirical studies questions the position of these sites from the Global South as arenas of reception and contest of global dynamics. These are sites where law and legal institutions have been engineered as laboratories of social control and social change, with reciprocal effects between the Global South and the Global North. These are also sites of revival where institutionalism is embedded in previous and parallel globalising dynamics.

As a substantive core to this collection, these six chapters foremost explore frontier zones left either invisible or doomed to the status of paradoxical encounters under mainstream legal globalisation lenses. In building their narratives, these six authors also engage in a process of distance-taking. They all share interdisciplinarity as a common strategy to push against mainstream tropes in their home disciplines. In their projects, thus, the stakes of (in)visibility are not simply a zero-sum game – between economic and political equality; informal and formal economies; the visual and the textual; religion and law; formal innovation and unscripted agency; successful or failed transplants.

In the **first** empirical chapter, Rachel Brulé, a political scientist, interrogates the relationship between economic and political equality which are usually studied in isolation. Rather, she argues, connecting the drivers of women's political participation in India can provide cues to answer a wider question about the relationship between representation and economic gender justice and equality. Legislative reforms equalising economic rights are common globally, with mixed results. Brulé considers the impact of quotas on women's rights in a crucial domain – property – by leveraging exogenously-set electoral quotas – 'reservations' – for women as heads of local government in India. Brulé's study finds that despite backlash that occurs and has to be navigated, political representation enables women to secure property rights and ensure that they are upheld. These findings confirm the power of political representation to not only claim institutional economic rights but also broaden their acceptance by changing perceptions of judicial parity.

In the **second** empirical chapter, Yugank Goyal, an economist, questions the resilience of the informality that structures the footwear cluster of Agra, which lies beneath the hyper-visible Taj Mahal. In the quest for a viable explanation, Goyal pushes against a prevailing economist binary between formal and informal economies. Rather, he underscores the entanglement between the caste system, family, and hierarchies between traders and shoemakers, that fosters trust due to a high degree of information symmetry on the market. His research excavates silences buried in the cacophony of markets – which, despite engaging more than half the world, continue to remain at the periphery of economic inquiry – thereby reconstituting our understanding of the invisible actors central to global institutions and the power they wield in upholding their legitimacy and survival.

In the **third** empirical chapter, Rahela Khorakiwala, a legal anthropologist and barrister, uses India's judicial iconography to unpack the relationship between courts, their buildings, and the public viewing and using them. Courts in the Global North, at least those without similar colonial experience, have been explored in this context, but the Indian subcontinent is yet to be investigated in terms of how the judicial iconography impacts the relationship of these courts with its people. Echoing earlier research, Khorakiwala underscores how judicial iconography in India has continued to evolve in the shadows of the empire in layered and complicated ways. Focused on the high courts in Calcutta, Bombay and Madras, all three emblems of the Raj, but all three also embedded in struggles over colonial memory, and justice's role in the present, Khorakiwala's story is also, therefore, about the politics of access to justice in contemporary India.

We lost Shamnad Basheer, one of India's foremost experts in intellectual property (IP) law authorities, during the course of this book's production. In the chapter he wrote for this project, the book's **fourth** empirical chapter, Basheer, uses, just as he did through much of his life, everyday actors and their possibilities for innovation (from multi-purpose rickshaws with special paddy-husking wheels, to traditional drugs that can cure oral cancer) to inform the country's diverse IP debates. His chapter offers a backdrop to better understand a set of informal innovations and their invisibility in light of mainstream standards of novelty and discovery. But like all things Basheer wrote about (and did), the ripple effects of the theory extend well beyond the specific innovations he highlights. The chapter cautions against the grander institutional tendency to superimpose mainstream models of innovation incentives (such as 'rights') on the informal economy, arguing that formalisation processes are likely to work to the detriment of their origin communities. The formalising trend also assumes that the same kind of incentives that work in the formal sector will necessarily work in the informal sector as well, and Basheer cautions against such a reductionist approach that could curb innovative processes in and from these organically creative communities. This is a theme we return to in many of the chapters in this book – a warning against using accepted legitimating logics as easy ways to understand processes in new sites.

Following this theme of being critical of the obvious, Maryam Khan's **fifth** empirical chapter uses the case of 'Islamic review' in Pakistan to illuminate the scholarship that views the rise of judicial power and 'political courts' as constrainers or inhibitors of more 'radical' religious demands. Focused on Pakistan's 'constitutional theocracy', this mainstream script tends to argue that the Supreme Court in Pakistan has played the role of counterbalancing the 'pro-religious' jurisprudence of the Federal Shariat Court. Looking at the operational structure and case law of these special courts Khan's makes two central arguments that cut against the grain: firstly, she argues that there is a good deal of harmonisation between the Federal Shariat Court and its 'secular' counterpart in judicial outcomes relating to constitutional rights; and secondly, that the hybrid design of the Federal Shariat Court is the primary explanatory factor for this harmonisation trend. These observations about the hybrid design and praxis of this Shariat Court then intuitively raise questions about how this institutional arrangement impacts its decision-making, and what, if any, effect it has on balancing Islamisation with democratic constitutional principles.

In the final **sixth** empirical chapter, Andres Palacios Lleras suggests an alternative approach to the history of competition law in Latin America. The established historical and sociological narrative construes the development of competition law as a progression from state interventionism to free markets and competition, embroiled in processes of legal transplants embedded in the neoliberal turn. Lleras challenges this narrative by showing it is harnessed to a (Western) conception of legal evolution, which reduces any departures to failures requiring subsequent fixes. Instead, Palacios Lleras argues that competition law regimes in Latin America as construed in mainstream scripts are mere mirages of the goals that contributed to their establishment. In doing so, he provides an alternative reading to the sense of inescapable doom that accompanies the failure of legal transplants in these postcolonial settings.

VI. The Six Courses in Dialogue: Reflections, Shadows and Refractions

As part of the iterative conversation of the *Long Table*, we subjected each of these substantive projects to a two-layered distance-taking and reflexive process. We asked each author of these empirical chapters to reflect on their own positionality. We kept these questions deliberately open-ended, so as to let contributors re-arrange and re-organise themselves the scaffolding of knowledge that they saw as their defining background and the limitations they were confronted with. What were they pushing against, and how? How did they conceive of their platform? We also asked them to reflect on their authorial voices, to the extent that they were willing and able to do: what had shaped them as scholars, and with it, their lenses? These six chapters are therefore the result, themselves, of an iterative process where the authors' own voices reflect and are the product of a multi-layered battleground.

Thus, Brulé walks the reader through her journey as a woman, Jewish, from New York, and the confrontation of her 'revolutionary quest for female empowerment' with an empirical site where, as a woman, she was both protected and constrained. Khorakiwala's beautiful rendition of the analogy with Kafka's *Before the law* traces and questions how her empirical material (and access to it) was fostered and controlled by her position as a woman and barrister. Goyal exposes the strength – and vulnerability – of being both close and empathetic to his empirical subjects: does it make his story more 'authentic', he asks, and what strands of responsibility does this entail? Basheer, for his part, suggests a radical break, suspending binaries at play in the legitimation/legalisation of innovation. Khan exposes her conflicted position as a scholar systematically called upon to redeem Pakistan's theocratic regime to outside audiences, and as a woman actively opposed to regressive *Shari'a* policies. Palacios Lleras, finally, invokes García Márquez's powerful imagination of mirrors and mirages to reflect on his own despair at the sense of inevitable doom espoused in his core discipline to account for the fate of legal evolution in Latin America.

Meanwhile, these chapters unveil tensions that become themselves (in)visibilised in the production of knowledge. Some contributors unequivocally straddle professional arenas – Khorakiwala, as an academic and a barrister, Khan, as an academic and an activist; all reflect on the inherent tensions born out of their gendered identity, their social and family backgrounds, their sense of (il)legitimacy and accountability. All, however, strive to build against – and beyond – binaries that they perceive as drivers in their respective fields.

It is precisely with the purpose of questioning these binaries that we invited respondents drawn from adjacent disciplines to reflect on these empirical and theoretical battlegrounds. Here, too, these response notes are the result of an iterative process. All of the respondents are similarly working on empirical sites dubbed peripheries of legal globalisation scripts. By inviting them to respond each to an empirical chapter, we were not, however, seeking an additional layer of substance – but rather that they subject these narratives to their own lenses, and that, in the process they also reflect on their own positionality.

We invited Danish Sheikh to respond to Brulé's work on political participation, as a lawyer and award-winning playwright specialising in LGBTQ rights in India. In his piece, Sheikh takes an introspective turn, reflecting on his own position as a queer rights activist and scholar and his own work on identity that employs humanistic bridges to the law rather than quantitative data, as is Brulé's tool. Pushing against the limits of commensurability, he admits: 'I grapple with archival envy', yearning for a 'reparative transgender archive' that could catalogue in numbers that which feels beyond his reach. During the course of this book, he started to navigate yet another praxis – as a graduate student in Melbourne, starting anew these quests for knowledge and their yields.

In his response to Khorakiwala's chapter on judicial iconography, Suryapratim Roy pushes her to distinguish between expression and dissimulation as ways of conceptualising the visual, to see the images in her work as words, to afford the visual artefacts discursive agency. This push is subtle; Roy is masterful with his words, but the pivot to re-territorialisation he calls for is a product of his own training as an international trade law scholar who draws on interdisciplinary epistemology in his own work.

Goyal's piece on the Agra informal economy is matched by two responses. In the first, Christopher Williams, a black law student, reflects on the frameworks it affords him to think about race in the American law school context, asking, meanwhile, how creating a space for critique is possible or affordable, 'if you are expected to only listen.' In the second, Fabio de Sa e Silva reflects on his own positionality as a Brazilian legal sociologist in the US, struggling with a platform reduced to that of 'area studies'. He ponders on the conditions under which non-hegemonic concepts can circulate. Beyond the candour of the question, he queries: how can we develop 'global fluency' without being the dominated of the dominant?

As mentioned above, we lost Basheer, one of our earliest collaborators and dearest friends, during the last round of edits to the book. The loss sat dark at the table, and while this was not a dialogue in the traditional terms, we matched his piece with two respondents to reflect on the ways in which silences and unrequited conversations can still offer engagement and echo well after certain ends. Amy Weissenbach, a sociology graduate student starting a PhD in the US uses Basheer's piece in her response, to think through the paradoxical power outcomes of innovation in her field of interest – synthetic biology – and the ways in which it is built around the principle of free flow of ideas and knowledge. For his part, Jules Naudet, a French sociologist specialising in social hierarchies and inequality in contemporary India, prompts the reader to reflect on the complex dialectic between emancipation and oppression which he recalls is at play both in the formal and in the informal sector. Weissenbach and Naudet would never have this conversation with Basheer in one sense, they would not trade notes and do edits and re-thinking in ways that other connected courses in this book were crafted. Still, their conversation lingers and, in a sense, lingers just as Basheer would have liked, without agenda and with the possibilities for interpretive multiplicities intact.

We similarly invited two contributors to respond to Khan's chapter. Gitanjali Prasad's response looks for parallels in Khan's work as she explores her own practice as a social worker providing assistance to defendants engaged in plea bargaining in the Indian legal system. The ideas of thinking about a meta south Asian court institutional practice alongside one another gave us a chance to complicate these narratives. As Prasad reflects on the discomfort of her position 'between the roles of researcher, activist, social worker and judge', it is clear that it is not just the systems being studied, but also the entry to such enquiry that mediates how institutional inequity is spoken about. In contrast to Prasad's tendency for seeking similarity, Stefan Kroll, a legal historian from Germany, picks on Khan's critique, arguing that it remains still too close to the binaries which she seeks to overcome. He suggests that it is necessary to not only challenge dominant models of law and legal practices, but also to see practices that deviate from dominant scripts as possible sources of innovation in a multi-normative world.

Finally, Palacio's lament about the state of competition laws in Colombia is framed in literary metaphor, and its response is matched in tone and analogy by Usha Natarajan's deep critique from a TWAIL perspective. Yet, Natarajan's piece also questions the end of the tale suggested by Palacio: 'one might be tempted to conclude', she argues, 'that competition law needs to be more fit for purpose. However, it is also possible to come to the end, as I did, with a sense that the purposes are themselves dysfunctional.'

How individual trajectories intersect with and echo that of contending theorisations within academic fields is precisely the question we asked refraction notes authors. Their pieces are stand-alone – as they were not responding directly to the empirical chapters and response notes – while being engaged in this relational conversation. These eight authors are well-known and established scholars – Marc Galanter, who authored the *Foreword*, Yves Dezalay and Bryant G Garth, Dave Trubek, Carrie Menkel-Meadow, David Wilkins, Eve Darrian-Smith, Kate Bedford, Kalpana Kannabiran.[50] We had crossed their paths sometimes as their students, as academic goddaughters, other times because we had read them, listened to them

[50] It is not lost on us that only one of these refraction notes is written by a scholar in India. As Greg Shaffer nudged us to consider, here too, the visibility of the institutional politics at play is crucial

and admired them. We invited them as agents who have each played a key part in building theory and knowledge about legal globalisation in the past decades.

Giving them carte blanche, we asked them for a snapshot of their own journey, inviting them too to lend themselves to a process of distance-taking and reflexivity on their own positionality as individuals and as scholars. We recount further, in the Conclusion to this volume, what we picked from their narratives; yet, Bedford's recalling that her journey was about 'collectively building ladders and, where necessary, shields' perhaps most fittingly encapsulates the threads woven by these pieces. This sentence is as much a cautionary tale about the necessity, and limits, of becoming gatekeepers into an academic field as a call for our collective responsibility *qua* scholars. It points to the delicate, sometimes tumultuous, balancing act of negotiating contradictions that are at once scholastic, political, gendered, and social; of producing knowledge by accepting that at times, the scaffolding of knowledge, just like Babel, *can* and *should* collapse, while also acknowledging the thread of responsibility that connects us collectively, and to the next generations.

VII. The Case for Conversational Thought Building

This book did not just emerge from a conversation, it *is* a conversation. The two humans who had that casual conversation have gone on to build a community around what was just a thought experiment, urging friends and once unknown colleagues to have a meta-conversation about conversations. We have made people take time out of their lives to meet us periodically, engage with us, engage with each other, and have conversations that don't quite fit in the traditional sense. In our exchanges with each part of our process of this book, we asked our authors to treat this like a dance – to pretend they were asked to join not so much to build scientific plausibility, but also to reflect on the process intuitively and interactionally, from within a safe space that they created for themselves and each other.

We recognise that this is not a usual academic book. We are grateful that this not a usual book. But we hope it offers a glance at the kinds of possibility that are present for academic collaboration and conversation. A hope that we can speak at each other, even if not in full sentences, and gain from the interaction, even when it does not look like a gain. That we can have these conversations with joy, with the possibility of expansion, without the constant end in mind. We can, as Gorris's film offers, expand our dinner tables beyond known rooms and have people join our everyday thinking so that we might have a communal transcendence – a

to observe. Who gets known and in what circles is a matter of position, performance, and power. It also reinforces the transnational limits of the field and makes us reflect about the kinds of choices we make in networks and community building. As another reader offered, inherent in this curation of the excluded are other kinds of exclusion. We do not think one book can include all, just as dinner tables and contexts are also limited. But in being self-reflexive about our choices of this curation, we have new tools to better understand the underlying processes at play.

collective effervescence, as Durkheim[51] would offer – that is greater than the sum of its logical parts.

We might have started these projects as naïve young scholars, looking to make a community of alterity within our known networks and grow exchange across communities we felt were not talking to each other. We tried to not just invite them to the dance, but also have them plan it, put up the decorations, pick the playlist, choose to listen to their headphones in the corner and not engage if that is what they wanted, etc. All of which is to say, our long table was set up to extend indefinitely without reason and without structure. But this is not the only table we have feasted on. The late Polish Nobel Laureate Wislawa Szymborska understood the debt we owe to these other tables well. In her poem 'Thank You Note' (2002), she offers a note of gratitude for all those she hasn't loved: 'it is thanks to them / that I live in three dimensions, / in non-lyrical and non-rhetorical space, / with a shifting, thus real, horizon.'

These other tables have similarly nourished us each over and over again, holding us concrete in three dimensions as we explored this bountiful project with our collaborators, friends, and interlocutors. We started this conversation eager for alterity but not grounded in structure to afford such access. These conversations would still have been had if we were not where we are now, but they perhaps wouldn't be in the form of this book, a structure of its own, a testament that holds the memories of these conversations as they are and have been, at these intersecting moments in time. Bringing people together requires structure, requires grant money, requires planning. And for this, there are debts of gratitude to be paid to structure to afford legitimacy to these conversations that might otherwise have been dismissed as flights of fancy. Over the years, alongside this project, we have also grown in our academic careers, written other things 'within our disciplines', extended other known conversations in the literature, landed tenure-track jobs, birthed (and god-parented) the most precious (human) baby. All those structures were vital, crucial, for our ability to nourish this project with the intentionality it deserved. And, in its own way, this book feels like an intended birth too. Of un-structured, incomplete, mosaics that allow directionless exchange as an end in itself. Of possibility beyond structure, even if birthed by and within it. Of queered collaboration and critique. Of a certain kind of alterity within the academy.

We hope it sparks and fuels your own discussions, duels, and dinner table exchanges.

[51] Emile Durkheim (1858–1917). French sociologist, commonly cited as the principal architect of modern social science.

Cover Note

GAIL TARANTINO

I am deeply interested in language – its rhythms, its codes, its musical quality. Recent bodies of work revolve around thinking about language and consider the meaning in a written text and their potential for interpretation and reinterpretation. The idiom to 'Read Between the Lines' was thought to have been derived from the use of 'disappearing ink', allowing messages to be hidden or concealed between lines of text. The rhythmic pace of reading, pausing, counting, and the spaces between informed my formalist approach. Inspired by the question of what is hidden and what is revealed, the work on paper '***What Will You Do / Do What You Will***' became an initial building block of the series, '***Reading Between the Lines***'. My 'Redaction Revisited' works on paper were conceived as a way to re-evaluate and digest a redacted document, becoming another entry into pondering 'reading between the lines'.

Although the published layout of 448 documents in the *New York Time*'s two-page of the Mueller Report[1] became a resource and initial launching pad, I refrained from translating word for word. Instead, using a bone folder, I inscribed an indented mark which helped me synthesise the content and supported a slower pace to absorb the meaning in the redacted documents.

While mulling over the theoretical ideas behind this book, *Invisible Institutionalisms*, my preliminary inchoate musings in creating *What Will You Do / Do What You Will* came into sharper focus upon revisit. I began constructing the piece in fragments and the textual word play arrangements of the piece became an initial inquiry and reflective question, discussing my role as a contributor to the book cover. I jotted down a few words that dovetailed with our mutual positionalities. Notes from one particular phone meeting resonated with me, synergistically: 'An inquiry into what is visible and invisible, what we may see or not see, what may be deliberately left out and the way we may encounter a text that is not yours, invisibility and presence that goes unnoticed. The subtly pencilled letters within

[1] Report on the Investigation into Russian Interference in the 2016 US Presidential Election.

the monochromatic palette were intended to be read and misread as they recede in and out of a viewer's focal point. What you may see and not see has its poetic power. My intention is that its textual reading did not begin as a political overture. However, in our ongoing toxic political climate, it may be interpreted and synthesised as a prompt for a call to action. All the works weave together ideas about the way we look for meaning that may get hidden or implied and is not explicit.

Course 1

BRULÉ AND SHEIKH

1

G-local Women Power: Local Female Representation and Property Rights in India

RACHEL E BRULÉ

Today, we live at the intersection of hyper-speed institutional change thanks to globalisation which increases the scope of opportunities for both integration and dissolution of prior structures and identities.[1] On one hand, rapid change enables integration of new knowledge across communities, with radically new opportunities for the advancement of individual and collective interests either in partnership with more transparent states, or with autonomy from authoritarian planners.[2] On the other hand, the striking inequality engendered by globalisation enables these same tools to support polarisation within and exit from the very communities that built transformative welfare states.[3]

In this context, I ask how we should expect equality, and its frequent shadow, backlash, to travel. I situate my work between two alternative theories of institutional change: top-down versus bottom-up. On the top-down side, Bardhan argues that the key mechanism at work is how elites arbitrate distributive conflicts.[4] As disparities between local elites and those with few social and economic resources grow, they stifle incentives for elites to relinquish goods or power.[5]

[1] KF Scheve and MJ Slaughter, 'How to Save Globalization' (2018) 97 *Foreign Affairs* 98–112; D Sorensen (ed), *Territories and Trajectories: Cultures in Circulation* (Durham NC, Duke University Press, 2018).

[2] J Scott, *Seeing like a State: How Certain Schemes to Improve the Human Condition have Failed* (New Haven CT, Yale University Press, 1998); P Evens and PRP Heller, 'The State and Development' (2018) 2018/11 *WIDER Working Paper*.

[3] RD Putnam, *Making Democracy Work: Civic Traditions in Modern Italy* (Princeton NJ, Princeton University Press, 1993); T Piketty, *Capital in the 21st Century* (Cambridge MA, Harvard University Press, 2014).

[4] P Bardhan, *Scarcity, Conflicts, and Cooperation: Essays in the Political and Institutional Economics of Development* (Cambridge MA, MIT Press, 2005).

[5] Bardhan argues that at high levels of socio-economic inequality, politically powerful individuals are likely to be elites locked in distributive conflicts that preclude meaningful collective action involving 'the weaker sections of society.' At lower levels of inequality, state policies to redistribute economic

On the bottom-up side, Daron Acemoglu and James A Robinson focus on power exerted by 'the masses'.[6] Where citizens pose a credible threat of revolution or costly unrest that would damage the economic and social interests of the elites who control de jure political power, citizens possess adequate de facto power to successfully demand change. This occurs when inequality is neither too high nor too low. This theory is most often used to explain democratisation, but it may also help us predict globalisation's heterogeneous micro-level impact. Both sets of theories suggest moderate inequality is conducive to transformative change in favour of social equality. At a time when globalisation makes 'moderate' levels of economic inequality increasingly rare within countries, this suggests that overt state attempts to improve social equality are becoming both more necessary and more likely to attract significant backlash. I seek to understand the scope of backlash to gender equality as well as the conditions under which we can transform resistance into support.

This chapter tells the story of how I arrived at one edge of the 'global periphery' – rural India – to enter a crucible of institutional change: one in which women's voices were changing the state from the household up. In 2008, I went in search of a revolutionary story about women's economic empowerment through national legal reform 'on the ground', from rural Andhra Pradesh in South India to the banks of the Yamuna River in North India's Uttar Pradesh and Haryana. I asked journalists, agriculturalists, politicians and activists to explain how a daughter's new, equal rights to inherit property worked for them. Bureaucrats, elected officials, and judges told me in adjacent breaths that laws were effectively implemented, and that nothing would change for generations. Indeed, many legal activists knew nothing of this 'transformative' reform. My perspective changed as I met women who organised in what is becoming a centripetal political force: all-female Self Help Groups. Some of these women are now successful as elected officials; some intentionally remain outside the state. I had naively assumed I would find that women's greater agency was the result of legislation declaring female and male inheritance rights equal. But instead, as I followed the steps of women steeped in the practice of female collective power, I found a resounding female political voice that had arrived on the scene long before.

This work is both a precursor and epilogue to my larger research agenda that explains how quotas mandating women's presence at the head of the local state have acted as powerful drivers in enabling women's economic agency – a model I call 'gatekeeper theory'.[7] As I *propose* extensions of this research to

power encourage political coalitions with a commitment to furthering socio-economic equality. See Bardhan (2005), n 4 above.

[6] Acemoglu and Robinson predict an inverted U-shaped relationship between equality and a salient form of institutional change: democratisation. They point to the de facto political power of non-elites as crucial. See D Acemoglu and JA Robinson, *Economic Origins of Dictatorship and Democracy* (Cambridge, Cambridge University Press, 2005).

[7] R Brulé, 'Reform, Representation, and Resistance: The Politics of Property Rights' Enforcement' (2020) 82(4) *Journal of Politics*: DOI: https://doi.org/10.1086/708645.

others less accustomed to pondering the gendered nature of power, I do so in the spirit of Aparna Basu's characterisation of women's history in India as 'an act of reclamation'.[8] Acknowledging women's central role in building India's grassroots democracy gives all women a way to acknowledge and value our voices in the building of collective political agency. In this chapter, I work to paint women's influence in realising political change expansively, as an act at the crossroads of multiple disciplines.

I begin with a minimal scaffolding to situate women's agency in the decision-making process of Indian democracy. This matters because of the polarised views about whether or not electoral quotas mandating women's political presence 'work'. Optimists claim that quotas can be shortcuts to building truly representative democracies, which may otherwise take generations.[9] Pessimists worry that quotas constrain 'lotteries of talent',[10] and that representatives may be fundamentally unfit to represent the substantive interests of groups who are descriptively 'like them'. Yet representation by people with similar backgrounds remains a powerful method of enabling members of disadvantaged groups to raise their voices and engage politically in contexts where they would otherwise mistrust state authorities, and can also catalyse innovative thinking by complex groups (such as 'women') when their political interests are not fully articulated.[11] The traditional view of women's quotas suggests they are imposed (by men) in response to 'men's ideas' about the ideal composition of India's democratic electoral institutions, rather than required by women's demands: this view supports concerns about the danger of quotas for a group of individuals – women – who are perceived to be not only unwilling but also unfit to compete in politics.[12]

To accurately take into account women's agency in drafting the blueprints for their political inclusion, I start by tracing the path I took, as a political scientist with training in development economics and anthropology, to learn the radical power of women's political representation in India. I next outline my 'gatekeeper theory' of women's political representation, to predict how women's electoral power matters for women's property rights. I conclude with a section that initiates a new round of theory-building about how equality 'travels' across the broad terrain influenced by globalisation and back into our understanding of where and how power is negotiated, bringing the potency of the invisible institutions which structure daily life into stark relief.

[8] AM Basu 'Women's History in India: A Historiographical Survey' in K Offen, RR Pierson and J Rendall (eds), *Writing Women's History* (London, Macmillan Press Ltd, 1991) 181.

[9] D Dahlerup and L Freidenvall, 'Quotas as a 'Fast Track' to Equal Representation for Women' (2005) 7 *International Feminist Journal of Politics* 26–48.

[10] J Mansbridge 'Should Blacks Represent Blacks and Women Represent Women? A Contingent "Yes"' (1999) 61 *Journal of Politics* 628–57.

[11] Mansbridge (1999), n 10 above.

[12] W Singer, *A Constituency Suitable For Ladies: And Other Social Histories of Indian Elections* (London, Oxford University Press, 2007) 99.

I. Speaking about Power

The question at the heart of my work is: how do formal institutions change the knotty terrain of our informal landscapes? Amidst revolutionary movements for dismantling inequality in our polities, economies, and societies, when and why does state intervention start to reshape hierarchy? At the micro-level, how do individual human beings and communities adapt to new legislation that contradicts resilient social norms?

Political science, which explicitly invites us to interrogate systems of power, is my chosen, disciplinary home. But in the investigation of systems, we political scientists often overlook the complexities of negotiating power outside the public domain of elected legislatures and campaign speeches. Thus, throughout my training I have sought alternative sources of insight about how power changes around the edges of the formal state. I find intellectual solace in scholarship from development economics, at its intersection with agricultural economics, behavioural economics, and the political economy of institutions. The brilliant, peculiar scholars who occupy this frontier are data scientists who care about precise empirical tests as well as anthropologists in disguise, gladly contemplating the qualities of a particular field, those who labour on it, and who benefits. Their work delves into the ideas and assumptions that drive individual behaviour: not only one's personal labour but how a person obtains, employs, and shares technology; what sort of insecurity modifies one's ability to profit from one's resources; which contracts are written down and which left unspoken; how intra-household power and privilege evolve in the shadow of higher-level political organisation. In addition, I find grounding in the work of legal sociologists who question the processes through which legal codes emerge, and the degree to which they reify – or destabilise – status quo power structures.

These interests have led me to build analytic skills that cross disciplines: supplementing traditional political science training with research design and data analysis techniques to maximise causal inference from economics, with skills of sustained inter-personal observation roughly called 'qualitative analysis' from anthropology, and with critical evaluation of the origin and implication of legal texts within larger systems of social, political, and economic power from law and society scholarship. Finally, feminist scholarship, while outside the explicit domain of my training, helps me understand the invisible contours of power that are still rarely acknowledged within mainstream political science. Each of these tools hones my sight.

In brief, I aim to understand the power of the state to change social norms. The work I describe here explores a radical legal reform with the power to alter fundamental social inequality in the world's largest democracy: reforms to equalise women's property inheritance rights. My initial research came from careful econometric studies grounded in economics: in particular, Sanchari Roy and the

World Bank.[13] Each acknowledged reform's complexities, but both were largely optimistic. Those at the World Bank made a simple argument: information held the key to improving the efficacy of new legislation. To check this logic, I returned to India – where I had recently lived for a year working with MIT's Abdul Latif Jameel Poverty Action Lab (JPAL).

At this point, my view was one of an American political scientist-in-training with copious advice from Indian, British, and American development economists, and an anthropologist and field manager's intuition that I would learn the most about fundamental puzzles by speaking to as many people as possible in situations of mutual trust. In practice, I experienced an uncomfortable dissonance between the guidance I received from political science, economics, and public policy versus the granular information others gave me in rural India.

On my journey as a relatively young, single, white woman with no biological family in India, speaking a rough, workable Hindi, I slowly built the scaffolding necessary for substantial field research. To the extent I succeeded, it was because people were kind enough to include me in their families. My first home in India was in Yamunanagar, Haryana, about two hours south east of Chandigarh, five hours north of Delhi, where I was invited into the home of one of my first respondents to, among other things, better understand conflict over property rights where the stakes were highest: at the well-irrigated, fast-urbanising national capital's periphery.

My welcome to this place transpired accidentally. Thanks to support from experienced journalists, I had been able to gather a family in the midst of a land dispute in the home town of the Editor-in-Chief of a major regional newspaper. I was at the early edges of my doctoral research and searching for a path into the private, inner landscape of individual identity and willingness to claim, share, and contest property, particularly inherited property. As a result, when the Editor-in-Chief's wife, a former schoolteacher, invited me to stay for tea and asked how long I would be in town, I told her that my timeline was open. Upon hearing this, she showed me the entirety of her home and invited me to live with them. Her husband agreed, and I enthusiastically accepted.

The language we use to describe home can only hint at the depth of human feeling that comes with being welcomed, in an absolute sense, into another family's world. What this newly married couple and their larger family gave me was an immense expanse of love, compassion for the vulnerable space of work and life I inhabited, an intellectual engagement that buoyed my confidence, and fundamental security in a town where the public presence of a single, white woman was neither welcome nor respected.

[13] S Roy, 'Empowering women? Inheritance Rights, Female Education and Dowry Payments in India' (2015) 114 *Journal of Development Economics* 233–51; K Deininger, A Goyal, and H Nagarajan 'Women's Inheritance Rights and Intergenerational Transmission of Resources in India' (2013) 48 *Journal of Human Resources* 114–41.

I learned a great deal from that fulfilling home and family, in which I remained about a month and a half on my first visit, and to which I returned as often as I could. Theirs was a love marriage, arranged by the bride and groom rather than their parents. They were each highly educated with independent earnings prior to marriage, broad, curious views of the world, and an inclination to reflect on their own places within it. Their marriage negotiations extended over years, and the union that eventually resulted was one that both the bride and groom valued immensely. They took time to cherish each other's presence in their lives. In addition, the husband's uncle, whose sons lived far away, also loved both bride and groom deeply, and did everything he could to support them.

This context, with many stars aligned to create a supportive family, threw their challenges into stark relief. Despite their non-traditional prior lives, when the couple married, powerful social expectations for female seclusion emerged from otherwise supportive men who acted to maintain their exclusive control over familial wealth. Under duress, the bride gave up her job in the school. This meant her excursions were limited to rare, ideally supervised, trips to the local marketplace for necessities. Her life quickly shrank to the edges of her home, such that even when she was outside, it was improper for her to say hello to former colleagues, let alone make eye contact with them. She negotiated informal tutorials for neighbouring young children within the household's inner courtyard, but her confinement within the boundaries of the household led her to experience physical pain so severe that she, an otherwise healthy woman in her early twenties, could not walk. Given her flawless English and Haryanavi, I suggested she keep me company in court as my translator. She hoped to join me, but acquiesced in the face of resistance from her husband. Later, when she happily became pregnant with their first child, a son, the physical boundaries of her world contracted further, and she was confined to her bed and limited to only the gentlest of movements to ensure the wellbeing of their future child. What I witnessed was the power of patriarchal norms around familial organisation to constrain equality – most notably in the domain of wealth accumulation – even in the face of a belief in each family member's equal worth.

Notably, there were many gaps in my vision. As one of vanishingly few 'white' females in a peripheral North Indian town, I was treated as someone to be guarded and protected, particularly from unknown men: those outside the family with whom I resided, in particular those whose land disputes I investigated with local officials and lawyers. In addition to limiting my observations of how men negotiated power amongst themselves, this may have created a Hawthorne effect of sorts: activating broader concerns about protection of women among the men with whom I interacted. If so, my view of power relations was likely skewed towards seeing men as more extreme defenders of patriarchal hierarchy than they were generally inclined to be. In addition, my residence with a relatively high status, highly-educated middle-class couple may have meant that I saw the backlash that comes alongside 'Sanskritisation' – which Srinivas theorised builds from the upwardly-mobile middle class – rather than more positive dynamics that may ensue for families who occupy more stable positions at the top or bottom of the social hierarchy.[14]

My world broadened immeasurably thanks to an offer by Jamuna Paruchuri, then the Director of Advocacy for the Hyderabad-based, government-run Society for the Elimination of Rural Poverty, to provide all the help I needed. She and her senior assistant, Aruna, invited me into their work of women's collective empowerment and their families. Together, we assembled a representative sample of women with high and low levels of literacy (relative to men in a given locality), from landholding and landless families, upper and lower castes, in villages with as well as without micro-finance groups. The last criteria helped ensure that Jamuna's organisational work did not bias my sample. Already, she had overseen the development of more than half a million Self Help Groups (SHGs) providing women with micro-finance across more than 28,000 villages in the state of Andhra Pradesh.[15] These interviews were sometimes individual and more often within focus groups. These meetings gave me the opportunity to compare experiences of women from radically different backgrounds, across a range of villages, within six districts whose proximity to the state centre varied considerably.[16] What I gained in breadth often required compromises on the intensity of questioning possible.

With Jamuna and Aruna's help, I witnessed a vast community of women who changed the fabric of the local state, economy, and community by mobiliing the support of their female peers. Their work started at the very edges of what was considered socially 'acceptable': often convening meetings at the doorsteps of their marital homes. They eventually supported a muscular public engagement by women as a unified political force, including with the state bureaucracy. Sometimes micro-finance itself spurred action. Other times life-changing events forced new solutions, in particular floods or factory expansions that left women and their families with neither land nor any alternative livelihood.

For example, one member of an all-women's SHG explained how female constituents' willingness to make a range of 'claims' on the state[17] improves with electoral quotas:

> After women's entry into the public space via reservations [quotas] for female Sarpaunches [Pradhans], women's public voice was reinforced by women who joined SHGs and village Social Action Committees. As a result, the village officials

[14] MN Srinivas, 'A Note on Sanskritization and Westernization' (1956) 15 *The Far Eastern Quarterly* 481–96.

[15] R Brulé, *Women, Power, and Property: The Paradox of Indian Laws for Gender Equality* (Cambridge, Cambridge University Press, 2020).

[16] These were Ranga Reddy, Krishna (both proximate to state centres of power), Anantapur and Khammam (at moderate distance from such centres), and Srikakulam and Visakhapatnam (in particularly remote locales). For more details, see Brulé (2020), n 15 above.

[17] G Kruks-Wisner, *Claiming the State: Active Citizenship and Social Welfare in Rural India* (Cambridge, Cambridge University Press, 2018).

> [became also responsible for certain [public] works in the village. So they, [Sarpaunches] invite us to their meetings, and we invite them to ours. In the past, we used to say something to the Sarpaunch but [he] didn't hear it. Today, women's voices are heard. Now Sarpaunches also counsel parents [as we demand] to stop child marriages … In some villages, Sarpaunches make many committees to improve sanitation, schools, road construction, and janmabhoomi (teams ensuring local enforcement of pensions, health, and empowerment programs). If people do not have the right records (aadar, for jobs or ration cards), they now inquire, make committees, and take action.[18]

This was a revolution in how I see the politics of daily 'domestic' life and those of the state. Following over two years of field experience which ranges from the northern banks of the Yamuna River in the Himalayan foothills to the southern banks of the Krishna River in Andhra Pradesh, I realised the importance of negotiating power *within the household.* I now recognise that neither the concept of the *household* nor that of individual influence are permanently fixed. Indeed, the moment when a new household is born – marriage negotiations – presents an enormous opportunity for radical shifts in household structure, including individual roles and the way an individual employs power. These changes have the potential to reverberate across generations, not only within the walls of the household but also in terms of when women exit the household, with whom they speak, and whether they raise their voices publicly or confine their actions to the quiet sphere of familial conversations in the kitchen or field. As one group of women in Andhra Pradesh explained when I asked them whether they expect their daughters' lives will be better or worse than their own: '*How can we know, our daughters aren't yet married*'![19]

For me, this overturned my notion of where political power resides. With the understanding that social power is intimately political, I realised that I too navigate power every day. I am doing so right now, as an academic 'tenure-track' mother who is equally serious about my intellectual and familial lives. As a political scientist who is committed to rigorous research design and analysis that meets the highest standards for causal identification in economics and political science, and to the field researcher's creed that research should respect and reflect the warp and weft of our daily lives. As a permanent outsider: a white, Jewish woman raised in a home in rural New York State by generations of strong, nomadic women and men, who finds deep connection among my adopted families in North and South India, Sri Lanka, and Egypt. What my field research teaches me is that my ability to simultaneously occupy these domains is central to my agency. This insight undergirds my theory of how women's representation influences individual agency.

[18] Personal interview with Padmawathi and colleagues in March, 2015, Krishna district, Andhra Pradesh.

[19] Personal interview with Focus Group Number 3, including longer discussion with Respondent Number 9 on 17 February 2011, in Ibrahimpatnam Mandal, Ranga Reddy district, Andhra Pradesh.

II. Gatekeeper Theory

How do women access social, economic, and political power in settings where multiple, interlinked systems prevent female influence and agency? More fundamentally: how does a low-status group challenge and destabilise what prior to that point had appeared to be a highly stable, inegalitarian system? To answer this question, I develop a theory of how altering women's political representation affects their economic agency.

I study the effect of political representation on women's ability to claim rights by examining landmark reforms that equalised Hindu women's and men's ability to inherit ancestral property. These reforms, amendments to the Hindu Succession Act of 1956 ('the HSAA' or 'the reforms'), were enacted State-by-State, beginning in 1976 and culminating in a national legislative mandate in 2005.[20] They equalised the rights of daughters to inherit a share of joint family property, in a ruling that affected roughly 400 million women.[21] The reforms are significant because inherited rights to property are a major stock of social, economic, and political power, and unequal inheritance rights sustain and magnify inequality.

Prior to reform, sons were the only children entitled by birth to inherit independent shares in ancestral property.[22] Reform retroactively assigned daughters and sons equal inheritance rights *upon birth*, conditional on a father's death post-reform.[23] However, the majority of land in rural India remains jointly owned despite the passage of more than a decade since the last round of these reforms. Why? Implementing gender-equal inheritance requires a revolution among elected government officials, bureaucrats, and family members, all of whom must change deeply entrenched behaviour, backed by strong social norms about property rights, politics, and the role of females in the family. Indeed, legislators promoted reforms not to bring about real change, but rather as symbolic gestures to solidify increasingly strong bases of female voters.[24]

[20] State-level amendments occurred in Andhra Pradesh (1986), Tamil Nadu (1989), Karnataka (1994), Maharashtra (1994), and Kerala's 1976 abolishment of the Joint Hindu Family.

[21] B Agarwal, *A Field of One's Own: Gender and Land Rights in South Asia* (Cambridge, Cambridge University Press, 1994); F Agnes, *Law and Gender Inequality: The Politics of Women's Rights in India* (New Delhi, Oxford University Press, 2000).

[22] The 1956 Hindu Succession Act granted daughters a symbolic right to an indirect share of their father's ancestral land. Sons retained their right to a direct share, as coparceners, in addition to an indirect share of their father's land. Amendments substantially increased the quantum of women's inheritance. See SA Desai, *Mulla: Hindu Law, 21st Edition* (Nagpur: Lexis Nexis India, 2010); Brulé (2020), n 15 above.

[23] The two other, rarely-utilized, conditions for eligibility are: the absence of a will, and partition of the ancestral land prior to paternal death. See Desai, *Mulla: Hindu Law* (2010). Deininger et al. estimate that 65 per cent of Indians die without writing a will. See Deininger, Roy, and Nagarajan, 'Women's Inheritance Rights and Intergenerational Transmission of Resources in India'. Partition is rare because all inheritors must first reach consensus about property distribution.

[24] Brulé (2020), n 15 above.

I find that where national constitutional amendments mandate women's electoral representation, gender-equal land inheritance rights create a fertile ground for reworking distribution of resources that reverberates throughout multiple, interconnected domains. Specifically, I consider the impact of women's political representation due to reforms imposed by the Indian state. In 1993, the 73rd and 74th amendments to the Indian Constitution were adopted. These mandated a three-tiered local governance system of Panchayats, or elected councils, with regular elections and quotas, known as 'reservations', for members of systematically under-represented groups: women and members of communities combating deep social stigma (Scheduled Castes and Tribes). I study the most decentralised of the three tiers, the Gram Panchayat, or elected village council. Constitutional amendments required that no less than one-third of elected Gram Panchayat heads (Pradhans, Sarpaunches, or Presidents) be female.[25]

Reservations represented a significant break with past practices of local governance.[26] They replaced traditional, appointed local councils of elders, which were male-run, with elected local governments supported by fiscal resources, regular elections, and quotas for traditionally excluded groups. The as-if-random nature of reservation implementation – which occurs sooner in some villages than others due to state-level rules – enables me to isolate the causal impact of these reforms on subsequent behaviour.[27]

Many of the prevailing narratives about quotas tend to minimise women's influence as organised political interest groups. Myths 'about women's disinterest and passivity in politics' are rampant.[28] Indeed, many in India subscribe to the notion that elected women are mere proxies for their husbands, who perform the actual work of governance; such a belief can be seen in popular terms for female heads of local government: 'sarpanchpati' and 'pradhanpati', which assume the un-elected husband (pati) is the 'real' leader.[29]

Yet women have been politically active since the dawn of India's contemporary political organisations. As of 1889, 'every meeting' of the most influential organisation advocating Independence, the Indian National Congress (INC), 'included some women … [who] were educated and politically knowledgeable and … were seeking very new public roles'.[30] Women were at the helm of organisations that

[25] In each electoral cycle, one-third of all *Gram Panchayats* are randomly selected to be eligible only for female candidates. Each federal State sets the procedures used to select and rotate quotas across GPs. For details, see Table 5.1 in Brulé (2020), n 15 above.

[26] L Beaman, R Chattopadhyay, E Duflo, R Pande, and P Topalova, 'Powerful Women: Female Leadership and Gender Bias' (2009) 124 *Quarterly Journal of Economics* 1497–1540; R Bhavnani, 'Do Electoral Quotas Work After They Are Withdrawn? Evidence from a Natural Experiment in India' (2009) 103 *American Political Science Review* 23–35; R Chattopadhyay and E Duflo, 'Women as Policy Makers: Evidence from a Randomized Policy Experiment in India' (2004) 72 *Econometrica* 1409–43.

[27] See Brulé (2020), n 15 above, for details on methodology, data, and analysis.

[28] N Buch, *From Oppression to Assertion: Women and Panchayats in India* (New Delhi, Routledge India, 2010) 9.

[29] Ibid.

[30] S Sen, 'Towards a Feminist Politics? The Indian Women's Movement in Historical Perspective' in K Kapadia (ed), *The Violence of Development: The Politics of Identity, Gender & Social Inequalities in India* (New Delhi, Zed Books, 2002) 475.

cemented political alliances for an Independent state, including the All India Women's Conference (AIWC), established in 1926, as well as the Women's Indian Association in Madras (WIA), and the National Council of Indian Women (NCIW). The strength of women's influence within these organisations cannot be understated. Indeed, amidst India's fight for independence, Gandhi's action to weaken and refocus women's political solidarity is one indication of female collective action's importance. Most notably, Gandhi worked to garner support for his protest against granting special electorates to 'members of depressed classes', known as his 'fast against untouchability' in 1932. This 'dramatically broke [the WIA's] demand for reserved seats and nominations'.[31]

After independence from British Colonial rule, the world changed. In Post-Emergency India, there is a particularly important but rarely discussed story. As Raka Ray explains, India's contemporary women's movement took root in mobilisation for radical protests against the state during the early 1970s.[32] Yet Chief Minister Indira Gandhi's declaration of Emergency rule in 1975 pushed many radical women's organisations underground.[33] After the Emergency's imposition, an array of women's groups emerged, including urban 'autonomous' organizations – broadly concerned with 'consciousness-raising' about gender issues and rural struggles for land rights – which brought women's demands for independent rights to the fore, most notably the Chipko and Bodhgaya movements.[34]

Women's political agency was central to the project of creating a state able to resist authoritarian control. As of 1977, organised political opposition emerged. Elections brought the new Janata Party (JNP) to power, thanks in part to 'autonomous' women's groups working to expand local political autonomy. The JNP instituted the Asoka Mehta Committee to 're-institute local self-government'.[35] The Committee recommended a new political terrain: giving *Panchayats* the power to tax citizens, run schools, and identify and solve core problems in rural villages. In the Committee's perspective, this would shift the balance of power away from the fiefdoms of local bureaucrats who 'would not easily be adjusted to working under the supervisions of elected representatives', and toward elected representatives.[36] These strategies were generally understood as means to break up status quo local power structures captured by local, male, landed elites in the service of new, male entrants to national government, including Rajiv Gandhi and Narasimha Rao.[37]

[31] ME John, 'Reservations and the Women's Movement in Twentieth Century India' in M Dhanda (ed), *Reservations for Women* (New Delhi, Women Unlimited, Kali for Women, 2008) 45.

[32] R Ray, *Fields Of Protest: Women's Movements in India* (Minnesota, University of Minnesota Press, 1999) 3–4. For a summary of the Indian women's movement, see: G Omvedt, 'Women in Governance in South Asia' (2005) 40 *Economic and Political Weekly* 4746–52.

[33] Ray (1999), n 32 above, 4.

[34] Sen (2002), n 30 above, 484.

[35] Singer (2007), n 12 above, 101.

[36] Asokha Mehta, *Report of the Committee on Panchayati Raj Institutions* (New Delhi, Government of India Ministry of Agriculture and Irrigation, Department of Rural Development, 1978), cf Singer (2007), n 12 above, 101.

[37] A Bohlken, *Democratization from Above: The Logic of Local Democracy in the Developing World* (Cambridge, Cambridge University Press, 2015) 85–91.

What deserves note is women's significant action at the ballot box, which shaped post-Emergency India's newly competitive democratic polity. This was clear in 1980, 'when Indira Gandhi focused serious attention on attracting women voters' to support her Congress Party.[38] This model of explicitly mobilising the female electorate diffused quickly. As of 1983, NT Rama Rao, heading Andhra Pradesh's newly-formed Telugu Desam Party (TDP), committed to support women via a range of policies, including implementation of women's reservations. In doing so, he garnered 'mass support from women voters' that propelled him into power, which he retained by implementing women's quotas.[39] Other parties took note and quickly followed suit. By 1991, the National Front (a broad coalition of parties including the TDP) advocated 30 per cent women's reservations in all government jobs, and by 1996, all party manifestos supported 30 per cent women's reservations in State legislatures and Parliament.[40] Women's importance for the political survival of successive Chief Ministers explains the state's decision to invest substantial political and material resources in signalling their long-term commitment to women by mandating they play a central role in elected local governments with real funds.[41]

Why should quotas requiring a woman rather than a man to sit at the highest local elected office make a difference in women's land inheritance? At the very least, state intervention changed the face of politics. Despite women's active participation in the movement for Indian Independence, 'it was easier to get arrested for supporting democracy (during the freedom struggle) than it was to get elected to the democratic institutions that Indian nationalists were fighting to obtain'.[42] These long-standing barriers to political office, combined with women's severe disadvantage in extra-household mobility, suggest that descriptive representation of women in politics may be a crucial tool for improving the quality of representative-constituent communication – and hence, representation of women's substantive interests.[43]

The elected position of the Pradhan is a crucial one. I call them political gatekeepers because in India, they are the most influential local politicians in a village. The Pradhan presides over the Gram Panchayat, and oversees implementation of public works, social justice projects, and land allocation. Large-scale surveys identify the Pradhan as the person most likely to be approached for assistance, regardless of the service requested.[44] They are key allies for individuals who want

[38] Singer (2007), n 12 above, 146.

[39] Singer (n 12 above) 103–48.

[40] Singer (n 12 above) 149–50.

[41] Singer (n 12 above) 106–7; Bohlken (2015), n 37 above, 99–103, 111; Sen (2002), n 30 above, 501–16.

[42] See N Chowdhary, BJ Nelson, KA Carver, NJ Johnson, and PL O'Loughlin, 'Redefining Politics: Patterns of Women's Political Engagement from a Global Perspective' in BJ Nelson and N Chowdhury (eds), Women and Politics Worldwide (Newhaven CT, Yale University Press, 1994), cf Buch (2020), n 28 above, 10.

[43] Mansbridge (1999), n 10 above, 641.

[44] J Bussell, *Clients and Constituents: Political Responsiveness in Patronage Democracies* (Oxford, Oxford University Press, 2019); Kruks-Wisner (2018), n 17 above.

to register crimes with the police; to acquire voting rights in a locality; or to secure formal title to land inheritance. Reservations for this position are game-changing because the Pradhan determines who controls the enforcement of all legislation in a given village.[45]

I argue that the simple act of mandating that women hold the highest elected position in their village government can generate a cascade of effects that run through this entire system. Traditionally, men used this political position to act as guardians of the status quo. When women occupy these seats, I find they change governance in three ways: they revolutionise how women occupy the public sphere, create new public spaces for women's benefit, and re-purpose private spaces. I will explain each briefly.

First, thanks to a mix of electoral and personal incentives,[46] many female Pradhans consider themselves personally responsible for increasing women's engagement with the state. According to one:

> We [not] only get to know about what happens in neighboring villages … We also keep a watch on what is happening in the world, which village is going what way, where people are happy. [As Pradhan] it is our job to make them [female constituents] understand … Slowly, I have brought the women out. It's my duty to explain and to tell them to improve. I have made them move ahead, little by little. My authority was such, no one ever said anything to me. So I took them out slowly, made them move about, to the office, to meetings, to attend, to discuss.[47]

A female lawyer explained how such information campaigns improve women's ability to claim rights:

> Formally, no one educates women about their [legal inheritance] rights, [except] those [female political] leaders and the [local] women's groups [they support. In contrast, when women are not the political gatekeepers] it is all about [women] being proactive and coming forward to contest their rights [alone].[48]

Secondly, female Pradhans open new space for women to raise claims in explicitly political fora:

> Earlier, [male] Sarpaunches (Pradhans) were opposed to women's organizations, and any form of women's organizing. Now, because women Pradhans are in power, they go

[45] PR Brass, *Theft of an Idol: Text and Context in the Representation of Collective Violence* (Princeton NJ, Princeton University Press, 1997); V Srinivasan, *Delivering Public Services Effectively: Tamil Nadu & Beyond* (New Delhi, Oxford University Press India, 2014); S Chauchard, *Why Representation Matters: The Meaning of Ethnic Quotas in Rural India* (Cambridge, Cambridge University Press, 2017); F Jensenius, *Social Justice through Inclusion: The Consequences of Electoral Quotas in India* (Oxford, Oxford University Press, 2017).

[46] For details on women's effectiveness mobilising voter turnout and competing as incumbents, see Brulé (2020), n 15 above.

[47] S Joshi 'Bitargaon' in B Datta (ed), *And Who Will Make the Chapatis? A Study of All-Women Panchayats in Maharashtra* (Calcutta, Stree Publications, 1998) 44.

[48] Personal interview with R.B., 7 January, 2017 at AV College, Hyderabad, Andhra Pradesh.

> sit with women in their sangha (groups). [Where female Pradhans are in power] lands are now being given in women's names, and gender issues are now being taken up.[49]

Third and finally, female gatekeepers bridge what are typically considered public and private spaces. In particular, they make the state an appropriate avenue for women to not only demand property rights but also to gain support for conducting private (and public) negotiations of what are often high stakes conflicts over the distribution of valuable, scarce rights. This begins with their willingness to meet constituents *inside* the home, and extends to their reshaping of female identity in public and private.[50] For example, as gatekeepers, women have altered parental attitudes about marriage in Haryana where one mother notes that she: 'not only gave up the ghunghat (veil) but also married off her two sons without taking dowry [from brides]' due to her female Pradhan's influence.[51]

Unsurprisingly, the potential for such sweeping change sets in motion varied forms of resistance. What is extraordinary is that women themselves are able to navigate and redirect challenges to their new authority. My research pinpoints a key window of opportunity for women to assert their rights around property and inheritance: marriage negotiations. Women who enter this point of social reckoning and recombination with powerful female interlocutors – female heads of local government who can advocate for their equal economic rights – are able to transform prior systems of power.

To explain how representation changes enforcement of women's inheritance rights, let me paint a simple, if overly general picture of life prior to inheritance reform. Broadly speaking, pre-reform, Hindu families provided ancestral wealth to daughters as monetary dowry and to sons as property. Diverse practices existed prior to British Colonial rule, including some that provided dowry as independent wealth to women in the form of 'stridhan'. However, Colonial legal reforms made stridhan illegal and uncommon. Today, dowry is considered the 'share' of a woman's inheritance that she brings to marriage, but this becomes the property of a groom and his parents alone.[52] Such notions of ownership have important consequences for married women's welfare. In the worst cases, the value of a woman is reduced to the size of her dowry, with dowries deemed insufficient used to justify

[49] Personal interview with Jamuna Paruchuri on 21 January, 2014, in Hyderabad, Andhra Pradesh, India.

[50] Joshi (1998), n 47 above; J Brown, K Ananthpur and R Giovarelli, 'Women's Access and Rights to Land in Karnataka', *Research Report* (Seattle WA, Rural Development Institute, 2002) 45; Brulé, 'Reform, Representation, and Resistance' (n 7 above); Brulé, *Women, Power and Property* (n 15 above).

[51] JaagoRe, '5 Women Sarpanch Leaders Showing India the Way Forward' (2014) *JaagoRe*, http://www.jaagore.com/power-of-49/5-women-sarpanch-leaders-showing-india-the-way-forward (accessed 30 June 2018).

[52] S Anderson, 'Why Dowry Payments Declined with Modernization in Europe but are Rising in India' (2003) 111 *Journal of Political Economy* 269–310; S Bhalotra, R Brulé, and S Roy, 'Women's Inheritance Rights Reform and the Preference for Sons in India', *Journal of Development Economics*, 10 August 2018.

abuse of a bride as extortion to extract further money. Cycles of violence often result, which can ultimately lead to the woman's murder.[53]

Reform assumes that families will provide daughters with substantial property, rather than dowry. This can improve female resources *and* familial wealth: it enables the child best-suited to manage property to specialise in this work (independently of gender) and increases the quality of marriage alliances, subsequently improving agricultural production and coordination. In the best cases, inheritance reform enables families to choose a Pareto-superior distribution of resources. Yet this tradeoff is impossible if a daughter has already received dowry. Given that roughly 90 per cent of Indian marriages in contemporary India involve the exchange of dowry, I assume that most daughters who married before inheritance reform have received dowry. Thus, I identify marriage negotiations as critical junctures, when the presence of a female gatekeeper can catalyse a daughter's effective claims to gender-equal inheritance rights.

For the subset of families with unmarried daughters who are eligible to benefit from reform, I find evidence that female Pradhans create welfare-improving 'integrative bargains' by simultaneously negotiating rights over multiple, valuable goods and services: dowry, rights to ancestral property, and obligations associated with these rights.[54] Put differently, daughters who encounter female gatekeepers prior to marriage can move away from one-dimensional trade-offs where claiming rights is a zero-sum game that reduces familial resources, particularly those of brothers ('narrow' choice bracketing)[55] to multi-dimensional trade-offs where a daughter's claim to substantial inheritance can benefit the entire family ('broad' choice bracketing). As a result, backlash diminishes and female empowerment extends across generations: reshaping inheritance and reducing female infanticide.[56]

In sum, where effective, gender-equalising inheritance reforms should reduce inequality. Yet there is good reason to believe that the success of economic reform is contingent on prior inequality.[57] Indeed, I expect resistance to female gatekeepers' enforcement of gender-equalising land inheritance reforms should track inequality across India. As a preliminary check of this theory's plausibility, I compare major States in Northern India (Rajasthan and Uttar Pradesh) with those in the South (Kerala, Tamil Nadu, Andhra Pradesh and Karnataka), in the West (Maharashtra and Gujarat) and the East (West Bengal). I find that moderate levels of socio-economic inequality do appear correlated with women's ability to secure land inheritance. Women are nearly twice as likely to inherit in States with

[53] F Bloch and V Rao, 'Terror as a Bargaining Instrument: A Case Study of Dowry Violence in Rural India' (2002) 92 *American Economic Review* 1029–43.

[54] Brulé, 'Reform, Representation, and Resistance' (n 7 above); Brule, *Women, Power, and Property* (n 15 above).

[55] See D Read, G Loewenstein, M Rabin, G Keren, and D Laibson, 'Choice Bracketing' in B Fischhoff (ed), *Elicitation of Preferences* (New York, Springer, 1999).

[56] Brulé (2020), n 15 above.

[57] Bardhan (2005), n 4 above; Acemoglu and Robinson (2005), n 6 above.

moderate levels of landholding per capita than they are nationally.[58] I also find tentative evidence of backlash against women's historical political empowerment across contemporary India: today, women are most likely to inherit land in States with below-average rates of women's historical political representation.[59]

III. Conclusion: How Equality Travels

The challenge that gatekeeper theory suggests for theories of institutional change is to acknowledge the influence that socially-disadvantaged groups (here women) wield thanks to one institution: top-down political quotas and the resistance that such 'gender shocks' can inspire. Backlash is particularly likely when insecurity is both material and social.[60] The stakes of this endeavour are high, as globalisation accelerates the pace and prominence of economic growth, just as it simultaneously narrows the strata of national populations able to benefit from that growth and increases the number of those in precarious positions, for whom any change in social, economic, or political status can have dire consequences. There is good reason to consider institutional unravelling at many levels, ranging from behaviour within the family (patterns of increasing female infanticide and refusal to care for ageing parents) to national support for authoritarian political leaders and parties – including India's Prime Minister, Narendra Modi, the militant Rashtriya Swayamsevak Sangh (RSS) that brought him into power, and their exclusionary agenda – who delegitimise India's broadening welfare state and its capacity to radically reduce inequality.[61]

Taking redistribution of power seriously leads to an important insight: local political institutions can productively engage with social norms to bring about progressive, egalitarian change at critical junctures where multiple paths are possible. However, this is hard and dangerous work. To be successful, reforms must take bargaining power seriously, and work to ensure claiming valuable rights and resources can occur in the context of integrative bargains across multiple

[58] While only 5 per cent of women inherit nationally, 9 per cent do in Karnataka and Maharashtra, where individuals own half an acre of land on average (in 2001, 0.57 and 0.51 acres, respectively, compared to a national average of 0.38, and maximum of 0.92 in Rajasthan). In these States, rural inequality hovers around the national mean (0.24), offset by above-average attempts to redistribute agricultural land. For example, Maharashtra distributed 77 per cent of land declared 'surplus' by 1996: higher than the national mean of 66 per cent, but lower than Tamil Nadu's 83 per cent redistribution. See Brulé (2020), n 15 above, Table 8.2.

[59] In 2017, women represented only 3 per cent of Members of Legislative Assemblies (MLAs) elected in the two States with the highest levels of female property inheritance: 7 per cent in Karnataka and Maharashtra, versus 9 per cent nationally. Brulé (2020), n 15 above, ibid.

[60] M Shayo, 'A Model of Social Identity with an Application to Political Economy: Nation, Class, and Redistribution' (2009) 103 *American Political Science Review* 147–74.

[61] Evans and Heller, 'The State and Development'; A Varshney, 'Democratic Subversion', *The Indian Express*, 16 December, 2019.

dimensions. Otherwise, members of vulnerable groups are, by the very nature of their status, at a disadvantage in the single-dimensional, zero-sum bargains that typically occur around rights. Equity-enhancing reforms are most likely successful when those responsible for advancing rights consider how to support the art of bargaining in the service of redistributing those very rights and resources. Such bargaining becomes only more important as globalisation makes negotiation – both locally and globally – a necessary act for survival in an ever-more-dynamic economic terrain.

Archive Envy

DANISH SHEIKH

> Since subject position is everything in my analysis of the law, you deserve to know it's a bad morning.
>
> Patricia Williams, *The Alchemy of Race and Rights* (1991).

Subject position is, amongst other elements, a function of time and space.

Starting in 2011, I worked with a collective of human rights lawyers in Bangalore engaged in litigation and advocacy on LGBTQ rights. My engagement with queer rights began with my own journey of coming out as a gay man in law school in Hyderabad, and the Alternative Law Forum gave me a space to build upon this trajectory once I'd graduated. At the Forum, my work included assisting with the constitutional challenge to anti-sodomy law in India which resulted, at first, in a defeat before the Indian Supreme Court in 2013.[1] In 2017, my interventions in advocacy moved to the theatrical space with a series of productions looking at the regulation of sexuality in India, a move which was accompanied by a shift to full-time law teaching where I brought these different strands of my work together.

I first read Rachel Brulé's work on the impact of electoral quotas on women's rights around the time India went to vote in its typically massive, seven-phase election. The grand narrative of the elections has involved tactics ranging from the underhanded[2] to the truly bizarre.[3] Somewhere on the margins of this frame are peripheral narratives seemingly extraneous to the broader story: accounts of unlikely poll booths[4] or candidates who are themselves at the margins (more on this last point shortly).

[1] *Suresh Kumar Koushal v Naz Foundation*, (2014) 1 SCC 1 (overruled by *Navtej Johar v Union of India* (2018), n 6 below).

[2] 'India's election campaign is racked by Dirty Tricks', *The Economist*, Kolkata, 1 March 2019: https://www.economist.com/asia/2019/03/21/indias-election-campaign-is-racked-by-dirty-tricks (accessed 26 June 2020).

[3] 'Unethical, gross violation of poll conduct: TMC, Congress write to EC over PM Modi's Kedarnath trip', *Indian Express* (New Delhi, 19 May 2019): https://indianexpress.com/elections/narendra-modi-kedarnath-trip-model-code-of-conduct-violation-trinamool-congress-election-commission-5735869/ (accessed 26 June 2020).

[4] Niha Masih, 'Election workers in India travelled 300 miles over 4 days to set up a polling booth – for one voter', *The Independent*, London, 18 April 2019: https://www.independent.co.uk/news/world/asia/india-election-vote-polling-booth-ladakh-himalayas-a8875921.html (accessed 12 July 2020).

During the weeks that India went to vote, I was putting together a workshop for transgender[5] rights activists from across the country at my law school. Over four days, this group would be exposed to a range of sessions on substantive and procedural laws that had a bearing on the LGBTQ community in India. My own session in this workshop was a reflection on new possibilities following the recent decriminalisation of queer intimacy in India.[6] Looking ahead in this presentation required looking back as well, and to this end I spent a segment of my allotted time talking about the difficulty of marshalling evidence in litigating the case before the Supreme Court (more on this as well, very soon).

Even as I prepared this workshop session, the students of my Legal Theatre course were putting together a performance for their final assessment. That production, titled Crooked Tree, would look at the gap between principle and implementation in the Supreme Court of India's decision in *NALSA v Union of India*:[7] a landmark decision on providing the right to legal gender recognition for transgender persons that has increasingly been mired in administrative tangles. One of the significant conflicts emerged with the judgment's omnibus directive to Centre and State Governments 'to extend all kinds of reservation (to transgender persons) in cases of admission in educational institutions and for public appointments'. This particular declaration was soon challenged by the National Commission for Backward Classes,[8] with the final position on reservations at an impasse five years later.

In this time, in this place, holding this position: what did it mean to experience Brulé's work?

A summary of her work will not do justice to the breadth of arguments she marshals, or the sense of navigating the different sources that come together to create her key propositions. I'll focus then on the elements that most leapt out at me from my vantage point of a queer rights lawyer-researcher who engages with theatre and more broadly, storytelling, as a space for embodying legal subjectivity.[9] I'll start with a section grounded in the difference between Brulé's core set of methodological approaches and my own, and go on to think through two examples of how this rumination on difference bounces off specific findings that Brulé makes. At its heart, I locate this difference as one of differing abilities to access and draw upon archives.

[5] Using the word transgender as an umbrella term in the Indian context requires also an acknowledgment that the umbrella is vast – a range of transgender communities exist in different regions of the country where, in addition to gender identity, community membership is located along the axes of caste, class and religion.

[6] *Navtej Johar v Union of India*, Writ Petition (Criminal) no 76 of 2016, AIR 2018 SC 4321.

[7] *National Legal Services Authority v Union of India* (2014) 5 SCC 438.

[8] Mario D' Penha, 'In Transition', *The Caravan*, 1 November 2014: https://caravanmagazine.in/perspectives/transition (accessed 26 June 2020).

[9] See G Calder, 'Guantanamo: Using a Play Reading to Teach Law' (2010) 142 *Canadian Theatre Review* 44.

I. On Numbers

I encountered Brulé's work as an empirical text about the impact of electoral quotas for women, with property rights serving as a barometer of impact. Her archive is vast and located across a dizzyingly broad array of sites, including the Population Census, the National Institute of Rural Development, and the Ministry of Agriculture and Farmers' Welfare to name only a few. The data for these sources is collected from records that go as far back as the year 1890.

Looking at the depth and breadth of information here, I was prompted to think of two possibilities: *First*, what if the *NALSA* judgment's deferred dream of reservations for transgender persons in education and public appointments had been realised and then extended further to the realm of electoral quotas? *Second*, if it had, how would one have navigated the question of impact and implementation there in the way that Brulé asks it here? How would one have marshalled together resources to ask analogous questions about how reservations for transgender persons in this domain might tangibly play out vis-à-vis access to property for transgender persons? Difficult as the first possibility is, it is the second question that truly gives me pause. To tell a story of impact is to employ information, to draw on archives, to creatively draw a line through the seemingly neutral maze of numbers. What does one do when those numbers don't exist, when they can't exist, when the archive is silent?

To ask questions about LGBTQ lives and the law in India is to hunt for answers in unyielding spaces. In 2013, when the Indian Supreme Court delivered its verdict criminalising the intimate lives of LGBTQ individuals, much criticism was directed to the following paragraph in particular:

> a miniscule fraction of the country's population constitute lesbians, gays, bisexuals or transgenders and in [the] last more than 150 years less than 200 persons have been prosecuted (as per the reported orders) for committing [an] offence under Section 377 IPC and this cannot be made sound basis for declaring that section ultra vires the provisions of Articles 14, 15 and 21 of the Constitution.[10]

The Court links the numerical minority of the community to its ultimate decision to deny that community its fundamental rights, a point that it was justifiably lambasted for. What is lost in this conversation is the fact that even within the limited prosecutions that the Court does acknowledge, only three out of the 200 prosecutions involved an instance of consensual sex involving either same-sex or transgender encounters.[11] It is difficult to locate queer persons in the archive.

[10] *Koushal v Naz Foundation*, (2014) 1 SCC 1.

[11] See International Commission of Jurists, 'Unnatural Offences: Obstacles to Justice in India based on Sexual Orientation and Gender Identity': https://www.icj.org/wp-content/uploads/2017/02/India-SOGI-report-Publications-Reports-Thematic-report-2017-ENG.pdf (accessed 26 June 2020). For a broader account of the other cases which largely involve non-consensual sexual assault involving men or minors, see A Gupta, 'Section 377 and the Dignity of Indian Homosexuals' (2006) 41(46) *Economic and Political Weekly* 4815.

It will continue to be difficult for a while. If the detailed queer archive is (at best) an aspiration for the future, what of the here and now? How might we even begin to have analogous conversations about impact, bargaining and backlash?

For now, that space is perhaps best responded to by deploying individual narratives. In placing those narratives alongside some of the ideas that Brulé's empirical work produces, perhaps we can formulate some preliminary intuitions about what this line of inquiry might produce. In the next section of this response, I'll take two narratives from transgender lives that speak to different elements of Brulé's work.

II. Narrating Rights

A. On the Campaign Trail

> The afflicted world in which we live is characterized by deeply unequal sharing of the burden of adversities between women and men. Gender inequality exists in most parts of the world, from Japan to Morocco, from Uzbekistan to the United States of America ... An enhancement of women's active agency can, in many circumstances, contribute substantially to the lives of all people – men as well as women, children as well as adults.
>
> Amartya Sen (2001)

An earlier version of Brulé's chapter began with the aforementioned quote by Amartya Sen. Even though the version in this volume no longer uses Sen's words in this manner, I find this a useful place to situate my comments. Sen here tells us how the enhancement of women's active agency has the potential to contribute substantially to the lives of all people. While this is not the core of Brulé's argument – which focuses more on the impact of women's quotas vis-à-vis women – it begins to resonate when she moves to talk about the backlash that arises following an increase in female political representation. Backlash, she finds, can be reduced through a series of tactics that ultimately reduce the 'cost' of reform to men. Later in the chapter, she invites us to think about how amassing and deploying bargaining power is an art rather than a fundamental, universal component of citizenship and to further think through how this art might evolve in the service of citizen empowerment.

For transgender electoral candidates in India, perhaps the rapid accumulation of civil rights serves as a cache of bargaining power in its own right, a leverage point from which to strategically approach empowerment. The 2019 election was the first one where transgender candidates could contest under their self-identified gender category, instead of placing themselves within the male-female binary.[12]

[12] Prior to this, transgender candidates had to contest under the gender binary. See for instance, the case of Shabnam Mausi, otherwise hijra-identified candidate who contested for the Madhya Pradesh Assembly under a female ticket. See 'Eunuch MP takes seat', *BBC Worldservice* (online), 20 March 2000, at: http://news.bbc.co.uk/2/hi/south_asia/668042.stm (accessed 26 June 2020).

There were five trans-identified electoral candidates in the 2019 election. Neha Dixit invites us to an on-the-road account[13] with one of them, Bhawani Nath Singh Valmiki, contesting from the state of Uttar Pradesh. In one incident on the campaign trail, an old man walks up to the candidate and her entourage: 'You are contesting elections, how will it benefit us?' A member from her entourage responds at first: 'Because it is the first time a *Kinnar*[14] is contesting your Lok Sabha seat'.[15] This is not enough incentive for the man, who asks how this will make a difference to him. At this point, Bhawani speaks up:

> I do not know if you know that it was only in 2014 when the Supreme Court of India recognised the third gender. It took us exactly seven years to mobilise and get our rights constitutionally. If we can win such a huge battle in so little time, we have some political and administrative capability to take up your battles too.

This answer appeals to the questioner, who notes how Bhawani is finally speaking like 'a true politician'. Bhawani can't productively use her transgender identity in a narrow-bracketed manner – and yet the amplification of her voice and electoral prospects here could possibly hinge on what the mobilisation work done to claim the identity in the first place has involved.

B. An Identity of One's Own

Brulé's chapter evaluates the impact of electoral quotas in the realm of property rights. Her evidence shows that quotas can improve women's economic wellbeing through spurring the enforcement of their fundamental economic rights to inherit property. The potential for this positive impact to occur is mediated by the point in their lives at which women gain access to representatives; the moment at which they have the most leverage to negotiate extra-legal arrangements for distributing inherited property.

Brulé goes on to distinguish her intervention from prior work: past research has considered the impact of quotas within the political domain, while her work allows us to rethink quotas as creating a new form of agency that leverages descriptive political representation – that is representation by people 'like me' – to expand access to economic and social power for members of groups who are traditionally excluded from both domains.

[13] Neha Dixit, 'Can trans woman and AAP candidate Bhawani counter UP's feudal patriarchy with religion?', *The Caravan*, 11 May 2019: https://caravanmagazine.in/politics/elections-2019-prayagraj-bhawani-ma-kinnar-aap (accessed 26 June 2020).

[14] A transgender community largely located in North India with a distinct socio-cultural identity, see UNDP India: Hijras/ Transgender Women in India: HIV, Human Rights and Social Exclusion (2010): https://www.undp.org/content/dam/india/docs/hijras_transgender_in_india_hiv_human_rights_and_social_exclusion.pdf (accessed 26 June 2020).

[15] Lower House of the Indian Parliament.

If the argument here is premised on access to property and the quota as a form of 'agency' to enhance said access, to bring conversation around transgender identity into this realm is to also bring in the question of gender as propertied attachment.[16]

For transgender persons in India, this notion of property gets filtered through the lens of difficulty in being able to access legal gender recognition, the barriers to which continue to remain daunting.[17] In a memoir about navigating her hijra identity,[18] A Revathi brings these two elements, of access and self-through-property, together in speaking of a bitterly contested property dispute. At one point, faced with the threat of losing her claim to her ancestral property because of her gender transition, Revathi approaches a lawyer with her father. The lawyer is calm:

> They can do nothing. When you are summoned to court and the judge calls out 'Doraiswamy' (Revathi's birth name) they'll look at you and ask if you are indeed him – they'll want proof. It is best that you come to court in a man's dress.

What appears to the lawyer to be a simple enough request is something that Revathi is unable to bring herself to comply with:

> I desperately wanted to be a woman. I put up with a lot for that … I felt that even if I am to die, let me die after having been a woman for a day at least. Now for property's sake, I'm not about to become a man, or cut my hair. None of that please!

The tangible property she might receive means nothing if it costs her, even temporarily, the intangible property of her identity.

III. The Invisible and Hyper-Visible

> You smooth an obituary, shelve two diaries, close as palms in prayer … Tonight you will turn and turn again, and think: it is her dust that I breathed in.

Anna Kisby's poem, which is framed as a response to Carolyn Steedman's writing on archive fever, thrums with the ache of the archive, its access to a past that exists as much in the fragments of dust on the page as it does in the written word. For the queer researcher the archival ache is as much for what cannot be found or recovered from the past. In some instances, it involves a desire to repair the record of the past.

[16] See for instance, D Cooper and F Renz, 'If the State Decertified Legal Gender, What Might Happen to its Meaning and Value?' (2016) 4 *Journal of Law and Society* 43. This article introduces the authors' project on prefigurative gender reform. They describe how the gender identity paradigm has come to understand gender as 'something authentic, and of value, which people hold, and which, like other kinds of personal attachment, they have a right to hold and have protected'.

[17] See International Commission of Jurists (2017), n 11 above.

[18] A Revathi, *The Truth About Me: A Hijra Life Story* (India, Penguin Books, 2010) 189.

The invisibility of transgender identity within one kind of archive stands in stark contrast with a kind of hyper-visibility that owes its roots to Colonial criminal law. Long before the census began counting transgender individuals, before the law began to place transgender identity in conversation with rights discourse, there was at least one archive which recorded transgender identity.[19] The Criminal Tribes Act of 1871 created a community of individuals perceived to be criminals by birth: following notification as a criminal tribe, all members of the community would have to register with the authority specified under the Act. Such registration would leave individuals marked with a presumption of guilt if they were found in circumstances indicating an opportunity for committing theft or robbery. An amendment to the Act in 1897 subtitled it as 'An Act for the Registration of Criminal Tribes and Eunuchs', where a 'eunuch' was 'deemed to include all members of the male sex who admit themselves, or on medical inspection clearly appear, to be impotent'. Any eunuch so registered who appeared

> dressed or ornamented like a woman in a public street ... or who dances or plays music or takes part in any public exhibition, in a public street ... (could) be arrested without warrant and punished with imprisonment of up to two years of with a fine or both.[20]

Even though the Act was repealed soon after India's independence from colonial rule, the identification of a certain kind of transgender body with notions of criminality continues.[21] And so even as I grapple with the archival envy in encountering Rachel Brulé's work and its deft and extensive use of multiple archives, I am left wondering about the possibility of a reparative transgender archive, a record of gradually accreting civil rights victories that embed themselves through the realm of numbers, a future catalogue of what will be gained.

Until then, we have stories.

[19] It might be argued that prosecutions under Section 377 of the Indian Penal Code, which criminalises 'carnal intercourse against the order of nature' constitute a parallel archive of criminality, with judicial observations and commentaries constructing the figure of the 'habitual catamite'. The Criminal Tribes Act however constitutes a much more direct example, with the figure of the eunuch explicitly foregrounded. For more on the archive as it pertains to s 377, see: A Arondekar, *For the Record: On Sexuality and the Colonial Archive in India* (Durham NC, Duke University Press, 2009).

[20] M Radhakrishna, *Dishonoured by History: Criminal Tribes and British Colonial Policy* (New Delhi, Orient Longman, 2001).

[21] Besides the manner in which individuals belonging to a range of transgender communities are at constant threat of public violence, the Criminal Tribes Act returned to haunt the community in the state of Karnataka with a 2011 amendment to the Karnataka Police Act that allowed for the creation of a register to suppress or control 'undesirable activities of eunuchs'. The provision has since been declared unconstitutional.

Course 2

GOYAL, DE SA E SILVA, AND WILLIAMS

2

Of Footwear Clusters, Community Ties, and Institutional Tenacity

YUGANK GOYAL

I. The *Hing Ki Mandi*

Most people in the north-Indian city of Agra do not draw their pride or livelihood from Taj Mahal. They rely on the bustling leather footwear clusters of the town. Behind the glistening, 'white' marble structure lie the 'unstructured', 'grey' markets where leather footwear has been manufactured and sold for centuries. This is the story of the *invisible* footwear cluster of Agra, which will take you beyond the scene of the *visible* Taj Mahal. And in doing so, this story will attempt to remove the parallax view[1] which confuses government with governance, the valid with the legal and perhaps order with globalisation.

Agra is the most important centre of (leather) footwear manufacturing in India. The city produces about 55 per cent of the footwear sold in Indian domestic markets and 22 per cent of India's total footwear exports. Around 40 per cent of the city's 1.7 million people are directly or indirectly involved with the footwear industry. While there are huge export houses and medium-scale businesses, an overwhelming majority of shoemaking labour is self-employed. These are artisans (also called as *dastakaar*), who work in their homes with their family members, making shoes by hand and selling their produce the next day in the wholesale market. By not-so-old estimates, more than two-thirds of the city's manufacturing units are located in household artisan-dominated communities.[2]

The wholesale market is called *Hing ki Mandi*, a huge bustling bazaar with hundreds of trading shops and units where artisans come in the evenings with

[1] I borrow the usage of the term from S Žižek, 'The parallax view: Toward a new reading of Kant' (2004) 8 *Epoché: A Journal for the History of Philosophy* 255.

[2] P Knorringa, 'Agra: an old cluster facing the new competition' (1999) 27 *World Development* 1587.

carts and rickshaws laden with shoes to sell.[3] The traders (wholesalers) buy these shoes and resell them to retailers in Agra and beyond. During the evenings, the market becomes a beehive of activity. Shoemakers (artisans) arrive and go into the wholesale shops, showing their products, and negotiations begin. If buyer and seller cannot agree on a rate, the shoemakers go to the next shop and so on. The market is crammed with vehicles, pedestrians, three-wheelers and rickshaws, and every tiny shop will be filled with a massive crowd of people getting business done. Everyone seems to know everyone else.

The chaotic comfort of familiarity, however, does not succeed in eclipsing the stress of business negotiations. One of the principal reasons is *trade credit*.

Traders buy the shoes but only pay for them months later. In other words, they purchase the shoemakers' products on credit, and this credit is rotated until the end of the supply chain. The trader will sell the shoes to the retailer on credit as well. Only when the retailer gets money from the end-customer, will he pay the trader. And then comes the turn of shoemaker. By this time, typically three months would pass. The shoemaker accepts this because it is the market norm. No trader – practically no one – will pay cash for his shoes.

Now businesses around the world run on trade credit. Here, however, it poses unique problems. *Firstly*, there is this issue of credible commitments, namely, what happens if the trader refuses to pay after three months. Judicial remedy is not quite available in such cases, due to its high transaction costs. *Secondly*, shoemakers have high cost of liquidity. And trade credit is typically offered by someone whose cost of liquidity is low, for obvious reasons. *Shoemakers need cash today to buy raw materials for making tomorrow's shoes. How do they access cash (or credit) for themselves if the trader only pays in three months?*

How does one solve these two problems? Looking at this market from the top, what solutions could one expect? If the 'one' solving the problem is the *homo economicus* – from the North Atlantic region, inspired by the selfish man (yes, this 'one' is assumed to be a 'he') – he will be devoted to enhancing his pleasures and unsurprised at the presence of institutions that help him attain it all. Perhaps, this 'one' thinks, the bank lends some credit to the shoemaker in the beginning, and the same credit can be rotated as the payment cycles kick in. Soon, the loop will be closed and the shoemaker can use his own savings to support the trade credit next time. A more realistic perspective might posit a moneylender coming in between, who will loan the outstanding amount to the shoemaker at an exorbitant interest rate and perhaps end up with the shoemaker eternally in his clutches. A more updated view could perhaps expect that globalisation will lead to the emergence of new capital and new investors in the market, who would absorb the trade

[3] The name literally means 'asafetida market' (asafetida is *hing*, the quintessential spice used in Indian food). Centuries ago, spice traders from Afghanistan used to come and sell their goods here. Hing can mask all other smells, so I think the market derived the name from the smell of hing. Of course no hing can be found here anymore, but like all old stories, the name's stuck.

credit and keep the cycle running. Another sophisticated perception could be that shoemakers may be part of some rotating savings and credit associations to absorb the risk.[4]

But it turns out, nothing like this takes place. I find in my fieldwork[5] that the *mandi*'s solution lies in what is known as a *parchi*, literally a (trade-credit) slip. Through this informal institution, the shoemaker finds a guarantor to secure his payment, as well as liquidity.

When shoes are sold, the trader issues the shoemaker a *parchi* which bears the trader's name, the amount due and the date on which this amount will be payable. The *parchi* is signed by the trader, and is offered as a promissory note. The trader will fulfil his obligation to whoever brings him the *parchi* on the due date. This solves the first problem of credible commitments.

Why do people trust the trader? In part it is because of the high degree of information symmetry prevalent in the market. Market players are very cohesive and close-knit. Traders often live in the same localities and often meet during social gatherings. Similarly, the shoemakers live in their ghettos and get together every day. The caste networks bring them closer – most traders are upper caste Punjabis, and most shoemakers are lower caste *Jatavs*. They all share stories, rumours, gossip and build information within their respective groups. Therefore, if a trader reneges on his payment, this news spreads instantly throughout the entire community. He loses trust. Shoemakers stop going to him for selling their shoes and other traders do not loan him money when he needs it. The loss of future earnings deters traders from cheating. Enforcement authorities are hardly needed. *Parchi* acts as a self-enforced contract.

What about liquidity? *Parchi* solves that problem too. Over time, informal financial intermediaries have evolved in the market, known as *aadhatiyas*. These middlemen buy the *parchis* from the shoemakers at a discount. On the due date, they go to the trader whose *parchi* they had purchased, and claim the amount. They earn their interest (which is the same as the discount they got the *parchi* at). The shoemaker gets liquidity. The trader gets the credit. This structure is illustrated in figure 1. The system resembles how commercial paper emerged historically. In many cases, the *parchis* act as currency as well, so that shoemakers can buy raw materials in the market using a *parchi* – again at a discount. The seller then becomes the intermediary himself.

[4] S Anderson and J-M Baland, 'The economics of roscas and intrahousehold resource allocation' (2002) 117 *Quarterly Journal of Economics* 963.

[5] I conducted the fieldwork during December of 2012, and January, April–August in 2013. I spent considerable time in the market, hanging out with shoemakers and traders in an interaction that loosely translates into participant observation. I hung out with 6 traders extensively but conducted unstructured interviews with 27 traders, 45 shoemakers and 4 intermediaries. Many of these meetings (and most of the meetings with shoemakers) were collective unstructured interviews rather than one-on-one. Almost all of the interviewees were second- or third-generation workers. Not everything that the fieldwork yielded is part of the chapter here.

Fig 1 Transfer of credit in Agra footwear industry (from left to right, aadhatiya, shoemaker and trader). *p* denotes value of parchi and *i* is the discount rate of the parchi that the aadhatiya charges the shoemaker

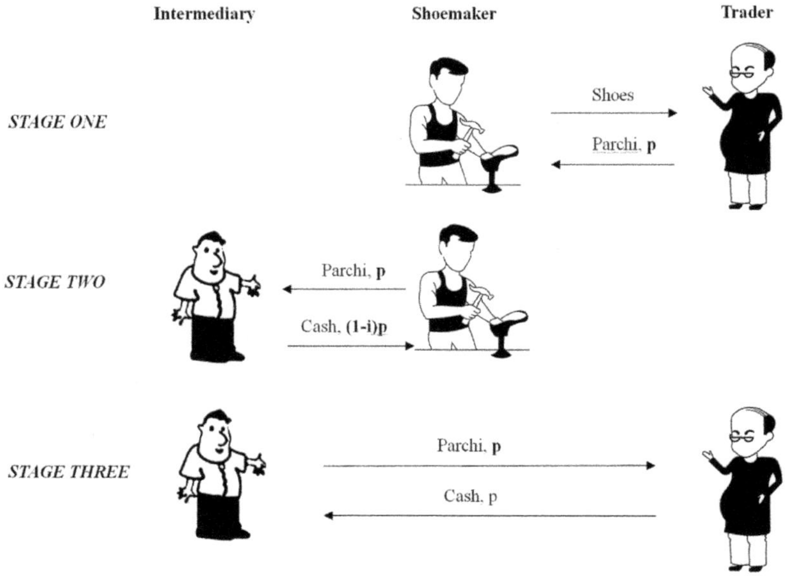

Even more fascinating: the discount rate will depend upon the creditworthiness of the trader. So if a trader is known to delay his payments or renege on his *parchi* promise, his discount rate would be higher than someone who paid on time. And since shoemakers want to sell the shoes to a trader with low discount rates, they will go to the most trustworthy ones. This means, if a trader wants to attract good shoemakers, he had better be trustworthy and pay on time. This way, without resorting to any legal means, the market has incentivised good behaviour and penalised breach of trust for a long time.

On specific days of payment (usually 5th, 10th, 15th and so on, of the month) the *mandi* is a sight to behold. Traders are running around making frantic phone calls to arrange funds to pay off the intermediaries against their *parchis*. No one has time to talk to you. The commotion and noise of people talking with each other and on phones is matched only with the indifference of chai seller hopping from one unit to the other. The *parchis* can be of varying amounts, and even big sellers (not just the artisans) sell their shoes on credit, when each *parchi* could be worth hundreds of thousands of rupees. Whoever has the *parchi* will get the cash. One trader told me 'On the day of payment, even if a dog comes with a parchi in its mouth, I will take the *parchi* and thrust the money in its mouth.'

My primary survey revealed that the average discount rate is 1.41 per cent monthly. Annually, this is five per cent higher than the bank's interest rate. Yet, people don't go to the bank.

When there are disputes, the local association of shoe traders will arbitrate. These are community elders who have also been successful shoe businessmen. They will draw up their own bankruptcy proceedings, which mimic those of the court, and award damages and offer liquidation as an option, where feasible. Power relations do come into the picture, but the associations need to signal trust to the market participants. Hence, cases of corruption or nepotism in the association are rather rare. Their decisions are binding to all. And people comply.

II. The *Aadhatiya*

The Agra footwear cluster's market structure is largely in line with the popular models, ranging from Lewis's[6] dual-sector to Ostrom's[7] self-governance. This means that the industry, according to Western mainstream economic theories, is considered to be composed of a formal sector, which – at least on paper – follows labour and tax laws, and an informal sector, which follows its own internal norms of transacting businesses. In reality, however, there is a continuum of formality and informality, reflecting osmosis of governance practices. I am not interested in labels and categories right now. First, dwelling on these is time consuming. Second, and more importantly, Western scholarship's desperate attempt to build a theory has resulted in Western definitions, leaving the remaining three-quarters of the world to push their realities in their prescribed definitional space. You get the picture anyway, and I am more concerned about functional equivalence.

The financial intermediary (*aadhatiya*) acts as a guarantor, the shoemaker as creditor, and the trader as debtor. The intermediary guarantees the debt repayment. But in the absence of legally binding contracts, how can he guarantee anything? So he goes a step further. He simply purchases the debt and clears off the credit. He does it at a discount which captures his risk, his cost of liquidity and the marginal cost of obtaining funds to buy the debt (*parchi*). Looked at differently, discount is therefore the cost of capital. The sale between shoemaker and trader sometimes takes place partly in *parchi* and partly in cash. This does not affect anything much though, because shoe-lots sold against *parchi* will command a higher price, since the price of the shoes carries the discount in it. But one must be wary of oversimplifying what is going on. The complexity of power relations, caste dynamics enmeshed with relational contracting and trust-based linkages complicate the market dynamics. The *parchi* system is an

[6] WA Lewis, 'Economic development with unlimited supplies of labour' (1954) 22(2) *The Manchester School* 139.
[7] E Ostrom, *Governing the Commons* (Cambridge, Cambridge University Press, 2015).

effective attempt to address power differences within the trust-based networks, but it cannot erase the residual complexities of power dynamics that continue to remain in the marketspace.

Since information is fairly symmetrical in the *mandi*, the costs of monitoring are low. As mentioned earlier, the trader who reneges on his payment is sanctioned through shoemaker boycotts. Why does a trader not run away, taking away all the credit he has accumulated? Well, this is a case of repeated interaction (invoking game theory here). Because the footwear industry in Agra is characterised by family units, there is no end-game state. A trader's credits have to be cleared by his sons and relatives, otherwise they will suffer too. The market keeps a close watch on everything. The discount rates of traders (their *parchis*) can go up if there is news of non-payment or delayed payment, if people learn about one of his consignments getting cancelled, or even if a wedding in his family is less lavish than expected.

Interest rates may move depending upon liquidity available in the market. During the times of credit constraints, particularly when there is a slump in the market, the interest rates increase. Liquidity constraint can also come in the time of festivals. One major festival in Agra – as in much of the country – is Diwali, which falls in the months of October/November. During these months, there is more work than can be handled. Everyone is in need of cash for procuring and producing more. This creates liquidity constraint, and increased demand for cash pushes up the interest rates. (Note that interest rates of *all* traders rise equivalently, so relatively speaking, they are all still at the same level.)

When one plots the discount rates across the 312 traders I secured the rates of, one realises the rates do not follow a normal distribution curve. A normal distribution curve shows us how random variables are distributed (for example height in a population). These curves are bell-shapes, because a few people will be short, a few will be tall, and most will cluster in the middle. Similarly, it seems sensible to expect a few traders (the most creditworthy) will have very low discount rates, a very few will be highly untrustworthy with high discount rates, and most will collect in the middle.

But we don't see such a pattern in the discount rates (see fig. 2). What could be the reasons? Our *homo economicus* might explain the lack of a 'normal' distribution in a variety of ways. Perhaps the traders are not divided continuously in the market; perhaps they are segregated. In other words, perhaps the shoes cannot be treated as homogeneous products. Alternatively, he may infer that there is always a trader for poor quality shoes who, regardless of his discount rate, secures shoemakers who make relatively inferior shoes, which are cheap and cater to customers of lower economic classes. There could be traders who only accept high-quality products, and so regardless of their interest rates, only good quality shoemakers come to them. Within these quality-cohorts, perhaps we would have been able to see some normal distribution, but that analysis was not conducted. Note that shoemaking is a type of handicraft here, so goods produced are dissimilar, thus attracting differential prices. Shoemakers are price takers in most cases.

Fig 2 Interest Rates scatter plot in ascending order of traders' interest rates

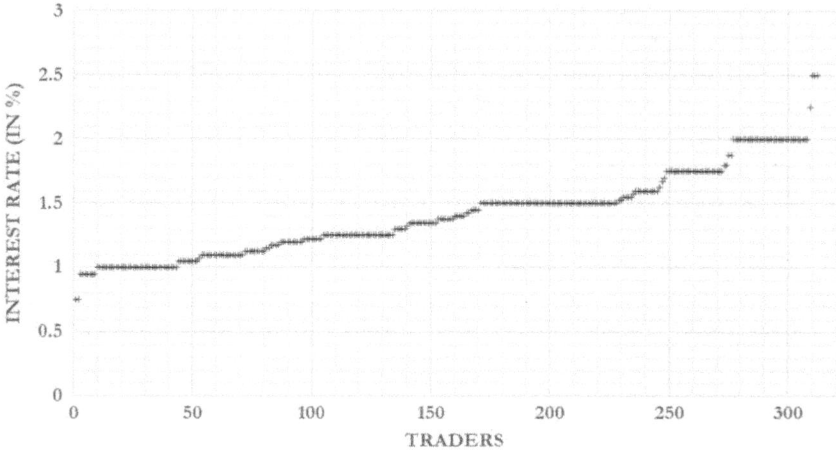

The scatter plot graph also shows peak interest rates at 1 per cent, 1.25 per cent, 1.5 per cent, 1.75 per cent and 2 per cent (points of 'flatness' in an otherwise rising curve). This may also simply mean that market has many traders with varying interest rates but there is a rounding off tendency in the values of interest rates, just to keep calculations simple.

An interesting feature of the market is that the interest rates almost hardly ever go beyond 2.5 per cent. Why would the interest rates have a ceiling, when in principle they could continue to increase with decreasing creditworthiness? Well, this is uncannily similar to the credit rationing performed by modern banks.[8] This is surprising. Research shows that banks ration their credit because of imperfect information, which is not the case here. But the intermediaries may put a ceiling on rates because, unlike banks, they find the risk is too high. Banks lend depositor's money. Here, intermediaries lend from their own money. Banking literature hardly engages with this central idea, that bank officers do not play with their own money. But in swathes of *invisible* informal markets, we know people have – to invoke Nassim Nicholas Taleb – their skin in the game.[9]

During the time of the survey, I discovered that almost all Indian banks doled out personal loans/advances at around 14 per cent per annum (minor deviations). Working capital loans were given at 11.5 per cent per annum for values below INR 500,000. For higher value advances on working capital, the interest rate hovered around 12.5 per cent. At this time, the government was also offering a Differential Rate of Interest (DRI) scheme, aimed at financial inclusion, which

[8] JE Stiglitz and A Weiss, 'Credit rationing in markets with imperfect information' (1981) 71 *American Economic Review* 393.

[9] NN Taleb, *Skin in the game: Hidden asymmetries in daily life* (New York, Random House, 2018).

offered loans up to INR 25,000 at a mere 4 per cent interest rate for those whose annual income was less than INR 35,000.

Even if we ignore the DRI scheme, intermediaries were offering credit at almost 5 percentage points higher than what banks offered. What encouraged shoemakers or traders then, to transact at higher interest? Whenever possible, unconstrained firms seek to borrow more from formal institutions because they are always cheaper. It turns out banks' interest rates may be low, but their *effective* interest rates are fairly high. Bank loans involve considerable processing delays, while shoemakers and traders need cash instantly. But even in the modern forms of banking that can process loans quickly, have reduced bureaucracy, and have high levels of informational challenges, one wonders why the cost of information to the bank is so high. Perhaps the knowledge about creditworthiness of the traders is a tacit knowledge embedded within the market, and for anyone outside securing the information is too difficult.[10]

Shoemakers' aversion to the bank also comes from two other factors. First, access to credit from banks is a cultural idea as much as a bureaucratic one. Studies have shown that migrants often do not have the same access to banks as native-born residents;[11] in addition, households which do not have bank accounts also tend to distrust banks. My interviews with traders and shoemakers point to the same findings. Second, bank officers are known to take bribes. My interviews with informal unit-owners and shoemakers revealed that the probability of bribery increases if the shoemaker belongs to a lower caste, if this is his first time in the bank with such a request, or if he has a smaller unit. In his brilliant work, Prakash explored how markets are mediated by caste-based structures and how Dalits routinely face discrimination in their efforts to access credit for their businesses.[12]

Caste is indeed a force in the industry in Agra as well. High levels of information symmetry, attributed to close-knit community living, are driven through caste-based networks. A vast majority of artisan shoemakers and shoe factory workers come from particular low status castes; or are Muslims. Most of the traders and factory owners are upper caste *Punjabis* and some *Baniya* Hindus. Practically everyone in the business leadership group is an upper caste (male). Each group is brought closer together by its caste network, which often creates narratives that challenge those of other caste network and enhance in-group loyalty. In this highly connected network, news of non-payment spreads like wildfire, and discount rates spike up instantly.

[10] M Polanyi, *The Tacit Dimension* (New York, Doubleday & Co, 1966).

[11] OU Okonkwo and A Paulson, 'What Can We Learn about Financial Access from U.S. Immigrants? The Role of Country of Origin Institutions and Immigrant Beliefs' (2008) 22 *World Bank Economic Review* 431.

[12] A Prakash, *Dalit Capital-State, Markets and Civil Society in Urban India* (Delhi, Routledge, 2014).

III. The *Jatav*

The story can't be complete without learning how it all came about. In Hindu's caste system, working with animal hides or leather has been considered highly polluting and therefore forbidden to upper castes.[13] Hence, upper caste Hindus have historically remained away from this work. Leather goods were made at household levels mostly by Muslims and a particular sub-caste of the untouchables, called the *chamars* (the Hindi word for leather is *chamra*, which is where presumably the word *chamar* comes from). In Agra, they are also called *Jatavs*. The shoe industry naturally flourished through those who *were supposed to* handle leather.

Agra has historically had a sizeable population of *Jatavs*.[14] Add to this the fact that Mughal rulers during the sixteenth and seventeenth centuries, who were great connoisseurs of art, craftsmanship and embroidery, as well as fine warriors (in need of leather boots), made Agra their capital. The skills for making leather footwear became more prolific in Agra. This tradition was further enhanced by the British, who brought shoe designers and stylists who worked with local artisans and added to the repertoire of local techniques (Agra was the capital of North Western Province during the mid-nineteenth century). This enhanced the skill-set of local *Jatavs* and the footwear business became lucrative.[15] But because of caste-based occupational segregation, the trade remained within *Jatav* families and Muslims, with Muslims being mostly the unit-owners and workers being *Jatavs* and Muslims. The artisans would occupy specific localities and work used to happen in clusters of neighbourhood – something we still see today.

The trade became even more important by the early twentieth century. Between 1899 and 1904, total exports of animal skin and hides increased significantly.[16] At around the same time, the first central shoe market was set up in *Hing ki Mandi*, which facilitated the trade immensely, allowing wholesale traders to sit at one place where both manufacturers and other merchants could come directly.[17] Shoemakers would buy leather in the open market, make shoes and then go to specific *mandis* (markets or local bazaars), where they would find an *aadhatiya*, or middleman. These middlemen would buy all the goods brought by a certain shoemaker, sell them off and charge a commission for themselves.

My interviews with families who have been in this trade for around a century suggest that the value of the commission in the early twentieth century would have

[13] RS Khare, *The untouchable as himself: Ideology, identity, and pragmatism among the Lucknow Chamars* (New York, Oxford University Press, 1984).

[14] *The Imperial Gazetteer of India, Volume V – Abazai to Arcot* (Oxford, Clarendon Press, 1908–1909), p. 76–77:. https://archive.org/details/imperialgazette05hunt/page/n3/mode/2up.

[15] See for example, S Misra, *Living and working conditions of laborers in leather industry in Agra.* Unpublished PhD thesis (Agra, Institute of Social Studies, Agra University, 1980).

[16] *The Imperial Gazetteer of India, Volume III – The Indian Empire: Economic* (Oxford, Clarendon Press, 1908), p 189: https://dsal.uchicago.edu/reference/gazetteer/pager.html?objectid=DS405.1.I34_V03_224.gif.

[17] Knorringa (1999), n 2 above.

been about 1.56 per cent of the total value. This was fixed, and did not depend upon volume. The commission was essentially a service charge paid to the *adhatiyas*, who take over the task of selling, enabling the shoemakers to concentrate on making shoes. This was highly localised affair. Shoemakers had very few markets, and due to the shortage of open markets with *aadhatiyas*, they had little incentive to expand their production or invest more time since the return on investments for shoes without such a system was sparse. Instead, shoe merchants from many parts of north India would come to Agra to place orders. Agra became an important centre for English-style men's shoes between the two World Wars, and by the time India became independent its products were being exported to Iran, Iraq and the East Indies.[18]

Partition-induced migration in 1947 changed these dynamics irreversibly. Punjabis migrated to India, while many Muslims moved to Pakistan – estimates suggest that about 14.5 million people were uprooted.[19] Many Punjabis settled down in the cities of north India, including in Agra. But because most of the affluent Muslims from Agra had left for Pakistan, the shoe industry began deteriorating as those who owned the units left the city.[20] When Punjabis arrived in Agra, they noticed that there were many skilled *Jatavs* and Muslims working as shoemakers. They also noticed that there was a lack of market connectivity, and that shoemakers were having a tough time finding customers since they could not travel far. The shoemakers themselves were having to act as shoe sellers, and selling came at the opportunity cost of making.

Punjabis are usually Hindus or Sikhs and they do not observe the strict forms of caste-based segregation. Therefore, working with leather was not a taboo within the Punjabi community as it had been for traditional upper caste Hindus. In addition, migrant communities in need of new livelihoods and income often engage in entrepreneurial initiatives. The potential of footwear trading in Agra caught their attention. They decided they could buy up the goods and sell them off to places far off, outside traditional markets, for a much better price. They began purchasing large quantities of shoes and began the system of credit. They would buy the goods on credit, sell them off in markets outside Agra, give the shoemakers their due and keep the rest for themselves. The only difficulty was the start of the cycle, during which traders were often penniless. Once the second round began, however, the chain of credit was triggered. Using these credit chains, Punjabis, over time, expanded the markets.

In time, the migrant traders became affluent and their reach began increasing. Starting from markets close to Agra, they extended their activity to cities far off across India. In the beginning, to absorb the shock of the credits, the traders themselves would act as *aadhatiya* intermediaries (for instance, a trader would have his brother do the *parchi* purchase at a discount). This ensured that the credit and cash

[18] Knorringa (1999), n 2 above.
[19] Census figures of 1951.
[20] Knorringa (1999), n 2 above.

remained within the family. Over time, however, new middlemen emerged who became the *aadhatiyas*. The institution got fossilised in history.

Peter Knorringa's work has been instructive to understanding this trajectory. Until the 1960s, production used to take place almost exclusively in household units, where self-employed *Jatavs* would manufacture shoes with the help of family members and sell the products to (mostly Punjabi) traders. Sometimes the shoemakers would manufacture shoes and go out to sell them; at other times the trader would place an order for specific shoe-type and quantity and the shoemakers would manufacture those shoes in a given timeline. These two systems still exist. There were very few organised factories, working exclusively by the second (order-fulfilment) system, that provided inventory for major traders in Delhi. In an extensive survey conducted in the early 1990s, Knorringa found that the organisational structure of Agra's shoe industry has remained unchanged since the '60s at a fundamental level.[21] Indeed, more than two-thirds of the shoe manufacturing units in Agra are located in *Jatav*-dominated localities. According to Knorringa's estimates, 'some 50,000 to 60,000 production workers, employed in around 4,000 to 5,000 mostly informal small-scale manufacturing units, would produce approximately 300,000 pairs of shoes.'[22] These production rates have significantly increased in last two decades.

It would be unfair to disregard the views on market structure offered by scholars in this regard. Lynch[23] and Knorringa[24] both noticed the distinct presence of a caste-based hierarchical network, fuelling generally hostile tendencies between the caste groups. I did not particularly find such a thing, at least not in the same vein. Sure, the *Jatavs* I spoke to talked about exploitation from traders who squeezed their margins by negotiating hard, but the traders also complained about shoemakers' 'laziness' and lack of work-ethic. These narratives have to be read against the prevailing order of sociology of businesses, whereby group loyalty and buyer-seller relationships become the dominant skeletons of thought. Agra is a legislative seat of the scheduled castes, of which *Jatavs* are one. This means only a scheduled caste representative can challenge and stand for political elections in the city – a policy that places substantial political power in the hands of the *Jatav* community. The line of thought that observes an antagonistic feeling between those who deal and trade on a daily basis cannot be too weighty, lest the market relations crumple under its weight. The continuous nature of the market, the tenacity of its institutions and indeed the flexibility with which these community ties and relations are built and rebuilt daily over gossip, negotiations and a sense of being-in-it-together dilute at least some of the standard assumptions one is tempted to make when looking at caste-based hierarchies in this

[21] P Knorringa, *Economics of Collaboration: Indian Shoemakers between Market and Hierarchy* (New Delhi, Sage Publications, 1996).

[22] Knorringa (1996), n 21 above.

[23] OM Lynch, *The Politics of Untouchability* (New York, Columbia University Press, 1969).

[24] Knorringa (1999), n 2 above.

market in particular, and India in general. There is something to be said about the near-absence of any large-scale protest or demonstration of one group against the other in all of Agra's history, despite Agra being one of the most communally strained cities in India, where newspaper stories on Hindu–Muslim tensions are disappointingly frequent. Caste-based group networks follow strict culinary or conjugal separation, or may exhibit vastly diverging economic status, and this may have structural causes. But whether the separation is the result of the structure of caste, or something else, one cannot make a claim with certainty. Discrimination cannot be ruled out, and it may be a necessary condition for the shoemakers' economic plight. One is, however, not sure if it is a sufficient condition. As I note above, discount rates are not dependent whatsoever on the caste of the shoemaker who was issued the *parchi*. At the same time, however, it does not seem implausible that caste-based networks might act as social insurance in other sorts of ways for the people in their respective groups.

IV. The Me and the Theory

And what makes my observations challenging the standard diagnosis of the problem merit any attention? It brings me to discover my own location. Paragraphs on 'method' in peer-reviewed journals have been assumed to echo academic rigour. This echo is deafening. It swallows all other minor – but perhaps more meaningful – din in the academic arena. The sound of experience is one such example. One cannot help but be reminded of Bourdieu's approach of reflexivity in this context.[25] Why would I capture this story, and if so, what is my own location with respect to its characters? A quick overview is in order.

James Mill (father of John Stuart Mill) wrote a treatise on the *History of British India*, in the early nineteenth century. One of the most influential books of the time, it was considered an authoritative text. It was often used by British (in fact mostly Scottish) governors who sought to visualise India based on the book's scripts and then followed those scripts to administer the country under imperial rule. How many times had James Mill – who wrote this authoritative text on India of the time – visited India? Zero!

Mill had responded to this criticism, suggesting that his non-visits made his analysis more objective. Back then, perhaps, this sounded like a valid claim. But Sen has reminded us that when Alberuni visited India in the eleventh century, he observed India's scientific achievements in much more detail than Mill could have done in his non-visiting capacity.[26] Guru and Sarrukai have recently explored the

[25] P Bourdieu, *In other words: Essays towards a reflexive sociology* (Stanford CA, Stanford University Press, 1990).

[26] A Sen, *History and the Enterprise of Knowledge* (Address to the Millennium Session of Indian History Congress, 2007).

vital question of whether those who have no lived experience have no right to theorise?[27] Thorny questions get starkly posed. One can write about oppression, but oughtn't we to lend our ears to at the oppressor's narrative on it too? Will the oppressed be able to capture the oppressor's viewpoint as well? Might a third-party observer be able to paint the most instructive picture?

I grew up in a slum in Agra. Frequenting shoe markets is not something one can take out of my childhood, though even if one did, little about my childhood would necessarily change from such withdrawal. In terms of class diversity, I think my childhood was rather unusual. My rustic engagements with friends at home, who might have been children of shoemakers, were matched by those with the elite English-speaking folks at school, many of whose fathers were traders at *Hing ki Mandi*. But except when I had to buy shoes from my friend's shops, I hardly ever ventured into the *Hing ki Mandi* maze. For most of my post-Agra life, the footwear cluster hung in my head as inconsequentially as an insignificant lesson in school – one I didn't care much about, but did not forget entirely either. Not remembering something is also a form of memory. Not being consequential is a type of consequence.

But my own history and network puts me in a unique position to gain access to the market more swiftly. By the time I returned for my fieldwork, my friends had become shoe traders themselves, and they would take me with them into the bottom-most recesses of the factories where I met workers, or to the surface of other units where I met the traders.

But I was conscious of not taking any notes from words of acquaintances. I learned about the *parchi* system accidentally, when a bunch of people were talking about it. I got intrigued and understood the phenomenon from friends, in a sort of participant observation method. But then I ventured out of my friend circle, in a snowballing technique, and spoke to so many others I had not known at all. In doing so, I collected all kinds of discount rates on *parchi*. At this stage, I was a member of the group leaning towards the outside, anonymous ring. During moments of doubt, I would squeeze back into the more comfortable space of friends' offices. How unalloyed I remained, or how much 'native' I remained during the course of my fieldwork, I am still to learn. But surely, I spent more time with *Jatav* workers, traders and their units than with my friends. My friends only let me in. After that, I was on my own. And my return to Agra after almost 12 years had been preceded by taking heavyweight courses in economic and social theories, and copious amounts of reading. Ignorance of theories is not a charge one could have easily put on me.

Does this make my account more authentic, and if yes, towards whom? Despite being from Agra, I remain an outsider to the trade, having no lived experience of what a shoemaker or a trader goes through. But more than a Western academic

[27] G Guru and S Sarukkai, *The Cracked Mirror: An Indian Debate on Experience and Theory* (Delhi, Oxford University Press, 2018).

who might visit the city during her teaching breaks and find solace in the thought of visiting Taj before making the *mandi* her research project, I have a certain sense of relational investment with the city, its inhabitants and surely the footwear cluster. So, while I may not be able to capture the pains and pleasure of cluster participants with as much accuracy as someone living the experience can, I can perhaps be sensitive to certain nuances that would not appear as important to a Western scholar. Or perhaps I will be quick to observe and then dismiss the dynamic which would be central to her analysis.

So for instance, how might scholars entrained in the dominant framework of globalisation and its supply-chain look at the cluster? Armed with Marxist, post-modernist or neoclassical tools, they would pounce on this story with a sense of purpose. How do we fit all these observations into the Holy Grail frames provided to us from the discipline we preach? Is it not clear there is a crystallised caste distinction between the traders and shoemakers? And surely, the trade credit is an oppressive mechanism imposed on the shoemakers by traders? Clearly this is a distinct set of narratives fitting into theories of the subaltern, and if one peeps behind the discount rates, one will observe the silence of the weak. Wait a minute, though, says someone else: this is all the most efficient way of organising resources, and the market has ingeniously designed the least-cost method to operate its transactions – if the discount rate is an oppressive mechanism, the rate would have been dependent on caste as well.

So how does one begin to theorise about the markets that characterise more than two-thirds of the world, while freeing these theorisations from the clutches of the dominant thoughts of the times? The old fable of looking for keys where the light is best is apt here. We may be tempted to read what we see in terms of the class struggle between the network of *dalit* shoemakers and high-caste Hindu traders. It is hugely exciting to see market mechanisms at work where information is freely available and we can effortlessly draw a textbook demand–supply graph. But we are not seeing a pent-up 'class war' sentiment or a costless information channel. The most crucial determinant in this model of market is the community-driven trust-based linkage that assists in the creation of tacit knowledge, offering vocabulary to the unwritten private ordering embedded within. There is no formal contract or property rights order, the cornerstone of any market-based mechanism; nor is there a conception of class struggle, or any third-party adjudication mechanism mimicking a Westminster-type model of separation of powers. The standard Econ 101 course curriculum is barely relevant to understanding what is going on here. This system's design is self-programmed, much like the complex adaptive system, with feedback loops being co-produced and altering the network, its designs and implications known to all. Information symmetry traverses through gossip and local networks.[28]

[28] JH Miller and SE Page, *Complex Adaptive Systems: An Introduction to Computational Models of Social Life (Vol 17 Princeton Studies in Complexity)* (Princeton NJ, Princeton University Press, 2007).

One must notice that the unit of analysis here is not individuals, but the social intermediating units like family, caste or even patrons and friends. So when a particular trader's daughter gets married, the lavishness of the wedding will affect his discount rates, as will news of the losses his son had in another business in another city. Conjugal alliances, observance and mutual respect of common religious practices, cohabitation in neighbourhoods, drinking sessions, and the mere act of 'hanging out' in the *mandi* – these are what builds a powerful inventory of tacit knowledge that acts as the repository of rules and obligations for market participants, materially affecting their wellbeing. And no one has a monopoly on this knowledge; no one can. We seem to be seeing some form of polycentric governance model.[29]

Cheating has a nonpecuniary cost as well, including good old social ostracisation. But more importantly, it does considerable damage to the reputation of the family (name). In fact that is a major driver. So is the idea of maintaining relationships. This relational dependence cannot be explained by monetary gains (or losses) alone either. It is socially, a heavy burden. Much of the motivation for maintaining relationships arises from a web of filial, moral and social obligations, more than from a market or power compulsion. One may want to connect these motivations in one way or another, but to ignore the intermediary aspects of religious, social, cultural ties – no matter how seamlessly that ignorance may fit our frameworks – is then to plaster the same old material onto a new type of brickwork. The look and feel will persuade an untrained observer, but the wall will not last long.

This underlying brickwork is a structure of complex social ties which have to be understood *as they are*, and not as they can look like in another mould. This dearth of comparibility is both because these structures would not have points of apt contrast within Western moulds and also because such moulds have not been around in Western scholarship for most part. Consider the ties of friendship, which cannot be crystallised in a codified definitional framework in the logical vocabulary of most Western scholarship. Similarly, the concept of neighbourhood cannot be cast into a definition either. Like friendship, neighbourhood is an accident; it exists in the mind although it manifests in our actions. It may or may not become a devotion. The boundary rules are unclear. Entry to it may be costless, but exit is emotionally costly.

V. Hvilsager

Agra's case reminds us of the privileges we must confront. One of the privileges is that we think in Euclidean fashion about everything that we see. Euclidean

[29] V Ostrom, 'Polycentricity (part 1)' in MD McGinnin (ed), *Polycentricity and Local Public economies: Readings from the Workshop in Political Theory and Policy Analysis* (Ann Arbor MI, University of Michigan Press, 1991).

geometry encourages us to fit the whole world into a set of axioms and theorems drawn out of those axioms. The scientific obsession with Euclidean thinking renders a vast swathe of humans untheorised – and I daresay, unattended. One needs to look at polycentric governance, the market as a complex adaptive system. An old fable comes to mind:

> A spider met a centipede while hurrying down the street.
>
> 'How do you move at such a speed, with all so many feet?'
>
> 'I do not have to contemplate to keep them all in line,
>
> But if I start to concentrate they're tangled all the time.'[30]

And that's the way to look at informal markets. The models of market and economics drawn from the West do not fit the rest – more than two-thirds – of the world. One must know that a vast majority of India runs like the Agra market described here, across a range of goods and services. People do not approach formal intermediaries like banks, the judiciary, or auditors and accountants, but find solutions in their home-grown indigenous institutions that have internal enforcement norms – and which are very, very effective.

Neoclassical economic frameworks bow to the supremacy of markets as the best way of ordering exchange in a society. After all, ownership and price govern every economic relation that can be imagined. But the claim that markets are a neutral way to organise exchange may be overstated. Markets and economic transactions, as we now know, are embedded in a range of social and political institutions which influence market dynamics rather fundamentally. The underlying structures of power, caste, and identities, informality, networks, and behavioural cleavages form the bedrock on which the market flows. Modern economic thought has paid little heed to how the texture of the canvas may affect the kind of painting that emerges over it. At the same time, Marxist lenses are of no great value either, in their deterministic Newtonian promise to explain anything they survey. The study of market participants as individuals amputates the broader interconnectedness they are part of, most visibly in societies like India. But to look at the society as a group of class members who, as a result of class exploitation, have alienated their subjectivity and are doing a job rather than giving meaning to their lives doesn't fit the observation wholly either. These models, drawing on the experience of the cold countries, blow steam over societies with hot climates, leaving little room for less spirited inferences to be drawn.

There is no desire to use broad brush-strokes here, or to deny the needlessness of existing blueprints. These blueprints offer useful analytical apertures to observe the world around us. And it would also be plainly wrong to say that the Agra story has absolutely no resemblance to any other similar model that fits the Smithian

[30] I thank Shivprasad Swaminathan for most engaging conversations on the idea of Euclidean thinking, and the spider-centipede fable. See, for instance, S Swaminathan, 'What the Centipede Knows: Polycentricity and "theory" for Common Lawyers' (2020) 40 *Oxford Journal of Legal Studies* 265.

or Marxian dream. Those models have a lot to teach us. But they cannot teach us everything. Flows of globalisation and of capital can be viewed fairly comprehensively using all these valuable models afforded to the world from Western universities. But the blind spots will remain, because the identity and behaviour of stakeholders in these models will be rigidly defined. Codification helps greatly in understanding the world around us. But it also truncates our understanding of the global. Must not the thrust of globalisation trigger various forms of organisational consolidation, constructing large formal firms that subsume all kinds of smaller household units? Must it not convert informally-held cash into bankers' vaults or computerised accounts? Must it not steamroll the variety of handiwork into standardised products? Must it not knock out informal intermediaries? And must it not whisk away the proverbial livelihoods of many artisans into the factories of China?

If one looks at the Agra footwear cluster's trajectory, only the last query has been answered. And even when Chinese plastic faux-leather footwear products flooded the markets, leading to massive closures of units in Agra, many small units and factories here exhibited great agility to adopt the new technology. In October 2016, the government of India, in an effort to clean the economy of 'black money' and encourage electronic payments, declared 86 per cent of its cash in circulation to be illegal tender, overnight. This had a catastrophic impact on the Indian economy, and in many ways crippled the informal markets which predominantly relied on cash.[31] As a rare experiment in monetary economics, it seemed to offer a textbook prediction for globalisation flows. But that's not what happened. In Agra, other than significantly eroding the working capital in the industry, the government's action brought about practically no change in the tenacious institution of *parchi*. Relational stakeholders, rather than contractual *homo economicus* were at play. Their collective adaptation at local levels has considerable lessons to learn from, for an alternative collective memory to emerge and be theorised, particularly in the light of the legality of everyday transactions and during moments of legal shift.

In the early '90s, anthropologist Prakash Reddy spent some time in a Danish village called Hvilsager. He was surprised to see that villagers hardly knew each other, and were largely living in microcosmic worlds of their own with almost no social network. At one point, Reddy noticed,

> Coming as I do from India, and born and brought up in a village, I am used to seeing people … But here in this village, not a single soul was sighted … The doors of all the houses were closed and created a doubt in me, as to whether this village had any people at all …
>
> In Denmark, only thieves and Jehovah's witnesses knock on people's doors without an appointment.[32]

[31] G Chodorow-Reich et al (2020) 'Cash and the economy: Evidence from India's demonetization' 135 *Quarterly Journal of Economics* 57.

[32] G Prakash Reddy, *The Danes Are Like That!: Perspectives of An Indian Anthropologist on the Danish Society* (Morke, Grevas, 1993).

Those who have visited or lived in India must be having a richly deserved laugh reading this.

After all, what is neighbourhood? Isn't it a spatial order that offers that cushion between the interiority of the home and anonymity of the large city?[33] And in that, it forces us to build some forms of relationships. Understanding neighbourhood beyond merely a spatial concept therefore is as important as understanding human nature. And the design of neighbourhood offers a unique entry point to observe the design of the culturally constructed market in Agra. Existing models in law fail to capture the analogical idea exhibited in the concept of neighbourhood. But one doesn't need to have been initiated into legal theory to recognise how amazing and uncaptured the idea of neighbourhood remains. When we get that, we will perhaps begin to get the vast majority of informal markets in the world. These spaces run on neighbourly sensitivities, and they may be mature enough not to confuse *work* with *job*[34] or *order* with *law*.[35] Both these distinctions are rather undertheorised in the Western canons.

That is why someone without a formal training in legal theory like myself is able to carve out the constructs of validity of the *parchi* system in the market. Elsewhere,[36] I have made an attempt to thrust a hybrid form of validity, squeezing it out of a Kelsen and Hart, but perhaps I am able to do that because I am myself a neighbour to the discipline of legal theory, just as I am to the site of my fieldwork. I am quite there, but not exactly there. Sometimes our neighbours and friends can see more about us than the people we live with!

[33] I thank Sadan Jha and Amiya Das for offering me with this fresh look at neighbourhood as a social construct.

[34] For Agra *Jatavs*, footwear is not simply an occupation or livelihood, but '*a family affair and a way of life*.': Lynch (1969), n 23 above, p 47. See also, NC Morse and RS Weiss, 'The function and meaning of work and the job' (1955) 20 *American Sociological Review* 191. But see also, RP Vecchio, 'The Function and Meaning of Work and the Job: Morse and Weiss (1955) revisited' (1980) 23 *Academy of Management Journal* 361.

[35] R Ellickson, *Order Without Law* (Cambridge MA, Harvard University Press, 1991).

[36] See, Y Goyal and P Westerman, 'A Short Note on the Validity of Rules Guiding Informal Markets' in P Westerman, J Hage, S Kirste, A Mackor (eds), *Legal Validity and Soft Law. Legal Validity and Soft Law* (Cham, Springer, 2018).

Three *Paise* and a Rough Agenda on How to Make the Invisible Visible

FABIO DE SA E SILVA

I was once told the story of a man who was desperately looking down at the ground, near a streetlamp. A passing woman asked, 'do you need any help?' The man responded, 'Yes, I have lost my car key.' The woman set out to help the man. After a while, having had no success in finding the key, she asked, 'Are you sure this is the place where you lost it?' The man responded, 'Actually it is not, but I felt like this is where I had to search, for it is where the light is.' As academics, we often find ourselves in a similarly bizarre state. Just like the disoriented man, we let ourselves be driven by the powerful light of certain theories and concepts, only to miss what we are looking for and that which can carry us forward.

This point is by no means new. From the sociologists of science of the 1960s,[1] to the more contemporary post-modern and post-colonial theorists,[2] multiple generations of scholars have encouraged us to rethink our scientific frameworks, acknowledge the ways in which they both enable and constrain what we see, expand our analytical imagination, and render more of our world visible. *But how do we make this all more than a scholarly cliché? What are some of the strategies that we could be using to achieve such ambitious goals? How do we search for our car keys beyond the glow of a streetlamp?* This book represents an effort to outline answers to these time-honoured questions in the specific realm of institutional studies – and hopefully will have implications beyond it. My modest contribution to such a project, or my few *paise* on the conversation the book seeks to foster,[3] stems from my closer reading of Yougang Goyal's chapter, entitled 'Of Footwear Clusters, Trade Credit, and Institutional Tenacity'. Goyal's work presents his readers with

[1] K Popper, *The Logic of Scientific Discovery* (London, Hutchinson, 1959); T Kuhn, *The Structure of Scientific Revolutions* (Chicago IL and London, University of Chicago Press, 1962).

[2] B de Sousa Santos, 'A Discourse on the Sciences' (1992) 15(1) *Review (Fernand Braudel Center)* 9–47; EW Said, *Orientalism* (London and Henley, Routledge & Kegan Paul, 1978); C Mohanty, 'Under Western Eyes: Feminist Scholarship and Colonial Discourses' (1988) 30 *Feminist Review* 61; A Quijano, 'Colonialidad del poder y clasificación social' (2000) 6(2) *Journal of World-Systems Research (Festschrift for Immanuel Wallerstein Part I)* 342.

[3] I am hereby playing with the Anglo-American expression 'two cents' by adapting it to the Indian monetary system, which forms the basis of the trade credit relationships described in Goyal's chapter.

many insights. In the context of this reaction, I highlight three of them – the three *paise* referred in the title.

***

The first *paise* involves what one could call the geopolitics of knowledge. Goyal looks at trade credit practices in the shoe industry in the Indian city of Agra. These practices entail multiple layers of institutional life, juxtaposed in peculiar ways. Individual manufacturers produce shoes and sell them to traders. Manufacturers do not get immediately paid, as traders need to sell the shoes first. But they do not walk away with their hands empty either. Traders issue the manufacturers with a 'parchi' (a note with the amount they owe and the date when such amount is expected to be paid). Manufacturers will discount these 'parchi' (at a given rate) with a third financial intermediary, the 'aadhatiya'. Later down the road, the 'aadhatiya' will cash in the 'parchi' with the traders. The whole system is cemented by a complex mix of trust, reputation, and class/caste hierarchies. As I read through Goyal's chapter, I imagined what would happen if it were delivered at any major academic conference in the Anglo-American world. My sense was that it would be received with great curiosity and engagement on the part of the audience, but that it would also be eventually treated as 'another exotic tale from a non-Western, developing context'.

I may have projected my own experience in this extrapolation, I concede. As an 'area studies' professor in a United States university, there is always a limit to which – at least initially – I feel capable of engaging my students and even peers in my research. This limit is set by how such students and peers believe my findings can be applicable to their 'modern' or 'developed' society. Needless to say, this line between modern/developed and traditional/developing societies is drawn arbitrarily, often based on idealisations of the core, Western countries and the spheres of privilege in which those interlocutors are situated.

A good example comes from my experience in teaching about Brazilian politics and institutions. In the wake of the major anticorruption initiative labelled *Operation Car Wash*, Brazil's image has become inevitably associated with corruption. Whether there is sufficient understanding of what such corruption entails is an entirely different story. Most, if not all of my students, come to class assuming that corruption in Brazil is both an outcome and an expression of the country's political 'underdevelopment'. After all, they will argue, Latin American politics is dominated by *caudillos*, Brazil has a history of 'patrimonialism', and although 'checks and balances' and 'rule of law' institutions exist, they are too young and immature.

All of this may – or may not – be true, but as we begin to unpack the issue at hand, the picture gets more complicated. Students learn, for instance, that most of the corrupt transactions documented in contemporary Brazil are meant not to fill up the pockets of 'traditional' and 'charismatic' leaders that the country lacks the means to hold accountable, but to pay for campaign expenses. The problem thus gets redefined in terms of undue influence of money in politics. We start discussing campaign-finance laws, and the reality of United States Political Action Committees and *Citizens United* is brought to bear. We eventually conclude that corruption may well be the same in both countries, but one gets coded as specifically problematic in ways that the other does not because of the cultural supremacy that gets afforded to the institutions at hand. I wonder if, in the absence of these extended conversations and efforts to bridge societal contexts and stereotypes, Goyal's chapter will be categorised as an extremely interesting but ultimately irrelevant read – not because of what it shows (which is potentially a lot) but because of what its readers may be un/able to see.

My second *paisa* concerns the place of concepts, frameworks, models, and theories in the processes of 'making the invisible visible'. As professional scholars, we must rely on previous concepts, frameworks, models, and theories to make sense of social phenomena and, in fact, it is our ability to do so – to speak to a known audience that cares to listen – that has allowed us entry into this profession. Visibility, then, is crucial in our lives. Yet, 'making the invisible visible' often involves pushing back against existing analytical repertoires and eventually producing entirely new ones. Goyal's chapter states this challenge with great clarity. Throughout his text it becomes undeniable that mainstream economics has very little potential to explain, or even describe the reality before him. Hence, he concludes:

> Markets and economic transactions … are embedded in a range of social and political institutions which influence market dynamics rather fundamentally. The underlying structures of power, caste, and identities, informality, networks, and behavioural cleavages form the bedrock on which the market flows. Modern economic thought has paid little heed to how the texture of the canvas may affect the kind of painting that emerges over it.

Taking up this task, however, is more complicated than enunciating it. One reason is because knowledge production itself is often entangled within (or lies on a 'bedrock' of) power. Law and society scholars, for instance, spent decades questioning the reigning understanding of law as a state-based, bureaucratised normative order. They argued that normative orders existed outside of the state, which also deserved to be analytically considered as 'law'.[4] In a context of economic nationalism and invigorated state sovereignty, their voices were generally marginalised. But, in the 1980s, neoliberal globalisation called for economic regulation to be reduced and decentered from the state. Suddenly, scholarship shifted its emphasis to 'non-state actors' and discovered the regulatory role of corporations, professions, 'epistemic communities', etc. Some conceptual features

[4] B de Sousa Santos, 'The Law of the Oppressed: The Construction and Reproduction of Legality in Pasagarda' (1977) 12 *Law & Society Review* 1; SE Merry, 'Legal Pluralism' (1988) 22 *Law & Society Review* 5.

of 'legal pluralism' thus became more widely shared;[5] yet, this does not mean that their critical and transformative potential was carried forward. The fragmentation of regulatory authority was taken for granted; the changes in power relations that underlay this process were less often scrutinised. Our scientific understanding of the 'law' certainly advanced, but always accommodated the larger power structures that, some will even say, the 'law' is ultimately meant to serve and protect.

Little I know of Goyal's home discipline, ie, economics. The momentum that the subfield of 'behavioural economics' is seemingly enjoying among his peers may nevertheless offer an example comparable to what we once observed in law and society. Behavioural economics questions core premises of 'traditional economics', namely the premise that we are 'rational' agents seeking to 'maximise utility'. It claims, instead, that our decisions on how to allocate resources are driven by social, cultural, psychological, cognitive, and emotional factors.[6] Broadly speaking, the project of behavioural economics is similar to what Goyal is calling for. In both cases, the end-goal is to place market transactions into a larger and more complex context, with differences, when existing, relating to the disciplinary traditions and 'toolkits' that each one is more tempted to draw from: psychology, neurobiology, and experiments for hard-core 'behavioural economists'; sociology, anthropology, and qualitative field research for folks like Goyal. Then again, research in behavioural economics has a clear comparative advantage. It is more likely instrumental to twenty-first-century capitalism, in which 'big data' and algorithms have become powerful tools to connect supply and demand and support a new age of mass consumption. This is probably why there are many more jobs and grants catering to behavioural economics than to the kind of work that Goyal is advocating, which I would call a 'political sociology of economic life'. The bottom line is, the more our attempts to 'make the invisible visible' challenge certain structures of power (eg: the hegemonic arrangements in race, class, and identity), the more obstacles we may find along the way.

My third and last *paise* concerns the discursive strategies by which the invisible can be made visible. Goyal's argument is laid out through an ongoing alternation of storytelling and analytical prose. Traditionally, there are a couple of ways in which these two can come together in academic work. In one of them, the mix simply follows stylistic purposes. Stories capture and maintain the attention of readers; yet the 'real business' is in the debates of concepts and theories. In another way, stories are used to present a 'puzzle' that is subsequently resolved through data, concepts, and theories. Finally stories that encompass mostly qualitative research output are used to generate new hypotheses or plant the seeds of new concepts and theories. Goyal does something quite different from other scholars insofar as

[5] RO Keohane and JS Nye Jr, 'Introduction' in JS Nye Jr and JD Donahue (eds), *Governance in a Globalizing World* (New York, Brookings Institution Press, 2000).

[6] CR Sunstein (ed), *Behavioral Law and Economics* (New York, Cambridge University Press, 2000).

he uses stories to constantly *challenge* some of the most dominant concepts and theories in economics.

One can easily anticipate what Goyal's critics will make of his endeavour. They will say that he is trying to invalidate proven concepts and theories on the basis of 'anecdotal evidence'. And they will technically be right, given the limitations of their vision. Goyal, however, has a trump card to play. His evidence is not anecdotal at all. 'The models of market and economics drawn from the West', he eventually states, 'do not fit the rest – more than two thirds – of the world'.[7] His use of stories is, in turn, a powerful way to convey this 'gap' in mainstream economics. *But how could richer academic conversations be promoted across national and cultural boundaries? How could non-hegemonic concepts, frameworks, models and theories be more legitimately invoked and employed in such endeavours? How could unconventional forms of communication of research findings be fostered in economics and beyond?* One could offer an easy answer by calling for research projects that look broadly into economic life across both the 'developed' and the 'developing' world. Attempts to understand the 'underlying structures … [forming] the bedrock on which market flows' based on a story of trade credit in Agra, India may find a hard time cracking the geopolitical and disciplinary mainstream of economics. *But what if trade credit in Agra is examined against the transactions that make up the modern, app-based shared economy, as in 'Uber'? Or what if it is examined against the logic of FEMA*[8] *credit-giving in post-disaster US cities?* Ambitious projects like these might be more able to reveal *what brings together* and *sets apart* these disparate market experiences, which, in turn, could help *decenter* dominant theories, methods, and narrative genres.

Yet I would be contradicting my deeper argument in this reaction if I were to expect that methodological decisions alone could disrupt geopolitical and epistemological hierarchies. There are larger forces limiting our ability and strategic interest in pursuing alternative 'scientific' pathways.[9] This is where Goyal's chapter begs for a bolder 'reaction' from those of us in academic institutions within the Global North; a 'reaction' that a few pages of a book could not encapsulate. To meet the challenge Goyal poses, we must create spaces where new questions can be asked – or older questions can be asked in different ways – and where issues of culture, history, and power are seen as vital for even the hardest issues of economic life and institutional development to be understood.[10] In these spaces, students *and faculty* would find an array of opportunities and resources to develop 'global

[7] They might not even fit parts of the West, as traditional economic structures are being transformed through changes in technology, while rising inequality is excluding many others from the formal market.

[8] Federal Emergency Management Agency.

[9] P Bourdieu, 'The Social Conditions of the International Circulation of Ideas' in R Shusterman (ed), *Pierre Bourdieu: A Critical Reader* (Oxford and Malden, Wiley-Blackwell, 1999 [1989]).

[10] I borrow this insight from my colleague Jonathan Stalling.

fluency', from language lessons to cultural activities, from short-term study tours to permanent platforms for collaboration and exchange with scholars and activists from the Global South.[11]

***

At this point, my senior colleagues and mentors may tell me to stop wandering around and focus on writing my next piece for a high-ranking US journal, for that is what is going to give me tenure. I wish I could urge them in turn to read Goyal!

[11] What turns out to be my main professional venture, the Center for Brazil Studies, which I cofounded and codirect at the University of Oklahoma, represents such an attempt of institution-building. For information on what the Center does, see: http://link.ou.edu/cis-brazil.

Searching for Space: Creating Room in Global Studies

CHRISTOPHER WILLIAMS

As a new entrant to the field of global studies in law and society, I've been trying to make sense of my uneasiness within these new surroundings. I've identified, after having read Goyal, that at least part of the discomfort has been with the relative domination that Western frames of analysis exert in the study of what is purported to be 'global'. Even in the few short months of being introduced to this literature through my own work on racial experience in the United States, I have been disorientated (perhaps as all new entrants are) by the mismatched impositions of Western understandings, and the false dichotomies that characterise our understandings of these comparisons. In my mind, this imposition feels inappropriate both because the tools employed do not always do the work at hand best *and* because I imagine it must discourage voices that otherwise have seats at the conversational table. This resultant invisibility and exclusion is not particular to international scholars any more than it is to other kinds of new actors, but as a recently minted law student embarking on doctoral study in sociology, I've been thinking more about the role of these actors in the periphery, and it is this reframing and hope with which I approach this response to Goyal's research on informal markets in Agra, a site I know little about but also felt a sense of solidarity with upon reading. As I will attempt to highlight throughout this response, perhaps global studies to be truly global will need to move past its positionality as global from the perspective of the West – a trap I found myself falling into periodically over the course of trying to respond to this chapter – to be more patient. I believe it is in willingness to learn and exchange solutions in a reciprocal fashion that we can acknowledge the importance of multi-dimensionality, and it is the constant commitment to re-centring voices that initially attracted me to this project.

Rather than restating Goyal's entire chapter, my response will engage with a few main takeaways that Goyal offers in an attempt to show the importance of creating room, using the inverse, and breaking down false East/West dichotomies that really just exist to privilege 'Western' over 'Eastern' contributions.

I. Animation of Discrimination

The most striking part of reading Goyal's piece to me was the way in which caste shaped (even if he did not claim causality about it) and impacted the market in Agra. Before reading the piece, I might have argued that understanding markets in Agra and by extension, India, could not have been understood absent caste. One would imagine that with caste being fundamental to how the market is experienced and transacted, using a frame that doesn't take account of caste glosses over both how the market actually works but more importantly how the market reproduces discrimination. Race, for me, operates in a fashion that is omnipresent and permeates everyday interactions. It is of course easy for me to note the ubiquity of race because of the prominence with which race has been salient in my life as a black person. It is through this lens that the obviousness of caste and its presence resonates with me, much like traditional frames resonate with me across legal, sociological, economic, political science etc, not taking into account the importance and salience of race. But Goyal's portrayal forces one to critically re-examine the use of one's traditional frames (here, my vision as a race scholar). At the same time, most racial analysis or stratification in general, happens in ways that do not pay attention to the conception of caste.

Like Goyal, albeit with different extensions, I find in my research on US legal education that the predominate frames surrounding its study fail to adequately capture the true nature of the entities they hypothesise about because they fail to meaningfully engage with the primary structures of discrimination at work there. Without adequately accounting for things such as caste and race in our frames, one could argue there is a fundamental breakdown of the ways in which we might be able to understand and meaningfully engage with oppression and its reproduction. For example, in the context of legal education most research might not consider the obvious (to me) possible connections between the experiences of black and *dalit* students. While invoking racial frameworks to think about caste oppression might feel natural, working with these concepts the other way has not always been seamless. This is not to say these categories are the same; they are certainly not. And they certainly do not do the same work. However, in my research, centring race and caste in an analysis of legal education has helped illuminate how legal education in India and the US hyper-reproduce hierarchies that reflect inherent societal discrimination. More importantly, such a framing has allowed space for connections to be drawn from these positions of similar oppression, thereby creating an opportunity for collaborative solution-building that borrows from the brain trust of *dalit* and black students.

Just as one cannot understand the markets in Agra without an understanding the nuanced overlay of the hierarchies that determine the actions of its individual actors and their imagined market audiences and counterparts, I argue that one cannot understand legal education without taking into consideration race and caste in both India and the United States. Race and caste cannot be considered as additive variables that can be added or substituted for each other; rather we must understand both if we are to understand the structure of legal education as it exists on a globalised scale. Some part of this is the institutional histories of these models: unlike race and caste perhaps, relationships between models of legal education exist as a function of the exportation of Global North structures. Further, due to the exportation of the model globally it is inappropriate to surmise the full understanding of the model by solely studying it within the US because the full extent of the model exists beyond just a US context: a recursivity that demands attention.

Goyal then offers me new ways to conceptualise and think about my own work. Viewing caste as something that can inform me, as a black law student in the United States, about race reveals connections about our respective positionality. It offers me that within the structure of legal education, despite differences, runs a common theme: thus problems, and solutions that *dalit* students use to combat the structure are now potential tools for black students and vice versa. I find that caste and race (similar yet different concepts) animate much of the outcomes in law school in both societies. While caste and race exist outside of legal education, they interact with legal education and produce outcomes in lockstep with inherent hierarchies existing in both societies. I am potentially able to learn from and take on the solutions deployed by *dalit* law students, even though race and caste are different, because of blacks' and *dalits*' shared position within the model. This interaction with Goyal offers another way to think about my engagement too: if, however, I don't consider the inverse, ie understand how caste informs how I understand race, I lose out on potential insight and solutions because information and understanding are only flowing in one direction and I'm merely imposing my own established understandings on something different. But as noted above, merely looking at just race doesn't capture the full extent of prejudice; thus I can't learn anything new if I do not take into account the specific ways and lessons to be learned from the structure's interaction with caste. Lastly, there is something to be said about how imperialism has crept into the ease with which US-based scholars such as myself use or impose Western frames to understand oppression.

Even for race scholars such as myself, the tendency is to understand anything that seems similar to race or ethnicity as operating under the same logics of race and ethnicity despite the fact that the concept is not race or ethnicity. Instead of learning perhaps a new set of logics and understanding attached to an identity category, we fall back on comfortable frames to help explain and understand phenomena. For me personally, in reading Goyal's piece, due to my orientation as race scholar, I zeroed in on the concept of caste, despite caste not being central to Goyal's analysis. Though the absence of the discussion of caste doesn't mean it isn't quite present. My keying into caste might provide the very example of imposing Western frameworks or ideological ways of thinking onto another context. While as a race scholar I may have wanted more discussion of caste, orientations that lead Western scholars to think only in our own terms have tricked Western scholars into believing that our own existing understanding of oppression and inequality in the West is absolute and superior. An example of this would be using what we know about race and merely imposing it on an Indian context and characterising it as applying also to caste, rather than opening up our own understandings as to how caste may help us understand our own logics of oppression and inequality related to race. Assuming that because we may fully understand race or a particular concept here, it must operate and fit into the same parameters there; and thus there being no need to consider what we might learn from another context.

II. Making Sense of Nonsense

Another important takeaway I want to highlight from Goyal's piece is how it makes sense of non-sense. By this I do not mean that Goyal's research is non-sense. Nor do I mean to suggest that Goyal does the work of making his work cognisable to the blind spots of predominate Western frames that usually render Goyal's subject matter unrecognisable. I use the phrase non-sense in reference to traditional Western frames that render Goyal's subject matter invisible, and to suggest that Goyal's work shows us why applying traditional frames in contexts where they don't belong is non-sensical. This highlights why it is imperative to not view information as existing in the silos of 'East' and 'West' and flowing only in one direction. Reducing reality to a one-directional framework or to one way of thinking because it is canonical, at best does a disservice to reality's complex multi-dimensionality; at worst it is an exercise in imperialist hegemony.

The first context in which Goyal displays this is that of the market in Agra itself. Goyal notes that the prevailing frame might view the markets in Agra as operating under a system whereby the banks lend credit to shoemakers to make shoes and eventually from profits accrued the shoemaker will be able to use savings to support trade credit in the future. Other predominate views might postulate that investors will buy up trade credit to continue the cycle or simply that shoemakers will form savings or credit associations that absorb their risks.

Goyal notes that none of these frames are applicable. This is because the particular market in Agra uses *parchi* (a trade credit slip) which is contextually specific device, not typically used in societies in the West. Further, this market is characterised and informed by caste and reputation, which can greatly influence whether a shoemaker goes to a trader to receive a *parchi*. As Goyal notes, the predominate economic frames cannot comprehend such interaction between the market, caste, and reputation because they themselves do not account for caste and reputation to begin with. As such, predominate frames as noted above cannot make sense of why the opulence of a trader's wedding might impact his bottom line in the market. Or why most traders are upper caste Punjabis, and shoemakers mostly lower caste Jatavs. Or why people reject financial institutions like banks and instead turn to their own created institutions with informal enforcement norms. This drives home the point that using a predominate frame, in Goyal's case one that centres banks, and markets' interactions with banks, would completely fail to explain Agra, where the individuals involved completely avoid banks.

Further, failing to take account of contextually specific variables, such as India's cultural context and informal enforcement norms, renders any theory insufficient to understand Agra. To miss these contextual variables results in a fundamental misunderstanding of what is occurring in Agra. What is occurring in Agra cannot be understood by applying the same frames that might be applicable in New York City and vice versa; which is why it is important that we must not rush to simply apply logics and frameworks that we are comfortable with in an effort to find our usual comfortable fit. As stated above, reality is complicated and multi-dimensional, and changes from context to context. There need to be spaces whereby we can sit and reflect on the specific contextual variables in an effort to learn from them. In some cases, this will mean that certain specific contextual variables are not transferable and in others it will mean that there is transferability. In the event that something is transferable, we must be aware of the direction in which information flows so as to maintain a shifting centre whereby information is equally diffused, retained, and valued.

As I reflected on Goyal's own search to subvert the traditional framework, I began to think of my own positionality. I'll borrow from Goyal here and pose the same question: *What makes my perspective merit any attention? What makes my own calls to pay closer attention to race and caste reciprocally matter?*

And the answer requires me to situate myself. After a couple of protests at the University of Missouri, I found myself in law school. On the eve of my first day of law classes, I was searching through the local Target store for school supplies. Presumably what any student would do before the first day of class. I remember vividly my anxiety that I needed to be over-prepared for the first day, partially because of first-day jitters and partially because as a black student I felt a sense of imposter syndrome. As I slowly filtered my way through various notebooks, highlighters, and pens, as every other back-to-school student in the store was doing, I suddenly felt like I was being gazed upon. As I turned around to verify my feeling, two elderly unknown white women approached me, peering at the notebooks in my hand. Before I knew it, one of the women said 'Starting school?'. Startled I responded 'Yeah.' To which the other woman replied 'Well that's just good for you.' To which her companion said 'Yeah that's good.' Frustrated and embarrassed I hurriedly left with a sense of deflation.

This experience was oddly emblematic of my interactions as a black law student with the law school model. It would not be the overt instances of racism that would come for me, although some black law students experience this. Mine were of the benign and benevolent kind: the kind that would make me the unqualified/qualified black expert on all things black in class; the kind that made other students avoid me and my fellow black students in the courtyard, whether we were soliciting more involvement from non-black students, actively inviting non-black classmates to our conversations, or, simply, hanging out; the kind that would lead to me being followed around at an LSAC forum[1] where I was recruiting other students because I didn't have the 'right look'.

Do these instances or my own black experience as a law student make my perspective 'the black perspective'? Certainly not by traditional standards, whereby all such claims need to be reduced to a variable and cross-referenced by the perfect number of interviews. But this 'scientific' approach has led to many harmful and frankly skewed perspectives about black law students, so why privilege it as an absolute good. And I do not claim ownership over the 'black' perspective, because I am just one person with one voice and the black experience is varied. Nevertheless I have moved through the model as a black student and there is yet and still something unique about being able to speak truth to power experienced and reflected upon. I speak not only from what I have intellectualised but from what I have had to sleep and wake up in every day for three years which can't accurately be reduced to a regression or an hour-long interview.

To be clear, I am not telling you, and my work does not attempt to tell you what the Indian law student experience feels like because I do not know what it feels like to be an Indian law student in India. I can only tell you what my own feelings are as a result of my own experience, much as I can't tell you what the experience of every black student who has ever gone to law school was like. I am not here attempting to say that because I have had the 'black' experience, I too have had the 'Dalit' experience. What my work *does* attempt to do is describe the space in which caste and race operate within US legal education and by extension the space in which Dalit and black law students operate within the model. I am not so much collapsing race and caste into one homogenous experience as I am describing a space within a shared structure that illuminates parallels and situated knowledge from oppressed groups experiencing similar phenomena.

I hope perhaps that analysing this shared space can give meaningful insight that can be harnessed by both black and Dalit students in solidarity with each other. My own experience helps inform connections I can see via the shared structural positionality of Dalit and black students. My approach does not fall in line with a pseudo-dominant approach that assumes 'race' is a superior analytical tool for understanding caste better. But drawing on Goyal, I search and wonder what might happen instead if one uses caste as a way to better teach lessons and illuminate untapped hidden answers about race. This might seem like a peculiar notion, since I have spent a lot of time stating how much I am not trying to equate caste with race, but now I am saying that it is possible for logics to be transferable from one to the other. I assure you that it's not a contradiction; it is indeed possible to understand and transfer logics from concept to concept without them being the same. The problem arises when scholars only understand and transfer

[1] Law School Admission Council.

logics in a unidirectional way and presume certain logics to be superior to others. Understanding caste as an instructive framework, and not just an entity that might be better understood by making it more palatable to Western scholars via race creates nuanced connections and forces those of us who have spent so much time imposing racialised frameworks on caste as learning objectives to look to reciprocate.

Course 3

KHORAKIWALA AND ROY

3

The Law, the Visual and Access to Justice in the Colonial Courts of India

RAHELA KHORAKIWALA

I. Introduction

As a law student in the Bombay High Court, I walked past carvings, statues, portraits, and inscriptions, without pausing to dwell on the images of justice that inhabited the juridical field alongside the precedents of justice (and injustice) being argued by lawyers in their courtrooms. Yet, I inherited a sense of pride in the history conserved in the Court, such that this sense of historicity was also part of my identity as a lawyer. It was when I encountered a wealth of literature on the iconography of justice, courtroom architecture and prolific images of justice, that I decided to research what law, visuality and culture in former presidency courts tell us about contemporary issues of access to justice. I borrow eclectically from a range of disciplines and sources – including visual studies, legal anthropology, aesthetics, legal theory and history – to frame my research.

My research more broadly (2019) looks at three high courts – the Bombay High Court, Madras High Court and Calcutta High Court – all from the erstwhile Presidency towns designated as centres of administration by the British. These three high courts were brought into existence at the same time, in July 1862, through Letters Patent issued by the then Queen, Victoria, which merged the several existing courts in each of these three towns under the ambit of one high court each. These were the first of the consolidated British judicial institutions, under the direct control of the British Crown, to be thus set up in colonial India. Although all three high courts were sanctioned and started their judicial work at the same time, the current buildings that these courts inhabit were built subsequently. The Calcutta High Court was completed first, in 1872, followed by the Bombay High Court in 1878, and the Madras High Court in 1892. The original buildings from the late 1800s are still the main court buildings for these three high courts. Therefore, there is a link between these three courts, having all commenced at the same time, under the same rules and regulations, but each having their own distinct identity. It is for this reason that I have selected these three high courts for my field research to represent the visual culture of courts in India.

Through my fieldwork in the former Presidency town high courts I analyse the intersection of law, visuality and culture. Observing these courts, I document the images of justice abounding in their precincts.[1] Using the intersection of multiple approaches and methods, I focus on how court buildings are structured in a way that hinders the physical access to justice. I am interested in exploring whether court spaces are neutral or if the judicial iconography has a symbolic effect in these spaces? How may we then define visual justice, or the relation between law and visual culture? In this chapter, I walk through these high courts asking these questions and highlighting different colonial practices that have carried forward to the contemporary era – creating and offering a recursive cycle of access to justice issues.

II. Law, Visuality and Culture

Visual justice as a concept, or more broadly, law and visual culture, draws upon different approaches and theories of iconography, semiotics and symbolism to reflect on law as a form of representation. Law is then not merely doctrinal, where black-letter law is treated as what the law stands for. Emphasising the relationship between law and the image, rather than only thinking of the law in terms of the written text, displaces the written word as the privileged way of defining law. Throughout this chapter, I argue that the law may be understood through its ocular representations which manifest in a variety of ways that are constitutive of what we understand by visual justice, or more broadly, the visual culture of law.

Taking judicial iconography as a starting point gives various allegories and images of law and justice a new meaning.[2] The symbolic power of law and justice is crucial to law's legitimacy. Rather than following a purely semiotic approach to law, therefore, I adopt a socio-legal method to understand the relationship between law and visual culture. This approach allows me to describe how the law establishes a judicial iconography that becomes a symbol of the majesty and dignity that it holds itself to.

In other words, I depart from the model of legal research that largely focuses on the rules of law, interpretation and the analysis of judicial decisions and associated

[1] For a detailed study of the various images of justice that abound the colonial high courts, see R Khorakiwala, *From the Colonial to the Contemporary: Images, Iconography, Memories, and Performances of Law in India's High Courts* (Oxford, Hart Publishing, 2019).

[2] E Panofsky, 'Iconography and Iconology: An Introduction to the Study of Renaissance Art' in E Panofsky, *Meaning in the Visual Arts* (Phoenix IL, The University of Chicago Press, 1982) ch 1, 26–54.

legislative enactments. Rather I argue that when a legal system is looked at in terms of its judicial iconography, then a new form of socio-legal research of the visual culture of courts becomes possible. This form of ethnography of the visual culture in courts engages with the judicial space, not only in terms of the law that is promulgated from its orders and judgments, but also through the regulation of the visual in the law, the symbolism of the courtroom as a performative space, and the constitution of the court as a theatre where justice is not only done, but must also be seen to be done.[3]

This ethnographic work focuses on the architecture of the courts, the dress worn by the various court actors, the debates over the language that the court uses and the official names of the court, along with the symbolism of the ceremony and ritual that is part of the court's daily routine. The avenues of analysis are not restricted only to the outwardly visual (ie what someone in the court sees) but also to the visual that is controlled through restrictions on photography and video recording – restrictions that speak, to borrow from Robert Cover, of the law's 'jurispathic' tendency to violently control competing images that challenge its legitimacy.[4]

In controlling the analytical imagery of the ways in which these spaces can be seen, the law manages to represent itself and create a visual culture of its own. Through this visual culture, the law creates a memory of itself that defines not only the present, but the past and the future as well. Judicial iconography not only conserves history and memory in specific ways, but also narrates a specific internal history about how law creates and negotiates its symbolic power. Therefore, the visual presentation of law, and in this specific case the courts of law, creates a history for itself that defines the meaning of judicial iconography for courts and acknowledges the presence of legal symbolism that alters the way the court is perceived, feared and venerated. While research on the judicial iconography of courts is prevalent across the world, in India it is a relatively nascent field of research.

The Bombay High Court, the Madras High Court and the Calcutta High Court have similarities and differences, and asking the same questions in three different spaces talks to the larger argument of the visual culture of courts that exists in the first three colonial high courts of India. Comparing the courts brings forward the alternating views on symbolism in courts of law and how law maintains an image of itself in order to control the environment within which it thrives. The three high courts therefore present what can be considered the first analysis of a developed visual culture of courts in India, which can then be taken forward and applied to other courts in India that have been constructed subsequently.

[3] P Goodrich, 'Law by Other Means' (1998) 10(2) *Cardozo Studies in Law and Literature* 111–16.

[4] R Cover, 'Nomos and Narrative' in M Minow, M Ryan and A Sarat (eds), *Narrative, Violence, and the Law: The Essays of Robert Cover* (Ann Arbor MI, The University of Michigan Press, 1995) ch 3, 139.

This research thus makes it possible for iconography and semiotics to enter the legal vision of India and exposes the courts of law to new debates and discussions. Certain inherent practices and procedures are integral to the existence and survival of the majesty and dignity of the law, and this has a subsequent effect on one form of access to justice. The question to be asked is whether the majesty of the law is critical to the way the law is revered and followed. If the answer is in the affirmative, then the visual culture of the court is of paramount importance, as it plays a crucial role in maintaining that image of the law from which it derives its power, dignity and respect – an image that directly affects how the courts are approached and perceived.

III. Ethnographic Work in the Three High Courts

In this section, I narrate my experiences in the field. Even though I had access to courts as a lawyer, my position as a researcher allowed me to appreciate how access to courts is regulated for people who are not part of the legal system.[5] In the Bombay High Court, it was fairly simple for me to approach judges, lawyers and court staff. Most persons were willing to communicate and answer questions. The Madras High Court was the most welcoming court in terms of academic research, as they provided access to various forms and modes of information, and persons in the court were approachable, amiable and in favour of an academic looking at their court. The Calcutta High Court was hostile at the start of the fieldwork but over time the court became more approachable and provided a trove of resources to aid in understanding the colonial legacy of the three high courts and how it has been carried forward in the post-colonial context.

In terms of the visual, images of law and justice abound in the interior and exterior of the Bombay High Court. There are numerous books that document images of the court through which these iconographic aspects can be studied.[6] The Bombay Bar Association, with a history of its own, is also active in bringing to the forefront the various images of justice that exist in the Bombay High Court. Tracing the history of the origin of the court and the creation of its structure, I asked present-day judges, lawyers and court staff about their visualisation of the high court as it stands today. The conversations with persons in the court have

[5] As a lawyer, dressed according to statute, one had access to the courts that were different if one were not dressed in this uniform – court entrances were different; what you could carry into the courtroom changed; and court staff's approach towards you was altered.

[6] For example, see R Mehrotra and S Dwivedi, *The Bombay High Court: The Story of the Building, 1878–2003* (Mumbai, Eminence Designs Pvt Ltd, 2004), D Chandrachud, A Mohta and R Dalvi, *A Heritage of Judging: The Bombay High Court through One Hundred and Fifty Years* (Mumbai, Maharashtra Judicial Academy & Indian Mediation Centre & Training Institute, 2012) and K Samant-Gupte, *Vakilnama: Celebrating 150 years of the Advocates' Association of Western India* (Mumbai, Advocates' Association of Western India, 2014).

informed my discussion and analysis of the symbolism and iconography of the apex court for that jurisdiction.

Having an association with the Bombay High Court as a law student and as a lawyer, along with living in Bombay city, my interaction with the high court stemmed from familiarity. This familiarity was restricted to the practices and procedures in the court. Definitively, in the past, I had not observed the Bombay High Court through the lens of judicial iconography, and my introduction to the visual field of law altered my viewpoint toward the court. The references to iconographical work and literature become clearly defined in the court spaces of the Bombay High Court. The attributes of justice come alive in terms of how the law visualises justice and the tools it uses to settle these debates. The majesty and dignity of the court is brought out in the large and small daily rituals, and in the same way that it imposes itself on court actors, the majesty and dignity manage to permeate through to all persons who enter its precincts.

Therefore, I would find myself bowing, not only while entering and exiting the courtrooms, but also while entering and exiting a judge's chamber after conducting an interview. I attended court dressed in black and white – sometimes Western formal wear and sometimes Indian. This uniform, which resembled that of a lawyer, provided me with a certain amount of legitimacy, but still not completely as I would not wear the lawyer's black robe or the prescribed white band. In the case of the Bombay High Court my uniform was not controversial, even though the actors of the court were clear that their uniform was a necessity to keep them apart from those who were 'outsiders'. Interactions became permissible when they were anonymous and when questions that were tagged as controversial were either not answered or approached with caution.

The didactic hierarchy of the court manifested in several ways, the most striking of which was my interaction with a judge who, upon seeing my interview request letter, decided not to speak with me, but chose to inform me of their decision in person. When I entered the chamber, the judge's first question was whether I had requested to interview judges in order of seniority. I was told to correct this action and then approach my judge-respondents as per the court-mandated hierarchy. On the other hand, junior judges, who had only recently been elevated to the Bench, were less concerned with maintaining the correct order of precedence and spoke to me freely about their dealings and interactions with the court. It felt as though they had not yet been completely formalised into the hierarchy of the court, and as soon as they were, a distance would be created between those who sit elevated and those who look up towards justice.

The sharing of personal stories and anecdotes was an interesting aspect of my interactions with lawyers and court staff in the Bombay High Court. The court was a space where they belonged and a space they identified with. This was also evident in the fact that most persons in the Bombay High Court had noticed the carvings and design work around the high court pillars, although they might not have known the significance or symbolism behind them. In contrast, in the Calcutta High Court, not everyone had observed the carvings that adorn the front façade of its building.[7] While attending a walking tour of the Bombay High Court, conducted by a conservationist architect, some attendees turned to ask legal questions related to the court. I was presented with an opportunity to talk about the 1908 *Tilak* trial,[8] jury trials and other explanations of the symbolism of the court that occurred through the presence of the idea of judicial iconography.

Therefore, the study of the judicial iconography is important for re-examining the meaning of justice in terms of the way it is projected. Beginning with observing this court, certain procedures appeared routine. However, when viewing the same processes outside of a familiar setting, in Madras and Calcutta, the processes developed as more than just daily rituals but things that assisted the courts in maintaining their legitimacy. I looked at the Bombay High Court first and then revisited it in light of my fieldwork in Madras and Calcutta, and the processes, procedures, signs and symbols within the Bombay High Court became more apparent and evident. These revisits allowed me to contribute more fully to the literature on how the image is represented in terms of law and justice by documenting the visual culture of courts layer by layer rather than just in a top-down manner.

The Madras High Court was the court that was most open and welcoming during the course of my fieldwork. The idea of a researcher writing about the high court was taken to positively and appreciated by most. Several people wanted to provide information for the purposes of spreading awareness about the court. Judges, lawyers and court staff willingly spoke to me and answered questions related to my research and even provided me with the available research material in certain cases. People in the court were well aware of the court's history and of its most popular symbol, the lighthouse on top of the high court building. Judges, lawyers and court staff described the high court passionately and several judges and lawyers were actively involved in restoration efforts to retain the original features and characteristics of the 1892 building.

While on one hand the court was open to research and allowed me access to various resources, on the other hand, the culture that permeated the court allowed for them to be curious about the status of a female researcher. While I had my set of questions for the court actors, every male respondent I interviewed had one common question in exchange: was I married? Some extended the question to whether I had children. One person offered me blessings in order to have a child soon. Though research and academic inquiry were supported, my respondents were surprised that this inquiry was being conducted by a woman alone. Many people asked me how my family had permitted me to come alone, and how I was able to do this research alone. Whether my formal black and white clothing was Western or Indian, the dress code I followed did not raise eyebrows nearly as much

[7] In both the high courts you can find carvings of flora, fauna and human faces, amongst other things.

[8] See R Khorakiwala, 'Memorializing history in the Bombay High Court' (2017) 1(3) *Indian Law Review* 269.

as the fact that I had been permitted by my family to research alone. It was interesting to see these dynamics play out within the court space where judgments were made based on curiosity.

While I sat in court and made notes or walked around and observed, many people would ask me my purpose and offer to help. Approaching individuals for interviews was permissible as long as I protected my respondents' anonymity. The Madras High Court was the most accessible court of the three in terms of how easy it was to approach judges, lawyers, and staff, as well as the availability of resources. While I was able to gather information in the other two courts, I faced the least resistance in the Madras High Court.

My observations of the court and its functioning over time indicated that the court personnel accepted that they had a colonial heritage but were ready to move ahead into a legacy of their own. Certain old practices, for example, following the distinction between solicitors and advocates, that have been abolished by statute, do not find customary following in the Madras High Court, although they are still practised in the Bombay High Court and the Calcutta High Court. The Madras High Court displays a strong sense of 'Tamil' culture, for instance, but it does not impose this wholly on an outsider. My inability to communicate in Tamil did not prove to be a hindrance in personal interactions. Therefore, this high court is unique in its capacity to maintain its own identity and still stand out as one of the first high courts to be established in India that continues its legacy and practices to-date. The visual field of law created by this high court encompasses several iconographical symbols, signs and characteristics that become representative of the visual culture of courts in India. In the Madras High Court, the original statues are juxtaposed with newer statues that have been placed post-Independence, which contributes to the legal consciousness of the court personnel and its visitors.[9]

Interviewing judges, lawyers and court staff in the Calcutta High Court allowed for a new space of understanding and discussion about the court built in the then-capital of British India. After the Bombay High Court and the Madras High Court, the Calcutta High Court presented me with an alternative perspective and mandated that different questions be asked and new propositions looked at.

My initial few days in the Calcutta High Court were marked by hostile experiences that challenged the method I had used to approach the field til then. While in Bombay and Madras I could approach interviewees directly, in Calcutta I needed a reference before approaching someone. Therefore, I had to create a different method for this field. The strongest reaction that I received was from the Judges' Library. Having been granted access to these libraries in the Bombay High Court and the Madras High Court, I took it for granted that the case would be the same in the Calcutta High Court. But when I approached the library for research

[9] For a detailed study on statues in the Madras High Court see R Khorakiwala, 'Legal Consciousness as Viewed through the Judicial Iconography of the Madras High Court' (2018) 5(1) *Asian Journal of Law and Society* 111.

work I was sternly informed that the entire space was a 'secret space' and that I had no right to enter it. I was asked to leave immediately. When I was later granted access through the assistance of a judge of the Calcutta High Court, the hierarchy of the court became stark. While the persons in the equation remained the same, the dynamics had now completely changed – I was welcomed by the same staff that had earlier restricted me and I was given access to all parts of the library.

The fact that the library had been described as a 'secret' space is important, as each person plays a role in visualising the judicial space and then attaches their own legitimising tools to this notion. Therefore, the idea of shrouding the law in secrecy works towards the law placing itself at a distance from where it can demand to be viewed in terms of its dignity and majesty. Even though I had crossed the barrier into the library and the high court became more accessible, secrecy was still at work. There were still several persons who chose not to answer all my questions and respondents refused to speak with me except on condition of anonymity. While the end result is the same, the means employed can be different based on individual perceptions.

Notably, most people at the Calcutta High Court did not have a lot of information about the history of the high court building other than the fact that it was designed on the basis of the Ieper cloth hall in Belgium. Several persons who entered the court on a regular basis said they had not observed the designs on the capital of the pillars that have carvings of foliage, human and animal figures and objects like books and musical instruments, among other things. Further, on the occasion of the 150-year celebrations of the Calcutta High Court, the pillars were painted and the original colour of the Caen stone has now been covered. Additionally, a walkway has recently been constructed that connects the main high court building to the centenary building of the high court. Due to its structure and position, it covers half of the front façade of the Calcutta High Court when looking left from the main entrance under the central tower. Therefore, when the high court is now looked at from the front, the full set of 24 pillars is no longer visible. The lack of observation of these iconographical symbols highlights how images of justice have different interpretational values for different observers and ties into the work of Erwin Panofsky and Roberta Kevelson on how iconography and symbolism have varied meanings for different viewers.[10]

Rules were followed in an unpredictable manner around the Calcutta High Court. One aspect that was important was the dress code. Although in the other high courts I did not need to wear the lawyer's black gown and the white band, it became a practical necessity in the Calcutta High Court. The rules allowed only lawyers to carry a bag inside the courtroom. Their definition of a lawyer was one who wore the gown and the band and although I was a lawyer, without the uniform I was denied entry. The court did not offer an alternative place to keep one's belongings and therefore access became a problem. Even when I wore the gown and band,

[10] For a detailed reading of Panofsky and Kevelson's work see Khorakiwala (2019), n 1 above, ch 2.

my dress remained a contentious issue in the Calcutta High Court. On one day I wore a blue and white striped shirt and a black jacket under the gown, and people repeatedly told me that I was incorrectly dressed and must leave the courtroom. A slight change in the white colour of my shirt and I was chided by lawyers in court by saying that either I should leave the courtroom or not wear the band and gown. This situation occurred enough times for me to re-check *The Bar Council of India Rules, 1975*[11] that prescribe the dresses or robes to be worn by advocates. These rules are written for advocates who intend to appear before the court. As I was not appearing before the judges, the rules being imposed seemed out of place.

Another issue I faced on access was with two books that I wanted to acquire. The Calcutta High Court had issued two souvenir volumes, one each on the occasion of the centenary and on 125 years of the high court. Initially I was told that the books were sold by one of the administrative offices of the high court. When I went there, the staff refused to entertain me. After several requests they said they had not seen these books before. After a few days of continuous requests, they located the books. When I offered to purchase the books they said since they had not sold them as far back as they remember they did not know what price the books should be sold at. They decided to seek permission from higher authorities. Once they had spoken to these authorities I was called in and informed they had decided not to sell the books at all as they are valuable for the high court. I tried to point out that the books had been located only upon my request, but instead I was offered a 'courtesy photocopy' of the books instead. After spending a week compelling them to locate the books and then being denied access, the entire process seemed to speak of the way the court maintained its legitimacy through different forms of denial.

The Calcutta High Court is a court that deals with its legitimacy in a different way from the Bombay High Court and the Madras High Court. A colonial legacy pervaded the processes of the court. In the end, I had the opportunity to speak to the maximum number of persons in the Calcutta High Court. Therefore, more often than not, when the law attempts secrecy, it wants to deny access to its interior so as to maintain an image of its exterior. This practice speaks of the visual culture of courts in India through the colonial High Courts as constructed by the British.

IV. Access to Justice

This ethnographic work forms the background to my research into the issue of access to justice. Access to justice can be interpreted in a multitude of ways – and here I will focus on how the law physically restricts the outsider as well as creating an image of constraint that limits access to the law. Kafka's parable *Before the Law* (1915) is a powerful reflection on this restricted access to justice for persons both

[11] Under the *Advocates Act, 1961*.

within and outside the law.[12] Even its title raises an important question: why is the text referred to as being 'before' the law? Is it possible that before the law there is lawlessness or that there is no law at all? What, then, is the position of a person coming towards the law or approaching the law? For our purposes, the relevant interpretation of this story is that when law exists or one is made to stand before the law, then the law creates restrictions and obstructions, generating alienation that, over time, becomes normalised. As a part of this 'normalisation' one begins to accept and believe that the law is meant to be guarded by a gatekeeper and therefore the onus of crossing the barrier created before the law is on the person approaching the law and not the person dispensing the law. This blockade also symbolises that, within this space, some people are always out and some people are always in. The distinction becomes categorical.

The access to justice argument fits into this narrative. The man from the country in Kafka's parable seeks his right to a day in court.[13] However, while the 'gate to the law stands open, as always' he encounters an obstacle to his access to the court in the form of the gatekeeper. In my fieldwork, the court buildings all have open and welcoming front façades. However, when one attempts to enter the Bombay High Court and the Madras High Court from these main entrances, it becomes clear that this entrance is restricted and strictly for the honourable judges of the high court only.[14] The entrance for those seeking to assist the law or access the law is on another side of the building. Even when entering there are restrictions based on whether one is a lawyer, a litigant or the general public. The entrance thus becomes the first symbol of visual control, along with a spatial and logistical control, exercised by the court.

An example of restrictions on access to justice for litigants is seen in *Sajid Ali v State and Others*[15] in the Delhi High Court, the case of a litigant summoned to a proceeding who was not permitted to enter the court premises as he did not have a photo identity card. Due to this, the litigant was not given a gate pass and was therefore denied access into the high court. The judgment in the case further refers to an earlier Order of the Delhi High Court in the same case, that states, 'The present case is one in a series of cases where it has been brought to our notice the difficulty being faced by the litigants in accessing the court system in the current gate pass regime'. The Order acknowledges that only for a want of a photo ID card, the litigant, who had travelled from far, was unable to enter the court premises and

[12] F Kafka, 'Before the Law' in *The Trial*, (trans) I Johnston, available at: http://johnstoniatexts.x10host.com/kafka/beforethelawhtml.html (accessed 30 June 2020). The parable is about a man who tries to gain entry to the law but is continuously denied the same by a gatekeeper. When the man is dying, the gatekeeper informs him that this entrance was only meant for him and will now be closed.

[13] ibid.

[14] In the Calcutta High Court, there is also a separate entrance that is restricted for use only by the judges of the high court. However, this is not the main entrance of the court; it is the entrance to the left of the main entrance.

[15] *Sajid Ali v State and Others* 2013 VII AD (Delhi) 670.

so to appear before the court in the said matter.[16] In this case, as is the case of the man from the country, a blockade is set into motion by the presence of the 'gate pass' and even though the person is a litigant in his own case, he is denied access to the court. Further, the court's reflection on the 'blockade' indicates how justice is blockaded by the systemic architecture of the court.[17]

As Kafka's narrative continues, the gatekeeper says that he is powerful but notes that even with this power he is the 'lowliest gatekeeper' and that 'from room to room stand gatekeepers, each more powerful than the last'. People who get past the 'lowliest gatekeepers' at the security entrance will encounter a court that is filled with them. Courts are structured in a didactic format, as noted by Goodrich, in which the hierarchy perpetrated by the court creates the second ocular register that places the law over everything that comes before it.[18] The structures of courts and courtrooms allow for the theoretical and physical hierarchy to be preserved and carried forward. In the high courts, courtroom number 1 (or the largest courtroom) is assigned to the Chief Justice of the court, who is at the top of the hierarchy. In the case of the Bombay High Court, this chamber propagates the hierarchy, with the judges seated in an elevated didactic position. Similarly, a lawyer in the Calcutta High Court commented that the judges of the Calcutta High Court are like teachers, the way they manage the court and correct the persons who present themselves before the bench. The hierarchy continues in the way the lawyers are positioned ahead of the litigants in the limited space of the court. Litigants and

[16] In its judgment, dated 3 May 2013, the Delhi High Court notes similar difficulties in accessing the courtrooms in several other cases. The judgment deliberates over judgments of the Supreme Court of India that mandate that any impediment to accessing the courtroom is an 'impediment to the fundamental and human right of access to justice'. The judgment reiterates that the judiciary in India follows the open-court principle, which creates transparency and reinforces confidence in the court system. The court also clarifies that the right to witness court proceedings is not restricted to litigants or parties listed in a case. It is open to third parties who wish to observe court proceedings also. At paragraph 29, the court asks, 'is it permissible to put in place a security regime that could have the effect of keeping members of the general public (including bona fide litigants) without identification documentation from accessing the courtroom?' The judgment concludes with directions to form a committee with representatives from the different high courts and government departments to create a regime that ensures persons can access court without compromising security concerns.

[17] The judgment discusses in detail the various difficulties that people face in procuring photo ID in India, along with the different laws that make it mandatory for people to attend court proceedings, thereby placing the gate pass provision in conflict with certain procedural laws. The court also provides examples of different institutions that have modified their rules to balance security concerns with access issues. An example they provide of this is the Delhi Metro Rail Corporation (DMRC), which handles lakhs (100,000s) of customers daily without impeding physical access through stringent identity requirements. Pointedly, the judgment notes (at para 34), that, 'We are still grappling with and struggling to overcome psychological, social, financial, technical, technological, geographical barriers to access to justice, and a security regime which provides for an absolute entry point barrier; it results in an exclusion which is complete'. The judges are clear when they say that they cannot permit the high courts and other subordinate courts to become 'privileged space[s]' accessible only to those with documentation. They state that the constitutionally protected rights of the people would be severely violated in such instances.

[18] P Goodrich, *Modalities of Legal Annunciation: A Linguistics of Courtroom Speech* (London, Weidenfeld and Nicolson, 1990).

the general public usually find themselves towards the bottom of the hierarchy of this internal courtroom structure.[19]

There is another internal grading system among the lawyers. Senior lawyers are always at the front and junior lawyers are behind. Further – and I noticed this across all the three high courts – if a senior lawyer enters the courtroom, the junior gets up and gives the seat to the senior lawyer. This is done without any explicit request; it is a given that a 'junior' in the system acts in this manner. The hierarchy is therefore well internalised and accepted as normal. The power structure that Kafka writes about manifests itself in many ways and in several spaces in the court structure.[20] In this example it is seen through the architectural structure of the court and its effect on the minds of the persons who function through these structures. The court has a multitude of gatekeepers, from the security officers who frisk people entering the court building to the court staff and security personnel positioned outside courtrooms who restrict entry based on various criteria. The gatekeepers also exist in the form of the persons who correct the dress code of lawyers and sometimes litigants in courtrooms, along with the people who deny information to those who ask questions about the court. Access to the courts of law therefore is restricted in a physical sense by these gatekeepers.

The idea of law being accessible does cross the mind of the man from the country in Kafka's parable.[21] He believes that 'the law should always be accessible for everyone' but the description and the image of the gatekeeper make him decide not to question his lack of access. The court uses such self-created images to create a sense of awe and distance. The image is so strong that a person approaching the court will think several times before entering the premises. When I spoke to several people who attended the exhibition celebrating 150 years of the Bombay High Court, they thought that the court had been opened temporarily for the exhibition – they did not know that it was open to the public. Numerous people, not from the field of law, were extremely pleased to have the opportunity to enter the high court and see it from inside. They were completely oblivious to the fact that the court is a public space and every person is in principle allowed to walk in and attend court proceedings. The categorical image of the court and the law – the feeling that one is always 'before the law' and must follow the restrictions placed either by gatekeepers or by the visual perceptions of the law – remains constant. Since the law is hidden in this sense from the outside, often one does not know how the court functions from within.

Instead, ideas of the internal functioning of the court are influenced by external perceptions, literature, journalistic reports, TV, Bollywood and regional cinema, and a general sense that the law is superior and therefore unknown. The fact that most of those I spoke with in the three high courts are not in favour of

[19] See L Mulcahy, *Legal Architecture: Justice, Due Process and the Place of Law* (New York, Routledge, 2011).

[20] Kafka, 'Before the Law', n 12 above.

[21] ibid.

photography, video recording or live telecasting of court proceedings is indicative of how the law still wants to maintain secrecy over its internal functioning and imagery. These modes of the ocular are not permitted in the court space, thereby restricting the internal image of the court from being externalised. Those on the outside therefore resort to alternative means of visualising the law, creating an ambiguity in the perception of the nature of the law. The law works towards maintaining this ambiguity, as it allows for it to control the image of its self. Therefore, when outsiders face the necessity of accessing the law, they approach it in awe and bewilderment as they are unaware of what lies 'ahead of the law'.

Kafka's narration ends with the man of the country still outside the door, aged and nearing his death, when the gatekeeper – who has apparently not aged – informs him that this particular entrance to the law was 'assigned only to you' and that he is 'going now to close it'.[22] The fact that the man seeking the law perishes without ever gaining entry while the person guarding it does not age further calls into question the principle of access to justice versus the modes of reaching it. While persons seeking to use the law might perish amidst the complicated use of legal language and court procedures, and the lawyer might get swallowed up by the dress code of black gowns and white bands, the law only grows to be bigger and more majestic at every step. The way the court is structured, in its physical form along with its rules and traditions, contribute to this feeling of awe towards the law and the courts. The judicial iconography that exists in the three high courts provides certain symbolic images of the law and plays a role in how the court is perceived. Being large structures, there is already a mixed feeling of awe and fear when one walks into the court for the first time. Many persons I spoke with during my fieldwork, from judges to lawyers and court staff, noted that they did have a sense of admiration when they entered the courts. Often those who had no prior interaction with the court felt this most acutely, sometimes even to the point of fear. For those who had been to court before or had been associated with the law before the high court became their workplace, there was admiration but not necessarily the fear, since the initial blockade had been crossed and they had moved to the other side.

While the physical aspect of awe plays a role, there are also rules and traditions of the high courts that contribute to this admiration of the law and prevent one from questioning its processes and methods. One such tradition is the use of the word *lordship* to refer to the judges. The term automatically elevates the judges to a superior, venerable position and reminds the persons accessing the law that they are amidst a hierarchy. While the use of this word is not mandatory it has become so much a part of the language of the court that it is used as a conjunction to complete sentences when speaking in court. While the kind of language and terminology used in courts is a large field, I specifically focus on the use of this one word and how it can make the language of the court confusing for someone who is

[22] ibid.

not part of the system. Another tradition of acknowledging the death of a lawyer by calling a '10.30' or a '3.30' in the Calcutta High Court and adjourning court proceedings for the day, can easily turn into a denial of access to law and justice; if the court closes for the day without prior warning, those already standing before the law face sudden adjournment of their case. Therefore, access is hindered by a tradition of the court.

There is a continuous discussion on the lack of space in the Bombay High Court – cases are filed in the court to resolve the issue – yet the largest courtroom remains unused, conserved as a site that memorialises the sedition trial of the freedom fighter Lokmanya Tilak. The actual operations of the law here take a back seat to the court's institutional history as remembered and recollected by the judges, lawyers, court staff and others. The legal history of the court identifies the law as documented in judgments, rules and regulations. The conflict between the institutional and legal histories of the court is brought to the forefront in the case of the sedition trial of Tilak that was held in the central courtroom of the Bombay High Court.[23] In my work, *From the Colonial to the Contemporary: Images, Iconography, Memories, and Performances of Law in India's High Courts*, I discuss in detail the way architecture and judicial iconography are significant in the colonial high courts of India and how history and memory are often reconfigured to materialise a specific pride and prestige and reflect on a recurring historical tension between Indian and British concepts of justice.[24]

Courtrooms in all three high courts were often crowded, especially in the mornings when additional matters had to be heard, or when there was an important case before the bench. When I asked people in court if the space in the courtrooms was sufficient, most felt that it was inadequate at certain times, depending on the matter to be heard. Some suggested that litigants and/or the general public should be excluded to ease the load of the courtrooms, pointing out that since the high courts were largely courts of appeal, litigants were not required to be present. Of course, this opinion was held by only a few interviewees, but it reflects how access to justice is denied at various levels.

In the Madras High Court, the judges enter the court premises using the same corridor as everyone else. Due to this there is a tradition of keeping silent and standing against the walls of the corridors when the judge walks past. When I encountered this practice for the first time, the whole process was confusing and unsettling: sitting on a bench, I suddenly heard the sound 'shh' as an indication of silence and several people looked at me sternly, telling me to stand up. When the judge walked past all present had to bow. After a while the process normalised and my reaction to the sound of 'shh' became a reflex. However, the existence of such performances is another obstacle in the access to justice.

[23] For the full debate on the intersection of law, history and memory in the Bombay High Court see Khorakiwala (2017), n 8 above.

[24] Khorakiwala (2019), n 1 above.

The three high courts of Bombay, Madras and Calcutta are large structures with a specific and unique judicial iconography that relates to their particular architectural requirements. They are colonial-built courts that have carried forward and merged into the Indian judicial system with the promulgation of *The Constitution of India, 1950*. These courts have certain rules and traditions that, coupled with their iconography, create a system of a semiotics of law. The existence of these signs and symbols of law creates a particular and unique visual culture for these courts that portrays the ambivalent relationship that the law shares with the image. Through the course of my research, I explore various registers at which the law controls its image. In this section, reading my ethnographic experiences along with the idea of access to law in Kafkaesque terms, I reach the conclusion that the current structures and rules and/or traditions of the court work in a direction that hinders citizens' path to reach the law and thereby eventually restricts the accessibility of the law. While the iconography, symbolism and traditions are a part of the image of the court through which it gains legitimacy, they are also a tool by which the court keeps itself at a distance. The two ideas therefore conflict with each other and create an alienation from the law similar to the kind faced by the man from the country. The juxtaposition of the law between access and denial challenges the very purpose of the court and therefore the high courts would benefit from a balanced rendering of access – where the man from the country not only stands before the law but is able to decipher and decode what the gatekeeper expects. It is only when he is able to accept what is 'normal' to the court that he can even begin to fathom the possibility of any access to that law, but the slips between his acceptance and actual and complete access still remain stark.

V. Conclusion

My access to the three high courts of Bombay, Madras and Calcutta allowed me to create a database of the judicial imagery and iconography that manifests in these spaces. The data creates an archive of the first three high courts of India. Further, it brings these three high courts within the same space and links them together in multiple ways. The ethnographical work is informed by the existing literature available in the field. Each court narrates a visual history that talks to its present and portrays the relationship between law and the image. The three high courts in my research create the same paradoxes and the research adds to the existing literature in this field.

The method of ethnographic fieldwork was important to this site of study as the imagery of the court can only be understood in the context of the functioning of the court and can be further classified by the conversations within the court. Being a part of the court processes allowed for me to become a part of the judicial space in order to understand the images of justice that the courts were creating and how they affected the way I have defined access to justice. Being able to look at the three high courts and analyse their data simultaneously was the primary source of information that was available to me as a resource. Being a participant observant to court proceedings created the space for me to be within and observe from outside. During the course of my fieldwork I interchanged my own roles between being a lawyer and being a researcher which allowed me to observe the court through different lenses and realise that identity plays an important part in the courts of law. The representation of this was brought out in the maximum through the prescribed courtroom dress. The 'uniform' of a lawyer became an important attribute of the fieldwork process, as it provided access of a different kind.

When accessibility is read in these terms, court spaces are then not considered to be neutral. In terms of the visual, the dress code is an important signifier and has a direct effect on the access to justice of court spaces. The dress allows the lawyers to become visible and therefore gain access, while the absence of the same makes litigants and the general public entering the court invisible. Within members of the legal fraternity, there are also insiders and outsiders, which is detailed through my own field experiences; for example, the denial of permission to enter the Judges' Library in Calcutta followed by the all-access permission granted subsequently. Through my presence in the field, I was able to identify the varied aspects that define visual justice and are perceptible in these high courts. While my larger project details the research as identified above, this chapter illustrates the tenuous relationship between the law and its own perceived image as witnessed in the colonial high courts of India.

The Visual Culture of Law in India: A Response

SURYAPRATIM ROY

Law might appear to be autonomously constitutive, but it is derivatively performative: people are constrained or facilitated depending on where they stand in relation to the constitutive forces behind legal expressions. A recent push for anti-Franco memory laws in Spain may be symptomatic of a cosmopolitan shift; however, this shift may be performative of material trends – the distribution of capital is no longer tied to the naturalisation of Francoist historical memory.[1] A similar mechanism is in play in European jurisprudence on social rights: the word 'social' is often used to privilege the claims of bounded communities in the centre over migrant workers from the periphery.[2] Looking at a legal text is perhaps not the best way of seeing the distributive role[3] of law.

Khorakiwala takes a different tack. It is important to literally *look* carefully before we see a text and call it law. Before we concentrate on the words that we see as law and engage in an investigative exercise on where the law really is, why don't we pause a bit over what we are looking at? Perhaps words are not the only starting point. What if the constitutive forces behind law find expression in pictures, architecture, dress? Further, if we are to pause for a bit over such *things*, then we might gain a better window into the real life of law. Words may be used to cover-up, confound or simplify. Perhaps buildings that house courtrooms tell us more about the architecture of law. Specifically, it may tell us quite a bit about the forces that shape and restrict access to justice. Khorakiwala runs with this insight. Invisible global interactions under colonial rule that shaped and persist in Indian law are revealed trenchantly through courtroom architecture and images of justice.

Accordingly, the visual culture of law is performative. We can also ask if and how it constitutes the relational through constraint or facilitation. Such an inquiry

[1] S Roy, 'Never Any End to an Event: Review article' (2018) 13 *Journal of Comparative Law* 132. See the Historical Memory Law (Ley 57/2007) *Ley de Memoria Histórica*, reversing the previous trend of oblivion, know as the Pact of Forgetting – *Pacto del olvido*.

[2] S Roy, Review of 'D Ferri and F Cortese (eds) *The EU Social Market Economy and the Law: Theoretical Perspectives and Practical Challenges for the EU* (Abingdon: Routledge, 2019)' (2019) 56(5) *Common Market Law Review* 1427.

[3] A first attempt at identifying distributive concerns in a particular regulatory instrument may be found in S Roy 'Distribution as the Organizing Principle of Environmental Regulation' (2018) 19(3) *German Law Journal* 649.

would not necessarily dilute the pervasiveness of the colonial project or shift our focus away from the visual, but introduce a functional positionality to map encounters that may explain that project's iterative bearing on the present.

My intervention in this brief response is in two parts. I wish to first appreciate Khorakiwala's contribution within scholarship on law and the image. In the process, I distinguish between expression, representation and dissimulation as ways of conceptualising the visual. Once we do that, we see the potential for words and images as artefacts that can capture, distort or replace the intention of the lawmaker. This is where the iterative nature of law that this project on Invisible Institutionalisms seeks to investigate may be best understood. Second, I suggest that, much like words, images may be assessed on their expressive effect. An expression may be effective in changing behaviour or not. Moreover, it may be subject to interpretation or not. It is here that I suggest that visual artefacts may foreclose discursive agency. If we were to view such agency as a primary good,[4] then it should be possible, at least in theory, to see how legal artefacts constrain or facilitate agency. This does not take away from Khorakiwala's contribution. Rather, it strengthens the need to understand the visual, as this sphere may not be susceptible to re-territorialisation as words may be.

I. Situating Khorakiwala's Contribution

A. The Visual and the Historical

Khorakiwala begins her contribution with walking past carvings, statues and portraits in the Bombay High Court without pausing to dwell on them, and I instantly revisit inside jokes, rings lawyers wear, how they curate files. This isn't accidental; legal ethnography invites stakeholders to graft visibility onto the invisible. Things become artefacts. The textual dominance in legal studies may have had something to do with the Protestant Reformation of the sixteenth century which turned against the worldly, sensual and potentially corrupt world of images – such images were not considered to be the appropriate business of law, which required the seriousness of text.[5] Thankfully, Khorakiwala is not alone in the revival of the worldly, sensual and corrupt in legal studies. Scholars such as Douzinas,[6] Goodrich,[7] and Halder[8] have utilised approaches Khorakiwala draws

[4] S Roy, 'Agency as Responsiveness', European University Institute Law Working Paper No 2016/04.

[5] C Douzinas and L Nead (eds), *Law and the Image: The Authority of Art and Aesthetics of Law* (University of Chicago Press, 1999); L Mulcahy, 'Eyes of the Law: A visual turn in socio-legal studies?' (2017) 44 *Journal of Law and Society* 111, 118.

[6] Douzinas and Nead (1999), n 5 above.

[7] Peter Goodrich, 'Specula Laws: Image, Aesthetic and Common Law' (1991) 2 *Law and Critique* 233.

[8] P Haldar, 'In and out of court: On topographies of law and the architecture of court buildings' (1994) 7 *International Journal for the Semiotics of Law* 185.

on (iconography, semiotics and symbolism), but the visual turn in socio-legal studies is on the rise. It is perhaps because of the ubiquity of the visual at the present time; the script does not drive the visual, as it were, but is useful only if it operates within the parameters of value determined by the visual.[9] The invisible scripts of the visual itself – the algorithms that drive them, the interface that renders them possible – are inescapable inquiries. It is opportune that scholars such as Mulcahy,[10] Resnik and Curtis,[11] Martin and Huygbaert[12] have fiercely excavated the visual from the margins of legal consciousness, and made it visible at its very front. Khorakiwala's contribution may best be described as akin to Martin and Huygbaert, or that of historical legal iconology. It is no surprise that her first footnote is a hat-tip to Panofsky,[13] best known for articulating the premise of iconology where values ascribe meaning to gestures, and further on, social and cultural forces that constitute such values. This entails an exercise in material investigation into such gestures and values, which explains Khorakiwala's interest in critical historical studies.

In relation to colonial encounters and processes that the visual may reveal, Khorakiwala prefers a more materialist inquiry of the colonial encounter. Such inquiry may be contrasted against the focus on indeterminate causation seen in recent scholarship on material legal history.[14] The preference for indeterminate causation on the part of scholars such as Tomlins draws on Benjamin's appreciation of the dialectical process of 'the observer's present' and past processes in the construction of perception.[15] The indeterminate causation approach is akin to speculative inquiries on legal imagination, that seek to dissolve the words/images binary, and concentrate on metaphors and imagery that mediate conceptual representations of political processes and normative choices.[16] In his essay on the evolution of critical legal history (CLH), Robert Gordon argued that CLH can no longer be thought of as an inquiry where historical accounts have something to say about law, but one where they are embroiled with law in an indeterminate kaleidoscope. It could be argued that Gordon was merely opening up space for law schools rather than social science and history departments to say things about law.

[9] The number of words inside a tweet, the role of writers collateral to the possibilities of familiar yet enhanced computer-generated imagery.

[10] L Mulcahy, *Legal Architecture: Justice, due process and the place of law* (Abingdon, Routledge, 2011).

[11] J Resnik and D Curtis, *Representing Justice: Invention, controversy, and rights in city-states and democratic courtrooms* (New Haven CT, Yale University Press, 2011).

[12] G Martin and S Huygbaert, 'Twenty New Contributions to the Upcoming Research Field of Historical Legal Iconology' in S Huygebaert, G Martyn, V Paumen, E Bousmar, X Rousseaux (eds), *The Art of Law. Artistic Representations and Iconography of Law and Justice in Context, from the Middle Ages to the First World War* (Berlin, Springer, 2018) 3–24.

[13] I couldn't resist this as Panofsky's paradigmatic example is 'A man raises a hat'.

[14] For a survey of these trends, see C Tomlins, 'What is Left of the Law and Society Paradigm after Critique? Revisiting Gordon's "Critical Legal Histories"' (2012) 37(1) *Law & Social Inquiry* 155, 158.

[15] C Tomlins, 'Historicism and Materiality in Legal Theory' in M del Mar and M Lobban (eds), *Law in Theory and History: New Essays on a Neglected Dialogue* (Oxford, Hart Publishing, 2016) 64.

[16] See for instance Z Oklopic, *Beyond the People* (Oxford, Oxford University Press, 2018).

In this respect, Khorakiwala's contribution and ethnographic-semiotic intellectual lineage may well serve a stronger functional purpose than the current form of the CLH movement, which is an autopoietic community,[17] ensconced in American law journals. It suggests that there are aspects of the Indian legal system that are set in stone – there *is* some such thing as colonial law, and there *is* some such thing as an enduring presence.

B. Approaches to Legal Visuals: Expression, Representation and Dissimulation

Khorakiwala seeks to provide accounts of materiality where abstract normative ideas as well as political forces have ubiquitous manifestation in matter and everyday phenomena.[18] To do so, she concentrates on visual expressions – something determinate is expressed or manifested – which she identifies using a critical historical lens. These two epistemic choices – *expression rather than representation* and *critical history* – may be complemented by a focus on Walter Benjamin's dialectical approach[19] and Latourian Actor-Network Theory.[20] In contrast to expression, representation implies that in the re-presenting, something new is created in the expression. Mulcahy is alive to the possibility of analysing the visual representations of law using the lenses of Latourian mediation:

> one wonders whether the work of contemporary socio-legal scholars interested in actor network theory might benefit from closer attention to the art object as a non-human actant which engages in the day-to-day construction of legal subjects … this type of work demands that serious attention is paid to the particular ways in which art and the image wield their power.[21]

The benefit from this line of inquiry would simply be that *the process of creating and perceiving the artefact has its autonomous construction of normativity.*[22] This, in turn, would open up nuanced and intersectional logics of the colonial encounter.

[17] The tendency of an autopoietic legal community to reject functionalism is found in Teubner's critique of Gordon. G Teubner, *Recht als autopoietisches System* (Frankfurt, Suhrkamp, 1989) 64.

[18] For a brief introduction, see HY Kang and S Kendall. 'Legal Materiality' in M Del Mar, B Meyler and S Stern (eds), *Oxford Handbook of Law and the Humanities* (Oxford, Oxford University Press, 2019).

[19] For an example, see Benjamin's dialectical approach to baroque art and architecture. W Benjamin, *The Origin of German Tragic Drama* (London, Verso, 1981) 66.

[20] B Latour, 'What is Iconoclash? Or Is There a World Beyond the Image Wars?' in P Weibel and B Latour (eds), *Iconoclash: Beyond the Image Wars in Science, Religion and Art* (Cambridge MA, ZKM and MIT Press, 2002) 14–37.

[21] Mulcahy (2011), n 10 above, 122.

[22] As Schlag puts it: 'Law is an aesthetic enterprise … We can "choose" to deploy an aesthetic in this or that moment. But by and large, the aesthetic operates through us – choosing us, enacting us, directing us. Meanwhile, as the aesthetics do their work, law happens'. P Schlag, 'The Aesthetics of American Law' (2002) 115 *Harvard Law Review* 1047, 1053.

Drawing on Goodrich's work on legal emblems, Haldar argues that the word 'representation' does not meaningfully capture the relationship between law and visual artefacts. Rather, he suggests what happens is a process of dissimulation: 'the visible surface of the image surrenders to and dissimulates an absent and prior cause.'[23] The surrendering of a surface to 'an absent and prior cause' is in keeping with Khorakiwala's analysis of the reality of colonial presence in Indian law despite its professed absence. Would the word 'dissimulation' add anything useful? Haldar has earlier described the word to mean 'a feigned order' – one where an artefact serves as a cover up function. At the cost of too broad an interpretive stretch, could it be that the representations of justice by the British administration were serving to cover-up some violence or injustice, or perhaps even an insecurity that was cloaked in regal architecture? Could it be that the cynical extraction of resources was sought to be legitimised through regal portrayals of justice? Might colonial legal architecture be a reflection of the attempt to precariously universalise law? As is clear, for instance, in the conflict between Lord Macaulay and Lord Elphinstone in how to formalise law,[24] Britain's construction of India as a site of effective hierarchical governance was in deep tension with prior law and social norms that coordinated collective life.

II. Normativity and the 'Justice' of Visual Culture

In section I, it was suggested that there is merit in exploring the constitutive potential of the legal artefacts beyond their performative role. Accordingly, this section touches on the normative hold of the visual, and the potential for visual justice.

A. Expressive Effects of the Visual

It was suggested above that Khorakiwala's approach points to the enduring presence of colonial law that the indeterminacy thesis of CLH scholars such as Gordon may not reveal. Having said that, there was a normative reason behind Gordon's intervention on indeterminacy. Disciplines other than law have something to say about constant legal forms, as law congeals some social practices and renders them regular. But, as Gordon argued, this does not mean that congealed legal forms have lasting determinate effects.[25] Does the architecture of the Bombay High Court have the same hold on its stakeholders now as it might have had in the

[23] P Haldar, 'A Gesture: A review of Peter Goodrich, *Legal Emblems and the Art of Law*' (2014) 8 *Law and Humanities* 304, 315.

[24] D Kolff, 'The Indian and the British Law Machines: Some Remarks on Law and Society in British India' in WJ Mommsen and JA de Moor, *European Expansion and Law* (Oxford, Berg Press, 1992).

[25] Tomlins (2012), n 14 above, 160. If the reader might forgive this reconstruction – just because it's congealed, does it mean it's sticky?

colonial project? Is it a compelling agent in the formation of the social imaginary? If not, then what might be the reason for identifying and rendering visible some artefacts over others? These questions are about the expressive function of legal artefacts, which in turn qualifies the epistemic preferences of the observer. This line of inquiry may add flesh to Khorakiwala's investigation into whether 'judicial iconography has a symbolic *effect* in these spaces' (emphasis added).

Scholarship on the expressive function of law has been limited to texts and legal decisions. The paradigmatic example is Lawrence Lessig's example of duelling in the American South.[26] Prior to the passage of a law that disqualified a dueller from holding public office, the act of duelling was honourable, and so to refuse it was considered dishonourable. After the passage of this law, the tables were turned, and refusing a duel was considered an honourable undertaking of legal duty, and thus no longer dishonourable. This, therefore, is an example of how law might change the social meaning of an act – the way a community understands a subject – which in turn leads to a change in behaviour. Criminalising a duel may not have had the same impact on behaviour, as it wouldn't have tampered with the class-based signalling attributed to it. Thus, the effects of two laws in dealing with the same issue are different owing to the distinct changes in the perceived social meaning, which in turn affects behaviour. The expressive effect lies in the effect that law has in altering the social meaning of one's actions. Given the textual orientation of scholarship on this issue,[27] the 'social meaning' appears to have a deliberative connotation. However, this is not necessarily so. There is no reason why a non-textual legal representation could not affect one's thoughts and actions by virtue of altering the social imaginary[28] within which people operate; rather, it adds nuance in appreciating the conjoined nature of words and images in shaping the perception of someone who comes in contact with the law. Drawing on the idea of relaxing the words/images boundary mentioned above, it appears that the image has expressive weight once it is congealed in textual metaphors such as *bonds* between people or a *gap* between community values and formal institutions.[29] I might suggest that Khorakiwala's research project would benefit from examining the expressive effect of the ethnographic vignettes that she identifies; this would also open up inquiry into the dialectical relationship between present observation and past processes.

[26] L Lessig, 'The Regulation of Social Meaning' (1995) 62 *University of Chicago Law Review* 943, 968–72.

[27] Several accounts on the subject may be found in Vol 42, Issue 1 (2017) of *Law & Social Inquiry*, which is dedicated to this subject.

[28] As Taylor notes, though social imaginary entails a common understanding, such understanding is tacit; the social imaginary 'can never be adequately expressed in the form of explicit doctrines because of its unlimited and indefinite nature': C Taylor, *Modern Social Imaginaries* (Durham NC, Duke University Press, 2004) 25.

[29] Oklopic (2018), n 16 above.

B. Visual Justice

When I first read Khorakiwala's contribution, I thought I knew what my critique was going to be. I would argue that it pays to explore the visual culture of law, but that that should not be confused with any sense of visual justice. Circumstance has led me to analytical legal scholarship, and the only way I know of bringing something to the table is to try and feel my way into where justice lies.[30] It is clear from Khorakiwala's account that sculpture, architecture and images contribute to a visual culture of dominance. This culture is revealed through her visual history of the colonial construction of legal institutions in India. There are no indications on how this culture may be overcome, thus precluding any meaningful possibility of visual justice. This line of reasoning, however, is hasty. Recent accounts point to the subversive potential of art and sculpture in perceiving law. Take for instance the destabilisation of the sovereign in Klimt's *Jurisprudence*,[31] or remoulding Justitia as black or working class or in need of legal counsel.[32] Through the beauty of anarchy or counter-stereotypic allegorical change, an image does point to the possibility of re-territorialising[33] the visual, thereby heralding the possibility of a very different iconological reading. The Panofskian querist in Khorakiwala might wonder whether the radicalisation of legal images gives way to a new dominance.

Notwithstanding the potential for re-imaging the visual, it still seems to me that the visual may not offer the same agentic potential as the discursive. Pictures and sculptures are set in stone, as it were. They have limited potential to add to legal iteration, and to that extent, appear to provide limited agency to actors wishing to overcome their meanings. The manifestation and perception of visual artefacts are in totality – there is a singularity to it, characterised by a dominant narrative. There could be revolutionary or radical visual change, but there appears to be no equivalent to ad-hoc or piecemeal constitutional interpretation, which in turn becomes part of the Constitution. I do not disagree with Khorakiwala that the Indian judiciary has not broken from its colonial past, and careful study of judicial iconography

[30] As often with the things we write, an unnoticed seemingly marginal struggle is often the most overwhelming. If critical scholarship has taught us anything, we should be careful in using pleasant abstractions to confound the explanatory power of nuanced scholarship. In this vein, trying to defend the characterisation of justice as a signifier went against every bone in my body; am I really arguing that a floating signifier could be a meaningful characterisation given that an indeterminate term would inevitably be co-opted by a hegemonic project? I soldiered on as I felt it important to highlight the inevitability of indeterminate and encompassing signifiers, and their emancipatory characterisation as sites of struggle. For a discussion, see S Roy, 'Justice as Europe's Signifier' in D Kochenov, G de Búrca and A Williams (eds), *Europe's Justice Deficit?* (Oxford, Hart Publishing, 2015).

[31] D Manderson, 'Klimt's Jurisprudence – Sovereign Violence and the Rule of Law' (2015) 35 *Oxford Journal of Legal Studies* 515.

[32] J Resnik and D Curtis, *Representing Justice: Invention, Controversy, and Rights in City-States and Democratic Courtrooms* (New Haven CT, Yale University Press, 2011) 32.

[33] For a conception of agency as countersterotypic reterritorialization, see Roy (2016). n 4 above, 18.

reveals the same. I do, however, think that the Constitution and decisions made by judges are not an instantiation of this lineage. Doctrinal changes such as basic structure and recognition of fundamental rights are brought about within the four walls of the constitutional text with its troubled past. However, they do provide agency to actors who would not have obtained them if legal texts or the law were appreciated in the terms in which they were constructed. Should law be assessed in originalist terms, then it seems to me that visual law would be on par with textual law. However, if there should be scope for an iterative functionality, then deliberative interpretation seems to be irreplaceable.

Course 4

BASHEER, WEISSENBACH, AND NAUDET

4

Formalising Informal Innovation: Engendering an Epistemic Injustice?

SHAMNAD BASHEER*

I. Introduction

Epistemic injustice is a term of art that connotes a type of injustice inflicted on people in their capacity as epistemic agents and 'knowers'. It was conceptualised by Miranda Fricker, who theorised two broad forms that it could take:

i) Testimonial injustice: where a speaker receives an unfair deficit of credibility from a hearer owing to prejudice on the hearer's part. Fricker cites the example of Tom Robinson, a character from the classic novel *To Kill a Mockingbird*, whose testimony (that he was innocent of the charge of raping a white woman) is not believed by an all-white jury, because of their prejudice against blacks.[1]
ii) Hermeneutical injustice: where someone has a significant area of their social experience obscured from understanding (others' or even their own), owing to prejudicial flaws in shared resources for social interpretation.[2] This injustice occurs when a person attempts to make sense of a social experience

* Editor's Note: As we explain in the Introduction, this 'course' went through a different process of reflection and conversational progress. The last set of edits that Basheer shared with us was in late April 2019, having read the earliest drafts of his respondents' responses that follow this chapter. No substantive changes have been made since then, to maintain the integrity of his voice as he wanted it to be shared, revealing another layer of potential meaning-making in these conversations: silence and early unplanned exits. As this chapter went to press, we were made aware of one other voice that helped create this chapter and was in conversation with Basheer's thinking at the time: his research associate Bhavik Shukla. Many thanks to Nihas Basheer for bringing Shukla's time and work on this contribution to our attention. Although there is no way of knowing (even when one *knows* or is in explicit conversation), from years of *knowing* Shamnad, this is exactly the sort of commitment to collaborations and less visible actors in processes that he would have wanted to exemplify and acknowledge. So I take the liberty of adding this substantive footnote on his behalf and to expressly acknowledge Bhavik for his time and thoughtful contributions to this draft. – SSB.

[1] See Miranda Fricker, *Epistemic Injustice: Power and the Ethics of Knowing* (Oxford, Oxford University Press, 2007), 23–28.

[2] Fricker (2007), p 148.

> but is handicapped by a gap in collective understanding – a hermeneutical lacuna of sorts that 'renders the collective interpretive resources structurally prejudiced'.[3]

Fricker contends that this second form of injustice arises from 'situated hermeneutical inequality', and the relative powerlessness of a social group to which the subject belongs. Consequently, the subject is not able to make sense of the social experience herself and is therefore handicapped in rendering it intelligible to others.[4] To this extent, there is an *unjust deficit of intelligibility*.[5]

Illustratively, a person might find it difficult to make sense of his own need to cross-dress in a society where gender stereotypes are strongly embedded and any transgression is seen as perverse or shameful. The subject is unable to make proper sense of his orientation, owing to the fact that those outside the traditional 'binary' model of gender (particularly the 'trans-gender' community) are prevented from making a full contribution to collective resources for social meaning. Consequently, the forms of understanding available for making sense of gender variance are crucially uninformed and distorted.[6]

Notions of epistemic injustice have also infiltrated the largely insular world of intellectual property ('IP'), mainly in relation to the cultural appropriation of indigenous heritage.[7] At its core, epistemic injustice occurs when the 'marginalised' are never really 'heard' by the 'mainstream', since their epistemic capacities are under-estimated and their testimonies given minimal credence.[8] As a result, the hearer misses out on something epistemically valuable, and the speaker suffers an injustice.

Against this backdrop, I wish to examine similar concerns that pervade the sphere of 'informal innovation'. Although this is not a term of art, I use it as a rough shorthand for a variety of innovative products/ processes in the informal economy, a 'shadow' economy that exists outside formal legal/ regulatory apparatus. I will elaborate on these definitional issues in the next section. For now, let me simply introduce the concept and key thesis I wish to advance in this chapter.

[3] Fricker (2007), p 155.

[4] Fricker, n 1 above, p 162.

[5] Miranda Fricker, 'Powerlessness and Social Interpretation' (2006) 3 *Episteme: A Journal of Social Epistemology* 99.

[6] Miranda Fricker, 'Epistemic Injustice: Power and the Ethics of Knowing: Precis' (2008) 23 *Segunda Epoca* 70.

[7] See Rebecca Tsosie, 'Cultural Challenges to Biotechnology: Native American Genetic Resources and the Concept of Cultural Harm' (2007) 35 *Journal of Law, Medicine and Ethics* 399; See also Erich Hatala Matthes, 'Cultural Appropriation without Cultural Essentialism?' (2016) 42 *Social Theory and Practice* 352, 353.

[8] See Katherine Hawley, 'Knowing how and Epistemic Injustice' in John Bengson and Marc Moffett (eds), *Knowing How: Essays on Knowledge, Mind and Action* (Oxford, Oxford University Press, 2012) 283, where the author states that 'One aspect of being a knower is being a giver of knowledge – 'The capacity to give knowledge to others is one side of that many-sided capacity so significant in human beings: namely the capacity for reason.' So wronging someone as a giver of knowledge – by perpetrating testimonial injustice – amounts to wronging that person as a knower, as a reasoner, and thus as a human being.'

Policy-makers often assume that the informal sector is better off when it 'formalises' in much the same way as the mainstream economy.[9] This logic extends to innovation too, where external agents seek to impose an IP-type regime on the informal sector in order to help it 'develop'[10] by 'appropriating'[11] the value of innovations through formal legal protection.[12]

I caution against this tendency to superimpose mainstream models onto the informal sector – especially given that scholars are questioning the value of such models to the formal as well as the informal innovation ecosystem.[13] Superimposing mainstream models onto the informal sector in this way reinforces an epistemic injustice, where the testimony of informal agents who 'innovate' is effectively ignored.[14]

Not only do we fail to understand informal agents' perspective (testimony), we do not even bother to elicit this testimony in the first place, even when such testimony could (ironically enough) contain valuable learnings for the formal sector. In addition, this failure ends up perpetuating hermeneutical inequality, in that our already prejudiced social understanding of innovation and appropriability mechanisms renders it difficult for informal innovators to make sense of incentives/ models that lie outside the mainstream script (such as 'divine channelling' experienced by a tribal healer, as outlined later in this chapter).[15]

[9] See Report V(1), *Transitioning from the informal to the formal economy*, International Labour Office, Geneva, pp 35, 36, http://www.ilo.org/wcmsp5/groups/public/---ed_norm/---relconf/documents/meetingdocument/wcms_218128.pdf; See Martha Alter Chen, 'Rethinking the Informal Economy: Linkages with the Formal Economy and the Formal Regulatory Environment', ECOSOC meetings, p 12, http://www.un.org/en/ecosoc/meetings/2006/forum/Statements/Chen%27s%20Paper.pdf; See Monami Dasgupta, *Moving from informal to formal sector and what it means for policymakers*, The World Bank, 20 September 2016, http://www.blogs.worldbank.org/jobs/moving-informal-formal-sector-and-what-it-means-policymakers, for argument in favour of formalisation of informal sectors.

[10] See Franziska Dübgen, 'Epistemic Injustice in Practice' (2016) 15 *Wagadu: A Journal of Transnational Women's and Gender Studies* 3, 4, for analysis of how the definition of development in mainstream debates prejudices marginalised countries; See also James Odhiambo Ogone, 'Epistemic Injustice: African Knowledge and Scholarship in the Global Context' in Anke Bartels, Lar Eckstein et al (eds), *Postcolonial Justice* (Leiden, Koninklijke Brill NV, 2017) 18, for an analysis of how the definition of knowledge prejudices post-colonial knowledge in mainstream debates.

[11] See Bronwyn Hall and Vania Sena, 'Appropriability mechanisms, innovation, and productivity: Evidence from the UK' (2017) 26 *Economics of Innovation and New Technology*.

[12] Jeremy de Beer, Kun Fu and Sacha Wunsch-Vincent, 'The informal economy, innovation and intellectual property – Concepts, metrics and policy considerations' (2013) WIPO Economic Research Working Paper No 10, pp 31–34; For the Indian context see Shamnad Basheer, 'An IP policy with no innovation', *The Hindu*, 17 May 2016, http://www.thehindu.com/opinion/op-ed/intellectual-property-an-ip-policy-with-no-innovation/article8607910.ece; See also G Krishnakumar, 'Experts come out against draft National IPR policy', *The Hindu*, 22 February 2015, http://www.thehindu.com/features/education/experts-come-out-against-draft-national-ipr-policy/article6922144.ece.

[13] See nn 14 and 15 below.

[14] See Harilal Madhavan, 'Innovation System and Increasing Reformulation Practices in the Ayurvedic Pharmaceutical Sector of South India' (2014) 9 *Asian Medicine* 153, for analysis with respect to Ayurveda in India; See also Rebecca Tsosie, 'Indigenous peoples and epistemic injustice: Science, ethics, and human rights' (2012) 87 *Washington Law Review* 1154, 1155, for analysis on how Native Americans face testimonial injustice in respect of claiming certain sites as spiritual.

[15] See Shamnad Basheer, 'Comment 6.3' in Erika Kraemer-Mbula, Sacha Wunsch-Vincent (eds), *The Informal Economy in Developing Nations* (Cambridge, Cambridge University Press, 2016) 284, 285;

II. Definitional Issues

What precisely is the 'informal economy'? And what does one mean by 'innovation'? Both these terms will be explored in brief below, before moving onto the central thesis in this chapter.

A. Informal Economy

Allegedly coined by an anthropologist, the term 'informal sector' was first used to describe the scope of unregistered economic activity in Accra, Ghana.[16] Since then, it has been popularised by many, primarily in the context of the 'urban' poor.[17]

In its current avatar, the term admits of multiple interpretations and meanings.[18] While some define it by highlighting the nature of employment, others emphasise factors such as incorporation, and the size and location of informal activities. In a witty exposition of the elusiveness of the concept, Jacques Charmes notes the various zoological metaphors triggered by the quest to define the informal economy:

> Hans Singer, one of the fathers of the concept in the early 1970s, compared it to a giraffe: difficult to define by usual standards but easy to recognise when you meet one (reported by Lubell 1991). It is not a giraffe, but a unicorn, replied Bruno Lautier (1990): the literature abounds with definitions, but you will never actually encounter it, because it does not exist. One could also compare it to a chameleon, for its ability to become invisible when the State or the law is too restrictive or inappropriate.[19]

See Martha Woodmanssee, *The Author, Art and the Market: Rereading the History of Aesthetics* (New York, Columbia University Press, 1994) 36–37 and Jarrod Welsh, 'Copyrighting God: New Cpyright Guidelines do not Protect Divine Beings' (2014) 17 *Rutgers Journal of Law and Religion* 139, 140, for analysis of how the formal sector has historically grappled with the informal sector in deciding copyright over divinely-inspired works; See also the decisions in *Oliver v Saint Germain Foundation* 41 Supp 296 (SD Cal 1941) and *Urantia Foundation v Maaherra*, 114 F 3d 955, 958 (9th Circ 1997) for further analysis of copyrightability of divine revelations in the US context; See the Judgment of 13 May 2014, Oberlandesgericht (OLG) Frankfurt, Case No 11 U 62/13 for recent adjudication on copyrightability of divinely-inspired work in Germany.

16 See Keith Hart, 'Informal Urban Income Opportunities in Ghana' (1973) 11 *The Journal of Modern African Studies* 68, 69. However, Hart acknowledged the existence of earlier studies on the 'economy of the street', including those by Henry Mayhew's work in Victorian London (Mayhew 1861–62) and WF Whyte's study in America (Whyte 1943).

17 See Nadini Gooptu, *The Politics of the Urban Poor* (Cambridge, Cambridge University Press, 2001) 2, for analysis of the author's study of urban India, where she notes that the informal economy was 'an overwhelming and enduring reality' in India.

18 See Barbara Harriss-White, 'Formality and informality in an Indian urban waste economy' (2017) 37 *International Journal of Sociology and Social Policy*, for discussion on different form of activities including small / primitive activity; unlicensed/ unregistered activity etc.

19 See Jacques Charmes, 'The Informal Economy: Definitions, size, contribution and main characteristics' in Erika Kraemer-Mbula, Sacha Wunsch-Vincent (eds), *The Informal Economy in Developing Nations* (Cambridge, Cambridge University Press, 2016) 13.

Indeed, for the most part, the informal economy lies below the state's radar.[20] Serge Latouche captures it best when he notes that informal sector operators are 'ingenious but not engineers, enterprising but not entrepreneurs, industrious but not industrialists',[21] suggesting thereby that their contribution cannot be captured adequately through the usual standards and norms.[22]

The above discussion illustrates the difficulty of pinpointing a precise definition for the term. However, a rough approximation can be found in a rather expansive definition adopted by the ILO: 'all economic activities by workers and economic units that are – in law or in practice – not covered or insufficiently covered by formal arrangements.'[23]

Under this definition, a significant part of the economic activity in developing countries would count as 'informal'. Illustratively, India's informal sector is said to constitute a whopping 81 per cent of its economy.[24] Similarly, the informal sector in Kenya constitutes 83.4 per cent of total employment.[25]

B. Informal Innovation

Notwithstanding a serious shortage of resources, the informal economy exemplifies a buoyant spirit of creativity.[26] Take India, for example, where

[20] See Ravi Kanbur, Sajal Lahiri and Jan Svejnar, 'Informality, Illegality and Enforcement: Introduction' (2012) 16(4) *Review of Development Economics* 511; See also Barbara Harriss-White and Anushree Sinha, 'Introduction' in Barbara Harriss-White and Anushree Sinha (eds), *Trade Liberalisation and India's Informal Economy: Macro meets Micro* (New Delhi, Oxford University Press, 2007).

[21] See Serge Latouche, 'Les paradoxes de la "normalisation" de l'economie informelle' (1989) 30 *Revue Tiers Monde* 227–33.

[22] See Charmes (2016), n 19 above, p 13.

[23] See International Labour Organization, Resolution concerning decent work and informal economy, 90th Session, para 3, 25/53 (Geneva, 2002): http://www.ilo.org/wcmsp5/groups/public/---ed_norm/---relconf/---reloff/documents/meetingdocument/wcms_080105.pdf; See Alter Chen (2006), n 9 above, p 2 for the extension of this definition 'to include the whole of informality, as it is manifested in industrialised, transition and developing economies'.

[24] See International Labour Organization, 'Women and men in the informal economy: A statistical picture', 3rd edn, (Geneva, 2018), p 88, http://www.ilo.org/wcmsp5/groups/public/---dgreports/---dcomm/documents/publication/wcms_626831.pdf; According to the Central Statistical Organisation (CSO) of India, all unincorporated enterprises an household industries (other than organised ones) which are not regulated by laws and which do not maintain annual accounts or balance sheets constitute the unorganised sector. The Directorate General of Employment and Training (DGET) defines the organised sector as comprising all establishments in the private sector, which employ 10 or more persons. By implication, the informal sector is comprised of enterprises with less than 10 employees. See http://www.dget.nic.in/content/students/employment-market-information-program.php.

[25] See Kenya National Bureau of Statistics, 2018, p. 39, https://www.knbs.or.ke/?wpdmpro=economic-survey-2018. This survey also states that this sector added 787.7 thousand jobs in 2017.

[26] See Anil Gupta, 'Innovations for poor by the poor' (2012) 5(1) *International Journal of Technological Learning, Innovation and Development* 28, 34–37; See also Jaideep Prabhu and Sanjay Jain, 'Innovation and entrepreneurship in India: Understanding jugaad' (2015) 32(4) *Asia Pacific Journal of Management* 843; Barbara Harriss-White, 'Innovation in India's Informal Economy' (2014) 1 *Social Development Forum* 2, 9–12; See generally Hemant Kumar and Saradindu Bhaduri, 'Jugaad to grassroot innovations: Understanding the landscape of the informal sector innovations in India' in Mammo Muchie et al (eds), *Informal Sector Innovations: Insights from the Global South* (London, Routledge, 2016) 113, 115–17.

innovations span a diverse array of technological arenas. Consider Gobind Deb Nath's multi-purpose rickshaw, where special wheels attached to the rear axle of the rickshaw can serve as paddy huskers, grass cutters, and bamboo mat cutters.[27] Or Remya Jose's exercycle-cum-washing-machine, which is essentially a cycle which when pedalled propels a wheel-shaped washing machine.[28] Or the countless number of medicinal innovators/ healers endemic in informal economies, such as Vellan Vaidyan (who features later in this chapter).[29]

All of these innovations are subsumed within the broad rubric of the term 'Informal Innovations', a term slowly gaining traction and[30] used even by the World Intellectual Property Organization (WIPO), the world's premier IP agency which commissioned a series of reports on this theme.[31]

But first, how does one define innovation? The origins of the term can be traced back to the Latin noun, *innovatio*, derived from the verb *innovare*, which means to introduce something new.[32] Today, the term admits of different meanings, depending on the context. A widely used definition is one proposed by the OECD, which describes it as the 'implementation of a new or significantly improved product (good or service), or process, a new marketing method [e.g. a novel product design], or a new organisational method in business practices, workplace organisation or external relations'.[33] The question is: should this be new to the world or new to the enterprise? Richard Nelson appears to suggest the latter: innovation, he says, is:

> the processes by which firms master and get into practice product designs and manufacturing processes that are new to them, whether or not they are new to the universe, or even to the nation.[34]

[27] See The National Innovation Foundation, Creative Eastern Himalayas, p 21: www.nif.org.in//dwn_files//creative eastern himalayas//Part I eastern himalaya.pdf.

[28] See Samar Halarnkar, 'Top Grosser *3 Idiots* to fund Real Life Inventors', *Hindustan Times*, Mumbai, 31 December 2009, www.hindustantimes.com//india-news//top-grosser-3-idiots-to-fund-real-life-inventors//article1-492261.aspx.

[29] See Basheer (2016), n 15 above, p 284, at 291; See also A Anoop, 'Many takers for tribal remedies, ancient cures, *The Hindu*, 23 May 2013, http://www.thehindu.com/news/cities/kozhikode/many-takers-for-tribal-remedies-ancient-cures/article4742534.ece.

[30] See Organisation for Economic Co-operation and Development, *National Intellectual Property Systems, Innovation and Economic Development: With Perspectives on Colombia and Indonesia* (OECD, 2014) 17; See also M Korzun et al, 'Innovations and agricultural exports: The case of sub-Saharan Africa' in Mammo Muchie et al (eds), *Informal Sector Innovations: Insights from the Global South* (Oxford, Routledge, 2016), for acceptance of informal agricultural innovation across the world.

[31] See World Intellectual Property Report: The changing face of innovation, 2011, http://www.wipo.int/edocs/pubdocs/en/intproperty/944/wipo_pub_944_2011.pdf; See also World Intellectual Property Report: Breakthrough innovation and economic growth, 2015, http://www.wipo.int/edocs/pubdocs/en/wipo_pub_944_2015.pdf.

[32] See JK Aronson, 'Something new Everyday: Defining innovation and innovativeness in drug therapy' (2008) 31 *Journal of Ambulatory Care Management* 65.

[33] See Organisation for Economic Co-operation and Development, 'The Measurement of Scientific and Technological Activities: Guidelines for Collecting and Interpreting Innovation Data: Oslo Manual' (OECD 2005) para 146.

[34] See R Nelson and N Rosenberg, 'Technical Innovation and National Systems' in Richard Nelson (ed), *National Innovation Systems: A Comparative Analysis* (Oxford, Oxford University Press, 1993) 4, 5.

Going by this wide definition, almost any informal product or process qualifies as 'innovative'. This abysmally low threshold defeats the very purpose of capturing the 'creativity' and inventive spirit associated with the informal sector. Therefore, for the purpose of this chapter, I will take the novelty threshold in the OECD definition to mean 'global' novelty,[35] a standard common to most patent regimes today.[36]

III. Formalising Informality?

Some policy-makers assume that the 'informal' economy needs to be moulded in the shape of the 'mainstream' by a process of 'formalising'.[37] In the specific context of intellectual property, this would mean that the value of intangible creations is 'appropriated' through formal legal protection; illustratively, patent registrations grant a near monopoly in some cases and are meant to incentivise further innovation. However, economists and scholars have contested this assumption even for the formal sector, citing the lack of compelling empirical evidence on this count.[38]

Given this uncertainty, it would be foolhardy to transpose the mainstream IP model to the informal economy, particularly when we know so little about it. The best we can do is to remove our filters of prejudice/ bias and open ourselves to 'testimonies' from the informal world. I detail some examples below. These are anecdotal no doubt, but one might find them a useful indicator of the plurality of views concerning innovation incentives and the appropriability narrative.

[35] See Shamnad Basheer and Annalisa Primi, 'The WIPO Development Agenda: Factoring in the "Technologically Proficient" Developing Countries' in Jeremy De Beer (ed), *Implementing the World Intellectual Property Organisation's Development Agenda* (Ottawa, Wilfrid Laurier University Press, 2009), for further elaboration on how under this standard, product designs and processes that are only 'new' to the company/entity/person and not to the industry, country or the world will not be considered.

[36] See Karla Shippey, *A Short Course in International Intellectual Property Rights: Protecting your Brands, Marks, Copyrights, Patents, Designs and Related Rights Worldwide* (California, World Trade Press, 2002) 124–30, for a glance at the 'novelty' concept in patent laws of various countries. It is to be noted that though the concept of 'novelty' is construed differently across Patent Offices, the lowest threshold on the spectrum ranging from non-obviousness to absolute novelty, is that the invention should identifiably be 'new' in the industry, country and the world.

[37] See n 9 above, for the international opinion on formalisation of the informal sector; See also Ministry of Labour and Employment, Government of India, Annual Report 2017–18, pp 224, 225, http://www.labour.gov.in/sites/default/files/ANNUAL_REPORT_2017-18-ENGLISH.pdf.

[38] See Jeremy Phillips, 'A Spanner in the Works – or the Spanner that Works? Patents and the Intellectual Property System' in Toshiko Takenaka (ed), *Patent Law and Theory* (Cheltenham, Edward Elgar Publishing Limited, 2008) 140; See also Andres Lopez, 'Innovation and Appropriability, Empirical Evidence and Research Agenda' in WIPO (ed), *The Economics of Intellectual Property: Suggestions for Further Research in Developing Countries and Countries with Economies in Transition* (Geneva, WIPO, 2009) 20–23; See especially Shamnad Basheer, 'The Invention of an Investment Incentive for Pharmaceutical Innovation' (2012) 15 *The Journal of World Intellectual Property* 7, 8; See Shamnad Basheer, 'The End of Exclusivity: Towards a Compensatory Patent Commons' (2018) 58 *IDEA: Journal of the Frank Pierce Center for IP* 229.

A. Stories/Lessons from the Informal World

(i) Mallesham: 'Compassion' Induced Creativity

Like other children from poor/ marginalised communities, Chintakindi Mallesham dropped out of school and began to holler around the house and his mother. That is when he noticed that his mother was doing back-breaking work trying to make saris.

These were no ordinary saris: but the famous Pochampally saris, a rare weave that boasted exemplary artistic ingenuity and had been handed down through several generations.[39]

Unfortunately, the process was extremely tedious and a concentrated effort of several hours resulted in a sari or two at the best. The young Chintakindi was heartbroken to see his mother suffer, so his mind began to wander and think through ways in which to help her. And soon enough, a creative light burst through, helped in no small part by Chintakindi's innate feel for science/ technology. He devised a contraption that would mechanise the process to some extent,[40] not only relieving human labour, but also resulting in a greater output per day.[41] The results were nothing short of spectacular, not just from a technological standpoint, but from the vantage point of how it transformed the fortunes of an entire community.

With the invention of Chintakindi's device, weaving became much easier and the output increased dramatically.[42]

Mallesham filed a patent for his device with the help of the National Innovation Foundation (NIF).[43] But if you ask him (as I did when I met him many years ago)

[39] See T Sucharitha, 'Rural Tourism Complex Bhoodan Pochampally Village' in Ramesh Kumar Miryala (ed), *Trends, Challenges and Innovations in Management – Volume III* (Hyderabad, Zenon Academic Publishing, 2015) 305, where the author states that Pochampally saris are made through the ikkat weave and its 'uniqueness lie in the transfer of design and colouring onto warp and weft threads first and then weaving them together'.

[40] See Rahul Anand, 'Meet Chintakindi Mallesham – The inventor of the Laxmi Asu Machine that relieved the pain of several Weavers', *The Better India*, 22 March 2011, http://www.thebetterindia.com/2564/grassroots-innovation-laxmi-asu-machine/.

[41] See Anand, ibid, to further understand the unique and useful nature of the invention. It is mentioned that the quality of the saris made with the help of the machine was better than the ones made manually. Moreover, in terms of saving time and increasing output, the machine proved to be an absolute boon. It reduced the time taken to weave a sari from 4 hours to just 1.5 hours, thereby enabling the women in the village to make 6 saris per day instead of the 2 saris they used to make which increased their income prospects.

[42] It bears noting that Pochampalli was registered as a geographical indication (GI) in 2005. [SB Note to self: *Give more details here and cite.*]

[43] See Umesh Anand, 'Self-taught inventor who made sari weaving safer', *The Civil Society*, 27 January 2017 (updated 24 September 2019): https://www.civilsocietyonline.com/mega-hall-of-fame/self-taught-inventor-who-made-silk-sari-weaving-safer/. The title of the invention is 'Thread Processing Machine' and was applied for under application number (1522/CHE/2009) on 29 June 2009. http://nif.org.in/innovation/laxmi_asu/9.

whether it was the thought of the patent that drove him towards this invention, he balks.[44] It was simply his love for his mother. Yet such 'compassionate' creativity finds very little mention in our mainstream debates on creativity and innovation.[45]

(ii) Vellan Vaidyan: A (Divine) Channeling of Creativity

What strikes you most about Vellan Vaidyan is the unassuming manner in which he treats his patients. But that demeanour belies a powerful ability to heal a variety of complex ailments, which brings thousands of desperate patients to him each month. A large portion of them are poor manual labourers, while others are somewhat better off but still cannot afford the more expensive hospitals. A few are like me, and have given up on mainstream medicine (allopathy) and its rather reductionist frame.

But more than finding a cure, I was interested in the myth behind the man and his alleged medical prowess. When I asked him about how he figured out cures for modern diseases, he answered:

> Our system is not a static one. We keep improvising just as modern medicine does.[46] I may not find the same herbs my grandfather used. I have to therefore figure out workable substitutes. Similarly, some of the ailments today were not known earlier. But the fundamental frame of disease and cure is still the same for us. I use the same frame, but adapt it to meet the requirements of today.

In many ways, Vaidyan's approach resonates with what constitutes an 'innovative' medical practice even today, an incremental method that adapts an older frame to meet a new exigency.[47]

[44] S Rama Krishna, 'Underdogs stunned to get Padma awards, as PM reforms nomination process', *The Sunday Guardian*, 29 January 2017, http://www.sundayguardianlive.com/news/8204-underdogs-stunned-get-padma-awards-pm-reforms-nomination-process, where it is noted that Mallesham thwarted efforts from MNCs to patent his invention, preferring to help the weaver community in general.

[45] See Anwesha Madhukalya, 'Moved by his mother's plight this Telangana school dropout invented a weaving machine', *Huffpost*, 5 January 2017, http://www.huffingtonpost.in/2017/01/05/moved-by-his-mothers-plight-this-telangana-school-dropout-inven_a_21648173/, where the author notes that Mallesham would be deeply affected by his mother's plight after every day's weaving work. Such work left her limbs sore and unbearable with pain. He invented the machine only in order to alleviate her sufferings; See Gupta (2012), n 26 above; See also Ivana Miranda, 'Young Inventor Lucca Riccio, US Patent and Trademark Office, http://www.uspto.gov/learning-and-resources/newsletter/inventors-eye/young-inventor-lucca-riccio, which documents the production of a bluetooth enabled microphone mask by a young boy who was inspired by his paternal grandmother's suffering; See Mina Holland et al, Africa Innovations: 15 ideas helping to transform a continent, *The Guardian*, 26 August 2012, http://www.theguardian.com/world/2012/aug/26/africa-innovations-transform-continent, for analysis of various inventions by the poor in Africa to facilitate their daily tasks and not for profit.

[46] See Basheer (2016) n 15 above, p 291 where the author divulges details of his personal interview with Vellan Vaidyan on 10 July 2014.

[47] See Alex Hankey, 'Ayurveda and the battle against chronic disease: An opportunity for Ayurveda to go mainstream?' (2010) 1(1) *Journal of Ayurveda and Integrative Medicine* 9–12, for analysis on how Ayurveda is used as a tool to fight modern diseases; See also RB Smarta, 'Holistic health through nutrition, diet, and nutraceuticals for prevention and treatment' in Dilip Ghosh and RB Smarta (eds),

Yet despite this similarity, there are fundamental differences between Vaidyan's 'informal' approach to innovation and the more mainstream 'formal' paradigm. For one, Vaidyan's is a more holistic approach that seeks to restore the body to its natural state/ balance than simply treating the symptoms, as allopathy routinely does.[48] Secondly, as opposed to an 'atomistic' reductionist method where the so-called 'active ingredient' is isolated and synthesised in the lab, Vaidyan and other traditional healers tend to use the entire plant or part (s) of it, as they believe in the concept of a 'life force' within the plant.[49]

Vaidyan also refuses to mass produce and sell medicines in the open market, and will only make the bare minimum amount that is required for the patient. But what intrigued me most was his notion of himself as a mere 'conduit' or channel of medical cures – flowing through him as if from a divine source, particularly for new ailments that confronted him for the first time. And it is for that reason that he refuses to charge for his services. Rather, he simply leaves a donation box outside his clinic for the public to contribute as they see fit. During my visit, I noticed several tattered notes of small denominations, no doubt left by the large swathes of poor patients that visited him. A crude form of 'crowdsourcing' one might say.[50]

Unfortunately, rather than drawing on these diverse models of compensating creators, our tendency is to transpose mainstream models of innovation onto the informal sector, reflecting a hermeneutical bias predicated on an innate sense of scientific superiority.[51] This tendency leads to grave epistemic injustice.

Pharmaceuticals to Nutraceuticals: A Shift in Disease Prevention (Florida, Taylor and Francis Group, LLC, 2017), for application of yoga in preventing and curing diseases.

[48] See John Neustadt and Steve Pieczenik, *Foundations and Applications of Medical Biochemistry in Clinical Practice* (Bloomington IN, iUniverse. 2009) 33, 34; See also David Miller, *Grow Youthful; Ancient Secrets, Modern Research* (Perth, Success Print, 2003) 55.

[49] See Marc Micozzi, *Fundamentals of Complementary and Alternative Medicine* (Missouri, Elsevier Saunders, 2014) 321, for understanding the concept of healing energies in plants. Traditional healers across the world believe that plants have 'life force' which is still to be understood in the conventional medicinal framework, and this energy promotes healing in addition to the plant's chemical constituents; See generally CN Fokunang et al, 'Traditional Medicine: Past, Present and Future Research and Development Prospects and Integration in the National Health System of Cameroon' (2011) 8 *African Journal of Traditional, Complementary and Alternative Medicines*; See also Michael Balick, *21st Century Herbal: A Practical Guide for healthy living using nature's most powerful plants* (New York, Rodale Incorporation, 2014), for analysis on the importance of 'life force' in the Far East countries.

[50] See Julia Bauer et al, 'The seven IP commandments of a crowdsourcing community: How self-organised norms-based IP systems overcome imitation problems' (2015) 1 *Academy of Management Annual Meeting Proceedings*, for elaboration on the concept of crowdsourcing in the IP sphere to mean contribution by the general community in arriving at a business decision. This piece further notes that crowdsourcing models usually result in innovation appropriation of the contributors by businesses.

[51] See Chidi Oguamanam, 'Pressuring "suspect orthodoxy": Traditional Knowlegde and Patent System' in Matthew Rimmer (ed), *Indigenous Intellectual Property: A Handbook of Contemporary Research* (Cheltenham, Edward Elgar Publishing, 2015) 315; See J Michael Miltenberger, 'Northern voices, northern waters: Traditional Knowledge and water policy development in Northwest Territories' in Alberto Garrido and Mordechai Shechter (eds), *Water for the Americas: Challenges and Opportunities* (Oxford, Routledge, 2014) 222, 223, for discussion on how science always makes a disadvantageous presumption about traditional means; See generally Stephen Bent, 'Herbal Medicine in the United States: Review of Efficacy, Safety and Regulation' (2008) 23 *Journal of General Internal Medicine*

(iii) Mansukhbhai: The Magic of Minimalism

For most of us reading this, a refrigerator is an absolute necessity, especially in this era of global warming, where food tends to spoil rather quickly.[52]

However, for large parts of India, a refrigerator is simply not feasible. Not only is it priced out of the reach of India's poor, it also requires a steady supply of electricity. Mansukhbhai Prajapati, who grew up in such a resource-constrained environment decided that this was not acceptable. Drawing upon ancient Indian wisdom, he invented Mitticool, a refrigerator-like device that does not require electricity. More importantly, it comes at a very affordable price tag for the poor consumer.

Mitticool draws upon the simple concept of evaporation: a concept applied for many centuries in Indian households where water was kept in earthen pots. Owing to the water evaporating through the pores of the earthen material, the remaining water in the pot was kept cool throughout. Using the same principle, Mansukhbhai built Mitticool from clay: it comprises an upper compartment filled with water (which evaporates and causes the cooling) and a lower compartment(s) to hold the vegetables/ fruits and other items to be kept cool. The device is reputed to keep vegetables/ fruits fresh for 2–3 days.[53] Almost as effective as a refrigerator, one might say; and without the need for any electricity.

Mansukhbai's inventive spirit teaches us that creativity knows no class or caste borders. It can come from the most severely resource-constrained settings. Indeed, constraints can actually induce creativity; a phenomenon that I label 'Constraint Induced Creativity'.

Mansukhbhai also teaches us that even in this age of consumerist excess, we do not always need the most expensive technology, intensive investments, or R&D to get socially impactful investments. In fact, given global warming and the ever increasing stress on the planet's limited resources, we are better off with inventions that consume less. Mansukhbhai's invention uses no electricity and is made of light weight biodegradable materials, so it presents no issue with waste disposal. It is made of earth (clay) which is where it gets its name from: 'Mitticool'.[54]

854–59; See Madhulika Banerjee, 'Local Knowledge for the World Market' (2004) 39 *Economic and Political Weekly* 91–93, for understanding how the perceptions advanced by modern science and medicine has driven people away from Ayurvedic medicine.

[52] See Christopher Furgal et al, 'Climate, Health and the Changing Canadian North' in VI Grover (ed), *Global Warming and Climate Change (2 Vols.): Ten Years after Kyoto and still Counting* (Florida, Taylor and Francis, 2008) 828; Renee Cho, How climate change will alter our food, Columbia University, 25 July 2018, http://www.blogs.ei.columbia.edu/2018/07/25/climate-change-food-agriculture/.

[53] See National Innovation Foundation, Mitticool Refrigerator, http://www.nif.org.in/innovation/mitti-cool-refrigerator/751, where it is mentioned that fruits and vegetables remain fresh without deterioration in their quality for a period of 2–3 days if preserved in Mitticool.

[54] See Mitti Cool, https://mitticool.com/product/mitticool-clay-refrigerator50-liter/, where the description of the refrigerator conveys that it is made of clay; See also G Zachmann et al, 'When and how to support renewables? – Letting the data speak' in Alberto Ansuategi et al (eds), *Green Energy and Efficiency: An Economic Perspective* (Heidelberg, Springer International Publishing, 2015) 292–95; See generally Mahima Kaushik, 'Exploring Renewble Energy Sources: Need of the hour' (2015) 1(3) *Delhi University Journal of Undergraduate Research and Innovation* 67; See Debabrata Das, *Biohydrogen Production: Fundamentals and Technology Advances* (London, Taylor and Francis Group, 2014) 2–12.

B. The Suitability of IP Norms

Limited as they may be, the above examples give us enough cause to doubt that the mainstream IP model of appropriating the value of 'inventions' will work well for the informal sector. Even assuming that one were to transpose some of the norms in these cases, they would require significant tailoring and adaptation. Let me illustrate this in the context of traditional medicinal knowledge.

(i) Traditional Knowledge: Individual v Community Inventorship

IP regimes across the world are modelled around the idea of the individual inventor or creator.[55] Traditional knowledge ('*TK*'), however, is housed within a community-based/ collective knowledge system.[56] This peculiarity primarily arises from the difference in conception of rights in indigenous communities versus the West.[57] In indigenous communities, individuals give primacy to group rights over individual rights, as they identify themselves through their group rather than as individuals belonging to a group.[58] Thus, most knowledge created in such groups is collectively created for the benefit of their members,[59] and is collectively owned by the entire community.

(ii) Traditional Knowledge Trade Secrecy

Patent regimes (the main legal instrument used to appropriate the value of an innovation) insist on 'novelty' and 'inventive step' as a precursor to protection. However, most community-based TK is guarded as a 'secret'.[60] To this extent, the one IP regime that comes close to suiting the informal context is trade secrecy. And yet

[55] See Mark A Lemley, 'The Myth of the Sole Inventor' (2012) 110 *Michigan Law Review* 710.

[56] See World Intellectual Property Organization, Intellectual Property Needs and Expectations of Traditional Knowledge Holders: WIPO Report on Fact-finding Missions on Intellectual Property and Traditional Knowledge (1998–1999), www.wipo.int//edocs//pubdocs//en//tk//768//wipo_pub_768.pdf; See also Gurdial Singh Nijar, 'Traditional knowledge systems, International Law and National Challenges: Marginalisation or emancipation?' (2013) 24 *European Journal of International Law* 1205–21.

[57] See Peter- Tobias Stoll and Anja von Hahn, 'Indigenous Peoples, Indigenous Knowledge and Indigenous Resources in International Law' in Silke von Lewinsky (ed), *Indigenous Heritage and Intellectual Property* (Alphen aan den Rijn, Kluwer Law International, 2008) 17.

[58] See ibid at p 18; See also Marco Odello, 'The United Nations Declaration on the Rights of Indigenous Peoples' in Damien Short and Corinne Lennox (eds), *Handbook of Indigenous Peoples' Rights* (Oxford, Routledge, 2016) 56, 57.

[59] See Martin Girsberger, 'Intellectual property rights and traditional knowledge: Background, Terminology and Issues arising' in Klaus Ammann et al (eds), *Methods for Risk Assessment of Transgenic Plants* (Basel, Springer AG, 2003) 76, 77; See also Deepa Varadarajan, 'A Trade Secret Approach to Protecting Traditional Knowledge' (2011) 36 *Yale Journal of International Law* 373, 374.

[60] See Manuel Ruiz Muller, 'The legal protection of widely shared and dispersed traditional knowledge' in Daniel Robinson et al (eds), *Protecting Traditional Knowledge: The WIPO Intergovernmental Committee on Intellectual Property and Genetic Resources, Traditional Knowledge and Folklore* (Oxford, Routledge, 2017) 122, 125; See also Christian Riffel, *The Protection against Unfair Competition*

this regime is the least studied and theorised.[61] More importantly, the mainstream model of trade secrecy is premised on the notion of 'knowledge' as capital for which value can be extracted through business transactions and the like. However, in a number of informal contexts, knowledge is not seen as a marketable/ tradeable commodity but as something more sacred.[62] The mainstream trade secrecy regime might not therefore be a great fit, but one would need to take account of this diverse view of knowledge creation and nurturing through generations.[63]

(iii) Discoveries v Inventions

The current patent system expresses a preference for certain kinds of creativity. Notwithstanding the high level of inventive thought that may accompany the discovery of a unique phenomenon of nature (such as a plant with rare medicinal properties), most legal regimes prohibit patents over 'products or phenomena of nature'.[64] And yet, in the context of the informal economy, a number of traditional medicinal systems may make use of such natural discoveries.[65] The patent system discriminates against such findings, by noting that they are but products or

in the WTO TRIPS Agreement (Leiden, Brill Nijhoff, 2016) 286, for analysis on TK and its secrecy; See Dr S Vedavathy, 'India case study – Protecting Yanadi Healers' Rights' in WIPO (ed), *Protecting Community Rights over Traditional Knowledge* (WIPO, 2005), for specific case study on India's Yanadi healers who protect certain TK with utmost secrecy.

[61] See European Union Intellectual Property Office, *Protecting Innovation through Trade Secrets and Patents: Determinants for European Union Firms*, July 2017, p 8, https://euipo.europa.eu/tunnel-web/secure/webdav/guest/document_library/observatory/documents/reports/Trade%20Secrets%20 Report_en.pdf; See also Mark Schultz and Douglas Lippoldt, 'Litigating Trade Secrets: An International Comparative Assessment of Civil and Criminal Trade Secret Enforcement' (October 2018) *The Sedona Conference Papers* p 3; See William Lesser et al, 'Intellectual Property Rights, Agriculture, and the World Bank' in Uma Lele et al (eds), *Intellectual Property Rights in Agriculture: The World Bank's role in assisting borrower and member countries* (Washington DC, World Bank, 1999) 11.

[62] See n 61 above, pp 19, 20; See also David Downes, 'How Intellectual Property could be a tool to protect traditional knowledge' (2001) 25 *Columbia Journal of Environmental Law* 279, 280, for analysis on how the Amazonian peoples considered a plant to be sacred to them and challenged its patenting on grounds of morality; See generally Ronald Trosper and John Parrotta, 'Introduction: The Growing Importance of Traditional Forest-related knowhow' in Ronald Trosper and John Parrotta (eds), *Traditional Forest-Related Knowledge: Sustaining Communities, Ecosystems and Bicultural Diversity* (Heidelberg. Springer, 2012) 16, 17.

[63] See Anthony Taubman and Matthias Leistner, 'Analysis of Different Areas of Indigenous Resources' in Silke von Lewinsky (ed), *Indigenous Heritage and Intellectual Property* (Alphen aan den Rijn, Kluwer Law International, 2008) 81–82; Srividhya Ragavan, 'Protection of Traditional Knowledge' (2001) 2(1) *Minnesota Intellectual Property Review* 1, 7–8.

[64] Illustratively, see Section 3(c) of the Indian Patents Act, 1970, which excludes from patentability the 'discovery of any living thing or non-living substance occurring in nature.' Similarly, in the US, courts have repeatedly held that: 'Phenomena of nature, though just discovered, mental processes, and abstract intellectual concepts are not patentable, as they are the basic tools of scientific and technological work. Monopolisation of those tools through the grant of a patent might tend to impede innovation more than it would tend to promote it.' See *Association for Molecular Pathology v Myriad Genetics, Inc* 569 US 576.

[65] See Daniel S Fabricant and Norman R Farnsworth, 'The Value of Plants Used in Traditional Medicine for Drug Discovery' (2001) 109 *Environmental Health Perspectives*, http://www.ncbi.nlm.nih.gov/pmc/articles/PMC1240543/pdf/ehp109s-000069.pdf; See also Maurizio Iaccarino, 'Western Science could learn a thing or two from the way science is done in other cultures' (2003) 4(3) *EMBO reports*

phenomena of nature. And yet these natural observations may be far from routine, and often are the products of a highly creative and observant mind. Consider the example of a rural school teacher from India who came up with the idea of using extract of naffatia as an herbal pesticide. Legend has it that a group of farmers were having tea one morning. When one of the farmers had to leave the group for a while, his wife covered his tea with naffatia leaves to protect it. Upon his return, the farmer drank the tea and fell ill almost immediately. His bloodstream was found to have high levels of toxicity and he barely survived. An observant school teacher noted that if the leaves were so toxic that merely covering a cup of tea with them could almost kill someone, they would perform well as an herbal pesticide.[66]

This is not to suggest that such discoveries in the informal economy ought to be patentable; merely that mainstream IP paradigms often exclude key parts of innovative processes that are endemic to traditional knowledge systems within the informal sector.

IV. Conclusion

'Epistemic injustice' strikes at the very root of what it means to be a truly plural and inclusive society: one where all voices are heard. Unfortunately, more often than not, the voices of the subaltern are shut out. This is particularly so in the technological/ innovation context, where we arrogantly assume that what works for the formal economy will necessarily work for informal communities as well.

This would not have been half so tragic, were it not for the fact that the mainstream IP regime does not even suit the formal IP ecosystem, as many have begun to realise.[67]

As the examples in this chapter demonstrate, the mainstream assumptions around innovation policy and incentives/ appropriability mechanisms may not hold good for the informal economy. For one, the mainstream script around IP and innovation centres significantly around 'pecuniary' incentives and the tantalising thought of a near monopoly in the market.[68] And yet, most stories

220, where the author states that 'Whereas Western science favours reductionist, mechanistic and quantitative methods, traditional knowledge observes natural phenomena from a global point of view'.

[66] See Anil Gupta, 'Roots of Creativity and Innovation in Indian Society: A Honey Bee Perspective' (August/Sept 1996) 12(1) *Wastelands News*, 37, http://www.sristi.org/papers/new/Roots%20of%20Creativity,spwd.DOC.

[67] See Ove Granstrand, 'Abbreviations', in Ove Granstrand (ed), *Economics, Law and Intellectual Property: Seeking Strategies for Research and Teaching in a Developing World* (Dordecht, Springer Science+Business Media, 2003) 559; See also Polk Wagner, 'Information wants to be free: Intellectual Property and the Mythologies of Control' in Ole Andreas Rognstad (ed), *Property Aspects of Intellectual Property* (Oxford, Routledge, 2006) 330.

[68] See WM Cohen and H Sauermann, Schumpeter's Prophecy and Individual Incentives as a Driver of Innovation (2014) 'http://papers.ssrn.com//sol3//papers.cfm?abstract_id=2254959&download=yes. See Speranta Dumitru, 'Are Rawlsians entitled to monopoly rights' in Axel Gosseries et al (eds), *Intellectual Property and Theories of Justice* (Basingstoke, Palgrave Macmillan, 2008) 67, for deliberation on the concept of monopoly in relation to IP rights.

of innovation in the informal economy showcase a significant array of non-pecuniary incentives.[69]

In fact, a number of scholars point to the existence of such non-pecuniary incentives in the formal sector as well,[70] casting doubt on the notion that intellectual property rights necessarily enhance the rate and range of innovations across all technology sectors.[71] Given this skepticism, it would be foolhardy to transpose the mainstream model (based largely on pecuniary incentives) to the informal sector.

Imposing such a flawed frame will also perpetuate a prevalent 'epistemic injustice', leading to further hermeneutical marginalisation.

Further, such an imposition may do more harm than good, in that a formalisation process could harm the very fabric of the innovative ecosystem endemic to such cultures. For one thing, a 'formalisation' process almost always entails a drive towards increasing production and scale. This could mean that traditional healers would be forced to reformulate their herbal compositions as 'pills' with longer shelf lives and to evolve treatment regimens that are quicker in redressing 'symptoms' as opposed to a longer and more sustainable 'holistic' approach. There are serious dangers in such 'reductionist' attempts to simulate the commercial success of the allopathic drug industry.[72]

Lastly, and most importantly, it is unwise to assume that the informal sector needs to learn from the formal sector and formalise as quickly as possible. Rather, the informal economy may have important lessons for the formal economy on a variety of fronts. This is particularly so around the notion of constraint-induced creativity and non-pecuniary incentives, which have been staple aspects of many informal communities for several centuries.

[69] See Fayaz Ahmad Sheikh, 'Exploring informal sector community innovations and knowledge appropriation: A study of Kashmiri pashmina shawls' (2014) 6 *African Journal of Science, Technology, Innovation and Development* 203–12; See also S Bhaduri and H Kumar, 'Extrinsic and Intrinsic Motivations to Innovate: Tracing the Motivation of "Grassroots" Innovators in India' (2011) 10(1) *Mind & Society* e27–e55; See n 47 above.

[70] See WM Cohen and H Sauermann, 'Schumpeter's Prophecy and Individual Incentives as a Driver of Innovation' in F Malerba and S Brusoni (eds), *Perspectives on Innovation* (London, Cambridge University Press, 2007) 73–104. The authors argue that non pecuniary incentives can take various forms such as the joy of invention or creation, peer recognition, satisfying a 'vision' or the opportunity to exercise autonomy or responsibility.

[71] See Brownyn Hall, 'Patents and Patents Policy' (2007) 18 *Oxford Review of Economic Policy* 568; Andrew W. Torrance and Bill Tomlinson, 'Patents and the Regress of Useful Arts' (2009) 10 *Columbia Science and Technology Law Review*, where the author states that 'Despite the economic logic of the conventional view, there exists surprisingly little empirical evidence to support the key assumption that patents do actually spur technological innovation'; See also Committee on Intellectual Property Rights in the Knowledge Based Economy, National Research Council of the National Academies, *A Patent System for the 21st Century*, Stephen A Merrill et al (eds) (National Academies Press, 2004) 81–130, www.nap.edu//catalog.php?record_id=10976, where the author states that '[t]here are theoretical as well as empirical reasons to question whether patent rights advance innovation in a substantial way in most industries'.

[72] See Ruiping Fan, 'Modem Western Science as a Standard for Traditional Chinese Medicine: A Critical Appraisal' (2003) 31 *Journal of Medical Law and Ethics* 213.

The examples cited in this chapter may be few and far between; but they do alert us to the fact that the mainstream narrative around innovation and IP may not necessarily suit the informal economy. One needs to understand this economy better. One way to do this is to open ourselves more to testimonies from within, so that we redress the deep-seated epistemic injustice that has plagued this sector.

Soliciting Testimony: The Challenge of Openness in the International Genetically Engineered Machine (iGEM) Competition

AMY WEISSENBACH

In his chapter, Shamnad Basheer explores how 'epistemic injustice' in innovation may occur where hegemonic evaluative frameworks (in his piece, intellectual property regulations) do not reflect how innovators perceive value in their own work. He writes that epistemic injustice occurs in two forms: testimonial injustice – where the perspective or 'testimony of informal agents who "innovate" is effectively ignored' – and hermeneutical injustice, where 'our already prejudiced social understanding of innovation and appropriability mechanisms renders it difficult for informal innovators to make sense of incentives/models that lie outside the mainstream script'. Basheer recommends that we solicit testimonies from these informal innovators to uncover 'valuable learnings for the formal sector' and mitigate hermeneutical injustice. My prompt is to consider how Basheer's argument relates to my own work experience: first, as a former student of synthetic biology, research assistant to a biosecurity scholar, and participant in and contributor to the international Genetically Engineered Machine (iGEM) synthetic biology competition; and now as an aspiring sociologist interested in the sociology of science, knowledge and technology.

I am curious about the politics of soliciting, providing, and translating testimony to define innovation as Basheer suggests. Something is new or 'innovative' insofar as it departs from or builds upon things that already exist. Innovation is thus regulated – both enabled and constrained – not only by the ways of knowing embodied in institutional environments and practices, or in the evaluative frameworks (eg intellectual property frameworks) imposed upon products of innovation by 'outside' actors, but also by how innovators draw upon existing ways of knowing to define their work. The language used to construct and translate testimony of innovation – understood broadly to include classification systems, standards, and information infrastructures, and the various ways in which these are encoded in common tools – at once enables testimony and constrains the form that testimony can take.[1] Given that there is some tension between the freedom to innovate with respect to a particular community and freedom from the epistemological assumptions of that community, I wonder if and when we should conclude that this tension results in epistemic injustice. Based on Basheer's definition of epistemic injustice, it seems that injustice should depend both upon the openness and flexibility of the particular language and/or criteria used to define innovation, and upon the extent to which there exist acceptable alternative communities in which to innovate and/or draw inspiration for innovation.

An innovator defines her work by reference to an established social history, and to speak to a community's history, she must use its language. The tension that results is evident in the sociology of scientific knowledge, where scholars scrutinise the social construction of knowledge, yet inevitably confront epistemological assumptions embedded in the language of sociology and of common speech. As historian and sociologist of science Steven Shapin pointed out in his 1995 survey of the Sociology of Scientific Knowledge (SSK) for the *Annual Review of Sociology*, the essential 'limits' of critics' 'skepticism about the categories of common culture' are those 'posed by the boundaries of communication':

> We can develop and put in place arcane languages, but we cannot ensure that others will hear us … If we wish effectively to speak to a specified community, we are obliged to share its realist idiom … That obligation is, properly speaking, a constraint.[2]

Though Shapin directed his response to sociologists, his observations apply to innovators across domains. The language used to construct and translate testimony of innovation is naturally a constraint, as its grammar regulates how the innovation is defined. This language, however, is also the thing that defines the innovation and makes it meaningful with respect to the community in question. It is in this sense, Shapin wrote, that '[t]he "cage" from which "escape" is sought is, in fact, a condition of such liberty as we enjoy'.

In theory, we might innovate with respect to any social history we choose. However, one community may lend us greater legitimacy and/or power to bring about our intended effect, and we may therefore feel compelled to speak using that community's language.[3] For example, I am entering my first year of a PhD in sociology, and I hope to publish in my discipline. In order to make a widely recognised contribution to the field (and improve my job prospects), I will aim

[1] On the sociology of standards, see generally S Timmermans and S Epstein, 'A World of Standards but not a Standard World: Toward a Sociology of Standards and Standardization' (2010) 36 *Annual Review of Sociology* 69; GC Bowker and SL Star, *Sorting Things Out* (Cambridge MA, MIT Press, 1999).

[2] S Shapin, 'Here and Everywhere: Sociology of Scientific Knowledge' (1995) 21 *Annual Review of Sociology* 289, 315.

[3] M Callon, 'Some Elements of a Sociology of Translation: Domestication of the Scallops and the Fishermen of St. Brieuc Bay' in J Law (ed), *Power, Action and Belief: A New Sociology of Knowledge* (London, Routledge and Kegan Paul, 1986); B Latour, 'Circulating Reference: Sampling the Soil in the Amazon Forest' in B Latour, *Pandora's Hope: Essays on the Reality of Science Studies* (Cambridge MA, Harvard University Press, 1999), 24–79; B Latour, *Science in Action* (Cambridge MA, Harvard University Press, 1987).

to publish in a top sociology journal. To do so, I must make my contribution understood by the community that journal represents. Though sociology is a relatively open discipline that accommodates many research methodologies and theoretical contributions, this task will inevitably impose some formal and informal constraints. My perception of my audience, and my interactions with editors and peer reviewers, will inform the language I use and the concepts I draw upon to define my work.

Though the constraints imposed by the epistemic community – here, the sociology journal's editors, peer reviewers, and audience – may create some kind of local epistemic limitation, insofar as the journal presents one way of understanding the world to the exclusion of others, these constraints are not in themselves sufficient to produce epistemic injustice. They do not inflict injustice upon me, for two primary reasons. First, there are many literatures that speak to the kinds of questions I might want to address: within sociology, in other academic disciplines, and beyond academia. This is partially due to the fact that sociology's boundaries are relatively porous where they border on other academic disciplines and practices of thinking and writing. I do not suffer testimonial injustice, insofar as there are multiple mainstream avenues by which I might communicate my ideas. I do not suffer hermeneutical injustice, insofar as I have plenty of literature I might draw upon to inform my work. Second, I do not currently feel that my testimony is meaningfully neglected or obscured by the various literatures available to me. As I am a white, US-born, second-generation academic positioned among elite universities, it is perhaps easy for me to identify with those working in sociology and neighbouring areas of practice, and unsurprising if I expect that my contributions will be heard in one of these areas.

However, there is also a more specific reason for my belief in the number and variety of avenues by which I might speak to social questions. I have known and sought help from generous mentors in diverse disciplines and occupations, respected in their fields, who helped me connect the language of their disciplines to my own personal experience, recognise my thoughts as insights, and develop an impression of myself as someone interested in and capable of contributing to their areas of work. Even now, with all my past experience and the resources of a PhD programme at my disposal, I am a novice, grappling with a new language and with fresh doubts about where and how I might contribute to the field before me. I continue to depend upon peers and mentors to help me recognise elements of my experience as knowledge and my reflections as ideas that can be productively explored through sociology. It took a mentor not only to tell me that I had something to contribute to this book, but to help me see *how* I might contribute. In other words, the epistemic tools we choose to use, and the extent to which we can use those tools to both innovate and express our ways of knowing, depend not only upon the availability and flexibility of the tools, but also upon the nature of our interpersonal relationships with more 'expert' knowers.

The political stakes of translation and inclusion may look different in highly technical areas where there are higher barriers to entry, and where scientists and innovators are more successful in making an epistemic project what Latour and Callon call an 'obligatory passage point' – a powerful site of coordination for multiple stakeholders who see the project as the most compelling or only vehicle by which to achieve their goals.

Synthetic biology is such an area where outcomes of research and development have wide impact and therefore involve many interested stakeholders. This is a discipline in which scientists and engineers apply engineering frameworks (mostly from computing) to biology in order to advance both bioengineering capacities and biological understanding.[4] The field promises to transform our relationship with biology, and research and development collaborations cross geopolitical boundaries, academic disciplines and industrial sectors.[5]

In this context, the international Genetically Engineered Machine (iGEM) synthetic biology competition treats standardisation and openness as mutually constitutive. The competition prescribes a set of standards and online infrastructure designed to facilitate sharing of scientific protocols and genetic 'parts' (or DNA sequences coding for specific cell functions) and to motivate work toward making biology easier to engineer, making it possible for those with less specialised expertise to assemble standardised genetic components into 'circuits'. iGEM's standards make the language and tools of synthetic biology more open and accessible, but specifically for those socialised into a computational mode of learning, collaborating and innovating. Like all standards, iGEM's contain their own evaluative frameworks and thus work to strengthen and extend the influence of a particular way of knowing in organising research and development. Synthetic biology is based on the premise that biology can and should be treated as an engineering discipline, and it thus cannot meaningfully incorporate testimony that counters this assumption. Clearly there is risk of epistemic injustice in synthetic biology where bioengineers reshape landscapes and organisms in spite of the protests of people who understand biology differently or find themselves without language to articulate opposition. With respect to innovation in this area, there is surely some form of epistemic limitation; however, it remains unclear to me when and where injustice is inflicted, and by whom.

iGEM began with the Synthetic Biology Working Group at Massachusetts Institute for Technology (MIT), the group that founded synthetic biology and articulated the initial goals of the field. Formed in 2003 as part of MIT's Artificial Intelligence Laboratory, the Group aimed to advance biological understanding, bioengineering capacities, and the social outcomes of technological progress by making biology easier to engineer.[6] Founding members Tom Knight and Drew Endy

[4] S Roosth, *Synthetic: How Life Got Made* (Chicago IL, The University of Chicago Press, 2017).

[5] JY Zhang, C Marris and N Rose, 'The Transnational Governance of Synthetic Biology: Scientific Uncertainty, Cross-borderness and the 'Art' of Governance', *BIOS Working Paper No 4* (London, BIOS (Centre for the study of Bioscience, Biomedicine, Biotechnology and Society) London School of Economics and Political Science, May 2011).

[6] Roosth (2016) n 4 above.

were inspired by the open source software movement, and they created an open online registry of 'BioBricks' (or DNA sequences) that were free: available for those who accessed the registry website to use and build upon, and requiring no payment. Thereafter, drawing inspiration from other student engineering competitions, Group members Knight, Endy and Randy Rettberg developed iGEM, a competition in which undergraduates could tinker with and build upon one another's designs for genetic parts, circuits and biological devices, testing and building out the Registry of Standard Biological Parts in the process. iGEM began in 2004 with five teams (from Boston University, Caltech, MIT, Princeton and the University of Texas, Austin) and grew quickly, fuelled by funding from the National Science Foundation.

iGEM soon became not only an annual summer competition but a de facto industry training programme, including undergraduate, graduate, high school, and community lab teams spanning the globe.[7] In 2018, iGEM drew 340 teams from 42 countries and five continents, for a total of over 5,000 participants.[8] Teams come from the world's premier research universities conducting work in synthetic biology, including those from the US, the Netherlands, Germany, France, the UK, India and China, among other nations. Each Spring, iGEM sends boxes of BioBricks as physical DNA to registered teams. Each summer, iGEM teams contribute to the Registry as they borrow, build upon, and create new BioBricks while designing their biological devices.[9] In 2012, iGEM became a non-profit foundation independent of MIT, taking over management of the Registry.[10] Today scholars, policy-makers, scientists, and industry representatives refer to iGEM as both a microcosm of synthetic biology and as an aspiring force for the field's advancement – in developing biological understanding and bioengineering tools, training future practitioners, and promoting attention to social norms about genetic engineering.[11] The competition has become a networking site among stakeholders in the discipline – including synthetic biology researchers at universities and research centres, industry representatives, social scientists, bioethicists,

[7] J McNamara, SB-Y Lightfoot, K Drinkwater, E Appleton, and K Oye, 'Designing Safety Policies to Meet Evolving Needs: iGEM as a Testbed for Proactive and Adaptive Risk Management' (2014) 3(12) *ACS Synthetic Biology* 983; E Frow and J Calvert, '"Can Simple Biological Systems Be Built From Standardized Interchangeable Parts?" Negotiating Biology and Engineering in a Synthetic Biology Competition' (2013) 5(1) *Engineering Studies* 42, 43; iGEM.org.

[8] 2019.iGEM.org.

[9] Drew Endy, 'Foundations for Engineering Biology' (2005) 438 *Nature* 449; Frow and Calvert (2013), n 7 above; Christina D Smolke, 'Building Outside of the Box: iGEM and the BioBricks Foundation' (2009) 27 *Nature Biotechnology*1099.

[10] parts.mit.edu.

[11] Smolke (2009), n 9 above; Zhang, Marris and Rose (2011), n 5 above; AW Betten, V Rerimassie, JEW Broerse, D Stemerding and F Kupper, 'Constructing Future Scenarios as a Tool to Foster Responsible Research and Innovation Among Future Synthetic Biologists' (2018) 14(1) *Life Sciences, Society and Policy* 21; D Stemerding, 'iGEM as Laboratory in Responsible Research and Innovation' (2015) 2(1) *Journal of Responsible Innovation* 140; Presidential Commission for Study of Bioethical Issues (PCBI), *New Directions: The Ethics of Synthetic Biology and Emerging Technologies* (Washington DC, 2010), 169–70.

legal scholars, and government representatives – many of whom support the competition as volunteers (often cycling through different roles), partners and sponsors.[12] In 2017, the iGEM organisation formally recognised its role in this regard, expanding its programming to serve a new 'After iGEM' alumni network.[13]

Cognisant of its commitment to openness and its position in an international and interdisciplinary field, iGEM has been careful not to institute overly prescriptive criteria. iGEM frames its main event as a 'Giant Jamboree', a 'celebration of everyone's efforts' rather than a competition. At the Jamboree, teams can win one of an unlimited number of 'medals' (Bronze, Silver, and Gold, delivered in the form of a paper certificate) by fulfilling various performance criteria. They can also win 'Awards' in diverse 'Best Of" categories, including 'Best Part', 'Best Therapeutics', 'Best Wiki', and 'Best Education and Public Engagement'.

However, to maintain its position and pursue its vision of openness and sharing in a rapidly developing field, iGEM must also standardise. Most critiques of iGEM concerned with inequality focus on how standardisation falls short, making judging non-transparent and providing less well-established teams with insufficient resources. Frow and Calvert describe how in practice, engineering frameworks only rarely align with the messy process of biology research, so iGEM teams often draw upon engineering metaphors only as framing devices: in conceptualisation and problem definition, and in final presentations.[14] Others have noted how winning teams at iGEM tend to be recurring participants from well-established and well-resourced research centres, who tend to 'avoid the uncertainties of the parts designed and/or characterized by others and choose to use new, ad hoc DNA parts for a specific purpose'.[15] These accounts suggest that the common 'shared' resources in the BioBrick repository may only have limited utility in producing successful projects, and thus may obscure primary sources of inequity just as they may create real opportunity at iGEM. Meanwhile, though BioBrick parts are free, and though technological advances continue to drive down other costs of research, participation at iGEM might still be prohibitively expensive for many who might wish to take part in it. In 2019, Jamboree registration cost US$5000, a sum that provides each team with a wiki,[16] a kit of frequently used BioBricks, a presentation slot and a poster location. This fee, however, did not cover the costs of research or of transportation and accommodation at the Jamboree. In 2014, synthetic biology researchers and former iGEM participants writing to *Nature Biotechnology* estimated the average cost per team at roughly US$20,000–US$50,000 per year.[17]

[12] Frow and Calvert (2013), n 7 above; iGEM.org.

[13] igem.org/Main_Page; after.igem.org.

[14] Frow and Calvert (2013), n 7 above.

[15] C Vilanova and M Porcar, 'iGEM 2.0 – Refoundations for Engineering Biology' (2014) 32 *Nature Biotechnology* 420, 422.

[16] A website that team members can collaboratively edit.

[17] Vilanova and Porcar (2014), n 15 above, 421; 2019.igem.org/Competition/Registration.

Where do we locate epistemic injustice at iGEM, and how do we address it? There appears to be an almost irreversibly hierarchical relationship between the ways of knowing that shaped synthetic biology's infrastructure and the ways of knowing that might be expressed through that infrastructure. Still, the most obvious and pressing sources of inequality at the competition seem to relate to unequally distributed information, training and resources, which might be remedied through the strengthening and extension of open standards and infrastructure like the BioBrick and the Registry. We might understand these standards and infrastructure as a mode to solicit testimony from those beyond the predominant research groups in synthetic biology.

As I continue to reflect on these questions, I think of Shapin, who writes, 'Intellectuals are not obliged to leap free from their culture in order to subject their culture to questioning'.[18] Perhaps the language we use need not perfectly reflect our understanding to provide us with sufficient tools to provide testimony. To the extent to which iGEM's BioBrick infrastructure constitutes a common language, greater standardisation and accessibility may give more innovators the language to express viewpoints that contradict and/or complicate mainstream synthetic biology research. My own experience suggests that epistemic openness will partially depend upon whether current experts in synthetic biology and neighbouring disciplines play generous mentors to newcomers, and whether they work to empower those currently beyond the practice. As a sociologist interested in innovating in my discipline, maybe my strategy should be to learn the language of the discipline as well as I can, while remaining in conversation with those beyond it. I might thus prepare myself (and help others) to generate insights that complicate and innovate upon mainstream sociological thinking, opening new avenues into the future.

[18] Shapin (1995), n 2 above, 315.

Are Informal Resilience and Formal Emancipation Necessarily Incompatible?

JULES NAUDET

The epistemic challenges of informality: Shamnad Basheer's legal approach to informal innovation, drawing upon the concept of epistemic injustice, opens an interesting line of social criticism. It reminds us of how restrictive it can be to define informal innovation from a mainstream perspective. Apprehending these innovations, sometimes referred to as *jugaad*, through the lens of the Intellectual Property framework necessarily leads one to negate the non-commercial relations within which they are embedded. Oftentimes, these innovations are indeed the consequences of motivations that escape the realm of profitability. Basheer gives three examples that suggest that they can be motivated by other aims. Be it the need to assist one's community peers, the need to improve a traditional form of therapy (that is itself embedded in non-commercial relations) or the will to move out of commercial relations.

In a way, the epistemic injustice to which Basheer rightly points is a derived form of what Pierre Bourdieu calls 'symbolic violence'. Such violence, Bourdieu argues,

> is perpetrated by those who, thanks to their knowledge of formalization and proper judicial manners, are able to put the law on their side. When they need to, these are the people who can put the most skillful exercise of formal rigor (*summum jus*) to the service of the least innocent ends (*summa injuria*).[1]

Law indeed produces violence by defining what is legal and what is illegal, what is true and what is false. Or what is innovation and what is not, who is an innovator and who is not; and, following on from this, which innovations can be commodified through Intellectual Property Rights and which ones cannot. Epistemic injustice is thus a derived byproduct of the symbolic violence of law.

If the force of law produces (epistemic) injustice, this necessarily suggests an important corollary that is not explored in Basheer's article; namely, that justice

[1] Pierre Bourdieu, 'The Force of Law: Toward a Sociology of the Juridical Field' (1987) 38 *Hastings Law Journal* 814, 850.

supposes inhabiting a common epistemic space. The force of law being arbitrary, producing symbolic violence and being based on epistemic asymmetries, genuine justice would thus require the capacity to understand the subjectivity of others. This would open interesting lines of inquiry regarding the nature of justice, but (un)fortunately this is not the aim of this short piece.

These clarifications about the underlying premises of Basheer's text being made, I see at least two directions in which to push the discussion of informal innovation further.

The first one consists in taking Basheer's analysis for granted and arguing that the epistemic injustice of which informal innovators are a victim is the sign that they actually resist processes of commodification. Informal innovation would then be a form of what Michèle Lamont and Peter Hall call 'social resilience'. They indeed argue that

> although neo-liberal initiatives improved the lives of some people, it also posed profound challenges to the well-being of many groups, communities and individuals, as more intense market competition reallocated resources and market logics worked their way into ever more spheres of social life.[2]

The capacity of these groups of people to sustain and advance 'their well-being in the face of such challenges' is what they call 'social resilience'.[3] This is somehow Basheer's point when he writes:

> The mainstream script around IP and innovation centres significantly around 'pecuniary' incentives and the tantalising thought of a near monopoly in the market. And yet, most stories of innovation in the informal economy showcase a significant array of non-pecuniary incentives.

Informal innovation would thus be a form of social resilience and of resistance to the oppression of the social order imposed by 'bourgeois environmentalism';[4] it should thus be praised and encouraged.

There are undoubtedly resilience and emancipating processes at work in the informal innovations Basheer discusses. Yet, another way to pursue the conversation would be to question the dualism underlying his analyses. In his chapter, Basheer indeed seems to imply that resilience is necessarily on the side of informality and that formality is necessarily on the side of commodification and oppression. There's a certain truth in that. But there's also more to it than that. And as a scholar specialised in social stratification and processes of inequality formation, I would have appreciated a more nuanced and complex discussion of these issues.

[2] Peter Hall and Michèle Lamont, *Social Resilience in the Neoliberal Era* (New York, Cambridge University Press, 2013) 2.

[3] Ibid.

[4] Amita Baviskar, *Uncivil City: Ecology, Equity and the Commons in Delhi* (New Delhi, Sage Publications and Yoda Press, 2019).

In a country where, as Basheer rightly points out, 'India's informal sector is said to constitute a whopping 81 per cent of its economy', conceptualising informality is indeed decisive and is the key to understanding how the unequal distribution of opportunities and resources operates. A sociology of social stratification processes in India necessarily implies a sociology of informality. And this constitutes a major epistemic challenge. As a sociologist conducting empirical research in India, I am too often confronted by the fact that we lack tools to address this issue. It is often skirted around, and not enough scholars openly reckon the need to rigorously question how to develop a sociology of stratification in a society whose economy is predominantly informal. With a hint of bad faith, we too often act as if our conceptual tools crafted in countries of the Global North were sufficient to make sense of the social processes at work in Indian society. They are not. But, on the opposite side, promoting the virtues of informality as a way to escape mainstream – and certainly Western – modes of thought is not a satisfying alternative to the shortcomings of our theoretical arsenal. It seems to me that Basheer's argument suffers from this lack of reflection of what informality does to stratification.

At the risk of being blamed of Eurocentrism or of statism, I think it is indeed important to remind oneself that informal innovation is certainly not the solution to the development issues many countries of the world face today. Let us not forget that informality is also a synonym of exploitation and oppression; that informality is often embedded in racial, patriarchal, classist and casteist modes of domination; and that there is also a certain potential for emancipation that comes along with formality. As Basheer himself reminds us in his long section on how to define the informal economy, the issue of the boundary between the formal and the informal sectors raises the question – among others – of the bureaucratic, legal and insurantial dimensions of economic activities.

And this legal framework is not limited to Intellectual Property rights. It also hides multiple invisible mechanisms that actually end up shaping the opportunity structure. There is, for example, the issue of safety and security standards or the issue of the certification of training. What I mean by that is that the question arises as to whether or not it is necessary to require certified training for workers who will be responsible for setting up and operating a crane, who will electrify a building in which hundreds of people may die in a fire or who will connect offices to a sewer system. What if Vellan Vaidyan, the healer whom Basheer presents, poisons his patients with his treatments? One should not forget that informality is also a potential source of health, safety and ecological risks.

One has to further look beyond the obvious – and often discussed – question of the legal protection of workers, clients or users of infrastructures. The absence of norms and imperative credentials – or the incapacity to enforce these norms and credentials – contributes to making the informal sector a poverty trap. It keeps workers away from education, quite simply because technical and technological education is not a compulsory and unavoidable prerequisite for access to employment.

So to come back to Basheer's quotation of Latouche, yes, informality is certainly an activity that is outside the radar of the state. But one should remember that it is outside of its radar because the state wants it so; because the state chooses not to regulate what it could regulate. The same state can sometimes choose, in reverse, to over-regulate and over-produce standards in other fields or sectors of activity, while being fully aware that economic actors will therefore choose informality to avoid regulation. The powerful ones then have the 'force of the law' with them and the weak ones are thrown into illegality.

There is a complex dialectic of both emancipation and oppression at play in the formal sector as well as in the informal one. Regulation can accelerate commodification processes but in other circumstances it can also initiate de-commodification processes and thus constitute the most efficient counterweight to market forces.[5] This variable geometry of state intervention and regulation suggests that expressions such as 'commodification' or 'neoliberalisation', by pointing at a unilateral direction of the course of events, may not necessarily be the best way to account for the contradictory processes that lead to the exploitation – or emancipation – of the subalterns. Basheer focused on the invisibility of processes in the informal sector. I would conclude by pointing out that the excess of attention to processes of informal resilience in turn can sometimes invisibilise potentialities of emancipation that exist in the formal sphere.

[5] Karl Polanyi, *The Great Transformation: The Political and Economic Origins of Our Time* (Boston MA, Beacon Press, 1957 [1944]).

Course 5

KHAN, PRASAD, AND KROLL

5

Islamic Review in Pakistan: Problematising the Divide between *Shari'a* Courts and their 'Secular' Counterparts

MARYAM S KHAN*

I. Introduction

Within the burgeoning scholarship on the global rise of judicial power, an influential thesis that makes a substantial empirical contribution to the phenomenon of 'political courts' posits that courts in constitutional systems that attempt to merge religious laws with liberal-secular notions of constitutionalism are rationally designed to constrain or even inhibit more radical religious demands in such societies.[1] These 'constitutional theocracies', the thesis asserts, empower courts to act as 'secularising' agents against global religious fervour, even as they exhibit features that are traditionally understood to be in conflict with liberal constitutionalism – such as assertion of divine sovereignty, establishment of a state religion, reliance on religion as one source of law (if not the chief or exclusive source), and judicial powers to review the conformity of laws with religion.[2]

Pakistan is a leading example of a 'constitutional theocracy'. Its current constitution – the Constitution of the Islamic Republic of Pakistan, 1973 (the Constitution) – declares Islam the state religion and the source of all laws, and

* I extend my deepest thanks to the South Asia Working Group at the University of Wisconsin Law School for invaluable comments on an earlier version of this work. I must also acknowledge the encouragement and critical input of participants and colleagues at a conference on 'Religion and the State' held in Tunisia in 2017 – co-organised by the Islamic Legal Studies Program (Harvard Law School), Arab Association of Constitutional Law, and Tunisian Association of Constitutional Law – where I was first invited to present on the subject and from which I drew my initial inspiration to write this chapter. Thanks also to Afiya Zia for her insights on Pakistan's feminist movement and Islamisation.

[1] R Hirschl, *Constitutional Theocracy* (Cambridge MA, Harvard University Press, 2010); R Hirschl, 'The Rise of Constitutional Authority' (2008) 49 *Harvard International Law Journal Online* 72, 80.

[2] Ibid.

establishes a parallel *Shari'a* court for, among other things, reviewing whether the laws of the country are 'repugnant to the injunctions of the *Holy Quran* and *Sunnah*' (the two primary sources of Islamic law). The 'constitutional theocracy' thesis argues that Pakistan's apex court, the Supreme Court of Pakistan (SC), has played an important role in counterbalancing the 'pro-religious jurisprudence' of the *Shari'a* court – known as the Federal *Shariat* Court (FSC) – and has provided a 'safety net' for moderate interests.[3] Three complementary and highly consequential claims are implicit in this argument: firstly, the belief that the FSC is a producer of an extreme form of religion-centric jurisprudence that is inherently in conflict with the larger constitutional framework in which all the constitutional courts, including the FSC, are generally embedded; secondly, that the SC has consistently played the role of a 'bulwark of secularism' vis-à-vis the FSC and its illiberal jurisprudence;[4] and thirdly, that despite the context of a dualist constitution, the application of Islamic laws is neatly compartmentalised within the *Shari'a* jurisdiction.

In this chapter, I aim to critically engage with the 'constitutional theocracy' thesis in the context of Pakistan. I do so with a particular consciousness of building theories from local sites in which institutions are situated and from which they emerge. Instead of viewing religious law and secular law as pre-determined and reified oppositional categories set up by the global narrative on 'theocratic constitutionalism', I aim to empirically observe the relationship between these laws through the interactions between the FSC and the SC (in its various jurisdictions) in the resolution of important constitutional cases within a broader historical, political, and institutional context. Based on the diversity observed in these interactions and the plurality in the outcomes of the cases under scrutiny, I argue that the two courts engage in a reciprocal process of resistance, accommodation and integration that is much more complex than essentialist notions of the *Shari'a* courts as 'Islamising' and non-*Shari'a* courts as 'secularising'. The dialectic between the two courts in Pakistan is as much a product of the absorption of liberal constitutional principles (such as Fundamental Rights) in the *Shari'a* jurisprudence as it is a result generally of the dual liberal–Islamic nature of the Constitution. Moreover, a closer study of the institutional design of the FSC reveals several interesting overlaps with the SC, both in terms of the judges and *ulema* (Islamic legal scholars) who sit on these courts and the fusion of this parallel system in the appeals process for Islamic review. In practice, these overlaps tend to considerably dilute the political and institutional binary perpetuated by a top-down global analysis of constitutional theocracies. Far from instantiating some kind of categorical or universal opposition or competition between secular and religious constitutional principles,

[3] R Hirschl, 'Constitutional Courts as Bulwarks of Secularism' in D Kapiszewski, G Silverstein and RA Kagan (eds), *Consequential Courts: Judicial Courts in Global Perspective* (Cambridge, Cambridge University Press, 2013), 318–22.

[4] ibid.

Pakistan's case shows that the role of courts in engaging with the liberal–religious duality in a constitutional theocracy is contingent on a multiplicity of intersecting factors. These include not just regime imperatives and institutional design, but also local histories of constitutional issues being adjudicated, the evolution of constitutional norms over time, and the broader socio-political context in which intra-judicial contestations happen.

This chapter is structured as follows. In rethinking positive theories of globalisation from the ground up, particularly in the context of Islamic constitutionalism and the sites of its emergence and institutionalisation, the next section (II) begins with an exercise in self-reflection. In it, I aspire to articulate my own positionality vis-à-vis my encounter with global theories as a constitutional scholar from a Muslim-majority country in the Global South, and what this foregrounding of one's location, both geographic and epistemic, can offer by way of reshaping the prevailing understandings of global theories. Against this reflexive backdrop, section III provides the background context to the broader structure of Islamic constitutionalism and its 'theocratic constitutional' features, the political origins of the FSC, and the interrelationship of the FSC with the SC or, more broadly, with what I refer to as the 'mainstream constitutional courts' in Pakistan to distinguish them jurisdictionally from the FSC. It also analyses the hybrid institutional design of the FSC that structurally integrates it into the mainstream constitutional courts and thus creates a major overlap between the two court systems. Section IV presents a typology of important constitutional cases with the objective of empirically observing the relationship between secular and religious laws through the interactions of the FSC and the SC. Based on a collective analysis of these cases, this section attempts to convey: (i) that the religious and the secular, far from being discrete legal categories, constitute each other; (ii) that both religious and secular laws are internally diverse and composed of competing liberal and illiberal strains; and (iii) that constitutional practice is a function of the larger socio-political context as much as of state policy and institutional design.[5] Section V recapitulates and synthesises the main themes and arguments in this chapter, and derives from them a set of theoretical propositions for approaching the study of legal globalisation.

II. Reflections on Positionality and 'Ground Up' Theorising

As a Muslim female legal scholar of post-colonial South Asia with educational experience and academic training in institutions of the 'Global North', I am acutely

[5] These observations variously draw from and are fortified by three cross-disciplinary works that touch on the liberal–Islamic duality in Pakistan: MJ Nelson, *In the Shadow of Shari'ah: Islam, Islamic Law, and Democracy in Pakistan* (London, Hurst & Co, 2011); AU Qasmi, 'God's Kingdom on Earth? Politics of Islam in Pakistan, 1947–1969' (2010) 44 *Modern Asian Studies* 6; JA Redding, 'Constitutionalizing Islam: Theory and Pakistan' (2004) 44 *Virginia Journal of International Law* 759.

aware of the local struggles around Islamic Constitutionalism and its institutions, both within and without the formal sphere of the courts. Because the globalisation narrative focuses exclusively on the state, the courts, and their formal logic, perceptions about the praxis of Islamic constitutionalism in a Muslim-majority context like Pakistan are premised narrowly on formal institutional contestations. For instance, nowhere in this globalisation narrative on political courts and Islamisation is there any serious engagement with the fact that resistance to Islamic constitutionalism in Pakistan was originally mobilised by a secular-liberal feminist movement in the 1980s[6] that continues to demand, among other things, the abolition of the FSC and the repeal of the draconian, anti-women *Hudood* laws that lie within its jurisdiction.[7] I profess my unequivocal support for this movement. Simultaneously, while I don't suffer many of the Islamophobia-related anxieties of Muslims in non-Muslim majority countries, I am not immune to the larger discriminating and dehumanising structures of globalisation discourse. Neither am I immune to the many contradictions of liberalism in post-colonial contexts, or to the persistent and opportunistic support in the West for military authoritarianism in Pakistan for proxy wars.

Hence, in my capacity as a Pakistani, 'Global South', scholar who routinely engages with her intellectual counterparts in the North on the basis of her academic training in and associations with institutions in the latter, I find myself treading an intellectual tightrope in representing Pakistan. On the one hand I am an abolitionist vis-à-vis the FSC – not only for the inefficiencies and conflicts it generates as a parallel judicial structure but, more importantly, for the potential it holds for the gross abuse of women's rights under the *Hudood* laws.[8] On the other hand, however much as this abolitionist stance may be equated with a secular or liberal worldview, in my mind it is wholly consistent with resistance to both the global onslaught of Islamic essentialism and the alienation and inequality resulting from liberal-constitutional frameworks in post-colonial societies. I am also, at the same time, critical of the state and the larger justice system for selectively instrumentalising Islam for their institutional and political interests even as they project an image of liberalism. This bundle of views is by no means self-contradictory or marginal among the urban intellectual classes of the Global South; on the contrary, it instantiates the complexities of identity politics in the globalisation context.

Yet, global theory on political courts tends to normalise a reductivism in which 'secular' and 'Islamic' occupy not just different but oppositional institutional

[6] See generally R Saigol, 'Feminism and the Women's Movement in Pakistan: Actors, Debates and Strategies' (March 2016) Country Study (Friedrich Ebert Stiftung, 2016): http://library.fes.de/pdf-files/bueros/pakistan/12453.pdf.

[7] See, eg M Lau, 'Twenty-Five Years of Hudood Ordinances – A Review' (2007) 64(4) *Washington and Lee Law Review* 1291.

[8] The FSC has two different jurisdictions: the *Hudood* jurisdiction, and an Islamic review jurisdiction. The analytical focus of this chapter is on the latter and how it relates to and interfaces with the judicial review powers of the mainstream constitutional courts.

spaces. This gap between complex reality and oversimplified and essentialising theory motivates a rethinking of theories of legal globalisation from the 'ground up'. By this I do not mean an inversion of the globalisation gaze – a mere overturning of the binaries of the globaliser and the recipient – but a recognition of the socio-political nuances and plurality of contestations and attitudes that are situated at the intersection of the local and the global. This 'ground up' theorising remains mindful of the powerful reality of global connectedness while introspecting about and critiquing the selective and monochromatic lens that the globalisation narrative uses to gloss over political context and local struggle.

The following sections III and IV present a case study on the FSC and its connections with the larger court system as well as the wider socio-political context in Pakistan. Premised on this case study, section V engages with the question of 'ground up' theorising on *Shari'a* courts and Islamic constitutionalism more broadly.

III. Islamic Constitutionalism in Pakistan

A. The Dual Character of the Constitution

The legitimating principle of Pakistan's Constitution is in many ways the ideology of Islam. Its Preamble reflects an attempt to merge a liberal democratic framework with Islamic principles in an historical context of political accommodation of a disparate set of constituents ranging from secularists to Islamic modernists to Islamic traditionalists.[9] An example of how liberal constitutional notions of freedom and equality sit alongside references to Islam is the Preamble's declaration that the political ideal of democracy is derived from a delegation of divine sovereign authority to the 'State of Pakistan through its people' and 'based on Islamic principles of social justice'. Other Islamic provisions include a declaration that 'Muslims shall be enabled to order their lives … in accordance with the teachings and requirements of Islam' (Preamble); a set of provisions to make the teaching of the *Holy Quran* compulsory (article 31(2)), secure the organisation of *zakat* (Islamic religious tax) (article 31(2)), prevent the consumption of alcohol (article 37(h)), and eliminate *riba* (usury or interest) (article 38(f)); a provision making it mandatory for the head of state or President to be Muslim (article 41(2)); a 'repugnancy clause' declaring that '[a]ll existing laws shall be brought in conformity with the injunctions of Islam … and no law shall be enacted which is repugnant to such Injunctions' (article 227(1)); and a chapter on 'Islamic Provisions' establishing an advisory body for making recommendations to the

[9] See, eg L Binder, *Religion and Politics in Pakistan* (Berkeley CA, University of California Press, 1961) 142–54.

Parliament on, among other things, whether a proposed law is repugnant to the injunctions of Islam (article 228). In addition, and importantly, the Constitution makes Islam the 'State religion of Pakistan' (article 2).

At the same time, the Islamic principles are grounded in a progressive framework for social and economic restructuring. This larger framework includes a recognition of labour rights, a commitment to broadening of the economic base, an expanded role for the state in regulating private wealth, and an express focus on securing gender equality. This progressive notion of Islam – centered on a social vision of 'an egalitarian society' (Preamble) – is most evident in the detailed chapter on 'Principles of Policy' that lays out a policy scheme for guiding executive and legislative functions (Chapter 2). On the one hand, the Principles iterate the state's role in enabling 'the Muslims of Pakistan, individually and collectively, to order their lives in accordance with the fundamental principles and basic concepts of Islam' (article 31(1)). On the other, they read like a socialist charter, directing the state to safeguard the rights and secure greater public participation of vulnerable and marginalised groups, including women, religious and regional minorities, and peasants and workers (articles 32–39). They emphasise the promotion of social justice (article 37), as well as social and economic well-being (article 38).

One feature of the original Constitution was that it left the *Shari'a* enforcement provisions non-justiciable. Moreover, the body constituted for making recommendations to the legislature on whether an existing or proposed law was repugnant – the Council of Islamic Ideology – had a purely advisory mandate. Hence, the nature of Islamic constitutionalism in the Constitution was one of 'political constitutionalism',[10] in that the locus of power for evaluating the 'Islamic-ness' of the legal framework was situated within the elected legislature. The FSC constituted a major departure from this original scheme of Islamic constitutionalism. Established in 1980, the FSC transformed the system to one of 'legal constitutionalism' in which a parallel judicial forum, composed of a combination of constitutional court judges and *ulema*, was granted Islamic review powers.[11] With the FSC in place, Pakistan exhibits the entire range of features observed in a 'constitutional theocracy': Islam as the state religion, Islamic injunctions as the source of all laws, and Islamic review. In fact, in global comparison, the FSC is truly distinctive. There is no other contemporary example of a parallel court invested with the exclusive power to judge whether any existing laws (legislated before or after the creation of the FSC) are repugnant to Islamic injunctions, and to render repugnant laws ineffective.[12]

[10] CB Lombardi, 'Designing Islamic constitutions: Past trends and options for a democratic future' (2013) 11 *International Journal of Constitutional Law* 615, 621–25.

[11] See, eg M Lau, *The Role of Islam in the Legal System of Pakistan* (Boston MA, Martinus Nijhoff Publishers, 2006).

[12] M Lau, 'The Re-Islamization of Legal Systems' in R Peters and P Bearman (eds), *The Ashgate Research Companion to Islamic Law* (Aldershot, Ashgate Publishing Ltd, 2014) 235, 236–37.

B. Parallel Constitutional Court Structure: 'Coordinate Constitutionalisation'

Both the SC and the FSC are 'constitutional courts' in that they exercise some form of constitutional review. In their political origins, however, they are markedly different. The SC and the provincial High Courts just below them in the judicial hierarchy derive their powers from the Constitution made by Pakistan's first democratically elected government in 1973, although they have a much longer ancestry in the pre-Independence colonial courts of British India. The FSC, on the other hand, is the product of executive decree by the military dictator, General Zia-ul-Haq, who took over power in a *coup* in 1977. General Zia 'suspended' the Constitution in 1977, but subsequently 'revived' it in 1985 with various unilateral amendments validated by a purged SC on the basis of the 'law of necessity'.[13] Those same amendments formally constitutionalised the FSC. Zia had multiple political, at times conflicting, motivations for setting up the FSC. Not only did he wish to appease and co-opt Islamists to crush political opposition, he also needed institutional mechanisms to restrain the autonomous tendencies of the mainstream constitutional courts and to discipline and marginalise rebellious judges in the latter. At the same time, he sought to circumscribe the powers of the legislature. After some initial experimentation, a parallel judicial forum seemed the best option for accommodating these complex agendas, albeit a pliable and closely controlled one.[14]

The result of all this constitutional engineering is that the FSC and the other constitutional courts function in parallel, each with its own jurisdiction and powers of judicial review. Thus, the system is one of 'coordinate constitutionalisation' in which 'a constitution incorporates Islamic law, laws of democratic processes, and liberal norms, placing them all on equal footing'.[15] Conceptualising Pakistan's constitutional system as a form of coordinate constitutionalisation acknowledges the fact that constitutional theocracies may take different forms depending on the relative powers of enforcement granted in respect of religious and secular laws across such contexts. The following discussion outlines the overall structure and composition of this coordinate judicial system, and fleshes out the respective powers of review and enforcement in the SC and the FSC.

The judges of the mainstream constitutional courts form the crème of the judiciary, and oversee a vast network of district and civil courts as well as various special courts and tribunals. They have historically been recruited partially from the professional legal bars and partially from the civil services, with more

[13] See, eg MS Khan, 'Genesis and Evolution of Public Interest Litigation in the Supreme Court of Pakistan: Toward a Dynamic Theory of Judicialization' (2014) 28 *Temple International and Comparative Law Journal* 284, 302–3.

[14] See generally Lau (2006), above n 11.

[15] IA Rabb, '"We the Jurists": Islamic Constitutionalism in Iraq' (2008) 10 *University of Pennsylvania Journal of Constitutional Law* 527, 531.

restrictive and higher bars on entry in the apex SC. Both legal practitioners and judges continue to receive training in what could be loosely described as a secular framework of legal education. They have no special knowledge or training in *Shari'a* or *Shari'a* law. Indeed, prior to the 1980s, there was no specially designated body of *Shari'a* law except 'Personal Laws' that were essentially codified religious laws limited to family and inheritance-related issues.

The powers of judicial review in the High Courts and the SC are grounded in an enforceable bill of rights known as the 'Fundamental Rights' (Constitution, Chapter 1). Following a familiar pattern of detail in post-colonial South Asian constitutions, the Fundamental Rights are broad-ranging and enumerated at length. The Constitution provides that laws that are 'inconsistent' with or made 'in derogation' of the Fundamental Rights are 'void' (article 8). Thus, when reviewing the general constitutional validity of legislation, the core question before these courts is whether the laws under scrutiny are consistent with the Fundamental Rights.

The Constitution endows the mainstream constitutional courts with different jurisdictions for enforcing Fundamental Rights, depending on where the dispute originates in the judicial hierarchy and whether it meets certain thresholds for adjudication. The most far-reaching and widely formulated of these is the 'original jurisdiction', with procedural and remedial powers dedicated to the 'enforcement of any of the Fundamental Rights'. Under this jurisdiction, litigants may circumvent the regular appellate structure and approach the courts directly for redress – in the case of the SC 'if it considers that a question of public importance with reference to the enforcement of any of the Fundamental Rights … is involved' (article 184(3)). The judicial activism of the SC has emerged largely from innovative judicial interpretations of its powers in its original jurisdiction, and has generated a vast body of jurisprudence commonly known as 'public interest litigation'.[16] All decisions of the SC – whether original or appellate – are 'binding on all other courts in Pakistan' (article 189). Thus, the SC is both a generalist and a constitutional court, and both an appellate and a first instance court (the latter in its original jurisdiction).

The FSC, on the other hand, is empowered – in addition to adjudicating cases under the *Hadood* laws in its general jurisdiction – to examine and decide 'the question whether or not any law or provision of law is repugnant to the injunctions of Islam, as laid down in the Holy Quran and Sunnah of the Holy Prophet' (article 203D). The FSC may do this either of its own motion (*suo motu*) or on the petition of a citizen or the government. If the FSC declares a law to be repugnant, it 'ceases to have effect' on a date specified by the Court, and the President is thereafter required to 'take steps to amend the law so as to bring such law or provision into conformity with the injunctions of Islam' (article 203D(3)). The FSC is barred from hearing Islamic challenges to the Constitution (article 203B(c)). At the same

[16] See generally Khan (2014), above n 13.

time, all other courts, including the SC, are barred from assuming jurisdiction over matters that lie within the power or jurisdiction of the FSC (article 203(G)).

Notwithstanding the FSC's exclusive jurisdiction over Islamic review, the mainstream constitutional courts are, not infrequently, seised of questions that directly or indirectly refer to Islamic law issues. For instance, various Islam-based arguments arise in the context of 'article 2-A' of the Constitution, a provision that has proved to be particularly controversial. Article 2-A originally constituted the Preamble to the Constitution, and essentially reproduced an early post-Independence constitutional blueprint from 1949, known as the 'Objectives Resolution', that articulated the political fundamentals of the Pakistani state. During the Islamisation project of the 1980s, this preambular provision was made a substantive part of the Constitution. Because article 2-A contains several references to Islam, it has generally muddied the waters of what constitutes the *grundnorm* – the Constitution as a whole or Islamic injunctions per se? – and its interpretation and reinterpretation over time has generated much conflicting jurisprudence on the status of Islam in the Constitution. This constitutional controversy is still not entirely settled,[17] and is perhaps the most ubiquitous instantiation of the dualist complexity of the Constitution. As such, the SC has exerted an indelible 'Islamising' influence on Pakistan's constitutional jurisprudence on the basis of article 2-A and other Islamic constitutional provisions.

C. Hybrid Institutional Design of the *Shari'a* Court System

In addition to the dual nature of the Constitution, there are two elements of the design of the FSC that, I argue, integrate it closely into the larger structure of the mainstream constitutional courts – namely the mixed composition of mainstream judges and *ulema*, and the fusion of the FSC with the SC in the appeals process for Islamic review. These elements give the court system a hybrid quality, so that there is considerable osmosis between constitutional rights and Islamic review jurisprudence.

(i) Mixed Composition of the FSC

In its current form, the FSC consists of 'not more than eight Muslim Judges', of whom not more than five must be former or serving judges of the mainstream constitutional courts, or qualified to be so. The Chief Justice of the FSC, who is among the five judges, has higher eligibility requirements: he/she must be a former or serving judge of the SC (or qualified to be so), or a former or serving permanent judge of the High Court (article 203C(3)). Given that the judges of

[17] See, eg U Ahmad, 'The Evolution of the Role of the Objectives Resolution in the Constitutional Paradigm of Pakistan – From the Framers' Intent to a Tool for Judicial Overreach' (undated) 5 *LUMS Law Journal*.

the FSC are recruited from a pool of former, existing or eligible constitutional court judges, they do not have any formal training in *Shari'a* law. The remaining members of the FSC – a maximum of three – are *ulema*. Although there might be a perception that these *ulema* are Islamic scholars with the requisite formal training in *Shari'a* law, their eligibility requirements are loosely and vaguely defined. Until very recently, *ulema* were required to be merely 'well-versed in Islamic law' to qualify for appointment. In 2010, the qualifications were enhanced to 'at least fifteen years' experience in Islamic law, research and instruction' (article 203C(3A)). However, this new standard is still fairly imprecise, and susceptible to significant variation in quality and competence. It does not clarify, for instance, whether *ulema* are required to have *legal* training, especially given that FSC members regularly encounter questions of law.

The constitutional provisions technically allow for the FSC to be constituted with judges in the minority. However, the judges typically dominate both the FSC as a whole and the benches composed for hearing individual cases. For FSC benches hearing Islamic review cases in particular – also known as '*Shariat* Petitions' – the required minimum is three members, one of whom must be an *alim*. The Chief Justice's office is central to the overall functioning of the FSC as it has exclusive authority to constitute benches for hearings.

Neither the judges nor the *ulema* of the FSC have tenure. They are to hold office for 'a period not exceeding three years, but may be appointed for such further terms as the President may determine' (article 203C(4)). Nevertheless, through a constitutional amendment in 2010, the FSC members now have at least security of term of office. Originally, the combination of executive powers of appointment with lack of tenure of FSC members was an integral part of the design of the FSC. The President had unfettered powers to transfer High Court judges to the FSC on the one hand, and to meddle with the FSC and influence its judicial outcomes on the other. From 2010 onwards, however, members of the FSC cannot be removed from office 'except in the like manner and on the like grounds' as a judge of the SC (article 203C(4B)).

(ii) Fusion of the FSC with the SC

Appeals lie from decisions of the FSC to a special bench within the SC known as the *Shariat* Appellate Bench of the Supreme Court (SAB). The SAB consists of three 'Muslim judges' of the SC and not more than two *ulema* to be appointed by the President to specific benches as 'ad-hoc members' from amongst either judges of the FSC or a panel drawn up by the President in consultation with the Chief Justice (article 203F). There are, thus, a number of important differences in composition between the FSC and the SAB. Firstly, the judges serving on the SAB must be sitting justices of the SC, not former judges or those qualified to be so. Secondly, while the number of *ulema* in the SAB may fluctuate between one and two, the number of judges in the SAB is fixed at three, so that SC judges always form the majority in the SAB. Thirdly, the *ulema* in the SAB are appointed on an ad hoc basis only for 'such period as the President may determine', and may or may not be from amongst the *ulema* serving on the FSC. This makes the position of the *ulema* considerably weaker than the SC judges in the SAB, who have tenure with a retirement age of 65 (article 179). It also makes them much more vulnerable to political influence than the *ulema* in the FSC.

There are other important ways in which the FSC is linked to the SC. One of these is the positioning of the Chief Justice of the SC in relation to the SAB. The Chief Justice exerts substantial control over composition of benches across the apex court, including on the SAB. It is the Chief Justice who nominates the 'Muslim judges' of the SC to the SAB, and also nominates the members from within the SAB – both judges and *ulema* – for hearing and disposal of individual cases. These sub-benches within the SAB may or may not include the *ulema* members of the SAB. In addition, the Chief Justice has the discretionary authority to direct that cases be placed for hearing and disposal before *all* the members of the bench. This overarching discretion may potentially determine judicial outcomes in the SAB in constitutionally salient or politically sensitive cases. Since 2010, the Chief Justice has also come to exert significant authority over the appointment of all judges and *ulema* to the SC (article 175A).

Clearly, while the FSC is a distinct court with a special jurisdiction, the SAB is an 'integral part of the Supreme Court'.[18] The SAB's judgments are understood to be the final word on matters of Islamic review, and to date the SC has not overridden the SAB on a matter within the SAB's exclusive jurisdiction. Taken together, all these factors – the dominance of the mainstream judges in the FSC and the SAB, the multiple avenues of control by the SC over *Shari'a* issues, and the SAB's status as a special SC bench with general powers of the apex court – suggest that there is a very broad institutional and normative overlap between what are otherwise perceived as two distinct spheres of religious and secular law.

IV. Complicating the Secular–Religious Binary

Pakistan's case study illustrates the very complex, reciprocal and at times competing processes in a constitutional theocracy of restraints on the application, but also the conscious accommodation, of *Shari'a* principles that in some way conflict with constitutional notions of liberal democracy. This complexity – demonstrated by the plurality of jurisprudential outcomes on different constitutional issues of high salience – problematises the prevailing thesis that constitutional courts in constitutional theocracies act as secularising agents of the state.

The following analysis presents a *precis* of four Pakistani constitutional cases spanning three decades that have had a defining impact (in two of the cases, the impact arising from the lack of a final outcome) on constitutional jurisprudence

[18] *Aziz Begum v Federation of Pakistan*, PLD 1990 SC 899.

that directly engages with issues of potential conflict between religious and secular law. With each case instantiating a different *type* of resolution of this conflict, the four cases together: (i) build a thicker, more nuanced picture of the layered interaction of these two spheres of the law, and (ii) bring into question the binary distinguishing the presumably well-settled categories of the 'religious' and the 'secular' in the global discourse on modern constitutional theocracies. The diachronic comparison of constitutional cases lends further credence to this chapter's central claim that the degree of overlap, or conversely opposition, between religious and secular law, and the manner in which this overlap or opposition is settled, are deeply contingent on an intersection of multiple factors. These factors include the larger political context, the nature of the secular–religious duality in the Constitution, evolving norms of constitutional interpretation, local histories of the issues being adjudicated, and the institutional design of the court system.

A. Case Type 1: Harmonisation of Religious and Secular Law

The first case relates to the freedom of religion of a religious minority, known as *Ahmadis*, who self-identify as Muslims. While there is a long history of socio-political exclusion of *Ahmadis* in Pakistan, a constitutional amendment in 1974 labelling them 'non-Muslim' ('2nd Amendment') was arguably the first major setback to their constitutional status as equal citizens of the state.[19] The gravamen of the anti-*Ahmadi* agitation was the allegation that *Ahmadis* were heretics because they eschewed belief in the finality of prophet-hood of Prophet Muhammad, a cardinal article of faith in mainstream Islamic thought. The case, which made its way to the FSC a decade after the 2nd Amendment, challenged laws introduced by the military regime of General Zia to criminalise the public religious practices of the *Ahmadis*. Essentially, the new criminal laws prohibited the *Ahmadis* from referring to themselves as Muslims, using Islamic epithets, and publicly proselytising, among other things.[20] These laws emerged not only in the thick of Zia's Islamisation programme but as a regime response to Islamist factions that had renewed calls for sanctions against the *Ahmadis*.[21] The laws also came on the heels of a controversial sequence of cases that had led to a judicial purge in the FSC and the inclusion of *ulema* in the membership of the Court.[22] Indeed, in the *Ahmadis*' case itself, the FSC bench was reconstituted before the final judgment.[23] The FSC

[19] See, eg CH Kennedy, 'Towards the Definition of a Muslim in an Islamic State: The Case of the Ahmadiyya in Pakistan' in DK Vajpeyi and YK Malik (eds), *Religious and Ethnic Minority Politics in South Asia* (New Delhi, Manohar, 1989).

[20] Anti-Islamic Activities of the Quadiani Group, Lahori Group and Ahmadis (Prohibition and Punishment) Ordinance 1984.

[21] See, eg T Mahmud, 'Freedom of Religion & Religious Minorities in Pakistan: A Study of Judicial Practice' (1995) 19 *Fordham International Law Journal* 40, 77–78.

[22] ibid.

[23] The reconstituted bench was composed of two judges (both previously High Court judges) and two *ulema*.

unanimously dismissed the petition on the ground that the laws in question were 'consequential to the Constitutional Amendment of 1974 by which the [*Ahmadis*] … were declared non-Muslims',[24] and that the prohibition on the *Ahmadis* was covered by the exception in the Fundamental Right to freedom of religion concerning 'maintenance of law and order'.[25]

The petition was abandoned in the SAB as the petitioners decided to pursue the Fundamental Rights route through the Lahore High Court, which meant that the FSC judgment, based on Islamic review, remained unchallenged. By the time the Fundamental Rights petition was decided on appeal in the SC in 1993, Pakistan was in the midst of a fragile post-Zia democratic transition. The SC held, in a 4:1 split decision, that the new criminal laws did *not* violate the freedom of religion of the *Ahmadis*.[26] The majority opinion of the SC approved of the FSC judgment, declaring itself bound by the latter on the question of Islamic validity of the laws under consideration, and likewise relying on a public order argument to uphold the prohibition on the *Ahmadis*' religious freedom. Contradicting its own recent precedent, the SC held further that the Constitution itself was subordinate to the injunctions of Islam by virtue of article 2-A.[27] It declared that 'every man-made law must now conform to the Injunctions of Islam as contained in Qur'an and Sunnah … Therefore, even the Fundamental Rights as given in the Constitution must not violate the norms of Islam'.[28] Thus, instead of testing the *vires* of the laws in relation to the Fundamental Rights, the SC adopted an FSC-like 'repugnancy' test.

The remarkable harmonisation of the FSC and the SC on the *Ahmadis*' religious freedom – on the basis of both jurisprudence and outcome – can best be explained by the historical context of opposition to and exclusion of *Ahmadis*, and the steady erosion of their rights over time. While the FSC judgment may be viewed as a conspicuous example of regime manipulation, the SC judgment reflects a progressive acquiescence, if not capitulation, to the constitutionalisation of religious exclusion and the persistence of antipathy and hostility towards *Ahmadis* from various segments of right-wing groups (many of them state sponsored). In this sense, the state and the entire judicial system is complicit in this progression, and there is no room to admit the argument that the SC has in some way exercised a secularising influence on radical religious demands for stripping a particular religious grouping of its right to equal citizenship. On the contrary, it has actively entrenched a precedent of religious discrimination.

[24] *Mujeeb-ur-Rehman v Federal Govt of Pakistan*, 1984 PLD FSC 136, 137.

[25] *Majibur Rehman v Federal Govt of Pakistan*, 1985 PLD FSC 8, 119–20.

[26] *Zaheeruddin v The State*, 26 SCMR 1718 (1993).

[27] In *Hakim Khan v Govt of Pakistan*, PLD 1992 SC 595, the SC had ruled that the Constitution, including the Fundamental Rights, could not be controlled by or subordinated to art 2-A or Islam.

[28] *Zaheeruddin v The State*, 26 SCMR 1718 (1993), 1775.

B. Case Type 2: Rupture between Religious-Progressive and Secular-Liberal Views

The second issue relates to the status of land reforms in Islam. A flood of cases challenging land reforms came up for adjudication in the FSC almost immediately after it was established in 1980. These petitions targeted laws that had been passed in the pre-Zia period, particularly those related to ceilings on ownership of agricultural land.[29] The Constitution (article 253), including the Fundamental Rights provision on property rights (article 24(3)), granted special protection to laws on land reforms enacted by Parliament. In line with these provisions, the FSC held that it was not empowered to declare repugnant constitutionally protected laws, and dismissed the petitions on account of lack of jurisdiction.[30]

The judgment was appealed to the SAB by a *waqf* – a kind of inalienable charitable endowment under Islamic law – that had lost land pursuant to the land reforms. The SAB's verdict came almost a decade later, in 1989. In what has become a highly influential judgment, one judge and two *ulema* on a five-member bench converged in the opinion that the land reforms were un-Islamic, as Islamic law did not generally countenance alienation of lawfully acquired property.[31] The dissenting opinions of the other two judges are important because they reveal something beyond the obvious fault-line between religious and secular legal viewpoints. The dissenting judges defended the land reforms also on the basis of Quranic injunctions relating to the concept of '*adl*' – a term denoting state intervention for creating a more just and equitable social order. One of them argued, for instance, that

> [I]n a society like Pakistan, which has been laid on feudalistic capitalistic principles for centuries, to reduce the gulf between the rich and the poor … it would be essential for the State to intervene … Accordingly even large scale intervention to restrain individual greed cannot be declared to be against the injunctions of the Holy Quran.[32]

Far from instantiating a religious–secular divide, the gulf between the majority and minority views on land reforms shows the internal diversity within Islamic thought on the question. Alternatively, and ironically, one can arguably view the opposing majority–minority views through a framework of liberal (pro-property rights) versus progressive (pro-state intervention) conceptions of government.

In 2013, a number of prominent politicians and intellectuals petitioned the SC to nullify the SAB judgment and declare the laws on land reforms valid. More than seven years later, the petition still awaits a proper hearing.

[29] See, eg CH Kennedy, 'Islamization of Real Estate: Pre-emption and Land Reforms in Pakistan, 1978–1992' (1993) 4 *Journal of Islamic Studies* 71.

[30] *Hafiz Muhammad Ameen v Islamic Republic of Pakistan, Shariat* Petition No. 2 of 1979.

[31] *Qazalbash Waqf v Chief Land Commissioner*, PLD 1990 SC 99.

[32] ibid.

C. Case Type 3: Engineered Outcome to Fit State Policy

The third case concerns the question of the conformity of the modern financial and banking system with *Shari'a*. Initially, Zia's regime placed a moratorium on the jurisdiction of the FSC to review fiscal laws, fearing the sweeping restructuring entailed by claims for a system of Islamic finance. It was only after the expiry of the moratorium, in 1991, that a full-scale contest made its way to the FSC. In a unanimous judgment, the FSC declared the prevalent interest-based economic system un-Islamic. The FSC adopted a broad definition of *riba*, declaring that it was prohibited in Islam in all its forms and manifestations, and laid down a plan for a multi-phased transformation to Islamic modes of financing.[33]

The FSC judgment was resisted by the post-Zia elected governments looking to liberalise the economy, and the matter went to the SAB on appeal. When the case was finally heard by the SAB in 1999 (the long hiatus ostensibly caused by the government's temporising), the SAB was unanimous in its affirmation of the FSC judgment.[34] The SAB gave the government two years to amend all the banking laws of the country in line with the prohibition on *riba*. Interestingly, the SAB judgment came in the immediate aftermath of a military *coup* by General Pervez Musharraf in late 1999, and was swiftly challenged by one of the aggrieved banks through a review petition. The government not only supported the petition but completely reconstituted the SAB bench (with the exception of one judge) that was to hear the review. This blatant judicial manipulation was in fact part of a large-scale judicial purge by the Musharraf regime between 1999 and 2000.[35] The new five-member SAB bench unanimously set aside the FSC and SAB judgments in 2002. The SAB remitted the case to the FSC for a re-determination of various issues that, it opined, lacked a 'definite finding'.[36] Not only did the FSC take more than a decade to commence proceedings in 2013, the matter is still pending a final decision.

Religion-based claims for elimination of *riba* have a long ancestry in Pakistan's constitutional politics. However, this prohibition has largely remained aspirational and unenforceable. The FSC judgment arose as an exception to this trend in the immediate aftermath of the Zia regime, when state patronage of right-wing groups had given sufficient valence to the issue that jurists sympathetic to Islamic activism had ruled in favour of an interest-free economic system.[37] Nonetheless, the

[33] *Dr Mahmood-ur-Rehman Faisal v Government of Pakistan*, PLD 1992 FSC 1. The FSC bench consisted of two judges and one *alim*.

[34] *Dr M Aslam Khaki v Syed Muhammad Hashim*, PLD 2000 SC 225. The SAB bench consisted of three judges and one *alim*.

[35] Khan (2014), above n 13, 315–16.

[36] Civil *Shariat* Review Petition No 1 of 2000, 22–24.

[37] The primary author of the FSC judgment was then Chief Justice of the FSC, Justice Tanzil-ur-Rahman – a judge who also had the rare distinction of being a renowned Islamic scholar.

government was successful in its attempts at keeping the issue *sub judice* til the judiciary strategically revived the *riba* appeal in the SAB in the context of a larger political confrontation with the government.[38] On the other hand, the quick and wholesale reversal of the SAB judgment under Musharraf was clear evidence of regime control.[39]

Thus, state policy, while adapting to the progressive build-up of judicial pressure to Islamise the economy, continues to be deeply opposed to any radical restructuring. To that extent, the state has used both extra-constitutional means (such as removal of judges and reconstitution of benches) and constitutional means (such as selective appointment of moderate *ulema* or strategic delay in judicial appointments) to inhibit, as much as possible, a judicial relapse to an all-encompassing declaration of repugnancy. Moreover, while the impending crisis has been averted for the foreseeable future, the government has adopted a policy of developing a parallel Islamic banking system that in many ways has taken the sting out of the demands for prohibition of *riba*.[40]

D. Case Type 4: Strategic Delay to Inhibit Constitutional Resolution

In 2006, during the Musharraf regime, the FSC took *suo motu* notice of gender-based discrimination in a citizenship law dating back to the 1950s. The provision in question denied citizenship rights to foreign husbands of Pakistani women while entitling foreign wives of Pakistani men to claim such rights.[41] The FSC framed the issue in a manner that seemed to go beyond the core inquiry of repugnancy to Islamic injunctions:

> whether or not the said provision of law … is discriminatory and repugnant to the injunctions of Islam *and violative of the principles of democracy, equality and social justice*, as enumerated and laid down in the Holy Quran and Sunnah' (emphasis added).[42]

While the government's response expressed anxieties about illegal immigration and national security, the case whipped up a storm of opposition to the citizenship law from human and women's rights organisations. In a unanimous decision

[38] See, eg CH Kennedy, 'Pakistan's Superior Courts and the Prohibition of Ribai' in RM Hathaway and W Lee (eds), *Islamization and the Pakistani Economy* (Washington DC, Woodrow Wilson International Center for Scholars, 2004), 108–9.

[39] Kennedy (2004), at 114.

[40] SJ Burki, 'Islamization and Private Enterprise: Can the Two Work Together? in RM Hathaway and W Lee (eds), *Islamization and the Pakistani Economy* (Washington DC, Woodrow Wilson International Center for Scholars, 2004), 54.

[41] Citizenship Act 1951 (s 10(2)).

[42] *In re Suo Motu* Case No 1/K of 2006 (Gender Equality), PLD 2008 FSC 1.

in 2007,[43] the FSC ruled that the provision in question 'is discriminatory, negates gender equality and is in violation of Articles 2-A and 25 of the Constitution … and also against international commitments of Pakistan and most importantly is repugnant to Holy Quran and Sunnah'. The judgment may be read in one of two ways. One interpretation is that the FSC, of its own motion, significantly extended the grounds for repugnancy to include constitutional provisions on social justice, the right to equality, and international law. The alternative reading – one that squares with the traditional understanding of the repugnancy test – is that the FSC considered these other relevant questions in light of Islamic injunctions. Either way, the FSC purported to expand its Islamic review scrutiny to the wider constitutional and international law terrain.

The government appealed the judgment the same year. The SAB, however, took up the appeal seven years later, in 2014, with delay that has become characteristic of the court in cases of high political salience. Since then, the SAB has indefinitely adjourned the matter, presumably because of national security concerns. Thus, paradoxically, while the FSC exercised its extraordinary *suo motu* jurisdiction to bridge the perceived gap between some of the more illiberal applications of Islamic law and liberal-constitutional principles on questions of gender equality,[44] the SAB has so far strategically delayed, on the basis of national security, what can be described as a liberalising impetus originating from the *Shari'a*-based jurisdiction.

V. Concluding Thoughts: Islamic Constitutionalism and Theories of Legal Globalisation

In the context of what is perceived to be an inherent tension between religious law and secular law in constitutional theocracies, there is an uncritical assumption that the two spheres of law are either ideologically and doctrinally oppositional, or politically or institutionally distinct, or both. This assumption frames the central argument of the literature on constitutional theocracies that mainstream constitutional courts in such contexts are invested with powers of judicial review to contain or curb the influence of religious law, and are thus 'secularising agents' of the state. Using Pakistan's example, this chapter argues for nuancing and reconceptualising this secular–religious binary as a complex, contextual, and overlapping relationship in constitutional theocracies. It advances this argument on the basis of three empirically observable phenomena in Pakistan: (i) the 'coordinate' liberal–Islamic duality in its Islamic constitution, (ii) the institutional hybridity of the court system, and (iii) the different, and at times conflicting, policies,

[43] The bench was composed of two judges and one *alim*.

[44] See generally I Yilmaz, 'Pakistan Federal Shariat Court's Collective *Ijtihad* on Gender Equality, Women's Rights and the Right to Family Life' (2014) 25 *Islam and Christian-Muslim Relations* 181.

strategies, and institutional interests at play in the politics surrounding constitutional jurisprudence and praxis.

What does breaking the secular–religious binary in constitutional theocracies mean for cases that can learn from it, borrow from it, and use it as a starting point for global theory? Three key propositions flow from the present analysis for approaching theories of legal globalisation in the context of a parallel *Shari'a* court in Pakistan, as well as the practice of Islamic constitutionalism in Muslim-majority states and the phenomenon of political courts more broadly.

Firstly, given the liberal–Islamic duality of Islamic constitutions, as well as the diversity within Islamic thought, global theory must adopt as its starting point the assumption – even if equivocally at the outset – that the categories of secular and religious laws and their institutional spaces in Islamic constitutional systems are interconnected and overlapping. In many ways, the duality of Islamic constitutions mirrors the bundling of political identity at the local–global intersection; while embedded in the local, they continuously engage with and respond to the global. To what extent and in what manner the interlocking liberal–religious framework manifests in the judicial resolution of constitutional-legal issues depends on institutional design as well as the broader socio-political context and contestations. In Pakistan, this duality has in practice ensured that the sphere of operation of Islamic laws is not confined within a special, parallel court jurisdiction. Thus, duality in constitutional design should not be mistaken for a binary.

Secondly, global theory must pivot from monolithic explanatory variables, like state policy and constitutional design, toward more complex and thick multivariate frameworks that additionally recognise the role of socio-political context and the multiple imperatives and institutional interests within which judicial contestations are embedded. Indeed, this widening of the lens is necessary even for the less ambitious purpose of a nuanced understanding of constitutional duality and design in constitutional theocracies.[45] Pakistan's case study unambiguously demonstrates that the state's agendas are dynamic, strategic and changeable, and that national security priorities can often conflict deeply with supposed concerns for 'secularisation'. Nor is the state the only player influencing the political logic of the courts.

Finally, global theory must consciously pushback on the temptation to focus exclusively and narrowly on formal inter-institutional interactions that, in the absence of context, are likely to mask and delegitimise struggles exogenous to the courts. In Pakistan, for instance, the spotlighting of the SC as a secularising force on the basis of a small and selective sample of formal law outcomes, both overstates the secular-ideological credentials of the state and the SC, and obscures the actual source of the secular-ideological challenge to Islamisation, namely, social movements centred on women's and human rights. That women's rights

[45] See, eg the mistaken reference to a SAB judgment as a Supreme Court judgment in Hirschl, 'Rise of Constitutional Authority' (2008), above n 1, fn 14.

groups – many of which are FSC abolitionists – were compelled to engage with the FSC's recent *suo motu* challenge to discriminatory citizenship laws is a conspicuous example of how *Shari'a* courts may in certain conditions mobilise issues across the liberal–Islamic divide, and conversely, how social movements, at times, pragmatically leverage such courts to achieve their goals. Thus, global and comparative theory can only begin to understand and accurately portray the local meanings and consequences of judicial–institutional contestations in constitutional theocracies if it extends its gaze to the wider social and political context.

Navigating Categories – Training, Positionality and Practice

GITANJALI PRASAD

Maryam S Khan builds the powerful case that the 'constitutional theocracy' thesis posited by Ran Hirschl – that constitutional 'secular' courts of the Supreme Court of Pakistan pose as a bulwark against more theocratic governance under the Shariat courts – needs to be understood instead as a complex 'reciprocal process of resistance, accommodation and integration', based in part on the hybrid structure of the Shariat courts and judicial appointments to these two sets of courts, which were created with the intent to be able to influence outcomes politically. Maryam illustrates these dynamic synergies through four significant empirical examples of how both the so-called 'secular' and 'non-secular' courts have arrived at judgments, influenced by factors that in addition to state policy and institutionalisation of laws, include local and national histories of the issues being adjudicated, the political context, and the changing norms of constitutional interpretation.

The author's important project is thus, at least in my mind, a statement against reducing the complex roles that these courts play into discrete categories, including into oppositional binaries of secular and non-secular, liberal and illiberal. This has given me a chance to reflect on aspects of research work that I undertook between 2014 and 2016 while working at a non-profit in Delhi, to examine the unequal outcomes of plea bargaining for petty offences through *Jail Lok Adalats* (JLAs) or people's courts in India, in prisons across three districts in Uttar Pradesh, India's largest and most populous State. The study found quantitatively that the JLA system, despite being part of a larger legal system that upholds free legal aid as a fundamental right, creates great inequity in terms of who is more likely to plea bargain. Demographic background drives the decision to plea bargain – level of education, level of informality of work, and (in one district where non-local surety was not accepted for bail) domicile.[1] Further, the system compounds the inequity for anyone arrested again in the future, as those who plead guilty make it to the list of 'history-sheeters', maintained in registers at every police station.

[1] G Prasad and M Satish, 'Exclusion from Access to Legal Justice' in *India Exclusion Report, 2016* (New Delhi, Yoda Press, 2017) 127, at p 139. Domicile is used here in the sense of the district of residence within an Indian State.

This context offers challenges in interrogating and breaking down how we think of a criminal justice system that is theoretically premised on the rights of the accused (including, but not limited to, the presumption of innocence, rights upon arrest and bail, the right to counsel, and fair trial guarantees, including protection from undue delays – all of which are essential to living a life of dignity). At the same time, these principles are balanced against administrative considerations of high case pendency rates and long trials, and the understanding of some that the liberty of the individual is more important than proving the innocence of mostly poor, daily wage earners incarcerated for these offences. Some of the questions that arise here are: *What are the assumptions we carry when we observe a system, engage with it, or try to make change in it? Is there value in interrogating different claims through a dialectical process to understand the basis of legal processes and their outcomes more clearly?*

Plea bargaining first came into practice in India in the form of sentence bargaining through *Lok Adalats* in prisons. At this time, it was not a part of the Criminal Procedure Code (CrPC), the main legislation that lays down procedure for the administration of substantive criminal law in India. It was adopted through an informal and arbitrary process, the result of a letter written by the Chief Justice of India, AS Anand, in 1999, outlining the need to provide 'speedy justice' to poor, under-trial prisoners and pre-trial detainees, and to reduce the jail population.[2]

Based on the process stipulated by the Chief Justice, the role of the legal aid lawyer shifted from that of a stakeholder who could uphold the rights of the accused, to that of an advocate who would argue that the prisoner should be released on the basis of their guilty plea. While he did not use the specific nomenclature of a JLA (directly translated as 'a people's court in prison'), he described its features and set its use into motion. This framing of the plea bargain as a 'people's process' is misleading, as the substantive character of the process by which justice is delivered departs from the participatory nature implicit in a people's court.

Relevant to this process of Alternative Dispute Resolution (ADR) through JLAs is Marc Galanter's important critique of legal pluralism in the context of

[2] Commonwealth Human Rights Initiative Report, *Liberty at the Cost of Innocence. A Report on Jail Adalats in India* (New Delhi, 2009) p 23 and Annexure A: https://humanrightsinitiative.org/publications/prisons/liberty_at_the_cost_of_innocence.pdf. In this letter, he stated: 'It is neither just nor fair that persons involved in petty offences should suffer incarceration much beyond the ultimate punishment merely on account of the fact that they happen to be poor and underprivileged … I, therefore, suggest for your consideration, that every Chief Metropolitan Magistrate or the Chief Judicial Magistrate of the area, in which a District Jail falls, may hold this Court once or twice in a month, depending upon the workload, in jail to take up the cases of those under-trial prisoners who are involved in petty offences and are keen to confess their guilt. "Legal Aid Counsel" may be deputed in jails to help such prisoners and move applications on their behalf on the basis of which the Chief Metropolitan Magistrate or the Chief Judicial Magistrate may direct the investigating agency to expedite the filing of the Police report … I feel, this exercise can go a long way in providing speedy justice to the poor under-trial prisoners and also reduce the jail population which is becoming a cause of concern.'

indigenous courts. Galanter stated that forums for ADR – of which there is a long and fairly endemic history in India arising from the Gandhian socialist tradition – are not necessarily more egalitarian than conventional courts, and he cautioned against championing them on the basis that they are less coercive, without looking at their functioning more closely. In their 2004 article, 'Bread for the Poor', Galanter and Jayanth Krishnan examined case resolution for civil litigation and provided a powerful critique of the pitfalls of informal systems of justice in India's hierarchical society, arguing that it reflects a paternalistic system of justice for the poor; they warn against using such systems in criminal law.[3]

In our observations of three JLAs across three districts in Uttar Pradesh, we found that procedure was not at all uniform, due in part to the fact that procedure has still not been codified, and because JLAs do not function as public courts.[4] In one plea bargaining session, the magistrate sat in the Jail Superintendent's office deciding which files to approve guilty pleas for, while the accused sat on their haunches in a line outside in the hot summer sun, with no interaction whatsoever between them and the magistrate.[5] Judges in the State were found to be provided numerical points for their disposal of cases through this method: four such successful disposals would give them the equivalent of one point for a case resolved through a completed trial.

In Ghaziabad, one of Uttar Pradesh's most economically developed districts, out of the 11 under-trial prisoners interviewed, not a single one had access to a lawyer at the time of the interview to access bail, and each had spent over two months in prison at the time of the interview. They had all resolved to plea bargain through the JLA, which took place on a weekly basis in this prison.[6] The prisoners provided different reasons for their decisions to plea bargain, including: not having the means to access a lawyer to apply for bail; being advised by other prison inmates that plea bargaining was a more fool-proof way of getting out of prison than hoping that a legal aid lawyer would assist them in accessing bail; not knowing that they had the right to access a legal aid lawyer or being wary of the process; facing significant social pressure from jail staff to plea bargain; and/or stating that what they thought to be the stipulated bail requirements would be beyond their means.

As part of their application, the accused are required to sign a form that states (translated from Hindi): 'The applicant is a poor helpless person with no support on his case. The applicant voluntarily accepts his guilt for this offence.' The judiciary continues to accept applications in this format, although it remains clear that there is little that is voluntary about the plea bargain, as the accused are typically

[3] M Galanter and J Krishnan, '"Bread for the Poor": Access to Justice and the Rights of the Needey in India' (2004) 55 *Hastings Law Journal* 789.

[4] While JLA procedures have not been codified, the procedures for plea bargaining have been stipulated in Chapter XXIA of the CrPC with the passing of The Criminal Law (Amendment) Act of 2005.

[5] G Prasad and A Lahiri, *Access to Justice in Uttar Pradesh – A Pilot Study in Five Districts*, p 114.

[6] Ibid, p 90.

living in precarity and unable to access a lawyer. The offences in these petty matters were mostly from inherited colonial laws/Special Acts dealing with 'preventive' matters – possession of a knife with a longer than specified permissible length of blade (2.5 inches), or possession of an unlicensed country-made gun, possession of alcohol above an amount of 2 litres, or of opiates beyond a certain amount.[7]

The plea bargain originates in British and American law, and has been borrowed as a means of swift redressal. But confusion arises as we realise that it is primarily being adopted as an administrative short-cut, and that more progressive provisions within the law to protect the first-time accused – such as releasing them on probation sans conviction under Section 265E of the CrPC or under the Probation of Offenders Act – are not utilised.

How, thus, are we understanding these processes and systems, and who produces and reproduces the binaries that we are confronting? Are they a result of political interventions that build upon global or regional processes, or are they more local processes and outcomes that get re-defined through a global lens? Maryam is able to interrogate the institutions she writes about from the socio-political perspective of a scholar who has spent many years as a teacher and researcher on law and related themes in the context of South Asia. My point of entry into this work was as a researcher, but as I went on, I found myself embroiled in an uncomfortable tussle between the roles of researcher, activist, social worker, and judge. This multiplicity of roles created ethical dilemmas at various points, including while we were trying to decide how to support two juvenile boys, who were wrongly arrested by the police as adults, and had been persuaded to plea bargain by other inmates (with the risk of establishing permanent adult criminal records) during the course of the research period.

It is likely that the origins of the Federal Shariat Court (FSC) and the Shariat Appellate Bench (SAB), and the fusion of the FSC's jurisdiction with the Supreme Court through the SAB, involved strong assumptions about what kinds of jurisprudential outcomes would manifest if these hybrid courts were *not* constituted. Similarly, those instituting plea bargaining into a system where criminal matters were resolved only through regular or summary trials likely assumed that the judicial system would continue to be slow, and people would not have reasonable access to legal justice while court pendency rates continued to increase – and that this was why such a system was needed. In the case of the courts in Pakistan, the politically powerful understood that without manipulation, the two court systems could theoretically produce different outcomes. Similarly, the upper echelons of the Indian judiciary believed that plea bargaining would be favourable administratively as well as support their articulations of what 'justice for the poor' should entail, ie, giving primacy to speedy justice over the fundamental rights of access to free legal aid and the legal principle of

[7] Arrests under these laws are colloquially described as preventive arrests by the police as they prevent further crime.

presumption of innocence.[8] The further irony remains that if someone had to appeal to the Supreme Court to uphold their constitutional right to free legal aid when denied it in the lower court, they would have to hire a lawyer, and have the socio-economic capital to achieve that access. The court cannot play the role of the last upholder of rights in such a system.

The principal actors or state institutions in these processes include Supreme Court judges and the *ulema* in the courts that Maryam writes about. In the context of plea bargaining, the functionaries include State Legal Services Authorities, prison superintendents, district court judges, lawyers, and the police. Significantly, both my work and Maryam's indicate that there are normative processes created through the actions of individuals across institutions with distinct, but often converging mandates that result in a certain resting point or status quo, within which the binaries tend to fade. In the context of plea bargaining in India, each of the primary institutional structures or actors has the ability to derail access to fair legal process, even though such process is a necessary part of their mandate.

The qualitative analysis in the study, which included interviews across every police station in five districts of Uttar Pradesh, showed that a number of these cases eligible for plea bargaining under Special Laws may have been false to begin with – fabricated in order to support the police in fulfilling their monthly targets for arrests, or to satisfy the public when a theft takes place and someone must be arrested for it. The interviews also pointed to caste and religious profiling by the authorities at the time of arrest, as indicated by their discriminatory attitudes and biases, and pronouncements of who is more likely to commit petty crimes. Analysis of 98 First Information Reports (FIRs) from three districts also indicated a great similarity in narrative, thus bringing into question the credibility of the basis of arrest, and also raising questions about the use of search procedures in public places. In over 50 per cent of the FIRs, the report contained a near-identical description of personnel encountering offenders by chance during their patrols, with the documented reason for suspecting the accused being that they quickened their pace on seeing the officers or tried to avoid crossing their paths.[9] When coupled with the finding that when they go to trial, these cases mostly result in acquittals in the absence of accurate police testimonies and documents, and the inequitable outcomes of plea bargaining based on certain demographic factors, this leaves the observer with a prevailing feeling of unfairness–both morally, and within the frameworks of the law.

[8] The Supreme Court of India has recognised the presumption of innocence to be a human right, although not a Fundamental Right in *Noor Aga v State of Punjab* (2008) 16 SCC 417. While most of the cases where the Court emphasised that presumption of innocence is a human right dealt primarily with issues of burden of proof, the principle applies as strongly to pre-trial detention and bail law. This was noted by the Supreme Court in *Vaman Narain Ghiya v State of Rajasthan* (2009) 2 SCC 281, where the Court recognised that the concept of bail emerges from the conflict between the power of the state to detain a person alleged to have committed an offence, and the presumption of innocence in favour of that person.

[9] *Access to Justice in Uttar Pradesh* (n 5 above) pp 51–54.

In the course of our research, we felt a constant push and pull to think about our role in engaging with these systems. How and where do we intervene with these legal and judicial systems that appear to be great monoliths without sufficient checks and balances, and which manifest as a by-product of social and political processes that are fundamentally anti-poor? Do we rely on quantitative and qualitative data that serve as hard evidence, recognising that the accused in these processes are usually informal workers with little social security, arrested under systems that we know to produce unequal, unjust outcomes? Or do we deploy moral arguments that try to connect with the idea of justice as a public good? Or try to push for local legal aid clinics with social work support through universities and colleges? Or as a lawyer, try to tangibly change outcomes by supporting the provisioning of legal aid? For the Jail Superintendent at the most corrupt of the six jails we visited, the answer was clear – he could not understand our desire to be there as researchers with a non-profit to advocate for better processes, and thought we were wasting our time. He stated simply that he thought I should do a PhD instead, a statement I admit I still have not fully understood. Throughout the process, we felt constantly questioned over our lack of formal legal education, and I have concluded it was a near-legitimate question. It led me to think that the only effective way to have credibility in a system like this is to study law, for which I recently completed my Bachelor of Law degree. As a reader, from my standpoint – despite Maryam's perceived physical distance from the site she explores – she has an unquestionable credibility as a scholar in her careful engagement with the laws she examines and how they empirically manifest in the context of the constitutional theocracy in Pakistan. It leaves me convinced of the need for a shift in the (binary of the secular–religious) conception of law, which she argues. Personally, this exercise has reinforced my commitment to solidarities that enable greater conceptual and practical connections, while further understanding what lends credibility to different kinds of interventions in legal globalisations.

Yet, at the same time, there is a need to acknowledge at this moment while writing this piece, that I am at the end of a long period of agonising – about how to express these ideas, and what to really say in response to Maryam's piece. I felt frozen for much of the process until a burst of activity emerged, and inadequate, as previously, for not having the requisite qualifications to undertake this process of contributing to scholarship on legal globalisation. The tension that remains for me in this context is whether there is a place for strong conviction and simultaneous insecurity of adequacy in these spaces of both intervening and theorising. What skills and ideas bring legitimacy to this process of writing? Who can be invited into these spaces of legal evolutions to theorise all that has not been written about?

The Judicial, the Secular and Beyond: Multi-normative Practices of Pakistani Constitutional Courts

STEFAN KROLL

I. Introduction: Neither Secularising nor Radicalising Agents

Scholars observing the resurgence of religion as a political force in constitutional systems offer disturbing analysis of the phenomenon: 'Virtually every major religious tradition has produced its own forms of extremism and growing disregard for the rights of "others".'[1] The permeation of religious extremism into political and legal institutions is a danger for free and plural societies worldwide. Against this background, Ran Hirschl's observation of a particular pattern of 'constitutional theocracies', in which constitutional courts serve as secularising agents who contain the impact of religious norms, sounds like a promising development that can at least secure a core set of fundamental secular rights. For the case of Pakistan, Hirschl concluded in 2010: 'The Supreme Court, while falling short of advancing a truly progressive human rights agenda by Western standards, has nonetheless served as a bastion of relative cosmopolitanism in an otherwise increasingly religious Pakistan.'[2]

But as Khan's chapter indicates, the reality seems to be more complex. While Hirschl too is not expecting the Supreme Court (SC) in Pakistan to 'operate in a political or ideological vacuum',[3] Khan shows 'that the degree of overlap, or conversely opposition, between religious and secular law, and the manner in which this overlap or opposition is settled, are deeply contingent on an intersection of multiple factors.'[4] Khan argues that in the case of Pakistan, differentiating religious and secular institutions is an artificial distinction, as the two are essentially hybridised. Therefore, she says, the concept of constitutional theocracies needs to be reconceptualised.

[1] Ran Hirschl and Ayelet Shachar, 'Competing Orders? The Challenge of Religion to Modern Constitutionalism (2018) 85 *University of Chicago Law Review* 425.

[2] Ran Hirschl, *Constitutional Theocracy* (Cambridge MA, Harvard University Press, 2010).

[3] Ibid, p 122.

[4] Maryam S Khan, 'Islamic Review in Pakistan: Problematising the Divide between Shariat Courts and their "Secular" Counterparts' (Course 5, above).

It is not entirely clear, however, in which direction the concept should be further developed. Khan is not interested in fundamentally rejecting the thesis that the constitutional courts act as secularising agents. For example, she could have deduced from her cases that the inter-activities of the courts favour an Islamisation of the law in Pakistan: 'Constitutional courts as radicalising agents' would have been an eye-catching title in a publishing market competing for attention. But it is precisely this kind of dichotomy, in this case of secularisation vs. radicalisation, against which her research turns. Khan is interested in closely describing normative expectations and practices, better understanding the interaction of allegedly different normative spheres and finally, against this background, questioning existing categories. As in my own work, in which I dealt with practices of a colonial court in Shanghai in the nineteenth century (the Shanghai Mixed Court),[5] Khan's aim is similarly not to illustrate the application or contestations of a particular normative model of *the* law. Her aim is rather to understand these practices as embedded in normative contexts which go beyond the law and which can only be partially described with reference to a particular model of the law, be it more statist or secularist.

II. Zooming Back and Forth: Macro- and Micro-Perspectives

Similarly to my research, Khan is arguing in favour of a context-sensitive perspective that seeks to go beyond an either/or logic of the religious or the secular and which aims at developing a more differentiated picture of the case. Reading more recent accounts of Hirschl, I would not expect him to generally disagree with this claim. In a co-authored piece with Shachar he describes clearly the 'considerable variation' of forms through which religion is integrated in constitutional structures.[6] Therefore, I read Khan's critique first of all as a methodological critique, a critique of the position taken by the observer and of the level of analysis. While, according to her reading, the concept of constitutional theocracies represents top-down analysis from a global perspective, Khan argues that a bottom-up local approach is needed.

In this sense, the chapter well represents the overall attempt of this volume to make visible so far invisible forms of institutionalisation. Khan is stressing the 'truly distinctive' nature of the Federal *Shariat* Court for example, instead of framing it within a broader universe of cases.[7] Such a classification as truly distinctive, however, has its limits with regard to a *generalisation* in the sense

[5] Stefan Kroll, 'Zooming in on Norm research: Towards a suitable scale for the Shanghai Mixed Court (2016) 5(2) Global Constitutionalism 383.

[6] Hirschl and Shachar (2018), n 1 above, 430.

[7] Khan, 'Islamic Review in Pakistan' – Introduction.

of a *reconceptualisation*. This kind of reconceptualisation of the 'constitutional theocracies' approach is a move that Khan is not taking just from her material but asking for as a more general move of the field. I remember that I myself was confronted with the objection that the description of the case of the Shanghai Mixed Court as unique would stand in the way of connecting it to conceptual discourses in political science and law, which aim at further developing theories instead of describing uniqueness. On the other hand, however, it also raises an important question of how conceptual innovations can emerge if they are not based on new and distinctive empirical material. The general approach pursued in this chapter and in the volume as a whole is so attractive, standing as it does for a theoretically informed research in legal sociology that at the same time is open to empirical irritation.

Both Khan and Hirschl come to the conclusion that there is an Islamisation of law in Pakistan that is incorporated and processed by the constitutional institutions. However, Khan observes a rather complex interaction, which needs to be described in its own right and then might lead to a process of conceptualisation rather than just re-conceptualisation. In other words, and maybe it is just a matter of terms here, the understanding of reconceptualisation is still too close to the concepts the research aims to transcend.

For me and my work, such an approach is both inspiration and challenge. As a social scientist trained at a European university, I am committed to a research process in which observations are closely linked to the current state of the art of the respective field – theories, methods, but also publication formats. It is true that there is an ideal of groundbreaking insights and theoretical upheavals. However, the structures do not promote this; rather they bring about gradual changes. It is therefore essential for academic innovation, however, to maintain an openness and curiosity for our objects that leads us beyond condensed discourses and paradigms – an openness and curiosity that characterises us not only as authors but also as reviewers.

III. The Concept of Multi-Normativity

But back to the chapter, what is needed at this point is a perspective which broadens our understanding of the interaction and convergence of the constitutional institutions in Pakistan. In this chapter, Khan highlights the '"hybrid" quality' and 'considerable osmosis between constitutional rights and Islamic review jurisprudence'.[8] A classical instrument for discussing the overlap between different normativities would be concepts of legal pluralism, the study of situations where two or more normative orders are applied in one social field.[9]

[8] Ibid, section III.C.

[9] Paul S Berman, *Global Legal Pluralism: A Jurisprudence of Law Beyond Borders* (Cambridge University Press, 2012) 13.

For the analysis of the present case, however, legal pluralism has shortcomings, which legal historians have described. According to legal historian experiences, centring the concept of law, which is described as a characteristic of legal pluralism, results in all other possible normative orders being lumped together into a large mass of non-law.[10] At the same time, the concept of legal pluralism, although it has developed in opposition to a unified perspective on law, has been described as paradoxically leading to such a unified perspective, which would hamper its ability to see or describe hybrid normative practices.[11]

As an alternative, legal historians introduced the concept of 'multi-normativity' which, in theoretical terms, appears to be more modest than the latest versions of legal pluralism.[12] The core idea of multi-normativity is to provide an analytical lens which allows for 'understanding law in the environment of other modes of normativity not structured by our idea of law.'[13] Furthermore, the approach of multi-normativity is also an attempt to focus on judicial practices in which different norms and socio-cultural contexts can mix, depending on the situation, and can mean a creative act of norm generation.[14] Against this background, I read the analysis of 'layered interaction' of religious and secular laws in this chapter, as an illustration of multi-normativity in which constitutional law is mixed up with religious normative expectations rather than actually containing them.

Furthermore, the chapter contains interesting perspectives on relevant actors in this context. In the research on constitutional courts, the central role of judges as actors is obvious. It is particularly striking here that in all considered cases (SC, FSC and SAB) the majority of judges have no formal training in *Shari'a* law. Only the *ulema* are formally expected to be experienced in Islamic Law but (for example) in the SAB their 'position is … considerably weaker than the Supreme Court judges'.[15] Returning to the thesis of secularising, one would expect that institutions which are composed with such a mixture of judges would indeed contain religious influences by constitutional requirements against the background of their training. However, as the cases show, this did not happen in the expected form.

[10] Thomas Duve, 'Was ist "Multinormativität"? Einführende Bemerkungen' (2017) 25 *Rechtsgeschichte – Legal History* 88, 91.

[11] Ibid, 92.

[12] In addition to the works of Duve see also the first use of the concept by Miloš Vec, 'Multinormativität in der Rechtsgeschichte' in Berlin-Brandenburgische Akademie der Wissenschaften, *Jahrbuch 2008* (Akademie Verlag Berlin 2009), 155–66.

[13] Thomas Duve, *European Legal History – Global Perspectives*, Max Planck Institute for European Legal History Research Paper Series No 2013-06. Working Paper for the Colloquium 'European Normativity – Global Historical Perspectives' (Max-Planck-Institute for European Legal History, 2–4 September 2013).

[14] Duve (2017), n 10 above, 94; Kroll (2016), n 5 above, 399–403.

[15] Khan, 'Islamic Review in Pakistan', section III.C.(ii).

IV. The Politics of Institutional Hybrids

What the cases show, however, is a high sensitivity to power shifts and political expectations. This is an indication that the legal sphere in this case has not established itself as an independent system, operating according to its own logic and rationality. In their decisions, the judges make themselves very strongly dependent on the specific conditions of the decision-making situation, in particular the political circumstances and assumed necessities. This becomes visible in case study three, in which the Islamic expectation is not implemented according to the decision, but, as it seems, not from a secular normative conviction, but because it is, practically, simply not possible. In the other cases, a clear expansion of religious influences can be seen in the interaction of the courts. But here too, it does not seem that the exchange of religious or secular normative sources has been the decisive factor, but also more general political expectations.

What becomes visible is that Islam does not appear here in its religious dimension alone, but also in its dimension as a political ideology that is ultimately superior to law and the Constitution. Khan writes this at the beginning of the chapter,[16] and the case studies very well illustrate this point, which can also be understood as a situation of de- or non-differentiation in which normative decisions transcend the expected differentiation of religious, political and legal spheres.

V. Invisible Institutionalism

How does this contribute to the approach of 'invisible institutionalism' as well as to law and society research more generally? A multi-normative approach allows us to deconstruct legal analysis that is too focused on state-centred understandings of the law. In this sense multi-normativity provides a more descriptive and context-sensitive analysis of the law and legal practices. Furthermore, it helps us to understand legal practices as practices for which non-legal normative expectations are also relevant, and to see those non-legal expectations as normal cases instead of defects. In terms of 'invisible institutionalisation', however, the multi-normative perspective does not provide very much in and of itself. The point here should be to ask what follows from multi-normativity. This leads us to the question of what are the consequences of individual practices. Under what conditions do they condense into new forms of institutionalisation? And what would be the central characteristics to describe these institutions – so that in the end also the 'multi' of normativity disappears in the perception of the actors?

These are difficult questions that I have had to struggle with in my own research. The basic question is, I think, how to use multi-normativity as a perspective not

[16] Ibid.

only of critique but also in more productive terms. In which sense does it help to produce new research questions that lead us somewhere? This, I suspect, is above all the point of intersection between multi-normativity and invisible institutionalism. The programme is not just aimed at challenging dominant models of law and legal practices but at seeing practices that deviate from those dominant models not as incomplete or incoherent, but as possible sources of innovation. For my own work, there are three more general or abstract questions which I have taken from this and which might influence my future work. First, while legal practices have to be understood according to the shared definitions of legal terms, at the same time they are highly context-sensitive. The challenge, against this background, is to understand legal change as a result of both the rationality of the legal system and its contexts. This kind of research is still interested in concepts and theory; however, the scope of the theories is rather limited and context-specific.

Second, most legal change is the result of evolution rather than revolution. Related discourses are therefore approaches that understand legal change as a gradual process. The difficulty lies in understanding at an early stage which individual practices are more relevant than others – precedents, so to speak – and therefore have a long-term impact. Finally, the background of the observation on multi-normativity is also the question of the autonomy of normative systems. This seems to be a process that varies. In some situations, law seems to us to be independent. In others, it appears to be superimposed by power dynamics. To describe and categorise this in more detail is another, very classical task of a sociology on the globalisation of law.

Course 6

PALACIOS LLERAS AND NATARAJAN

6

Competition Law in Latin America: 100 Years of Solitude

ANDRÉS PALACIOS LLERAS

In 'One Hundred Years of Solitude' Gabriel Garcia Márquez depicts the fate of the fictional town of Macondo as being tragically foretold since its foundation; a city of mirrors that gradually becomes a city of mirages. Beyond being a wonderful piece of fiction, the novel can be read as a map of both local culture and collective self-understanding: an exercise in soul searching, perhaps, regarding the promises and pitfalls of Latin America's convergence with the West. The fatalistic tone of this novel echoes other manifestations of 'Latin Americanism', not least its legal and political cultures. Among these is a recurring theme of Latin American law that it never seems to live up to foreign standards. While the origins of law in this region are often traced back to the early days of the European colonial rule, the law is never as good as it is in Europe. 'The Failed Law of Latin America'[1] is, as Jorge Esquirol aptly put it, a common narrative for framing the history of law. Like Macondo, the fictional town in the novel, Latin America is heir to some of the most notable facets of Western culture and, at the same time, replicates some of its darker, unappealing attributes. And just as Macondo was conceived as a city of mirrors and became a mirage, Latin American law draws considerably from foreign law, but often only to fall prey to several of its mirrored shortcomings.

In this chapter I use the history of competition law regimes in Latin America to develop an alternative reading of why and how Latin American law fails. Rather than adhering to the standard view – Latin American law is a poor, misguided reflection of the laws of other, more developed jurisdictions – I claim that Latin American law fails when it becomes unable to address the goals that provide its foundations. This failing is often the result of convergence processes aiming to

[1] J Esquirol, 'The Failed Law of Latin America' (2008) 56 *American Journal of Comparative Law* 75–124.

close the gap between local and foreign laws and policies, by ignoring or downplaying local goals and perspectives that shaped the laws in the first place.

The experiences of Chile, Colombia and México offer a history of competition law in this region that provides an alternative to the 'failing Law of Latin America' narrative. Competition law regimes (CLRs) have developed considerably over time in this region, much for the better. These regimes were originally moored in constitutional doctrines about the 'social function' of private property, as well as in economic doctrines regarding development and industrialisation. While observers differ in their assessments of how stringently these regimes were enforced in early days, it is generally agreed that it was not enough. The neoliberal wave of the 1990s amended the outlook of these regimes by making them focus on fostering markets. Furthermore, since the early 2000s local and global actors have been aiming at the convergence of local CLRs vis-à-vis the regimes of the United States (US) and the European Union (EU). This can be evidenced in the redefinition of enforcement priorities, the coupling of leniency regimes and higher fines, and the adoption of criminal sanctions.[2] I find this more recent convergence process problematic because it prizes a single goal – efficient competition enforcement – at the expense of the rights of citizens and their empowerment. Hence, by aiming to become more like the regimes of other jurisdictions, CLRs in Latin America run the risk of becoming mirages of what they could have been; very much like the fictional town of Macondo.

This chapter is structured as follows. In section I, I provide a brief summary of the development of CLRs in Latin America, focusing mostly on their goals. In section II, I show the underlying conflict between the protection of citizens and the enforcement of the CLRs in the name of efficiency and effectiveness alone. In particular, I will show how a focus on efficiency and effectiveness for their own sake risks creating self-serving competition authorities that disregard and discourage the effective protection of citizens-as-consumers. In section III, I will present some tentative explanations of why the actors involved in competition enforcement promote this harmonisation process. In each of these sections I will draw upon the CLRs of Chile, Colombia and México as examples. While one can hardly claim that these regimes are completely 'representative' of the Latin American experience with competition law, they are illustrative of the kind of issues and problems found in this region. Finally, in section IV, I offer some conclusions.

[2] J Peña, 'The Consolidation of Competition Law in Latin America' (2011) *Antitrust Chronicle* 1–4; A Palacios and J Gutiérrez-Rodríguez, 'Una Nueva Visión Sobre Los Orígenes Del Derecho De La Competencia Colombiano' (A New View on the Origins of the Colombian Antitrust Law) (2015) 11 *Revista Derecho de la Competencia* 137; A Palacios, *Competition Law in Latin America: Law, Politics, Expertise* (University College London, 2016) PhD Thesis.

I. The Origins of Competition Law Regimes in Latin America

The history of competition law in Latin America is related to the constitutional movements that took place during the first three decades of the twentieth century. The constitutions and constitutional amendments of these decades addressed economic phenomena – from private property to labour – differently to their nineteenth century predecessors.[3] This can be appreciated in the adoption of a 'social function of private property' doctrine in the Mexican Constitution of 1917, the Chilean Constitution of 1925, and in the 1936 constitutional amendment to the 1886 Colombian Constitution. In general terms, the 'social function of private property' doctrine was conceived originally by French legal realists such as Leon Duguit.[4] This doctrine was used in Latin America to justify limits to private property, and direct the exercise of property rights for the benefit of society as a whole.[5] It can also be appreciated in the establishment of regulatory regimes, subject to oversight by a country's president, and enforced by administrative bodies. These changes at the constitutional level – socially-oriented constitutional foundations for private property and the development of a bureaucratic apparatus in charge of enforcing administrative regulation – laid the groundwork for the development of CLRs.[6]

The constitutional foundations of CLRs explain the administrative ethos of these regimes across Latin America during the early twentieth century. Overall, the original goals of the CLRs were to promote industrial development and prevent anticompetitive behaviours that harmed other firms and citizens-as-consumers. In particular, the concern for other firms and for consumers is expressly manifested in the original drafting of article 28 of Mexico's 1917 Constitution and of article 1 of Colombia's Law 155 of 1959. Proper competitive behaviour came to be a particular manifestation of the 'social function of private property'.[7]

Although some Latin American adopted CLRs much earlier than others – México's 1917 CLR predates those of Chile and Colombia by four decades – they had several common features. First, the content of the regimes was quite open-ended, for they were based on general prohibitions against conduct that harmed competition but did not enumerate specific acts. Secondly, the regimes also provided enforcers with considerable discretion to exempt particular agreements or behaviours deemed anti-competitive but necessary. Thirdly, the enforcers

[3] R Gargarella, *Latin American Constitutionalism 1810–2010: The Engine Room of the Constitution* (New York/Oxford, Oxford University Press, 2015).

[4] See MC Mirow, 'The Social-Obligation Norm of Property: Duguit, Hayem, and Others' (2010) 22 *Florida Journal of International Law* 191–226.

[5] H Wiarda, 'Law and Political Development in Latin America: Toward a Framework for Analysis' (1971) *American Journal of Comparative Law* 434–63.

[6] Palacios and Gutierrez-Rodríguez (2015), above n 2; Palacios (2016), above n 2.

[7] Palacios (2016) above n 2.

themselves were administrative bodies with little political and economic independence, tightly bound to the executive branch and under the purview of presidents and ministers.[8] The administration of competition was, under this general scheme, one of several regulatory alternatives that governments could use to foster development and industrialisation.

Overall, Latin American CLRs were local manifestations of a global phenomenon; they were not 'parochial' regimes, but rather local articulations of policy ideas regarding political control over private economic power that were then in circulation around the world. Evidence of this can be found, for example, in the government draft of Colombia's Law 155 of 1959. This draft suggests that a CLR was necessary to keep up with the competitive challenges posed by industrialisation and the presence of multinational enterprises, and expresses the importance of keeping up with similar regimes in more than a dozen countries. In fact, the belief in 'administering competition' that lies at the core of these regimes was aligned with the experience in other countries during the first decades of the twentieth century. In particular, the institutional experiment of entrusting administrative agencies with the enforcement of CLRs dates back to the enactment of the United States' 1914 Federal Trade Commission Act. It is also worth pointing out that the Colombian law included institutions 'borrowed' from other jurisdictions, such as the Sherman Antitrust Act of 1890 and the Clayton Antitrust Act of 1914 (both also from the US), including a general prohibition regarding monopolisation and merger control.

The three main features of the first Latin American CLRs – open-ended provisions, considerable administrative discretion and little political and budgetary independence – have prompted criticisms by several commentators. Julián Peña, for example, argued that these first regimes were too vague and were hardly enforced.[9] Others, like Rudolf Hommes, argued that the Colombian CLR was hardly enforced because the same body in charge of enforcing this regime was authorising price agreements between competitors.[10] These criticisms have become part of the 'official' story of these regimes, and they are casually reproduced by international organisations like the Organization for Economic Cooperation and Development (OECD), which invest considerable resources in closing the gap between Latin American CLRs and the 'best practices' drawn from the US and the EU.

We should assess the merit of these criticisms carefully. To begin with, there is very little empirical research about the levels of enforcement by the bodies in charge of such matters. The most comprehensive research regarding Chile, for example, shows active enforcement since the creation of the enforcement bodies – the *Comisión Antimonopolios* in 1959 and the *Fiscalía Nacional Económica* (as

[8] Ibid.

[9] Peña (2011), above n 2.

[10] R Hommes, 'Regulation and deregulation in Colombia. Much Ado About Nothing?' (1997) 40 *Revista Desarrollo y Sociedad* 133–84.

it is known today) in 1963 – albeit with variations.[11] Secondly, the criticisms implicitly assess these regimes against an unspecified standard that is analytically and historically thin: that competition law should only be about reprimanding inefficient anti-competitive behaviours and authorizing pro-competitive mergers. However, this view ignores that the CLRs, as they were adopted, were also about fostering cooperation between firms and promoting industrial development, even if this meant sacrificing inter-firm rivalry or negatively affecting consumer welfare. Hence, while these criticisms warn us against developing a rosy view of the origins of CLRs in Latin America, they lack factual support, and are based on a standard that is not explicit or accurate for assessing these regimes.[12]

The 'neoliberal turn' of the 1990s provided ample ground for reforming CLRs in Latin America. Based on criticisms such as the ones mentioned above, and a desire to establish a new understanding about the role of states in markets, reformers across Latin America brought forth a new generation of CLRs. These new regimes evidenced the influence of the EU's competition law regime and US antitrust law; as such the regimes can be understood as manifestations of 'institutional syncretism'.[13] In very broad terms, they followed the EU's formula of having explicit legal mandates detailing the forbidden conduct, and 'borrowed' the concept of abuse of dominance. From the US these regimes 'borrowed' the semi-independent enforcement agency, and a law and economics approach to the analysis of the forbidden conduct, agreements, and mergers. Hence, for example, one can find references to authors such as Robert Bork and Richard Posner by Méxican and Chilean individuals that were participating in the implementation of the new regimes.[14]

México's 1992 *Ley Federal de Competencia* exemplifies the changes in competition law that took place during the 1990s. In 1982, México was the first Latin American state that defaulted on its financial obligations with foreign banks; this triggered a new payment schedule coupled with important regulatory modifications, which changed drastically this country's economic outlook. President Miguel de la Madrid (1982–88) began to implement these changes; however, the more drastic changes were undertaken by President Carlos Salinas de Gortari (1988–94). Among these was the adoption of a new CLR in 1992. A group of government lawyers and economists prepared the draft of the new regime, which incorporated new substantive provisions as well as creating a new enforcement body, the *Comisión Federal de Competencia*. These officials met with different actors, including OECD officials and business associations, before submitting the new draft bill to the Mexican Federal Congress. The bill was presented with a note of manifest urgency by the President, and it was discussed and approved in December 1992, roughly one month after it was submitted and without any

[11] D Furnish, 'Chilean Antitrust Law' (1971) 19(3) *American Journal of Comparative Law* 464–88.

[12] Palacios (2016), above n 2.

[13] For this concept, see D Galvan, *The State Must Be Our Master of Fire: How Peasants Craft Culturally Sustainable Development in Senegal* (Berkeley CA, University of California Press, 2004).

[14] Palacios (2016), above n 2.

major changes.[15] The new competition law distinguished between absolute and relative monopolistic practices; the former – in particular cartels – are per se forbidden under US antitrust law, while the latter (such as vertical agreements) are subject to a 'rule of reason' analysis. Also in the US mould, the *Comisión Federal de Competencia* was a semi-autonomous body composed of several commissioners who decided about the investigations without any formal attachment to other governmental institutions. These institutional changes were presented as a new dawn for competition enforcement in México.[16]

The experiences in Colombia and Chile during the 1990s were less successful than their Mexican counterparts. In Colombia, article 333 of the 1991 Constitution established a right to free competition and a mandate for the state to prevent or curb the abuse of dominance. The government of Cesar Gaviria (1990–94) planned to adopt a completely new regime, but decided not do so, for it feared that the proposed regime would flounder in Congress due to the pressure of business groups. Instead, the government used the temporary legislative powers given to it by the 1992 Constitution to draft a decree in which – under the pretence of amending the structure of the agency in charge of competition law enforcement (the *Superintendencia de Industria y Comercio*) – it introduced new, detailed prohibitions (including abuse of dominance) and procedures for investigations and fines.[17] In spite of this effort, competition law enforcement did not pick up its pace. Instead there was a backlash against the new CLR, and during the government of Ernesto Samper (1994–98) it became hard to find anybody to direct the *Superintendencia.*[18]

In Chile, the end of the military regime of Augusto Pinochet (1972–90) gave little space to consider reforms to the CLR, which had been put in place by the military regime in 1972. But by the late 1990s, Chile had experienced two decades of neoliberal regulation, and local actors realised that this regime needed amendments regarding the independence of the prosecutor – the *Fiscal* – and the *Comisiones*, the bodies in charge of deciding about the legality of anticompetitive conducts. The changes began in 1999 with a law that empowered the *Fiscal*, and then in 2003 a new law replaced the *Comisiones* with a special judicial tribunal, the *Tribunal de Defensa de la Libre Competencia.* This tribunal adjudicates on the investigations brought by the *Fiscal.*[19]

[15] G Castañeda, 'Orígenes, Avances y Dificultades De La Política De Competencia En México (1993–2003)' in P Garcia Alba, L Gutierrez and G Torres Ramirez, *El Nuevo Milenio Mexicano.* Tomo 3 *El Cambio Esstructural*, Universidad Autónoma Metropolitana, 2004) 337; G Castañeda, S Levy, G Martinez and G Merino, 'Antecedentes Económicos Para Una Ley Federal De Competencia Económica' (1993) *El Trimestre Económico* 230–56.

[16] Ibid, Castañeda et al (1993).

[17] Palacios (2016), above n 2.

[18] 'Desidia por las Superintendencias', *El Tiempo* (16 October 1995) https://www.eltiempo.com/archivo/documento/MAM-426560 (accessed 5 July 2020).

[19] P Bernedo, *Historia de la Libre Competencia en Chile 1959–2010* (Santiago de Chile, Fiscalía Nacional Económica, 2013).

It is hard to overstate the changes that took place in Latin America in the 1990s, especially as one considers these countries' CLR trajectory during the following decades. The amendments introduced in Chile, Colombia and México *after* the 1990s can be considered more as amendments than as entirely new regimes. These amendments are focused on improving the autonomy and performance of the enforcement bodies. They do so by (i) raising the sanctions that can be imposed on parties found guilty of infringing the laws, including the establishment of criminal sanctions for certain anti-competitive behaviours, (ii) focusing on cartels, and (iii) establishing leniency regimes that enable whistleblowing by cartel members in exchange for partial or full immunity. The increase in sanctions and the criminalisation of cartels go hand-in-hand with leniency regimes; these provide firms engaged in anti-competitive behaviour with incentives for whistleblowing so that they can escape the increasingly expensive consequences of being investigated and sanctioned by the enforcement authorities. The increase of administrative fines and the adoption of leniency regimes were introduced by law in México in 2006 (amended in 2011) and in Colombia and Chile in 2009. In turn, the criminalisation of certain behaviours (like cartels) occurred in 2009 in Chile, and in 2011 in México and Colombia.

As I explain below, the changes that took place after the 1990s are subverting the goals that CLRs were meant to serve, such as promoting industrial development and punishing anti-competitive conducts and agreements that harmed other firms and consumers. Notwithstanding their enforcement records (about which there is little information), the original regimes offered consistency between their goals and their means, and especially between such goals and constitutional mandates. This is not the case of the changes that are now taking place. These changes are decoupling CLRs from their legal and constitutional moorings, as detailed in the next section.

II. Enforcement Effectiveness vs Citizen Empowerment: The Precarious Balance of Leniency Regimes in Latin America

The changes that have taken place recently in the landscape of Latin American CLRs are about sticks and carrots; higher fines and criminal punishments for cartels, coupled with leniency programmes. As this section will show, the implementation of these changes is creating a sort of constitutional moral hazard, for they contribute to benefitting enforcers at the expense of citizens and competition at large.

The idea of establishing more drastic punishments for cartels draws largely from their negative effects upon consumers, and so it seems hard to challenge; however, this is not the case with granting leniency to cartel members because they collaborate with the enforcers. Leniency regimes are based on the premise that cartels are fragile because their members have strong incentives to 'cheat'. This is so because artificially high prices benefit cartel members with higher volumes of output the most; however, high prices can only be maintained artificially if all cartel members agree to reduce their output. Hence, cartelists have an incentive to increase their output secretly to deceive their partners and benefit from the earnings resulting from artificially higher prices. Leniency regimes take advantage of this particularity by inducing cartel members to inform authorities about the cartel and its participants.[20] In the US, in exchange for providing authorities with valuable information regarding the cartel, the first 'whistleblower' may obtain complete amnesty, no criminal convictions for their employees involved and no damages payments (if they collaborate with plaintiffs before or during the preparation of civil litigation). The benefits for later whistleblowers are considerably less generous.[21]

The adoption of leniency regimes, and the subsequent efforts to improve their effectiveness, only make sense when considering their underlying assumptions. The single most important assumption is that cartels are the most harmful of all anti-competitive practices, as famously stated by the OECD in a 1998 Council recommendation.[22] Hence, from a competition policy perspective, enforcers should give priority to fighting cartels over other, supposedly less harmful practices, such as abuses of dominance or vertical restraints.

This assumption about cartels reflects a value judgement that is hard to justify for all possible scenarios. Cartel members restrict competition in order to obtain the additional surplus resulting from 'artificially' high prices; however, this is the same surplus that dominant firms aim to capture when they become monopolists in a market. Hence, the nature and scope of the social harm cartels cause is not analytically different from the harm caused by monopolies. In addition, the threat of new firms entering related markets and other market dynamics serve to discipline cartels just as they do monopolists. All things considered, the possibility that cartel members cheat among themselves suggest that cartels can be more fragile than a monopolist simply because the latter is not plural in composition, and therefore has lower oversight costs.

Enforcers across the globe claim that leniency regimes are very important tools – perhaps the single most important one – for the investigation and prosecution of cartels. Most of the former officials, litigators and academics that study these regimes concur. Enforcers have a vested interest in defending the

[20] G Spagnolo, *Divide Et Impera: Optimal Leniency Programs*, CEPR Discussion Paper No 4840 (2004) (Stockholm School of Economics. Centre for Economic Policy Research).

[21] United States Department of Justice 'Frequently Asked Questions About the Antitrust Division's Leniency Program and Model Leniency Letters' (November 2008 – Updated 2017): https://www.justice.gov/atr/page/file/926521/download.

[22] Organisation for Economic Co-operation and Development, *Recommendation of the OECD Council Concerning Effective Action Against Hard Core Cartels* (1998): http://www.oecd.org/daf/competition/2350130.pdf.

programmes they enforce; however, some of them have the data to support their enthusiasm. For example, in a 2016 public statement, former Acting Assistant Attorney General Renata B Hesse of the Antitrust Division at the US Department of Justice described the fines that were imposed in recent years, including the single, highest-grossing fine ever imposed under US antitrust law – a US$2.9 billion fine imposed on the participants of the 'auto parts' cartel.[23] She went on to assert that 'Our leniency policy remains the criminal program's single-most powerful case generator, and continues to serve as an example to our partners around the globe as they develop and improve their own.' Litigators and academics tend to have a less rosy view about the effectiveness of these regimes. In broad terms, one line of research analyses the conditions under which leniency regimes can be effective; such research is often premised upon existing leniency regimes.[24] A second line of research addresses the effectiveness of leniency programmes in terms of cartel detection and punishment, duration, and so on.[25] Both of these research areas are quantitative in nature and assume certain similarities across leniency regimes. There is, moreover, a third line of research that addresses core institutional issues often ignored in the previous two, and this line therefore is more cautious about the real effectiveness of leniency regimes.[26] This research addresses issues such as the political economy underlying the adoption of leniency regimes[27] and procedure issues,[28] to name a few.

The trade-offs between the public benefits vs private gains offered by leniency regimes can be analysed separately. Firstly, leniency regimes create incentives for competition enforcers to act deceptively. This is so because these regimes can be used by enforcers to have 'easy wins' and bolster the numbers of convictions and fines, thus conveying the impression that their work is socially beneficial. Such enforcement decisions make leniency regimes too generous, effectively lowering the private costs of participating in cartels in the first place; the regimes themselves become under-deterrent and less effective than they could otherwise be.[29] This situation can also occur when enforcers over-rely on their leniency regimes, for example by getting information *only* from whistleblowers and not undertaking their own fact-finding enquiries. Such enquiries can produce first-hand

[23] Renata B Hesse, 'Can there be a "One-World Approach" to Competition Law?', Chatham House Conference on Globalization of Competition Policy, 23 June 2016, London: https://www.justice.gov/opa/speech/principal-deputy-assistant-attorney-general-renata-b-hesse-delivers-remarks-chatham-house.

[24] See JE Harrington Jr, 'Optimal Corporate Leniency Programs' (2008) 56(2) *Journal of Industrial Economics* 215–46.

[25] See eg, J-R Borrell, C Garcia, JL Jiminez and JM Ordonez-de-Haro, '25 Years of Leniency Programs: A Turning Point in Cartel Prosecution' (January 2019) *CPI Antitrust Chronicle*.

[26] For a review see G Spagnolo and C Marvão, 'Cartels and Leniency: Taking Stock of What We Learnt', *SITE Working Paper Series*, 39/2016 (Stockholm Institute of Technology).

[27] F Haines and C Beaton-Wells, 'Ambiguities in Criminalizing Cartels: A Political Economy' (2012) 52(5) *British Journal of Criminology* 953–73.

[28] Wouter PJ Wils, 'Leniency in Antitrust Enforcement: Theory and Practice' (2007) 30(1) *World Competition: Law and Economics Review* 25.

[29] Spagnolo and Marvão (2016), above n 26.

information that may bring about either further convictions or, at the very least, critical appraisals of the information provided by the whistleblowers themselves. Furthermore, under-deterrence casts a shadow over the performance and accountability of competition enforcers when measured in the number of convictions and the amount of fines. In particular, such data are not enough to make a causal claim that because of the leniency regime enforcers are deterring and punishing cartels effectively, because it cannot reliably identify other cartels that could have been detected and were not so.

The incentives that leniency regimes create for enforcers vis-à-vis the public also explain, in my view, why antitrust enforcers are not sympathetic towards private enforcement, that is, when the affected parties file claims before judges asking for damages of their own accord. While leniency regimes' convictions and the amount of the fines imposed enable enforcers to appear effective in the public's eyes, private enforcement that leads to substantial damages awards robs them of their spotlight. Hence, it is understandable that enforcers prefer to devote their efforts to strengthening leniency regimes that contribute to their public image.

A similar issue involves the balance between effective public enforcement and citizens' right to seek redress via private enforcement. Policy-makers acknowledge that private actions can undermine cartel participants' incentive to fully disclose their participation in such arrangements.[30] This is so because whistleblowers may benefit from amnesty or reduced fines as per the applicable leniency regimes, but still risk exposing themselves to private enforcement lawsuits. This is a 'wicked problem', for a policy choice that favours public enforcement would have to limit private enforcement to be sufficiently enticing, but a policy choice that favours private enforcement would render leniency regimes unappealing, and therefore ineffective.

This problem may not be as wicked as it looks.[31] Some scholars argue that, in theory, a socially optimal leniency regime can incorporate both public and private enforcement. This can be done by granting full leniency to the first whistleblower and reducing his or her liability vis-à-vis damages awards, while at the same time establishing joint and several liability for the remaining cartel members and granting access to all pertinent documents to civil claimants. This arrangement holds out the possibility of limited damages awards as an incentive for filing for leniency quickly and facilitates information-gathering for victims seeking for reparation.[32] We disagree; granting full leniency to the first whistleblower firm enables it to keep the benefits of the anti-competitive conduct it participated in, thus rewarding cartelisation *via* whistleblowing. In this sense, full leniency can be used

[30] Organisation for Economic Co-operation and Development, Working Party No 3 on Co-operation and Enforcement. *Challenges and Co-ordination of Leniency Programmes – Background Note by the Secretariat* DAF/COMP/WP3(2018)1.

[31] P Buccirossi, C Marvão, and G Spagnolo, 'Leniency and Damages', CEPR Discussion Paper DP10682 (June 2015).

[32] Ibid.

strategically by the first whistleblower firm to legally keep the otherwise illegal proceedings from the cartel it belonged to; it turns illegal earnings into legal ones by administrative fiat. This solution comes across as both inefficient and immoral. A better solution is to convey the message that cartelisation is wrong and that whistleblowing is desirable, but that collaborating with the authorities does not compensate for the social harm resulting from abusing the trust consumers place in markets.

The EU's Directive 2014/104/EU[33] is a clear example of a policy choosing to side with public rather than private enforcement and the victims. Article 11(4) states that immunity recipients are jointly and severally liable to parties injured directly or indirectly by their conduct only when full compensation cannot be obtained from other cartel members. Article 6(6) states that national courts cannot order the disclosure of the evidence in the leniency statement or the settlement submissions. Furthermore, article 7(1) states that evidence presented before a court that can be traced back the documents mentioned in article 6(6) to be considered inadmissible. Hence, while the Directive maintains joint and several liability for cartel members, it actually prevents damages claims, as it limits the information available for victims to prove wrongdoing.

Leniency regimes in Latin America support the idea that public enforcement should take priority over private enforcement activities – and therefore that enforcers are more important than citizens. These leniency regimes have been constructed in such a way that enforcement bodies affect whether citizens may file suits against cartel members. Setting aside the issue of how to achieve a balance between public and private enforcement, it is unclear how a policy choice that privileges public enforcement can be justified according to the consumer and citizen protection mandates of the different constitutions.

México's leniency regime is a case in point. Article 28 of the 1917 Mexican Constitution (as amended in 2013) prohibits agreements that force consumers to pay 'exaggerated prices' or that grant advantages to a few individuals at the expense of the public at large or a particular social class. The article also states that the law should protect consumers and enable them to organise in defence of their interests. In spite of this mandate, the 2014 Federal Economic Competition Law statute seriously curtails injured parties' access to information and limits the term within which they can file lawsuits. Article 125 states that the Commission is under no obligation to share information that investigated parties and leniency applicants identify as confidential, and article 103 explicitly mentions that the very identity of the investigated party or leniency applicant can be held confidential. In turn, article 134 limits the opportunity injured parties have to file their respective claims before the specialised courts; this can only be done before the Commission

[33] Directive 2014/104/EU of the European Parliament and of the Council of 26 November 2014 on certain rules governing actions for damages under national law for infringements of the competition law provisions of the Member States and of the European Union.

issues its ruling on the investigations it has conducted. Furthermore, the ruling issued by these specialised courts only determines whether or not the defendants are liable; if they are, claimants have to begin a new, different procedure asking for damages (known as *acción indemnizatoria*). Hence, injured parties face considerable difficulty in identifying whom to sue because of the confidentiality rules in the law, and once they do so, they still have to go through multiple trials to obtain damages. This institutional arrangement benefits managers and other personnel of investigated firms, as a 'class', over consumers. Notably, a 2018 OECD report on México's leniency regime notes that 'confidentiality is one of the Program's core principles, which limits the Commission's ability to increase the Program's transparency'.[34]

In Chile's leniency regime, however, public enforcement efforts are intertwined with private enforcement – but not for the best. Article 19 of the 1980 Constitution states a right to equal treatment under the law and forbids arbitrary differences (see also article 22). However, the CLR creates such a difference precisely by subjecting private enforcement to the enforcement agenda of the *Fiscalía*. According to Chile's CLR, both the *Fiscalía* and harmed parties can file claims against parties that have presumably violated the law. Leniency beneficiaries are identified by the *Fiscalía* before the Competition Tribunal, and it is the latter that decides whether these accused parties can obtain benefits. However, leniency provides amnesty only from criminal charges, not from damages awards. If the Competition Tribunal rules in favour of the harmed parties, claimants would still have to file a separate lawsuit for damages – the *Fiscalía* does not have procedures for the imposition of fines. Such an arrangement discourages both leniency applicants – who do not know whether they will benefit, or in what amount – and harmed parties, who still have to undergo a separate procedure to obtain a damages award. Therefore, it is unclear to what extent the benefits extended by the leniency regime actually induce applications.

Colombia's CLR works differently from those of México and Chile. Under article 2 of the 1991 Colombian Constitution, the state has the duty to facilitate the material conditions for citizens' full enjoyment of their rights. In turn, article 333 grants every citizen a right to free competition. This right is a collective right according to article 88 of the Constitution, and hence can be protected via collective actions. Even so, there is a considerable gap between the constitutional mandate established in article 333 and the development of Colombia's CLR at the level of laws and decrees. To begin with, it is unclear as a matter of law if individuals that have been injured by anti-competitive behaviours may file for damages. This is largely because the legislative development of this CLR has focused mostly on public enforcement. Article 11 of Law 155 of 1959 explicitly

[34] Organisation for Economic Co-operation and Development, Working Party No 3 on Co-operation and Enforcement. *Roundtable on Challenges and Co-ordination of Leniency Programmes – Note by Mexico* DAF/COMP/WP3/WD(2018)9.

allows injured parties to file claims for damages; however, it is unclear whether this article remains in force, for it has been amended and partially repealed by later laws. Consumer associations have pursued collective action before the courts, but in not a single case has the court ruled in their favour. The legislative developments of this CLR, mostly Decree 2153 of 1992 and Law 1340 of 2009, deal only with public enforcement activities. Hence, individual and collective claimants are in a sort of legal limbo; individuals do not know if they even can ask for damages; collective claimants know that they can, but find an inhospitable response from the judges. In contrast, public enforcers have a neatly established regime that details the nature, scope and breadth of their procedures – including the leniency regime.

In spite of the emphasis on public enforcement, the results of the leniency regimes here considered are far from spectacular. México's leniency regime, arguably the most successful of the three,[35] is nonetheless subject to several critical observations regarding its transparency and saw a considerable drop in leniency applications during 2017 (a phenomenon that is hard to explain).[36] Chile amended its regime in 2016 by raising fines and introducing new sanctions for cartel members; there is little information about whether these changes brought more leniency applications or deterred cartels from taking place.[37] The results of Colombia's leniency regime are similarly equivocal. This regime was not even applied until four years after its establishment, and the number of filings has been considerably lower compared to other Latin American countries. Furthermore, the adoption of criminal sanctions for some anti-competitive behaviours (for example, collusion in public procurement) meant that leniency applicants were treated differently under administrative and criminal law in a way that made the whole institution unappealing.[38]

I believe that there is considerable room for improvement regarding these leniency regimes and this may be a worthwhile cause. However, it remains unclear why the implementation of these regimes has meant, as a matter of legal design, limiting the rights of injured citizens to damages in the first place. This is particularly evident when we consider the goals underpinning the CLRs, in particular the goal of protecting and empowering consumers. Under these institutional arrangements, it is enforcers, rather than consumers, who benefit more from leniency applications.

[35] Palacios (2016), above n 2.

[36] OECD (2018), *Note by Mexico*, n 34 above, para 18.

[37] See Organisation for Economic Co-operation and Development, Working Party No 3 on Co-operation and Enforcement. *Roundtable on Challenges and Co-ordination of Leniency Programmes – Note by Chile* DAF/COMP/WP3/WD(2018)3.

[38] See Organisation for Economic Co-operation and Development Working Party No 3 on Co-operation and Enforcement. *Roundtable on Challenges and Co-ordination of Leniency Programmes – Note by Colombia* DAF/COMP/WP3/WD(2018)14.

III. The Buendía Family: Enforcers and the Making of Latin American Competition Law Networks

How did these changes to the CLRs come to be? While it is certainly the case that the trajectory of the CLRs of Chile, Colombia and México has been determined by a mix of local and international institutional factors, the development of international networks composed of individuals and organisations played a considerable role in this process. In particular, leniency regimes appeared in Latin America during the 2000's – in 2006 for México and 2009 for Chile and Colombia – largely as a byproduct of the activities developed in this region by the OECD and by the International Competition Network (ICN).

The importance of these networks can be appreciated better by resorting to the history of international competition law – or lack thereof. In contrast with other areas of law that regulate trade at an international level, there is no global CLR. There have been several attempts to establish such a regime, including the 1948 'Havana Charter for an International Trade Organization' and the 'Working Group on the Interaction between Trade and Competition Policy' that was established during the Singapore round of the World Trade Organization. The US expressed skepticism towards the initiatives proposed by the discussants in this 'Working Group', which were mostly developing states, and eventually withdrew its support. However, the US did not stop at expressing its discontent. It also sought the support of the OECD, which in 1998 issued a highly influential recommendation in line with US policies, such as the premise that prosecuting cartels should be the highest priority. The 'Working Group' was dropped by the WTO General Council in 2004.[39] The US also decided to establish the ICN as an informal global network of competition authorities in order to address the international challenges of anti-competitive cartels.[40]

The efforts to develop an international CLR reflect an increasingly important concern for jurisdictions, like the US and the EU, that are driving globalisation. The absence of international coordination mechanisms diminishes the effectiveness of each regime and limits the effectiveness of each enforcement agency. This is because anti-competitive practices such as cartels often operate across national boundaries, and their consequences often spill-over multiple jurisdictions. Such a practice will be ineffectively prosecuted by each individual enforcement agency acting on its own (assuming they do so at all). In addition, the effectiveness of any given leniency regime depends crucially upon the existence and effectiveness of other leniency regimes in the jurisdictions that compose the affected market; this is especially the case when it comes to the management of sensitive information.

[39] World Trade Organization, *Working Group on the Interaction between Trade and Competition Policy (WGTCP) – History, Mandates and Decisions* (2019):https://www.wto.org/english/tratop_e/comp_e/history_e.htm, accessed 6 July 2020.

[40] E Fox, 'Linked-In: Antitrust and the Virtues of a Virtual Network' (2009) 43(1) *International Lawyer* 151–74.

A network of enforcement bodies may address these issues effectively, especially if it enables enforcers from different jurisdictions to coordinate their activities.

It is important to note that the benefits of establishing such a network are considerably higher for more active enforcers, like the US and its European counterparts, than for less active ones. This is because, as the example of the leniency regime suggests, the level of enforcement raises the vulnerability that enforcers face vis-à-vis the activities of other agencies engaged in similar activities. Hence, the development of a network based on cooperation between different enforcement agencies can be both an overall improvement *and* a politically-motivated strategy deployed by states, like the US, that benefit the most from such coordination.

By the early 2000s the OECD had increased its presence in Latin America. The strong anti-cartel policies and the adoption of leniency regimes in this region can be traced back to OECD recommendations made even before countries like Chile and Colombia became member states. The particular case of Colombia is telling: the draft of Law 1340 of 2009, which introduced leniency to this country's CLR, refers to OECD recommendations; a first review of Colombia's CLR appeared in 2009 and a second one in 2015.[41] Colombia became an OECD member in 2020. Chile has been a member since 2010; however, a recommendation to add leniency to Chile's CLR can be traced back to a 2004 OECD peer review.[42] Moreover, the OECD has also teamed up with the Inter-American Development Bank in producing said peer reviews and regularly organises events for enforcers via the 'Latin American Competition Forum', established in 2003.[43] (The ICN has not adopted such a regional emphasis, but nonetheless several enforcement bodies are members of this institution[44] and together they have also organised activities in the region.)

This network of institutions has become a hospitable environment for those Latin American professionals that received a foreign education in the US, Europe or the United Kingdom. To begin with, this network places them in positions in which they can mediate between foreign and local actors. In addition, aspects such as an education based on law and economics, a mastery of languages such as English, and common acquaintances or educational affiliations, allow these individuals to bridge the cultural and contextual gaps that separate them from their peers in other enforcement agencies or multilateral organisations, like the OECD and the International Development Bank.[45] Moreover, these networks open new

[41] Palacios (2016), above n 2.

[42] Organisation for Economic Co-operation and Development and Inter-American Development Bank, *Competition Law And Policy in Chile A Peer Review* (Paris, OECD, 2004).

[43] See http://www.oecd.org/competition/latinamerica/.

[44] See https://www.internationalcompetitionnetwork.org/members/?location=south-america.

[45] Regarding Latin American lawyers and economists, see M Fourcade-Gourinchas and S Babb, 'The Rebirth of the Liberal Creed: Paths to Neoliberalism in Four Countries' (2002) 108(3) *American Journal of Sociology* 533–79; Also Y Dezalay and B Garth, *The Internationalization of Palace Wars. Lawyers, Economists, and the Contest to Transform Latin American States* (Chicago IL, University of Chicago Press, 2002).

worlds of opportunities for these individuals. As the individual CLRs converge, these opportunities extended beyond their jurisdiction of origin, and include different positions in other jurisdictions and in multilateral bodies – from advisers to litigators. Even if they decide to work for the private sector after belonging to these networks, they are able to navigate the hurdles posed by public and private enforcement of CLRs more effectively than other individuals lacking such experience.

Looking at the bigger picture, the adoption and subsequent reformation of CLRs in Latin America after the 1990s, and the special importance given to fighting cartels through leniency regimes, evidence a convergence of CLRs towards a new set of international 'norms'. It is unclear, however, that this convergence will contribute to protecting the rights of individuals or promoting competition. So far, they have contributed more to advancing the agenda of competition enforcers, without clear benefits for harmed parties, citizens and individuals at large.

IV. Conclusions

The preceding pages can be read as a nostalgic criticism against a process of institutional transformation, as Latin America – exemplified by Chile, Colombia and México – becomes further immersed in the world economy. Most of the competition law regimes might have been initially based on ideals such as promoting local development, enhancing market competition and protecting citizens as consumers. However, time has not been kind to these goals, nor to the rules they supposedly embody. As these regimes converge towards their US and European counterparts, they have become increasingly less in touch with their original goals and, in doing so, have neglected citizens and their rights. These regimes are transforming, striving to achieve a foreign agenda that has little in common with their original goals.

There are good reasons to go beyond this feeling and consider the consequences that result from the convergence of CLRs towards the international 'norms' constructed upon the regimes of the US and the EU. These reasons are related to the promises that are part of Latin America's constitutional democracy and may contribute to the development of a more critical approach to competition law and theory.

First, the choice to focus public enforcement on fighting cartels via leniency regimes has come at the cost of citizens' rights to access to justice and reparation for their loss. Just like Macondo, CLRs are in danger of becoming mere mirages. There is a considerable gap between the goals of these regimes when they were established and the goals they aim to achieve now; this gap results from foreclosing the constitutional foundations of CLRs and gearing them towards serving the status quo. In turn, the rights of consumers *as* citizens are trumped in the name of administrative effectiveness. When comparing the benefits for market participants against the limitations of consumers, it is unclear how such a gap can be justifiable under the applicable constitutional law mandates of each of these jurisdictions. The full extent of the citizen's rights should be taken seriously by enforcement agencies; after all, they are bound by their constitutions, and the constitutional adequacy of their decisions contributes importantly to the legitimacy of CLRs. Furthermore, being able to ask for damages as reparation for a harm before a court is essential to what democracy is about.[46]

Second, leniency regimes bring about real ethical dilemmas that enforcers and policy-makers seldom discuss openly. One such dilemma is about the incentives that leniency regimes create for enforcers. How do we know that enforcers are not providing excessive benefits in hopes of accumulating easy wins that will bolster their public image? Even if leniency regimes are functioning properly, how do we know that the burdens consumers must assume because of cartels are less than the social benefits obtained? What if leniency can be used strategically to affect rival firms? Might it become a strategic punishment that cartel members use when they detect cheating? In that case, rather than deterring collusive behaviour, these regimes may lead to an extended game of 'musical chairs' where fines are imposed when the music stops.

Weighed against all these considerations, it is not clear that decoupling CLRs from their constitutional values is worth it. As citizens, we simply do not have enough information to assess whether the more recent changes in CLRs are merited, or if they are working as expected. Clearly, enforcers have every incentive to say that they are, and may provide many statistics concerning the number of cartels disclosed, the number of fines imposed and their towering amounts. However, it is doubtful that the enforcers have earned the trust of the citizens they supposedly protect, for they seem keener on keeping cartelists on good terms than on promoting relief for the affected parties. This subversion of the roles reminds one again of Macondo; its tragic fate was made palpable when the military arrived to protect the plantations companies and their owners during the labour disputes with the unions – and not the other way around.

Finally, the changes in the CLRs have contributed to the development of a network for professionals that participate in the changes criticised in the preceding pages. This author is, as can be expected, part of this network; Colombian of origin, bilingual, and alumnus of prestigious law schools in the US and in England. However, I am also skeptical of the network, its institutions and members. I believe that a research agenda aiming to assess the trajectory and enforcement of these CLRs can contribute to reshaping the network in ways that are more congenial to certain values at the heart of the Latin American legal tradition, such as fairness and equality. Just as in other jurisdictions, such as the US, there is a resurging interest in antitrust law and fairness, I believe Latin Americans should embark on a similar path, but on our terms and with our own references.

[46] See SW Waller, 'Antitrust and Democracy' (2019) 46 *Florida State University Law Review* 807–60.

Mirrors, Mirages, and the Development Myth

USHA NATARAJAN

Palacios analogises Latin American competition law with Márquez's famous Macondo, a town of mirrors destined to become a city of mirages. After a century of emulating Western legal regimes, competition laws in Mexico, Chile, and Colombia have become illusory: laws are untethered from their purposes, outcomes mismatched with goals. As an international lawyer coming from a postcolonial milieu and working in the Global South, I found Palacios' tale compelling while also possessing an undercurrent of the predictable. There is a sense of inevitability that accompanies postcolonial legal failure. Palacios acknowledges an underlying fatalism that 'we will never be as good as the West'.[1]

Coming from a law and development background – I worked on UN law reform projects in Asia before taking an academic job in the Arab region – I developed an early and close acquaintance with this fatalism and the challenges of sublimating it. I am part of a movement called TWAIL (Third World Approaches to International Law) that demands an international law that is responsive to the diverse needs of peoples across the Global South, a discipline more truly international.[2] Our aims are not new: we build on the legacy of Third World international lawyers that have struggled for the same since the advent of the postcolonial state. While we stand on their shoulders, the strategies of the past had some pitfalls that are also our inheritance. With this personal history, perhaps it is unsurprising that I read the shortcomings in Latin American competition law as symptomatic of the broader law and development failures of the postcolonial state. Underpinning postcolonial fatalism is the deeper problem of fetishism: devotion to the Western development model despite repeated disappointment.

In *One Hundred Years of Solitude*, Palacios identifies an apt metaphor for pondering development dilemmas. Márquez's superlative panorama of the paradoxes of postcoloniality resonates across space and time. Over my decade of teaching law and development in Cairo, contemplating why Arab peoples still

[1] Jorge L Esquirol, 'The Failed Law of Latin America' (2008) 56(1) *American Journal of Comparative Law* 75.
[2] Usha Natarajan, John Reynolds, Amar Bhatia and Sujith Xavier, 'Introduction: TWAIL – On Praxis and the Intellectual' (2016) 37(11) *Third World Quarterly* 1946.

struggle for liberation so long after attaining formal independence, I have found solace in Márquez's ability to utter all our realities and make us feel less alone. Just as Márquez transcends history and geography, Latin American development theorists, from the *Dependistas* to the Decolonialists, influence postcolonial regimes across Africa, Asia, and the Pacific. Against this backdrop of development economics, I read the competition law regime Palacios describes as one facet reflecting a much broader conundrum facing peoples across the Global South. From hyperbolic increases in inequality to the changing climate,[3] from wage stagnation and debt to the sixth mass extinction of species,[4] from unemployment and labour unrest to institutionalised corruption,[5] from violence and unhappiness to mass displacement,[6] from conflict and insecurity to drought, famine, deforestation, and desertification,[7] the failures of the dominant development model are proliferating and overwhelming. Any attempt to address them requires a return to fundamentals: What is development and who decides? Third World international lawyers regularly revisited this question over the last century and their history is indispensable to formulating effective strategies today.

In one sense, the question was answered for us long ago, because the postcolonial state's sovereignty was conditional on commitment to the Western industrial development model.[8] Postcolonial states could to some extent negotiate a position along the economic spectrum from right to left (capitalism, communism, or non-alignment during the Cold War) but none could forfeit a commitment to industrialisation. Societies that refused to capitulate were denied sovereignty, as evidenced most clearly by the continuing struggle of many tribal and Indigenous peoples for self-determination.[9] Once postcolonial states echoed Western development goals, industrialisation became normalised as a pursuit beyond question. Over time, additional requirements were added to mitigate the dark sides of industry such as rampant inequality, labour exploitation, and environmental degradation. Development was initially measured purely through

[3] Oxfam, *An Economy for the 99%* (Oxford, Oxfam, 2017); Intergovernmental Panel for Climate Change, *Global Warming of 1.5%* (Geneva, IPCC, 2018).

[4] Oxfam (n 3 above); Intergovernmental Science-Policy Platform on Biodiversity and Ecosystem Services, *Global Assessment Report on Biodiversity and Ecosystem Services* (Bonn, IPBES, 2019).

[5] International Labour Organization, *World Employment and Social Outlook: Trends 2019* (Rome, ILO, 2019); Transparency International, *Corruption Perception Index 2018* (Berlin, Transparency International, 2018); UNODC, *Global Study on Homicide 2019* (Vienna, UNODC, 2019).

[6] UNODC (2019), n 5 above; J Helliwell, R Layard and J Sachs, *World Happiness Report 2019* (New York, Sustainable Development Solutions Network, 2019); International Organization for Migration, *World Migration Report 2018* (Geneva, IOM, 2019).

[7] International Institute for Strategic Studies, *Armed Conflict Survey 2019* (London, IISS, 2019); Center for Research on Economic Development and UN International Strategy for Disaster Reduction, *Economic Loss, Poverty & Disasters: 1998–2017* (Brussels, CRED, 2018); UN Environment Programme, *Global Environmental Outlook 6* (Nairobi, UNEP, 2019).

[8] Usha Natarajan, 'TWAIL and the Environment: The State of Nature, the Nature of State, and the Arab Spring' (2012) 14(1) *Oregon Review of International Law* 177.

[9] Usha Natarajan and Kishan Khoday, 'Locating Nature: Making and Unmaking International Law' (2014) 27 *Leiden Journal of International Law* 573.

gross domestic product,[10] but by the 1980s it was also measured in terms of the ability to meet 'basic needs',[11] by the 1990s assessments included metrics of 'human development',[12] and since the 2010s we have seen its latest incarnation in the form of 'sustainable development'.[13] But at the heart remains industrialisation and economic growth as inevitability, not choice.

This conception of development originates in the European Enlightenment, when Europeans began to equate social progress with efficient exploitation of nature to fuel industry, for the purposes of limitless economic growth and scientific innovation.[14] Before the Enlightenment, European understandings of social evolution were diverse, ranging from the Aristotelian notion of the recurrent rise and fall of civilisations[15] to the Augustinian conception of a single rise and fall of humankind from Eden to the apocalypse.[16] Pre-Enlightenment European doctrines were diverse but they shared a belief in the inevitability of civilisational decline, whether precipitated by natural forces, divine will, or moral degeneracy. Only upon the Enlightenment did European thought embrace the possibility of *limitless* civilisational progress.[17] This premise underpins the contemporary global economy: all states and peoples can and should continuously strive to develop, from richest to poorest, because there are no natural, divine, or social limits to growth. Resting on assumptions of resource abundance and scientific ability to transcend natural limits to growth, the contemporary development myth asserts that development opportunities are endless, so even the very richest should always strive for more.

European conquest of the non-European world pre-dated the Enlightenment by several centuries, but it was no coincidence that the heyday of colonialism occurred alongside the Enlightenment and industrial revolution in Europe. Labour and resources from the colonies were an integral part of fuelling industry in the imperial heartlands.[18] In Europe, new notions about societal progress were taking form alongside increasing exploitation of non-European life,

[10] Elizabeth Dickenson, 'GDP: A Brief History', *Foreign Policy* (3 January 2011) www.foreignpolicy.com/2011/01/03/gdp-a-brief-history/.

[11] Paul P Streeton, 'Basic Needs: Premises and Promises' (1979) 1 *Journal of Policy Modelling* 136.

[12] UN Development Programme, *Human Development Reports*: www.hdr.undp.org/en/content/human-development-index-hdi.

[13] UN Department of Economic & Social Affairs, *Sustainable Development Goals Knowledge Platform*, www.sustainabledevelopment.un.org/.

[14] Gilbert Rist, *The History of Development: From Western Origins to Global Faith* (trans, P Camiller) (London, Zed Books, 2014).

[15] WD Ross (ed), *The Works of Aristotle Vol 9* (Oxford, OUP, 1966), 'De Generation et Corruptione' 335, 336.

[16] Saint Augustine, *City of God* (trans H Bettenson) (Harmondsworth, Penguin, 1984), 392, 495, 500, 1091.

[17] Rist (2014), n 14 above, 35–40.

[18] A Stanziani, *Labor on the Fringes of Empire: Voice, Exit and the Law* (London, Palgrave-Macmillan, 2018); GK Bhambra, 'Undoing the Epistemic Disavowal of the Haitian Revolution: A Contribution to Global Social Thought' (2016) 37 *Journal of Intercultural Studies* 1; M Badia-Miró, V Pinilla and H Willebald (eds), *Natural Resources and Economic Growth: Learning from History* (New York, Routledge, 2015).

leading to convenient conclusions about hierarchies of societal evolution where European life was assumed to be the pinnacle.[19] Herefrom stemmed the now-familiar tropes of the civilising mission, the white man's burden, and the dual mandate: the non-European was exploited not merely to fuel European industry but ostensibly for the non-European's own good, to inculcate knowledge of inferiority and hope of transformation into European likeness.[20] The contemporary development myth is a legacy of these tropes, with terminology such as 'least developed', 'developing', 'emerging', 'developed', and so on naturalising longstanding hierarchies and directionalities; albeit today these are stripped of racial and cultural connotations and sanitised by the cold calculus of GDP, HDI, and SDGs.[21]

The postcolonial moment arrived earlier in the Americas, more than a century later in the former territories of the Ottoman Empire across the Middle East and North Africa, and later still across most of Asia, Africa, and the Pacific, reflecting European assumptions of social hierarchy. Societies had to earn sovereignty through proximity to the European norm.[22] Thus, those societies most closely resembling Europe (whether through cultural proximity, as with settler colonies in the Americas, or through capitulations, as with Japan) achieved independence sooner, with others undergoing an independence process that directly inculcated the Western development myth.[23]

A commitment to Western development necessitated mirroring those Western legal frameworks that enabled such economies in the postcolony. Though shackled by the prerequisites of sovereign statehood, some Third World leaders were suspicious of the Western development model. Most famously, both Gandhi and Fanon warned against the structural violence embedded in the developmental state.[24] But there were also postcolonial leaders who favoured industrial development, accepting the Enlightenment premise that industry was the best way to meet the greatest variety of human needs.[25] While such leaders were cognisant of the exploitative economic system they were entering, they believed in changing the rules of the game to make it fairer. At the forefront were Latin American *Dependistas* that influenced postcolonial economies,

[19] Peter Fitzpatrick, *The Mythology of Modern Law* (London, Routledge, 1992).

[20] Antony Anghie, *Imperialism, Sovereignty and the Making of International Law* (Cambridge, CUP, 2005).

[21] HDI = Human Development Index; SDGs = Sustainable Development Goals. Dickenson (2011), n 10 above;, UNDP (n 12 above); Rist (2014), n 14 above.

[22] Antony Anghie, 'Colonialism and the Birth of International Institutions: Sovereignty, Economy and the Mandate System of the League of Nations' (2002) 34(3) *New York University Journal of International Law and Politics* 513; Usha Natarajan, 'Creating and Recreating Iraq: Legacies of the Mandate System in Contemporary Understandings of Third World Sovereignty' (2011) 24(4) *Leiden Journal of International Law* 799.

[23] Natarajan and Khoday (2014), n 9 above, 588–91.

[24] Mahatma Gandhi as quoted in Leela Gandhi, *Postcolonial Theory: A Critical Introduction* (Sydney, Allen & Unwin, 1998) 20–22; Frantz Fanon, *The Wretched of the Earth* (New York, Grove Press, 1963).

[25] Rist (2014), n 14 above, chs 7–9.

the G-77, and the Non-Aligned Movement in the 1950s, 1960s, and 1970s.[26] But the *Dependistas*, the New Left, and most postcolonial development theorists never questioned whether the game was worth playing. One of the few exceptions was the Self Reliance movement, whose goal was not industrial development but freedom from dependency and debt;[27] though in the very few places where it was attempted, self-reliance proved either unsustainable (such as Nyerère's Tanzania) or deteriorated into painful isolationism and extreme authoritarianism (such as Mao's China, Communist Cuba, and North Korea).[28]

Unfortunately, attempts to rewrite the rules of global economy in a fairer way ultimately did not work either. Decades of Third World solidarity – across the 1950s as epitomised in the Bandung Conference,[29] the 1960s through the doctrine of permanent sovereignty over natural resources,[30] and the 1970s with calls for a New International Economic Order[31] – all ended in abject failure by the 1980s when sovereign debt crises brought state after state in the Global South to its knees at the mercy of international lenders controlled by powerful Northern elites. From the 1980s onwards, international lenders offered debt relief conditional on states undergoing structural adjustment – a process as painful as it sounds.[32] By the 1990s, with the collapse of the Soviet Union, the victory of globalised capitalism, and the putative end of history, there was an untrammelled neoliberal push for law reform across the Global South under the mantra of *privatise, deregulate, liberalise* that continues to this day.[33]

Lacking Márquez's dexterity in compressing centuries of cause and effect into a single text, it nevertheless seems evident that contemporary Third World strategies could learn from this history. Indeed, Palacios does precisely this, tracing the evolution of Latin American competition law through the aforementioned development eras and delineating the growing mismatch between competition law's aims and its actions. At the end of his tale, one might be tempted to conclude that competition laws need to be more fit for purpose. However, it is also possible to come to the end as I did, with a sense that the purposes are themselves dysfunctional. Latin America's industrialisation, rapid economic

[26] Fernando Cardoso and Enzo Faletto, *Dependency and Development in Latin America* (Oakland, University of California Press, 1973); André Gunder Frank, *Latin America: Underdevelopment or Revolution* (New York, Monthly Review, 1969).

[27] Julius Nyerère, *Freedom and Socialism* (New York, OUP, 1968); Johan Galtung, Peter O'Brien and Roy Preiswerk (eds), *Self-Reliance, A Strategy for Development* (London, IUED, 1980).

[28] Ibid; Okwudiba Nnoli, *Self-Reliance and Foreign Policy in Tanzania* (New York, NOK, 1978).

[29] L Eslava, M Fakhri and V Nesiah (eds), *Bandung, Global History and International Law* (Cambridge, CUP, 2017).

[30] General Assembly Resolution 1803 on Permanent Sovereignty over Natural Resources, UN Doc A/5217 (1962); Nico Schrijver, *Sovereignty over Natural Resources: Balancing Rights and Duties* (Cambridge, CUP, 1997).

[31] Charter of Economic Rights and Duties of States, UN Doc A/RES/29/3281 (1974); Declaration on the New International Economic Order, UN Doc A/RES/S-6/3201 (1974); Mohammed Bedjaoui, *Towards a New International Economic Order* (New York, Holmes & Meier, 1979).

[32] Rist (2014), n 14 above, 171–78.

[33] Rist (2014), n 14 above, 171–78.

growth, and extreme wealth is accompanied by exponential inequality and dire poverty,[34] environmental destruction,[35] crime,[36] racial injustice,[37] ghettoisation,[38] corruption,[39] unstable governance,[40] and mass displacement.[41] Disturbing trends include felling of rainforests at the rate of two football fields per minute,[42] assassinations of environmental activists,[43] in some years higher regional deaths from homicide than global deaths from armed conflict,[44] and some of the world's biggest displacements.[45] These are not side-effects to ameliorate by returning to basic principles of development. Rather, they are the product of those principles. The Western development model has failed and postcolonial societies must decide what societal progress looks like on our own terms.

Peoples across the Global South are rethinking development. Indigenous peoples across Latin America posit 'alternative developments',[46] the Decoloniality movement advocates strategic delinking from the ongoing operations of colonial power,[47] and TWAILers try to learn from their past.[48] The challenge is immense, swimming against the tide of centuries of development fetishism, and the erasure of alternative imaginings of good life. Even when surrounded by past failures, it is tempting to believe the next law reform project will make things better, with faith beyond reason or experience.[49] Like Gatsby 'we beat on, boats against the current, borne back ceaselessly into the past'.[50]

[34] UN Economic Commission for Latin America (CEPAL), *Latin American Economic Outlook 2019* (Mexico, UN CEPAL, 2019); UNDP, *2016 Human Development Report for Latin America and the Caribbean* (New York, UNDP, 2016).

[35] UNEP, *GEO-6: Regional Assessment for Latin America and the Caribbean* (Nairobi, UNEP, 20).

[36] UNODC (n 5 above).

[37] UN CEPAL, *Social Panorama of Latin America 2018* (Mexico, UN CEPAL, 2019).

[38] Jeffrey Gutman and Nirav Patel, *Addressing Spatial Inequity in Latin American Cities*, Brookings Institute (20 March 2018). www.brookings.edu/research/addressing-spatial-inequity-in-latin-american-cities/.

[39] Transparency International, *People and Corruption: Latin America and the Caribbean* (Berlin, Transparency International, 2017).

[40] UN CEPAL, *Quadrennial Report: 2030 Agenda for Sustainable Development in Latin America and the Caribbean* (Mexico, UN CEPAL, 2019).

[41] UNHCR (UN Refugee Agency), *Global Focus: Americas*: https://reporting.unhcr.org/americas.

[42] Jonathan Watts, 'Deforestation of Brazilian Amazon surges to record high', *The Guardian* (4 June 2019): www.theguardian.com/ world/2019/jun/04/deforestation-of-brazilian-amazon-surges-to-record-high-bolsonaro.

[43] Global Witness, *At What Cost? Land and Environmental Defenders Annual Report 2017* (London, Global Witness, 2018).

[44] 'Latin America's Homicide Epidemic', *The Economist* (11 April 2018): www.economist.com/graphic-detail/2018/04/11/latin-americas-homicide-epidemic.

[45] UNHCR, *Global Focus: Americas*: https://reporting.unhcr.org/americas.

[46] Roger Merino, 'An Alternative to "Alternative Development"? *Buen Vivir* and Human Development in Andean Countries' (2016) 44(3) *Oxford Development Studies* 271.

[47] Walter Mignolo, *The Darker Side of Western Modernity: Global Futures, Decolonial Options* (Durham NC, Duke University Press, 2011).

[48] George Galindo, 'Splitting TWAIL?' (2016) 33(3) *Windsor Yearbook of Access to Justice* 37, 39.

[49] Rist (n 14 above) 211–37.

[50] F Scott Fitzgerald, *The Great Gatsby* (New York, Simon & Schuster, 2018 ed [1925]) 180.

Márquez saw his continent as haunted by the past, like the ghosts that frequented Macondo throughout its evolution. He said solitude was not merely the experience of unending sorrow and suffering but the impossibility of expressing these truths.[51] Thus, he explained his recourse to

> [p]oets and beggars, musicians and prophets, warriors and scoundrels, all creatures of that unbridled reality, we have had to ask but little of imagination, for our crucial problem has been a lack of conventional means to render our lives believable. This, my friends, is the crux of our solitude.
>
> … it is understandable that the rational talents on this side of the world [Europe], exalted in the contemplation of their own cultures, should have found themselves without valid means to interpret us. It is only natural that they insist on measuring us with the yardstick that they use for themselves.
>
> … The interpretation of our reality through patterns not our own, serves only to make us ever more unknown, ever less free, ever more solitary.

Literature and art across the Global South reverberate with a multitudinous cacophony of hopes and dreams, exposing the impossibility and undesirability of a single shared development myth. By making space for diverse social desires, laws could do more than endlessly reiterate false promises of economic development through marketplace competition. In a world increasingly characterised by the inequality and isolation that Marquez discerned, laws can help rebuild social interconnection, mutual understanding, and justice.

[51] Gabriel García Márquez, *The Solitude of Latin America*, Nobel Lecture, 8 December 1982 (translation): www.nobelprize.org/ prizes/literature/1982/marquez/lecture/.

Refraction Notes

A

Opportunism and Reflexivity: Researchers Playing Double Agents to Study the Double Game of National Legal Elites in International Competition

BRYANT GARTH AND YVES DEZALAY

Our collaboration began after we met at a Law and Society Association (LSA) Annual meeting[1] in Chicago in the mid-1980s and then again a little later at a conference on alternative dispute resolution in Boston. Bryant was charged at that conference with presenting and commenting on Yves' work on ADR in France, and Yves' paper focused on international commercial arbitration. Bryant liked the paper and mainly commented that this arcane topic needed research beyond Paris. Yves agreed but said there were no resources available on his side. Together (with another collaborator who dropped out) they submitted a National Science Foundation grant proposal, which was funded. Bryant then moved fortuitously from Indiana to the American Bar Foundation (ABF) – based in Chicago – in 1990. We then had the funding to begin our research and our actual collaboration.

We decided to conduct the first interviews jointly – contrary to what was on the grant proposal – to work out our approach. One of the very first interviews in New York – with a partner of a top law firm introduced to us by an ABF Board member – mapped the field of arbitrators for us by saying that there was a division of labour among arbitrators between 'grand old men' – leading French and Swiss professors typically – necessary for high-stakes disputes, and a younger generation of 'technocrats' who could be counted on for more routine arbitrations. He then named them and gave us a strong point of entry into this world.

[1] See https://www.lawandsociety.org/.

The timing of entry into the world of international commercial arbitration was propitious. Yves was already in the course of research into the great transformations that were taking place in European economies and legal fields in association with the growing presence of multinational corporate law firms (published in 1992).[2] The Big Bang in 1986 involving deregulation of financial markets in London was one key event. There was also the related rise of global mergers and acquisitions and intense litigation over such activities led by corporate law firms in New York City armed with new legal technologies such as the 'poison pill'.[3] The Big Five accounting firms were also rapidly expanding their legal presence globally, helping to intensify competition and fuel expansion by law firms. US and British corporate law firms began to expand their global presence substantially, led in Britain by the newly-named Magic Circle.[4] The rise of international commercial arbitration was closely related to these events.

These events did not easily match with the existing legal sociology or law and society approaches to studying the legal profession. The leading approaches at the time were Richard Abel and Philip Lewis, drawing on Magali Sarfatti Larson[5] and focusing on comparative study organised around the issue of market control. Terence Halliday and Lucien Karpik, on the other side,[6] looked toward comparisons of lawyers as political actors on behalf of liberalism. One side attacked the claims of the legal profession to serve the public interest and the other supported it. There was also interest in the large law firm as an institution of growing importance in the United States, as seen in the work of Galanter and Palay (1991).[7] None of these theoretical approaches spoke to what we saw in the transnational field emerging around international commercial arbitration. Yves of course had trained under Pierre Bourdieu, but Bourdieu had written little on the legal profession (1986),[8] and that early work was very European based, focusing on the law professors and pure law.

Bourdieu was interested in the transnational, however, as he noted in his preface to our collaboration *Dealing in Virtue*.[9] He also commented on our different

[2] Y Dezalay, *Marchands de droit: La restructuration de l'ordre juridique international par les multinationales du droit* (Paris, Fayard, 1992).

[3] A poison pill is a structural manoeuvre used as a defensive tactic by a target company to prevent or discourage hostile takeover attempts. Poison pills allow existing shareholders the right to purchase additional shares at a discount, effectively diluting the ownership interest of the would-be acquirer.

[4] The Magic Circle is an informal term describing the five top-performing London-headquartered multinational law firms.

[5] R Abel and R Lewis (eds), *Lawyers in Society* (3 volumes) (Berkeley CA, University of California Press, 1988–89).

[6] T Halliday and L Karpik (eds), *Fighting for Political Liberalism: Europe and North America from the Eighteenth to Twentieth Centuries* (Oxford, Clarendon Press, 1998).

[7] M Galanter and T Palay, *Tournament of Lawyers: The Transformation of the Big Law Firm* (Chicago IL, University of Chicago Press, 1991).

[8] P Bordieu, 'The Force of Law: Toward a Sociology of the Juridical Field' (1986) 38 *Hastings Law Journal* 805.

[9] Y Dezalay and B Garth, *Dealing in Virtue: International Commercial Arbitration and the Construction of a Transnational Legal Order* (Chicago IL, University of Chicago Press, 1996).

national and scholarly positions as a research strategy for studying a transnational field. We represented two legal traditions, he suggested, competing for ascendance in the international arbitration field, and we brought different national and disciplinary points of entry – French sociologist at CNRS[10] and US Director of the American Bar Foundation (itself confused by corporate lawyers with the American Bar Association) – that exposed us to, and allowed us to develop, the cleavage behind what our early interviewee noted – European 'grand old men' versus 'technocratic' arbitrators. The latter, we later saw, meant arbitrators attuned to US law firms' interest in making arbitration into US-style 'off-shore' litigation; the former were elite arbitrators seeking to find the right resolution according to their experience and interpretation of the *lex mercatoria*. The double game associated with our identities facilitated rich interviews around this fault-line in the field. Incidentally, we have continued doing the interviews jointly through all our projects in order both to enrich the interviews and to allow for fruitful discussion afterwards.

Dealing in Virtue was welcomed in law and society in part because it helped launch research topics such as legal globalisation, judicialisation and transnational legal fields. Our approach was novel and interesting to law and society scholars, but it did not fit especially well or influence the prevailing paradigms of research on law and the legal profession within law and society. We next began to do interviews for a study of the emergence of the field of international human rights, but we switched when we found too much similarity to international commercial arbitration.

Our next research project, represented by the book on *The Internationalization of Palace Wars*,[11] went deeper into the impact of US-style globalisation in national settings, a sub-theme of the later chapters in *Dealing in Virtue*. NAFTA, the trade agreement for the US, Mexico, and Canada, was a link also to the role of internationalised dispute resolution. Our original proposal aimed to cover three continents, with two countries from each of the three. Preliminary research suggested, however, that even within Latin America, differences among countries made four countries – Argentina, Brazil, Chile and Mexico – sufficient. We tried a few interviews with military representatives, but our best points of entry continued to be: lawyers and law professors, with those over 40 speaking French as their second language and those under 40 speaking English; economists, with access to various 'Chicago boys' and their counterparts through the ABF's University of Chicago economists; and an outstanding group of sociologists connected to Yves and Bourdieu. In Brazil and Chile, in addition, we followed the stories of US law and development, in which some of our friends, such as David Trubek, were major players willing to point us to their contacts.

[10] French National Centre of Scientific Research.

[11] Y Dezalay and B Garth, *The Internationalization of Palace Wars: Lawyers, Economists, and the Contest to Transform Latin American States* (Chicago IL, University of Chicago Press, 2002).

The *Internationalization of Palace Wars*, published in 2002, therefore extended the French-US strategy that Bourdieu observed to explore the development and export of neo-liberal politics into Latin America, which led to the expansion of corporate law and the take-off period of human rights law as well. It showed that 'palace wars' in the North were exported to the South, and that events in the South such as the purported success of neo-liberalism in Chile, are used for legitimacy in the North. The book depicted the political move away from the stronger, European model of the state and law toward a greater focus on private markets and competition emanating from the 'Chicago Boys' and their allies in the United States and elsewhere. This book was translated into five languages, but within the US law and society community it was not as well received as the first book.

Retrospectively, we understand that reaction and also, from our point of view, believe we hit a kind of cul de sac with this book in terms of future research. Our theoretical approach, built on Bourdieu and on our own ability to explore the global competition between Europe and the US over legitimate models of governance and law, limited how deeply we could go into national and transnational topics such as human rights and alternative dispute resolution. We felt that a deeper understanding of the colonial roots and legacies of the profession in Latin America would have been useful.

From the perspective of law and society, for very different reasons, we were placed in a kind of niche – studies of elite lawyers – that by definition was outside the law and society mainstream.

There are the two poles that still dominate the mainstream of the law and society field, especially in the United States, but of course influential elsewhere. One pole, which we certainly did not fit, is that involving those who wish to help legal policy-makers by presenting them with rigorous social scientific research. This approach corresponds to a division of labour which allows those researchers to gain a place in policy discussions but avoid posing questions about the structure of the field in which is inscribed the process of political decision-making. The social science researchers confine themselves mainly to quantitative analyses with given objectives. The political and professional stakes that weigh on the themes and the categories are, if not hidden, at least bracketed for the purpose of the research. Within the broad law and society field in the US, the spin-off of the Society for Empirical Legal Studies[12] from the Law and Society Association well reflects this division.

In contrast, those who work on the themes that are much more political play less on the scientific register and much more on their engagement in the service of causes for which ideological legitimacy imposes tactical imperatives and self-censure on the researchers. The fact that they are engaging in the service of great causes preempts all forms of reflexive distance, since it might appear as a criticism of the actions of the activist professionals – even a kind of treason.

[12] https://www.lawschool.cornell.edu/sels/.

Further, these allies play a determinant role, as much for the definition of the objects and the themes of the research as to validate the results. The support and recognition – or mild criticism – of the activist legal practitioners attests to the value of the scholarly analyses. Central to the legitimating rhetoric around these cause lawyers and social movements is the purity of the activists. The favoured movements for these studies are locally- and not globally-inspired, and they come from the grassroots rather than a more complex mix of individuals bringing strategies and resources to the movement. And ideally, from a law and society perspective, they are to be studied bottom-up to best learn and support their authentic voices. Work such as ours, which did not purport to find and give voice to these 'emancipatory' groups, went very much against the law and society grain – easy to set aside as a sociology of elite lawyers. Indeed, our work in Latin America revealed the close connections at times between emancipatory groups and business groups whose main focus was social control.

From the perspective of our own research interests and agenda, in any event, we found that the best way to move forward in our own scholarship was to reinvest, especially in social history. In particular, the works of scholars focusing on the genesis of the legal profession in the medieval era, including Harold Berman, whose work is from the 1980s,[13] and James Brundage, whose seminal work was published in 2008,[14] were extremely helpful for the geneses. On the other side were scholars on empire, including recent work of Lauren Benton and *Rage for Order*, with Lisa Ford, published in 2016 and focusing on the British Empire.[15]

This look backward at geneses of lawyers and colonial legal exports adds a dimension we could not cover in *Palace Wars*. It shows the origin in the medieval era of a cosmopolitan legal elite in Bologna, representing aristocratic, meritocratic, and scholarly capital. Close to medieval feudal and religious power and later emerging state power, they used their mix of capital and the prestige of rediscovered roman law texts to serve as brokers among different economic and political groups. Following the legacies of this cosmopolitan elite facilitates, in the term of Berman, 'broadening the focus from palace wars to palace revolutions'. More specifically, this investment allows research into political and legal changes and later echoes, facilitating much richer inquiry into continuities and changes in national legal fields. It also facilitates a better examination of colonial legacies, since the European approaches were exported into Asia, where we next focused our study. Colonial legacies can also be examined in relation to new imperial or hegemonic challenges.

[13] Harold Berman, *Law and Revolution: The Formation of the Western Legal Tradition* (Cambridge MA, Harvard University Press 1983); Harold Berman, *Law and Revolution II: The Impact of the Protestant Reformations on the Western Legal Tradition* (Cambridge MA, Belknap Press of Harvard University Press, 2003).

[14] James A Brundage, *The Medieval Origins of the Legal Profession: Canonists, Civilians, and Courts* (Chicago IL, University of Chicago Press, 2008).

[15] L Benton and L Ford, *Rage for Order. The British Empire and the Origins of International Law, 1800–1850* (Cambridge MA, Harvard University Press, 2016).

The competitions that can be examined with this framework produce multi-colonial and hegemonic stories, not just the competition between Europe and the US that organised *Dealing in Virtue* and *Palace Wars*. In contrast to leading comparative works on the legal profession, it enlarges the focus to interconnected legal histories rather than examinations of one country or another. The additional investment, from our point of view, facilitates a deeper understanding of the background and context behind stories of change, continuity, and the reproduction of legal and social hierarchies. Our book on *Asian Legal Revivals* builds on the new approach and goes much deeper into colonial legacies to make sense of the very different 'revivals' of law after the Cold War in Asia.[16] As with *Palace Wars*, we adapted our focus on specific countries. We began with aspirations to cover China and Japan, but we determined that they we could not compete with the relatively large body of specialists on those countries. We added India after initial interviews in Korea suggested that linguistic barriers there might limit our research, even though we overcame that to a great extent through the work of an outstanding Korean student who worked with Yves in Paris. We also added the Philippines when our studies of the US Foreign Policy Establishment revealed so many connections to US colonial management in the Philippines. As with respect to *Dealing in Virtue*, *Asian Legal Revivals* also won the LSA's Herbert Jacob prize, but it also goes against the LSA grain in the ways mentioned earlier.

We are now finishing a book that builds on the Asia research and goes deeper into this examination of legal hierarchies relating to colonialism. Drawing on the history of the cosmopolitan elites built in medieval Bologna initially and shaped further on the Continent and in Britain before exportation, the book will examine not the revival of law after the Cold War but the explicit clash of conservative colonial hierarchies with a neo-liberal legal revolution emanating from the United States. This revolution is associated with exportation recently of the US hybrid model for education and hierarchy. It combines the Continental model of limited access to universities (in the US, elite universities) with the US meritocratic ideology (which in practice rewards mainly those with resources to excel in the relevant tests) that limits access to prestige careers such as those in corporate law firms. The European colonial model exported earlier operated in part through co-optation of local elites brought into colonial governance – as in Korea and Hong Kong. It was maintained and in part revived through complex strategies combining family capital, as in India, and quasi-familial relationships such as the Judicial Institutes in Japan and South Korea. In China and Japan, the model developed through mimicry under the pressure of the European imperialists.

The new phase of law and development, in contrast to the US-led movement in the 1970s and 1980s, is led now by importers in Asia. This phase builds on the much larger presence of corporate law firms in Asia and the general spread of

[16] Y Dezalay and B Garth, *Asian Legal Revivals: Lawyers in the Shadow of Empire* (Chicago IL, University of Chicago Press, 2010).

neo-liberalism. But we can see through our deeper historical approach that the contest now is between legal elites embedded within existing Asian legal structures and importers drawing on the recipes from multinational law firms and places like Harvard Law School to challenge those elites and their practices. Interestingly, this fight, as it turns out, is a reprise of where we began our collaboration in *Dealing in Virtue*. There, too, the contest was essentially between elite, meritocratic, corporate law firms versus the European guardians of the temple. The new work looks at the same fight, except that the legal revolution from the US confronts different hierarchies – not just grand professors – in the different countries. We are confident now that the more historical approach we bring today illuminates this important contest, and indeed that this time that we can bring insights to China and Japan that are novel and credible to the specialists.

B

Reflections on the Value, Risks, and Obligations of a Career as a Misfit

KATE BEDFORD

I. Introduction

I came to this collection on *Invisible Institutionalisms* quite late, after meeting one of the editors at a talk. When she asked me to contribute a reflection on my journey to being a senior person with a gatekeeping role in my field, I thought she had mistaken me for someone else, not least because I am never entirely sure which field is mine and which I'm temporarily grazing while the landowner builds a better fence. Nonetheless, I found myself intrigued by the book. In particular, I was drawn to (i) its determination to use experimental forms of writing and scholarly community-building to help reframe law and globalisation debates, and (ii) its explicit focus on the shadows and peripheries, and its emphasis on the related need to enlarge our academic gaze beyond the usual topics.[1] In particular, as a scholar originally trained in development, I share the sense of puzzlement and, occasionally, frustration – expressed in several contributions here – about why and how dominant conversations about law and development became so narrow, instrumentalist, and uncritical of law.

My befuddlement in part stems from the fact that I have been trained in several different disciplines, and that I fit awkwardly in all of them. I was trained in interdisciplines (development studies and gender studies) before a PhD in political science in the US. I had some short-term teaching jobs wherever I could get them, an interdisciplinary post-doctoral fellowship position, and then – quite miraculously – a permanent job in the UK's leading critical law school, at the University of Kent. As a result, my reflections on the law and globalisation field are not disciplinarily-located. They cluster, instead, around a more cross-cutting theme: the value, risks, and obligations of focusing on what are understood to be the margins of a

[1] See Swethaa Ballakrishnen and Sara Dezalay, Introduction to this volume.

field. In this short piece, I seek to explain my investments in those margins, and discuss the benefits I have gained from them. Simultaneously, however, I seek to be reflexive about the costs. A career spent researching topics considered marginal carries advantages, risks, and attendant duties to others: for me, it is crucial to keep those all in view together.

The key lesson that I take from this reflection about the value of circulating structurally-aware, collectivity-bolstering, self-deprecating accounts of ourselves. For me, those accounts may be helpful interventions in an academic sector prone to instead tell stories about individual geniuses, with neat and tidy career trajectories. As Patricia Ewick and Susan Silbey noted in their account of narrating law in everyday life, passing on stories about individual acts of non-compliance – however small – is a collective enterprise.[2] The stories acquire value as they circulate; this is why it is so important for researchers to repeat stories that are told to them for these purposes. As they put it:

> [R]esistance is enabled and collectivized, in part, by the circulation of stories, narrating moments when taken for granted social structure is exposed and the usual direction of constraint upended, if only for a moment. By telling stories of resistance, actors name and thus expose 'what goes with-out saying' … By narrating those moments when they were able to best power, actors extend temporally and spatially individual acts of resistance.[3]

An individual contribution to an academic book is not, by any stretch, an act of resistance. But what intrigued me about this book was, in part, that it sought to reframe law and globalisation debates by using experimental forms of writing, including reflection pieces. For those reflection pieces to help build our *collective* strength to do things otherwise, they are perhaps best framed in a dual way: as invitations to be honest about our (sometimes extensive) personal experiences of failure, and also as opportunities to diagnose the structural factors explaining success. Duties stem from that diagnosis. The value of senior people circulating their career stories is thus less about autobiography, and more about identifying the obligations that such people owe to others being, increasingly, excluded from academia.

II. Accounting for the Investment, and the Return

Broadly speaking, my research is on gender, law, regulation, development, and political economy. One key strand of my work is on the role of multilateral

[2] Patricia Ewick and Susan Silbey, 'Narrating Social Structure: Stories of Resistance to Legal Authority' (2003) 108(6) *American Journal of Sociology* 1328.

[3] Ewick and Silbey (2003), 1329.

institutions in shaping sexuality.[4] More recently I have being trying to rethink law and development debates, and chronologies, from a gender and development perspective.[5] I tend to take a somewhat off-centre starting point in this strand of work. For example, in looking at the relevance of sexuality to the World Bank, I chose not to focus on areas of development lending that were already marked as sexualised, such as HIV/AIDS or reproductive health. I focused instead on the way that sexuality – particularly *hetero*sexuality – was a useful analytic category within Ecuadorian export promotion loans involving floriculture (flower-farming), and efforts to strengthen institutions in the aftermath of Argentina's 2001 economic crisis. In a similar vein, rather than starting from an analysis of contemporary gender and development practices centring law reform as a key priority, I went backwards and sideways to see what, if anything, some canonical gender and development texts published between 1970 and 1989 said about law. This, I hope, offers some critical distance on the present moment, allowing us to tell a different, more critical story about the role of law in gender and development.

A second strand of my work is on gambling regulation and its relationship to our theories of risk, consumption, and welfare.[6] A few years ago, partly inspired by the 2008 financial crisis, I began to research the relationship between gambling and capitalism, a relationship that has intrigued critical law and political economy scholars for a very long time but that needs some feminist-inspired rethinking. Specifically, I have used the game of bingo to reflect anew on the relationship between gambling, gender, regulation, and political economy. Bingo is a lottery-style game that is especially popular, in many parts of the world, with older, working-class women. I argue that bingo offers important, wide-ranging lessons about the role of regulation in shaping the gendered interaction between capitalist and more-than-capitalist economies. By way of analogy, Ann McClintock (1995) was not a scholar of soap,[7] Leela Fernandes was not an expert only on jute,[8] Cynthia Enloe's (2014) theoretical contribution was

[4] eg Kate Bedford, *Developing Partnerships: Gender, Sexuality and the Reformed World Bank* (Minneapolis MN, University of Minnesota Press, 2009).

[5] eg Kate Bedford, 'Law, Gender, and Development: Potent Hauntings' (2020) 13(1) *Law and Development Review* 229. Published online November 2019, available at: https://doi.org/10.1515/ldr-2019-0066.

[6] eg Kate Bedford, *Bingo Capitalism: The Law and Political Economy of Everyday Gambling* (Oxford, Oxford University Press, 2019); Kate Bedford, 'Regulation and Resistance in Canadian Bingo: A Socio-Legal Account' (2018) 30 *Journal of Law and Social Policy* 11–35; Kate Bedford, 'Bingo Regulation and the Feminist Political Economy of Everyday Gambling' (2016) 13(6) *Globalizations* 801–14; Kate Bedford, 'Letting the right ones in: Whitelists, jurisdictional reputation, and the racial dynamics of online gambling regulation' (2016) 34(1) *Environment and Planning D* 30–47; Kate Bedford, 'Regulating Volunteers: Lessons from the Bingo Halls' (2015) 40(2) *Law and Social Inquiry* 461–90.

[7] Anne McClintock, *Imperial Leather: Race, Gender, and Sexuality in the Colonial Contest* (New York, Routledge, 1995).

[8] Leela Fernandes, *Producing Workers: The Politics of Gender, Class, and Culture in the Calcutta Jute Mills* (Philadelphia PA, University of Pennsylvania Press, 1997).

not banana-specific,[9] Inderpal Grewal (1999) was not just interested in Barbie dolls,[10] and Michael Fakhri's book (2014) is not solely about sugar.[11] Through soap, jute, bananas, dolls, and sugar, these academics provided new insights into empire, labour politics, international relations, transnational cultural economies, and trade law. I use bingo to provide new insights into the state regulation of diverse (gambling) economies in a similar way.

In this regard, I insist on the broader relevance of bingo to work on law and political economy not (solely) to justify a misspent youth, but also because I have learned the importance of questioning disciplinary parameters. Critical scholars have long demanded that colleagues working in the mainstreams of their disciplines be more reflexive about who is positioned as offering meta-theoretical, universally-applicable work, versus who is understood to be doing applied, empirical, or case-study research with, it is alleged, limited academic or geographical reach.[12] In an earlier reflections piece, written for a politics journal,[13] I agreed with James Scott's (2010) warning that U.S. politics scholars risked extinction unless at least half of their reading was outside the discipline:[14] I now tend to think the same of global law academics. Not only must legal theorists 'learn how to honor empirical work' for the lessons it offers them,[15] but the sites, and cites, for many allegedly universal theories about law, development, and globalisation must expand.

Being reflexive about the value of non-mainstream work also requires us to grapple, collectively and *intellectually*, with self-deprecation and its valuable role in the stories we are telling about ourselves and our fields of study. I have spent a lot of time thinking about that lately, because self-deprecation is a defining feature of bingo. When researching the game's regulation in different parts of the world, I lost count of the times I was told – by clearly skilled and dedicated people responsible for running or regulating the game – that bingo wasn't hard to organise, or call, or play, or manage. It's not rocket science, or brain surgery, I was assured. I was struggling with a way to write seriously about bingo that took account of this deeply classed and gendered self-deprecation. In the end, I chose to analytically foreground it as a significant theme in its own, conflicted terms. I argued that bingo – as a practice and lens – gives us a privileged vantage point on diverse economies, and the crucial role of the state in shaping them, in

[9] Cynthia Enloe, *Bananas, Beaches and Bases: Making Feminist Sense of International Politics*, 2nd edn (Berkley CA, University of California Press, 2014).

[10] Inderpal Grewal, 'Traveling Barbie: Indian Transnationality and New Consumer Subjects' (1999) 7(3) *Positions – Asia Critique* 799–827.

[11] Michael Fakhri, *Sugar and the Making of International Trade Law* (Cambridge, Cambridge University Press, 2014).

[12] eg Gayatri Spivak, *Outside in the Teaching Machine* (London and New York, Routledge, 2012).

[13] Kate Bedford, 'Reflections from a Visitor' (2013) 9(4) *Politics and Gender* 484–88.

[14] James Scott 'Theory Talk #38: James Scott on Agriculture as Politics, the Dangers of Standardization and Not Being Governed', Saturday, May 15, 2010: http://www.theorytalks.org/2010/05/theory-talk-38.html.

[15] Gayatri Spivak, *Outside in the Teaching Machine* (New York, Routledge, 2012 [1993]).

part *because* it is populated by people who insist that they are nothing special. This is neither to make a virtue of self-protecting acts of humility, nor to associate modesty solely with shame. Alongside the fears of being mocked by others that may provoke (some of) us to pre-emptively laugh at ourselves, there can be gentler, kinder, more quietly self-assured reasons to not take ourselves too seriously. However, to root our discussions of law and regulation here, in the self-effacing shadows of Las Vegas, is to upend dominant ways of seeing market-making. Roulette-playing wolves of Wall Street cede the stage to bingo players stubbornly squatting in back rooms of social clubs when the manager wants them gone. Glamorous casino-ised spectacles fade out to rainy afternoons in northern English seaside arcades, or evenings in rural Canadian games in which the jackpot prize is a packet of part-defrosted chicken thighs. Faith in cutting-edge algorithms to prevent harm is eclipsed by the day-to-day gendered and classed labour of knowing your regulars. Our discussions of diverse (gambling) economies, and the state's role in shaping them, get more grounded, more complex, more feminist, and – hopefully – more analytically significant as a result.

The value of research at the margins of disciplines is thus in part, for me, about the potential to disrupt dominant academic, legal, political, and economic stories. In my case, I tell a new story of gambling and political economy centring mutual aid, not commercial operations. However, the value of a marginal(ised) focus is also about disrupting the notion of a canonical disciplinary story, with an earnest citational honouring of forefathers (rarely mothers), and a linear temporality of origins, developments, moments, waves, occasional crises, and progress. For example, in a recent article on gender, law, and development,[16] I drew on the approach to narrating feminist pasts offered by Clare Hemmings (2011), of how we collectively learn, craft, and pass on stories about feminism, as social movement and intellectual canon.[17] Wanting to explore 'how we might tell stories differently', she suggested that we force absent presences back into our stories of feminism, to bring the 'half-forgotten' back into conscious theoretical consideration.[18] This process, one she terms recitation, involves revisiting material previously encountered, as part of an effort at 'unforgetting', of making visible what is already there, of inquiring after the 'obscured dimensions of the present'.[19] In the afore-mentioned article, I applied Hemmings' approach to gender and development debates about law. However, bingo is another helpful example. It is globally widespread, yet almost entirely ignored in academic debates (including about gambling), and, for me, it provides us with a vital *lens* on law and political economy. The mutual aid dimensions of the game offer an entry point to a new history of gambling law and policy, for example, oriented to actors such as unions and working men's clubs.

[16] Kate Bedford (2020), n 5 above.

[17] Clare Hemmings, *Why Stories Matter: the Political Grammar of Feminist Theory* (Durham NC, Duke University Press, 2011).

[18] Hemmings (2011), at 16 and 23.

[19] Hemmings (2011) at 180 and 181.

Moreover, precisely because it is widely dismissed as a joke, bingo is worth taking seriously. In this respect, an epistemological orientation to the margins stems from an abiding interest in what we can learn from the mundane, unspectacular, and laughably ordinary.

III. Risks and Attendant Obligations

Since we were asked to be reflexive about our career trajectories, it behoves me to say that my diverse (inter)disciplinary location was not always actively chosen. At one point, armed with my dissertation on heteronormativity and development, and my offer to teach courses on critical political economy, I tried to get a job in US political science. Strangely enough, it didn't call back. I had a book contract with a leading university publisher, and considerable teaching experience, but I didn't fit. It was a blessing, though not one I saw at the time, when the rent was due and the car died. Thanks to feminist referees and mentors, I ended up instead in Kent Law School, a place proudly welcoming of misfits. A few months into my new role, I anxiously scheduled a face-to-face meeting with a senior female colleague to confess that my article had been rejected from a leading disciplinary journal: despite having two positive reviews, the editor felt it was too critical of the development institution involved, and had failed to address mainstream debates in the field (the piece was on gender). I expected to be told to redouble my efforts to get an article into a top-ranked journal of that kind. Instead, having read the piece and the feedback, my colleague laughed. She told me that I had no need to adapt my work such that it'd be published in that venue, unless I wanted to, and that the school didn't care where I published so long as what I did was good. Unsurprisingly, I stayed in that institution for many years. When it came time to take the next step, I moved to Birmingham Law School, again with the help of feminists as referees, mentors, and space-creators.

I relay this brief career trajectory because I agree with those arguing that we need to honestly discuss our failures, mistakes, and disappointments, and the accidents that shaped our paths.[20] This can be one strategy to help counter-balance the myth that successful academic careers are heroically steered by brilliantly strategic individuals. Mine, in truth, was reliant on accident, luck, and the systemic over-work of senior women as referees, heads of school, mentors, and reviewers.

[20] See in particular bell hooks' reflection on her complex feelings after receiving tenure (in *Teaching to Transgress: Education as the Practice of Freedom* (New York, Routledge, 1994), and the collection *Secrecy and Silence in the Research Process: feminist reflections* (Róisín Ryan-Flood and Rosalind Gill (eds)) (London/New York, Routledge, 2010). See also the powerful accounts of the systemic production of what are often mis-understood as individualised experiences of academic 'failure' by, inter-alia Erin Bartram (http://erinbartram.com/uncategorized/the-sublimated-grief-of-the-left-behind/); Marie-Alex Thouaille (https://blogs.lse.ac.uk/impactofsocialsciences/2018/03/01/is-pursuing-an-academic-career-a-form-of-cruel-optimism/); and Ben Freeland (https://medium.com/@benfreeland/confessions-of-a-failed-academic-bdd40d7a174b).

If I am being honest, though, it was probably not strategic to have written monographs on sexuality, or bingo. The risks of a focus on what are considered marginal fields of study are real: it is crucial to keep them in mind, without investing too heavily in the ego-wounds that may accompany the (re)minding. I was told by a prospective supervisor that he hoped I was independently wealthy because I'd never get a job in a US Political Science department if I did a dissertation on sexuality. He was, of course, correct: I didn't. However, having been supervised by an excellent academic team at Rutgers, I won a dissertation prize from the gender section of the American Political Science Association that helped me get a job outside the discipline, and for which I remain extremely grateful. (I am judging a similar prize now: it takes weeks of work, which I am ashamed to admit I did not realise at the time). I doubled down on the inclination towards the margins in my later work: not only is gambling a side-lined topic overall, but within it I chose to centre a game that is, for many, a joke rather than topic of seriously scholarly consideration. For a time, I renamed the research grant I was leading, on bingo, 'the career suicide project'. The originality and rigour of the research was not a problem, but stopping people laughing for long enough so that I could explain the broader significance of the findings to debates about law, regulation, and political economy was a challenge. An early draft of a book proposal was rejected within a day or so; the broader contribution to the discipline of law was a concern. Again I found a home for it – the book (with a much better proposal) was just published by OUP[21] – but I spent a long time worrying that this time I really would get sacked.

Were I a different person, the takeaway lesson here might be about being scared but doing it anyway. But that seems simplistic to me, flying in the face of the intellectual inheritances that have most powerfully shaped my work: the ones that teach us to look beyond the individual as the key causal factor. In reality, senior roles in academia – like in other professions – are mostly the result of structural inequality, where privilege masquerades as merit. When that is not the case, collective support, and the structurally-conditioned resource context, play the key roles. On the collective support side, I had senior feminist role models to whom I looked for guidance. They showed me how to respond to rejection and failure with humour and kindness, and how to practise academia in ways that counteract hierarchy, isolation, and competition. When I first arrived at Kent, after many years in the US, I noticed how senior academics made the tea for seminar meetings, and washed up afterwards. The practical and symbolic importance of senior people putting the kettle on can never be underestimated, in my view.

The structural support side is somewhat harder to articulate: as Bowker and Starr noted many years ago, infrastructure often becomes visible only in its

[21] See Bedford (2019), n 6 above.

breakdown.[22] I was the first person in my family to go away to university.[23] My access to university relied on a decent school on my council estate, and free access to higher education. The council housing is now privately owned, the school is now a sports academy, and UK students are charged nearly £30,000 in tuition fees for a three-year undergraduate degree. If I were a young person now, I would not be able to attend university.

My later degrees, in the US, were reliant on scholarships: without them, I would have neither a MA nor a PhD. I was granted the visas I needed, as an international student, to study and then work. When I started my first permanent job, in Kent, I had adequate research time, and funding: I could finish my first book, travel internationally to a few key events that were crucial for research networks, and pull together a large grant application, with the proactive support of more senior colleagues who were not burnt out. In turn, politically and economically enabled 'luck' played a key role in winning that grant: at that time (2013), there was more money. Since then, I have seen many, many research grants that were as good as mine be knocked back.

I also benefited, in my own research, from the intellectual curiosity and engagement of excellent PhD students, from around the world. We could attract such students to Kent, in part because we could sometimes help fund their studies. Since then, funding has been squeezed, and international students face onerous and expensive immigration hurdles that make it far harder for them to study in the UK.

Relatedly, I could delay my last book proposal for 18 months, until I was sure I had a much stronger empirical and conceptual case for bingo's broader significance, because I worked in a place where research management was underpinned by a principled commitment to patiently nurturing quality. Senior people stood in front of junior colleagues to shield them from the worst impulses of some top-level university managers. If I'd been measured based on what businesses, legal professionals, governments, or large development institutions want from academics, I'd probably have been sacked, or at best moved off an academic contract that gave me time for research. In short, my perseverance was institutionally enabled. If any trails were blazed, it was by those who built the ladders that got people like me into university, who fought for research as a core component of what defines a university, and who stood up for the interests of junior colleagues, including postgraduate research students.

[22] Geoffrey C Bowker and Susan L Starr, *Sorting Things Out: Classification and Its Consequences* (Cambridge MA, MIT Press, 1999), 35.

[23] My mother had done a distance learning degree as an adult, at a time when those courses were available at very low cost.

In summary, then, the key lesson I have taken from this invitation to reflect on my own journey is not primarily about my scholarship, or its place with the law, development, and globalisation field. Rather, it is about the obligation that I feel I have – as a scholar whose research on the margins didn't (so far) result in career suicide – to do for others the work that made my own career possible: collectively building ladders and, where necessary, shields.

C

Genealogy of a Globalised Socio-Legal (and Feminist) Scholar

CARRIE MENKEL-MEADOW*

I have written often about 'Durkheimian epiphanies' in socio-legal studies[1] – those moments when factual patterns of data or observations are suddenly illuminated to cast a different hue to the colour of legal conclusions or legal institutions. For me, the beginning of my socio-legal career began when, as a young poverty lawyer (while my political scientist husband was studying multiple quantitative methods at the University of Michigan), I read the classic empirical study of *The American Jury*.[2] How could I prepare a case solely on the basis of legal doctrines and evidence presented when different decision-makers (judges, juries) would bring to their decision-making their personal, social, political and economic backgrounds?[3] I was sociologically trained at Columbia University to know that what we see, believe and think depends a great deal on where we come from – socialisation is a major determinant of opinions, beliefs and behaviours. The law is neither totally 'neutral' nor 'rational' in its making, interpretation and enforcement. I was 'hooked' on the more rigorous and complex field of socio-legal studies – the

* Thanks to my partner in research and all else, Dr Robert Meadow (political scientist among other things!) and to Swethaa Ballakrishnen and Sara Dezalay for including me in this multi-generational globalised conversation.

[1] C Menkel-Meadow, 'Durkheimian Epiphanies: The Importance of Engaged Social Science in Legal Studies' (1990) 18 *Florida State University Law Review* 91, and C Menkel-Meadow, 'Uses and Abuses of Socio-legal Studies' in N Creutzfeldt, M Mason and K McConnachie (eds), *Routledge Handbook of Socio-Legal Theory and Methods* (New York/London, Routledge Taylor & Francis, 2019).

[2] H Kalven, Jr and H Zeisel, *The American Jury* (Boston MA, Little, Brown, 1966).

[3] I later used this work in my teaching of Trial Advocacy for many years, to make students aware of the a priori or socialised 'generalizations' that decision-makers bring to their assessments of facts and law. This should affect how opening and closing speeches and all else in between take account of how jurors (and judges) process information. These observations also lead me to abandon trial work for alternative dispute resolution, as I became a great sceptic of whether there ever was anything like 'the truth' to be found in a contested trial, with only 'two sides of a story' to be presented. The 'brittleness' of trial work does not work well with the greater complexities of social science variance. C Menkel-Meadow, 'The Trouble with the Adversary System in a Post-Modern, Multicultural World' (1996) 38 *William & Mary Law Review* 5–44.

contextual study of law and legal institutions as made by differentiated human beings.

When, a few years later, both my husband and I were junior scholars at two different branches of the University of California (UCLA and UC San Diego), we embarked on our first collaboration on a study of how poverty lawyers allocated their scarce resources (time) to represent an almost limitless number of worthy clients. Our multi-tiered and triaged methods (observations, qualitative interviews and quantitative data gathered from time sheets) received National Science Foundation support. Our work was championed by then NSF Law and Social Science Program Director, Felice Levine, who insisted that I (a law professor whose school, at the time, didn't much care about empirical research or grants) received equal credit for this work. (More on that below. In those early years – the 1970s – the institutional support of feminist and scholars of colour, however limited, was necessary for the development of a growing diversity of scholars, now championed by a more international Law and Society Association[4] than when I first joined in the early years.) Our aim was to see how lawyers who had values other than maximising incomes allocated their work and make decisions about what was important – 'social change' cases or individual case service, then a big political issue in federal allocation of funding for legal aid.[5] We had another 'Durkheimian epiphany' when Ronald Reagan was elected President and various conservative government officials wanted to use our study to show how 'political' poverty lawyers were and attempted to de-fund the Legal Services Corporation.[6] In the ongoing debates in the socio-legal field of the 'pull of the policy audience' – the desire to use data for social good,[7] the need for more theoretically and scientifically-neutral crafted questions and research programmes, and the use or 'co-optation of social science' for political or law reform purposes,[8] we felt the chill of political (mis)uses of our work, and after publishing a few reports of our work, refused to testify in settings that might have encumbered the LSC funding cycle.[9]

I next turned to two different kinds of socio-legal projects. As an individual scholar and one of the first generation in the American clinical legal education movement, I noted, from my practice experience, that winning lawsuits

[4] The Law and Society Association, founded in 1964, is a group of scholars from many fields and countries, interested in the place of law in social, political, economic and cultural life: https://www.lawandsociety.org.

[5] C Menkel-Meadow and RG Meadow, 'Personalized or Bureaucratized Justice in Legal Services: Resolving Sociological Ambivalence in the Delivery of Legal Aid for the Poor' (1985) 9 *Law & Human Behavior* 397–413.

[6] The United States' publicly-funded provider of civil legal aid, founded in 1974.

[7] C Seron, 'The Two Faces of Law and Inequality: From Critique to the Promise of Situated, Pragmatic Policy' (2016) 50 *Law & Society Review* 9–33.

[8] C Menkel-Meadow and B Garth, 'Process People Power and Policy: Empirical Studies of Civil Procedure' in P Cane and H Kritzer (eds), *Oxford Handbook of Empirical Legal Research* (Oxford, Oxford University Press, 2010).

[9] Ironically, one of the Reagan's administration staffers in this project was a conservative classmate of mine in law school who was active in trying to defund LSC in the 1980s.

did not necessarily solve problems or reduce human suffering. Cases might be won on technical or Constitutional grounds, but without sufficient funding or governmental support, prison, schools, welfare systems, health care and workplaces did not move to eliminate discrimination or injustice or poverty. It was when parties (even adverse) came together to try consensually to negotiate outcomes (and seek financial support and political buy-in) that more creative (not necessarily legally brittle) solutions could be sought. I began to focus on how other disciplines (diplomacy, political science, economics, psychology, anthropology, sociology, decision sciences, urban planning, among others) studied problem-solving and decision-making – law was only one means for social change and not necessarily the most successful, efficient or humanitarian. My first major law review article on problem-solving negotiation, informed by many different disciplines in addition to law,[10] was originally rejected by all law reviews because it was unconventional and there was little legal doctrine in it, but when published, won the first Center for Public Resources Scholarly Paper award (1984) for the new field of dispute resolution. I had helped to articulate the theory of a new legal and social movement to recognise and use many methods of dispute resolution (negotiation, mediation, arbitration and later a variety of processual hybrids)[11] in addition to or in substitution for litigation in order to both resolve legal disputes and seek productive solutions for the future, not just resolve conflicts of the past. I had helped to create a new field!!

Eventually, this move outside of the mainstream of conventional legal scholarship led to my globalisation as a scholar, teacher and practitioner[12] as I began to be asked to practise, lecture, teach and conduct research on 'A' (now not only alternative, but appropriate, accessible, aspirational) dispute resolution in many countries outside of the US (Canada, Norway, Switzerland, France, the UK, Ireland, Italy, Paraguay, Argentina, Brazil, Israel, Belgium, Singapore, China, Australia, Mexico, Costa Rica, Nicaragua, Chile, Germany, the Netherlands, Spain, and Russia).

As a woman coming of age in the 1960s, I was also an early feminist – beginning with conventional goals (wanting to be the first woman senator from

[10] C Menkel-Meadow, 'Toward Another View of Legal Negotiation: The Structure of Problem Solving' (1984) 31 *UCLA Law Review* 754–842.

[11] C Menkel-Meadow, L Love, AK Schneider and M Moffitt, *Dispute Resolution: Beyond the Adversarial Model* (Aspen Casebook series) (New York, Wolters Kluwer, 2019).

[12] I should mention here that I was already a 'globalised' person as my parents, German Holocaust refugees, raised me with many European, not American, customs and values. Sadly, although I have studied many languages, I was of the immigrant child generation that focused on assimilation (in the 1950s) and so although I read several languages, I am more American in my mono-lingualism than I should be with my personal background and scholarly interests. I was raised in the 'Ethical Culture' religion – a secular humanist religion founded by philosopher Felix Adler in the late 19th century in the United States and my childhood Sunday School education was studying a different religion of the world every year. Margaret Mead, the anthropologist often delivered lectures about the great variations in social organisation throughout the world at the New York City (Manhattan) chapter, near her post at the Natural History Museum in New York City. See: https://ethical.nyc/.

New York – a feat later accomplished by Hillary Clinton[13]). At university, however, I was more radical, joining Students for a Democratic Society and participating in the Columbia University Student Protest of 1968 (protesting, among other things, the racist plan for a gymnasium blocked off from Harlem, the industrial-military complex and research on campus in support of the Vietnam War, and disciplinary proceedings for more radical students who had occupied buildings and had been arrested[14]).[15] In the middle of that life-changing time, I was not alone in noticing that the men were dominating the political meetings and asking the women to make the coffee and paint the signs. Columbia Women's Liberation was born in the crucible of that social movement and quickly moved across the street to the women's college I was attending, Barnard College of Columbia University, which became one of the first centres of feminist scholarship and women's studies. I was mentored by distinguished sociologist Mirra Komarovsky, one of the first female sociologists to win international acclaim for her studies of gender in the family, marriage, workplaces and scientific institutions.[16] Barnard became a hotbed of feminist literary, sociological, anthropological (original home of Margaret Mead[17]) and political theory and activism.[18]

So, building on my feminist work in legal studies, I began to look at the role of women in the legal profession and participated in the feminist project of remapping legal doctrine.[19] My then colleague, Rick Abel (at UCLA), along with

[13] This is not as totally far-fetched as it seems. I am only alive today because my mother's family was part of the Lehman family (Herbert Lehman was both Senator and Governor of New York State) which worked to achieve sponsorship for immigration from Germany during the Nazi regime for its family members – a form of privilege within that horrible human tragedy. My family history and education did teach me to be a civil rights lawyer and to do what I could to work for the elimination of discrimination and injustice wherever I could and that is why I went to law school, in an era when women were just beginning to do so in more than token numbers. My class, for example had about 30 women in a class of just over 200 in 1971.

[14] P Cronin (ed), *A Time to Stir: Columbia '68* (New York, Columbia University Press, 2018).

[15] This is really where my mediation career began, as I joined a group of students who slept outside on bricks on the campus for days, hoping to prevent the University from calling the police and committing violent arrests. We were not successful – the police came, there were bloody arrests, and the revolution was over – but although I was not arrested, I participated in the legal efforts for arrested and disciplined students and even tried to mediate with the University officials and New York City police (I was 18 at the time).

[16] Professor Komorovksy and I remained in touch for many years and we had a robust and wonderful afternoon tea some years later when we argued about my feminist 'difference' work, C Menkel-Meadow, 'Portia In a Different Voice: Speculations on a Women's Lawyering Process' (1985) 1 *Berkeley Women's Law Journal* (now *Berkeley Journal of Law, Gender and Justice*) 39–63, (based on the work of psychologist Carol Gilligan, C Gilligan, *In A Different Voice: Psychological Theory and Women's Development* (Cambridge MA, Harvard University Press, 1982)) with which she whole-heartedly disagreed – she was an 'equality' feminist, having 'made it' in the old-fashioned male dominated profession!!

[17] Margaret Mead (1901–78) was an American cultural anthropologist who featured frequently as an author and speaker in the mass media during the 1960s and 1970s.

[18] At the time, Barnard College also produced more women doctors and scientists than any other liberal arts college in the United States.

[19] C Menkel-Meadow, 'Mainstreaming Feminist Legal Theory' (1992) 23 *Pacific Law Review* 1493.

Philip Lewis (University of Oxford), had organised a multi-year, multi-national study of comparative legal professions. As a diverse group of international scholars reported on the development of the legal profession in many different nations, one trend seemed universal, with varied impacts – the growing number of women in the legal profession – so I was commissioned to analyse the data and reports from all the country reports and write about emerging gender themes. Another Durkheimian epiphany!! Women were entering the legal profession in growing numbers all over the world, but (just as Margaret Mead had noted in her anthropological studies decades earlier[20]), what women did in each national legal system was structured by how professional work was valued, with women usually being in the least prestigious or valued jobs – occupational segregation was occurring even as women were entering the most significant professions. In some countries where court advocacy was important, the prosecutors and trial lawyers were still mostly men; in the United States, where corporate and transactional work was most valued, there were few female partners in major elite law firms. In those countries where civil servants and judges could use meritocratic criteria to advance (and get state subsidised childcare), eg, Germany, women were more likely to be judges than in other countries. I argued that not only should we observe this gender segregation by numbers but also study whether the increase of women in the profession might actually change both the practice of law (more mediative, problem-solving practices) and legal doctrine itself (not only for 'women's issues', but even for more conventional legal concepts, like property and contract[21]), a project on which I am continuing to work.[22]

Feminist theory was also having an impact on socio-legal studies generally. In the early 1990s I co-edited a special issue of the *Law & Society Review* on gender in socio-legal research with then editor of LSR, Shari Seidman Diamond (law and psychology scholar) which looked at feminist content, epistemology and methods in studies of law and legal institutions.[23] Gender served as a category of both social analysis and data, but feminist theory actually reoriented questions that were being asked and interpretations of data (eg, perceptions of 'facts' in sexual abuse cases, as well as women's ways of seeing and 'knowing' evidence and communication patterns and decision-making[24]).

[20] M Mead, *Male and Female: A Study of Sexes in a Changing World* (New York, William Morrow, 1967).

[21] C Menkel-Meadow, 'The Feminization of the Legal Profession: The Comparative Sociology of Women Lawyers' in R Abel and P Lewis (eds), *Lawyers in Society: Vol. 3 Comparative Theories* (Berkeley and Los Angeles, University of California Press, 1989).

[22] C Menkel-Meadow, 'Feminist Legal Academics: Changing the Epistemology of American Law Through Conflicts, Controversies and Comparisons' in U Schultz et al (eds), *Gender and Careers in the Legal Academy* (Oxford, Hart Publishing, 2021).

[23] C Menkel-Meadow and SS Diamond, 'The Content, Method and Epistemology of Gender in Sociolegal Studies' (1991) 25 *Law & Society Review* 221.

[24] C Menkel-Meadow, 'Women's Ways of 'Knowing' Law: Feminist Legal Epistemology, Pedagogy and Jurisprudence' in M Belenky, B Clinchy, N Goldberger and J Tarule (eds), *Knowledge, Difference and Power* (New York, Basic Books, 1996).

Both my dispute resolution and feminist legal studies work led to invitations for comparative research and lectures in other countries as both of these intellectual movements developed traction in other parts of the world. When I moved to Washington DC to teach at Georgetown University in 1992 I continued my domestic work (including consulting for the Clinton administration on a variety of dispute resolution topics) but began to work more globally. I did immigration asylum representation with students in Georgetown's clinical programme and, given the large foreign student LLM programme at Georgetown, I began to teach students from many other nations, including from Asia, Europe, Africa and South America. Beginning in the late 1990s I began to teach and mentor younger scholars on those continents in their home countries, as well as Georgetown, and became heavily involved in the globalisation of legal education in a variety of ways.[25] I spent over a decade teaching a variety of courses in Latin America in a variety of programmes (Chile, Argentina, Brazil, Costa Rica, Nicaragua and Mexico) in which I studied transitional and restorative justice,[26] advised governments and lawyers on dispute system design issues,[27] and was able to see first-hand the somewhat contentious dialogue and interactions of the 'transplants' of the Global North (and its traditional justice institutions) and the Global South (often contributing more complex forms of restorative, reparative, and transitional justice (or not!)). Truth and Reconciliation Commissions as a hybrid form of legal process actually originated in Bolivia and other Latin American countries, even if South Africa's TRC has received a greater part of global attention.

In 2008, Georgetown Law Center, along with 12 other law faculties, founded the Centre for Transnational Legal Studies (CTLS) in London, a programme for law students to study law comparatively together with faculty and students from around the world and different legal traditions. I taught with civil law and mixed system (eg, Israel) faculty, as well as common law faculty from four different continents. As faculty director of the programme, I taught courses in transnational legal theory, comparative law and international dispute resolution, attempting to introduce socio-legal approaches to law study in a comparative environment. This wonderful programme, where none of the students were 'home', allowed an amazingly multi-cultural and multi-jural approach to the study of law, legal institutions and the world's problems. On one of our first student gathering nights, Germans and Israelis took off together for a pub crawl, to continue to discuss our 'Global Practice Exercise' (a problem I had drafted involving international environmental

[25] C Menkel-Meadow, 'Have Law Books, Computers, Simulations, Will Travel: The Transnationalization of (some of) the Professoriate' in B Garth and G Shaffer (eds), *The Globalization of Legal Education: A Critical Study* (forthcoming).

[26] C Menkel-Meadow, 'Process Pluralism in Transitional/Restorative Justice: Lessons From Dispute Resolution for Cultural Variations in Goals beyond Rule of Law and Democracy Development (in Argentina and Chile)' (2015) 3(1) *International Journal of Conflict Engagement & Resolution* 3–32.

[27] C Menkel-Meadow, 'Are There Systemic Ethics Issues in Dispute System Design? And What Should We (Not) Do About it: Lessons from International and Domestic Fronts' (2009) 14 *Harvard Negotiation Law Review* 195–231.

and employment disputes in an international commercial arbitration), demonstrating some of the new generation healing old global wounds. On the other hand, global legal education does not always move in one 'progressive' direction. For example, a forceful group of Israeli students managed to convince some liberal European students that maybe sometimes torture could be justified to thwart terrorism. In this multi-cultural programme I studied Shar'ia law and led a faculty seminar on Amartya Sen's *The Idea of Justice*, which culminated in a multi-jural review article,[28] as well as an edited book on Amartya Sen's contributions to jurisprudence, deliberative democracy, comparative constitutionalism and law and development.[29] CTLS has been home to a variety of new generation courses and studies on human rights, language policy, humanitarian law, Artificial Intelligence, privacy, and technology law, as well as international business and finance policy. The programme's efforts to be comparative and deal with new subjects each semester, with different faculty and students, allow a flexibility to the curriculum and development of new knowledge and legal frameworks that likely surpass the more rigid institutional homes of participating teachers and students. I have now taught at six of the founding schools on four continents and have been able to see how modernisation, globalisation, internationalisation and tradition are getting 'mixed up' with the growing cosmopolitanism of modern legal education and scholarship. All CTLS students have undertaken their law studies in multiple countries and legal jurisdictions. (How Brexit will impact both CTLS particularly and cosmopolitan legal education more generally remains to be seen.)

I conclude this contribution with a note about my most recent work. As a result of my international dispute resolution work (and strong and not much mentioned here, interdisciplinary law and literature interests), I am now working with a colleague (Italian) who is a mediation and socio-legal scholar, on a study of Elena Ferrante's *My Brilliant Friend* series of novels (*Neapolitan Novels*),[30] in the original Italian, *Mi Amica Geniale*, to study exactly the kinds of issues this volume interrogates. Ferrante's women grow up outside of Naples and span the turbulent period of Italian politics (including socialism, communism, and organised crime) from the late 1950s to the present. Professor Maria (Marica) Moscati and I have engaged in field trips to study the 'neighbourhood' (rapidly changing, now including Chinese immigrant workers making 'Made in Italy' leather goods) as well as literary and legal analysis of the different 'informal' approaches to conflict 'handling' (not resolution) demonstrated in the novel. As formal law and government are mostly absent from Mafia-controlled streets (until some political activists are actually 'disappeared' by the state [through imprisonment and violence]), we are studying the power of informal processes and patterns of

[28] C Arjona, A Jamal, C Menkel-Meadow, V Ramraj, and F Satiro, 'The Many Senses of Sen: A Review Essay' (2012) 8(1) *International Journal of Law in Context* 155–78.

[29] C Menkel-Meadow, V Ramraj, S Routh and A Thiruvengadam, *Amartya Sen and Law* (London, Taylor & Francis, 2020).

[30] E Ferrante, *My Brilliant Friend* (Europa Editions, 2012), Book One of *The Neapolitan Novels*.

conflict in a dramatic culture with women's stories at the centre. Surprising to us (and probably to our eventual readers), our multi-disciplinary, multi-cultural, feminist influenced perspectives are illuminating that conflict and gender are very complicatedly related to each other (in different contexts). As Ferrante notes, '[w]hile men were always getting furious, they calmed down in the end, women who appeared to be silent, acquiescent, when they were angry flew into a rage that had no end.'[31] As informal feminist power is currently manifesting itself in many fora (eg, the #metoo movement) we have a perfect laboratory both to study 'invisible institutions' and processes within a fictive world that illuminates the particularity of locations not always studied traditionally by socio-legal scholars (young girls growing into adulthood in a lawless and male dominated world) and to map the ways that power and conflict modalities are far more complex and variegated than traditional theory (and practice) would have it. Perhaps, in some settings, and often with fewer harmful global consequences, women may make more conflict than men, with each other, and with those who both torment and love them, as human agency takes more complicated and less predictable forms, away from dominant theoretical and Global North legal and narrative scripts and schemas.

As the new generations of globalised and cosmopolitan socio-legal scholars go forth to study places that haven't been studied, conceptualised or well documented before, with a more diverse set of researchers and frameworks, we will be able to explore more sites of human activity, outside of conventional socio-legal locations, with a more complex set of actors and perhaps different explanatory ideas.

[31] Ibid, 38.

D

Learning to be a Legal Anthropologist

EVE DARIAN SMITH

I left Australia in 1990, disillusioned with my three-year stint as a corporate lawyer in what was then the largest law firm in the country. My secondment to BHP to essentially help dupe Indigenous communities in South Australia into allowing uranium mining on their lands was the last straw. Earlier as a graduate student I had stumbled on a book in the library by Sally Falk Moore and was entranced. This was at a time before the internet existed and I had to look up what university she was at in a huge tome in the library. I wrote a letter to her on an electric typewriter asking if I could come and study with her in the United States.

I loved learning from Sally and particularly her class titled 'Anthropological Approaches to Law' that she taught to hundreds of sceptical Harvard law students, engaging them in cargo cults in the South Pacific, rituals among New Guinean tribes, and stockpiling yams in the Trobriand Islands. I remember the students' shocked sensibilities when she told them that if they were ever lost in the bush without water it was okay to drink one's urine. Despite moments of satisfaction, I gradually become alarmed by the discipline's generally apolitical stance. I wanted to study the historical legacies of colonial racism and injustice as they intersected with the fast-moving changes of a new legal world of supranationalism that talked of transnational flows of goods, services and people, and the concurrent delinking of sovereignty, territory, citizenship and democracy. It was the early 1990s, the Maastricht Treaty has just been passed, and there was much optimism about the European Union. I wanted to study what ordinary people thought about the so-called New Europe, and how they imagined themselves navigating an emerging pluralist and overlapping legal landscape. How was the EU going to reshape the concept of sovereignty?

However, for such a study I did not have the analytical and theoretical framework or even the vocabulary. It is hard to believe but back then the word globalisation was rarely used (as late as 1995 I had a senior colleague rush down the corridor and agitatedly ask 'what is all this nonsense about globalisation?'). Apart from lack of vocabulary and analytical concepts, a major problem was that there was no study I could point to as a model to help me explain what I wanted to do. When I talked about my research, everyone said that I was doing was a study of nationalism. But I insisted that I was not, that I was trying to explore processes that were impacting nationalism but were not framed or contained by the nation-state as the unit of analysis.

In addition to not being able to theoretically explain what I wanted to study, my methods appeared to be all wrong. I was being trained to be a legal anthropologist engaged in ethnographic research. Anthropologists traditionally do ethnographies of people in far-away lands, in small villages where they can chart kinship ties, map linguistical genealogies, and thoroughly immerse themselves in another 'culture'. Given these localised methods, how could one do an ethnography of unfolding European legal processes?

I am not sure what made me so obstinate. Maybe my experience as a volunteer in a legal aid office in Melbourne, where I had listened to Greek and Turkish migrants talking about their very different understandings of law, gave me an early appreciation of the cultural dimensions of legal engagement. I surmised that developing a supranational EU legal system was not going to be easy. I was stubborn and pushed on, deciding that I would study the building of the Channel Tunnel as a focus for analysing shifting responses in England to the 'penetration' of the island nation by the European Union. I wanted to reverse the intellectual gaze and apply postcolonial theory to the perceived colonisation of Britain by the New Europe. I was fascinated by people's responses to the debates for and against the EU, and the different reactions to new opportunities such as those emerging in Scotland. I was particularly interested in how the opening of borders and the transfer of goods, services and people were creating new opportunities, as well as concurrently fostering the closing of minds and sowing seeds of nationalist discontent that would – decades later – fuel the Brexit movement.

Fortunately, at the University of Chicago where I ended up doing up doing the doctorate, my advisor, John Comaroff, let me explore research topics without interference. After receiving funding, I flew off to England to do fieldwork under the supervision of Peter Fitzpatrick who graciously did not grill me about my nebulous research plans. I wrote like a mad woman, and in 1995 finished the dissertation and was very lucky to secure an anthropology job at the University of California Santa Barbara. A year later, Susan Silbey, then President of the Law and Society Association, gave what I considered a mind-blowing public address titled 'Let Them Eat Cake: Globalization, Postmodern Colonialism, and the Possibilities of Justice'.[1] I was totally convinced that I wanted to study law and globalisation and that a socio-legal department was where I wanted to be. And so shortly after receiving tenure in 1999, I packed up my office and moved to an adjacent building to chair the Law and Society Program. The next year – much to my complete

[1] S Silbey, 'Let Them Eat Cake: Globalization, Postmodern Colonialism, and the Possibilities of Justice' (1997) 31 *Law & Society Review* 207.

surprise – my book *Bridging Divides*[2] received the Law and Society Association book prize for being an innovative ethnography of law and globalisation.

I. Law and Globalisation – Challenging Modernist Assumptions

Over the ensuing decade I read widely and became increasingly dissatisfied with the literature on globalisation, with its obsessive recounting of 'time-space compression' and the world's increasing integration through transnational flows of labour, markets, technologies, products and so on. Most of the literature – then and now – argued that globalisation, and the increasing mobility of goods, people, capital and information, was driven by the economy and coincided with emerging markets in Southeast Asia and the BRICS countries. Within law and society scholarship, studies of law and globalisation largely reinforced the determinist model of market forces driving legal innovation.

Throughout the early years of the new century there emerged a small but growing body of law and society scholarship on international arbitration, internationally oriented law firms, transnational legal fields, international policing, international human rights, international legal education, international constitutionalism and so on. Most of this scholarship raised new research questions and advanced theoretical frameworks. However, almost all of it ultimately relied upon a comparative state framework that sought to place US-based scholarship on a specific topic up against its counterpoints in Asian, Latin American or European countries. The state-centrist model was largely taken-for-granted, as was the notion of law being geopolitically bounded to coincide with modernist assumptions of territory, jurisdiction, sovereignty and legal actors as identified by national affiliation. I believe this limited intellectual imagination largely reflected the economic and political dominance of the United States on the world stage at the time. And I believe it also reflected the rather staid and self-satisfied disciplines of law, sociology, criminology and political science that form the training of the majority of US law and society scholars.

I found myself increasingly arguing against the inherent state-centrism within the emerging body of so-called law and globalisation scholarship. This led me to challenge the conventional law and society approach that takes 'law' and 'society' as pre-existing and fixed analytical frames, which seemed to me no longer viable in a world of overlapping and competing legal systems and emerging alternatives of non-state legal power. It also led me to become increasingly frustrated by scholarly investigations that overlooked the voice of ordinary people impacted by global

[2] E Darian Smith, *Bridging Divides. The Channel Tunnel and English Legal Identity in the New Europe* (Berkeley CA, University of California Press, 1998).

forces. Much of the emerging literature was about companies, agencies, arbitrators, lawyers, judges and investors, and when scholars did conduct interviews these tended to be with (white male) legal elites. This rubbed me up the wrong way. I am not arguing that a legal elite is unimportant, but to study them alone is to tell only part of the story.

I hold a very strong belief that socio-legal scholars cannot ignore the myriad ways that globalisation affects people. This includes a relatively small, cosmopolitan, plane-hopping elite as well as the many millions of ordinary people from various classes, cultures, ethnicities, and regions of the world impacted by forces beyond their control such as climate change, mass migration, and surveillance capitalism. To me a global socio-legal perspective means adopting a 'global imaginary' that destabilises our modern linear understandings of what law is, where law appears, and how law works. This requires us to be mindful of legal processes that impact elites and non-elites in the Global North and Global South. This is a matter of ethics, but it is also necessary if scholarship produced in the Euro-American academy is to remain relevant. My book *Laws and Societies in Global Contexts* was the outcome of this line of thinking.[3] It did not sit particularly well with most US-based law and society scholars, but despite that was well received in other socio-legal communities and from what I understand is taught in law and society programmes around the world.

II. Diversifying Scholarly Communities

In my efforts to push back against intellectual parochialism and the assumed superiority of the Euro-American academy, I fought hard to make the Law and Society Association more accessible to non-Western scholars as well as minority scholars trained within the United States. As a three-time elected trustee member, this became my constant goal, to broaden and diversify attendance at annual meetings and help minority and non-US scholars participate in the governance of the Association itself. Alongside other scholars fighting the same cause, the international membership of the Association has steadily increased. This has been enabled through grants and giving awards to scholars from less wealthy parts of the world to offset the costs of travel and so on. Another important milestone was the election of Laura Gomez to be President of the Association in 2009, the only scholar of colour at the time to have achieved this stature since its founding in 1964.

My efforts to help diversify and internationalise law and society scholarship are not made without self-interest. As already noted, I believe that without a constant interrogation of our taken-for-granted assumptions and willingness to learn

[3] E Darian-Smith, *Laws and Societies in Global Contexts* (Cambridge, Cambridge University Press, 2013).

from those with different worldviews, mainstream socio-legal scholarship will become irrelevant. In pointing this out, I have been pejoratively called a 'scrappy Australian' a few times by senior scholars. More positively, I have been involved in many wonderful conversations over the years with (typically) junior researchers, many from the Global South, seeking to engage on issues of legal pluralism and non-Western legal processes. One of the joys of getting older is that I can help these early career scholars with advice on how to publish, where to present their work, and how ultimately to be acknowledged as having something important to add to socio-legal conversations.

Another pleasure is witnessing the rising prominence of legal anthropology as a critical field of inquiry. When I started out many years ago, legal anthropologists were a very marginalised subset within socio-legal circles. There were only a few people studying the cultural dimensions of legal processes, let alone doing bottom-up ethnographic research that took seriously ordinary people's insights about law. Since then, legal anthropology has seen somewhat of a resurgence as more scholars start appreciating that the universalistic assumptions embedded within Western law are no longer tenable or effective in practice. While I rarely identify myself as a legal anthropologist, I am very pleased by this general reception to insights about power, racism and law that legal anthropology tends to point to.

Within and beyond anthropology, a surge of critical scholarship is now engaged with questioning the degree to which global processes – however articulated – may be impacting how people think about law and its legitimacy in the first place. A case in point is today's crisis of democracy and the rise of global authoritarianism that underscore the woeful inadequacies of our prevailing modernist state-centred paradigm. Similarly, catastrophic futures wrought by climate change, surveillance capitalism, mass migrations and pandemics call for imagining a very different kind of global legal order that can no longer dismiss the majority of the world's population. In this vein I have been very involved in promoting the emerging field of Global Studies in the United States and in many other parts of the world. Global Studies is a critical interdisciplinary field that embraces the social sciences and humanities, all the while acknowledging the deep histories of colonialism, imperialism, and capitalism that shape our contemporary moment. Global Studies views legal processes as one dimension of complex interactions that occur across a local–global continuum. As a result, law and globalisation is now being studied by a new generation of scholars who may not belong to law schools or identify with law and society scholarship at all. This expansion of intellectual work beyond socio-legal networks promises new thinking about law in a global world from which we can all benefit. I am personally very excited by the possibilities, though I imagine there may be some who are not. The key for law and society scholars, particularly those trained in the Global North, is to be flexible and inclusive thinkers and embrace potential critique rather than dismiss it. This is because we are all necessarily facing a 'global turn' in our thinking about law – whether or not we are willing to admit it.

E

Living in the Contradiction: Globalisation and its Discontents

DAVID M TRUBEK

I have engaged with some aspect of globalisation for much of my career. But I seem always to find myself at the intersection of competing and contradictory impulses about the processes and their impact, trying to manage my ambivalence, and living in the contradiction between different visions and possibilities.

I started my academic career in the 1960s. Fresh from working in the field as a USAID lawyer,[1] I hoped to build an academic specialty in 'law and development'. I saw this as an emancipatory project: by building legal systems in developing countries we would foster political liberty and help reduce poverty. My initial idea was to apply modernisation theory to build positive knowledge about law's role in development. This, I thought, would guide legal transplants from advanced countries and chart the way for other reforms. But no sooner had I launched this effort than I found myself criticising the entire enterprise as ethnocentric and neo-colonial. By the 1970s I had emerged as a major critic of my own earlier efforts.

As I learned more about 'law' and about 'development', I found myself confronting contradictions. While in an earlier article I had used liberal legalist principles to attack the military regime in Brazil,[2] by the mid-1970s I was questioning whether we could or should export these same principles.[3] Later, I championed globalisation as a way to lift millions out of poverty and welcomed the rise of international economic law as an instrument of global integration, but then helped launch a critical examination of the effects these laws were having.[4] I helped manage a major

[1] The United States Agency for International Development (USAID) – a US government-run international development agency.

[2] HJ Steiner and DM Trubek, 'Brazil: All Power to the Generals' (1971) 49 *Foreign Affairs* 464–79.

[3] DM Trubek and M Galanter, 'Scholars in Self-Estrangement: Reflections on the Crisis in Law and Development Studies in the United States' (1974) *Wisconsin Law Review* 1062–1102.

[4] A Santos, C Thomas and DM Trubek, (eds), *World Trade and Investment Law Reimagined: A Progressive Agenda for an Inclusive Globalization: A Progressive Agenda for World Trade Law*, (London, Anthem Press, 2019).

study of corporate lawyers in developing countries[5] but I have remained sceptical of claims that their rise would foster democratic values. I devoted a lot of time to helping Brazilian lawyers adapt to globalisation and then pointed out that this was reproducing hierarchy.[6]

One could put these contradictory behaviours and views down to an unwillingness to make decisions or a desire to have things both ways. Or they could be seen as a mature recognition of the complexity and contradiction inherent in social life and an effort to navigate it. Could my effort to live in and try to manage contradiction have something to do with my family origins, which included contradictory and competing values and traditions? My mother's roots went back before the American Revolution and included both Protestants and Catholics who lived in the South; my great grandparents had a farm on the Chattahoochee River in western Georgia. My father's family were recently-arrived German-speaking secularised Jews from the Baltics, living in the New York City area; my paternal grandfather had a Doctorate in Chemistry from the Riga Polytechnic and a Medal from the Tsar. In my family there was a tension between my father's success in business and his affinity for left-wing politics, and a latent ambivalence in my mother's efforts to be a conventional suburban housewife while thinking more like the semi-bohemian artist she had been – and still was at heart.

My sense of contradiction could be further affected by the feeling of being an outsider that my family's anomalous position helped foster in the posh upper-middle-class WASP suburbs where I grew up and went to school. Or it could be a result of the tension between my desire to manage big enterprises and create and reform institutions while at the same time maintaining a critical sensitivity. But for whatever reason, I often found myself living in the contradiction when it came to globalisation. To better understand how that felt, let me recount a couple of episodes.

A. Promoting Law and Development and Learning about its Global and Structural Embeddedness

I started thinking about the relationship between laws from the North and 'development' in the South as a lawyer for USAID. When I started at USAID in

[5] I served as co-director of the Project on Globalization, Lawyers and Emerging Economies (GLEE): https://clp.law.harvard.edu/clp-research/globalization/. For an overview of this project and its major findings, see D Wilkins, DM Trubek and B Fong, 'Globalization, Lawyers and Emerging Economies: The Rise, Transformation, and Significance of the New Corporate Legal Ecosystem in India, Brazil and China' (2020) 61 *Harvard International Law Journal* (forthcoming). HLS Center on the Legal Profession Research Paper No 2019-1.

[6] DM Trubek and C Alves, 'Legal Education Failures, Spontaneous Bypasses, and the Reproduction of Hierarchy in Brazil: Some Preliminary Thoughts' (2020) *Brazilian Journal of Institutional Studies* (*Revista de Estudos Institucionais*) (forthcoming).

1962, I shared the common view that developing countries needed 'modern laws' and that meant laws from the US. Also, working for the USAID Mission to Brazil from 1964–66, I was frustrated by the government lawyers I engaged with. Whilst I was taught that law was flexible, they saw it as rigid. Whilst I was taught that lawyers should be problem-solvers, they seemed happy to create obstacles and step away. So I cheerfully embraced modernisation theory, supported legal transplants, and promoted the reform of Brazilian legal education along US lines as a way to create 'modern' (read US-style) lawyers.

I thought the 'law and development' enterprise was an emancipatory mission, promising both freedom and an escape from poverty. That led me to help found the Yale Law School Program on Law and Modernization with a massive grant from USAID. The Program, the first organised effort to construct an academic field of law and development, brought together lawyers and academics from all over the world with US social scientists and Yale Law School professors and students.[7]

As the Program developed and we learned more about what was going on in the developing world, doubts crept in. The first were practical. Struggling with barriers to the import of US laws, we began to question the neo-evolutionary narrative that lay behind the transplant enterprise. I came to appreciate the local embeddedness of legal orders and the local specificity of developmental solutions. I realised that economic reform through law was a much more challenging task than we had thought, and came to understand the limits of foreign experts and expertise.

The second doubts were political: I had thought that making Brazilian law more modern and helping Brazilian lawyers become more problem-oriented would – by that very fact – be promoting liberal and democratic values as well as economic efficiency. But I learned that a more flexible law and more pragmatic lawyers can as easily support authoritarian legalism as foster democracy. Indeed, I was forced to take seriously the view that the very legal formalism that had shocked my Yale Law School post-realist sensibility was as likely to be a source of resistance to authoritarianism as was US pragmatism.

These doubts about the original law and development idea were reinforced by contacts with people in the Yale Program, including social scientists like Laura Nader and Marc Galanter and advanced students like Francis Snyder, Duncan Kennedy and Boaventura de Sousa Santos. In seminars, conferences and working papers they criticised our early ideas about modernisation theory and about law's role in development. Ironically, the Program that USAID funded to lend academic support to its programming in law became a leading source of critique of its efforts. This critique was crystallised in the article I wrote with Galanter entitled 'Scholars in Self-Estrangement: Reflections on the Crisis in Law and

[7] This program operated between 1968 and 1975 and received over US$1 million from USAID. See R Abel and DM Trubek, 'Inventing the Field of Law and Development: The Short Happy Life of the Yale Program in Law & Modernization' (forthcoming).

Development Studies in the United States,' which is to this day the most widely cited article in the field.[8]

While all these things started my gradual move away from the initial law and development movement, it took a major change in my whole frame of reference to cement that transition. This came about through my exposure to Immanuel Wallerstein. B.W. (Before Wallerstein) I, like many others, thought of 'development' as something contained within each country. External forces could help – that is where foreign aid came in – but the structures impeding development were internal and the changes needed came largely from within. And then along came Wallerstein. I first heard him speak at the Latin American Studies Association sometime in the 1980s. He made a devastating critique of modernisation theory and set forth a new way of thinking about 'development'. Wallerstein posited an integrated world system; rejected the idea that the nation-state was the proper focus for analysis; drew attention to transnational structures that constrain development; and questioned the ideal types of 'tradition' versus 'modernity' and the related assumption that all countries must follow a single path of evolution.[9]

It took a while for this to sink in. But I remember sitting by the beach in Recife, a city in Brazil that was once part of the Dutch and then the Portuguese empire, had been affected by the English and French, and was now under US influence, and thinking: *We have to start all over.* The process we want to change, the tools we hope to use, indeed, our very identities, are created by, and caught up in, complex global structures. Unless we understand that, we will understand nothing and change nothing. By the time I had digested Wallerstein and all the rest of the emerging critical ideas, I had come a long way from the simple export of US law and legal education.

Was it time, I thought, to chuck the whole thing? If 'development' could really be a mode of capitalist exploitation of the periphery, containing, within its very structure, limits on equitable growth in the Third World (as it was then called), what was left of the idea of law and development as an emancipatory enterprise? Were academics like myself no more than representatives of a hegemonic global capitalist class, and our Third World counterparts, mere compradors?

This led to a period of soul-searching. I could not deny that the Wallerstein model caught elements of the reality around me. When added to the other critiques it made me question the whole project I had launched during my time in Brazil. Can I live in the contradiction between the emancipatory vision that animated me in the first place and the complex reality that had been revealed? Should I get out of this business and take up something less fraught?

[8] Trubek and Galanter (1974), n 3 above. For a discussion of the history of the article see Ruth Buchanan, 'A Crisis and its Afterlife: Some Reflections on 'Scholars in Self-Estrangement' in G de Burca, C Kilpatrick and J Scott (eds), *Critical Perspectives on Global Governance* (Oxford, Hart Publishing, 2014); See also DM Trubek, 'Law and Development: Forty Years after "Scholars in Self Estrangement"' (2016) 66 *University of Toronto Law Journal* 301–29.

[9] Carlos A Martínez-Vela, 'World Systems Theory' (2001): https://web.mit.edu/esd.83/www/notebook/WorldSystem.pdf.

In the end, I decided to stick with it and continue my practice as a law and development theorist and reformer. I recognised the power of global capitalism and its possible negative effects. I saw that law and development efforts could be used to support authoritarian regimes. I saw the effects of global and transnational structures. But I rejected the determinism and fixed hierarchies of the world-system model. I stayed with my initial vision and looked for ways that emancipatory goals could be pursued *within* these structures.

I felt there was a need for a critical approach to law and development. I saw the importance of documenting both the exercise of power and resistances to it; the failures of transplants and the successes of alternative approaches to reform; the limits of exporting liberal principles and the ways rights could still be protected. I thought it essential to help students entering the field of law and development to understand the mission, grasp the complexity, and learn, as I had, to live in the contradiction.[10] I worked with others to ensure that critical approaches to law were embedded in the law and development enterprise and these discourses became available world-wide.[11]

B. Welcoming Globalisation and Critiquing International Economic Law

I started my encounter with development studies and policy in the era of Import Substitution Industrialization (IRI). The IRI era was marked by closed economies and state-led growth. Like modernisation theory, IRI saw the national economy as essentially a closed space: the aim was to build industry to serve that space. Because local markets were seen as weak, the state was expected to fill the gap at least temporarily. To carry out this project, the state had to occupy key sectors of the economy, subsidise private firms, and close the economy to imports of competing industrial products while 'infant industries' grew up behind tariff walls. As a lawyer working in Brazil I encountered the Law of Similars, the legal embodiment of ISI and an elaborate system designed to keep 'similar' products – from cars to Scotch whisky – out of the local market.

But then came the 'Asian miracle' which ushered in the age of export-led growth (ELG). Simultaneously we saw the neo-liberal turn in development strategy. The

[10] DM Trubek, 'The Owl and the Pussy Cat: Is There a Future for Law and Development?' (2007) 25 *Wisconsin International Law Journal* 235.

[11] See Duncan Kennedy, 'The Globalization of Critical Discourses on Law: Thoughts on David Trubek's Contribution' in de Burca, Fitzpatrick and Scott (2014), n 8 above. A major ally in this effort was the critical enterprise launched by David and Duncan Kennedy at Harvard and currently institutionalised as the Harvard Institute for Global Law and Policy. This group supported work that led to DM Trubek and A Santos (eds), *The New Law and Economic Development: A Critical Appraisal* (Cambridge, Cambridge University Press, 2006). I also have been privileged to work with critical law and development scholars in Brazil, especially the informal network led by Mario Schapiro and Diogo Coutinho that is based at the FGV Law School in São Paulo and the University of São Paulo.

result was that both state-led growth and ISI policies were challenged: opponents argued that the state was not capable of making efficient choices and ISI led to inefficient domestic industries. They promised that neo-liberalism would unleash the power of domestic and global markets. By opening markets and reducing the heavy hand of the state, a global market would arise that would make the most efficient use of scarce resources. ELG, at least as managed by the Asian Tigers,[12] would create world-class industries that could compete in advanced markets, harnessing the buying power of affluent societies to the task of eradicating poverty in the Global South.

The ELG and the neo-liberal era brought about a global shift: countries like Brazil, India and China which had been committed to state-led growth and ISI gradually liberalised their economies, privatising State Owned Enterprises, lowering tariff barriers, and facilitating investment from advanced countries including investment to create industries that would export to the advanced markets. Technological changes made global value chains possible, connecting workers in the poor countries with markets in advanced ones.

Globalisation held out promise of freedom from want. It transformed the Asian Tigers and allowed China to bring millions out of poverty. Overall, like law and development, globalisation seemed to be an emancipatory enterprise. I welcomed the creation of new field of law, called international economic law (IEL), which emerged to encourage and govern transnational flows and maintain pro-market policies. I supported efforts in Brazil and elsewhere to adapt legal education to the demands of a globalised economy. Becoming Dean of International Studies at the University of Wisconsin–Madison in the 1990s, I sought to orient the University's resources not just to the study but also to the facilitation of globalisation. This involved creation of global studies programs in several parts of the University, including the Law School, the Medical School, the Business School and the Institute for Regional and International Studies. I worked with colleagues in universities around the world to develop global and transnational approaches to law.

I would have been glad to be called a 'globalist'. And then came Milanovic's Elephant Curve.[13] Like Wallerstein before him, Bronco Milanovic led me to rethink earlier ideas and see the complexity of global processes. His research on the distributive effects of globalisation brought to light troubling effects of a process I had championed with such enthusiasm. Milanovic's chart showed

[12] The four Asian countries that underwent rapid industrialisation between the early 1960s and 1990s: Hong Kong, Singapore, South Korea and Taiwan.

[13] B Milanovic, *Global Inequality: A New Approach for the Age of Globalization* (Cambridge / Boston MA, Harvard University Press, 2016); see also Facundo Alvaredo, Lucas Chancel, Thomas Piketty, Emmanuel Saez, Gabriel Zucman, 'The elephant curve of global inequality and growth' (December 2017): https://wid.world/document/elephant-curve-global-inequality-growth-wid-world-working-paper-2017-20/.

that almost all the poor in developing countries, except those in the poorest countries, had benefited immensely from globalisation. But he also showed that the working- and middle-classes in the advanced countries had fallen backwards as the rich there and everywhere soared ahead. As the academic literature on the distributional effects of globalisation grew, evidence of these trends began to emerge in the popular press. We saw that some regions in the advanced world had been devastated by the effects of global trade while others grew precipitously. We saw that the neo-liberal attack on the state and on social protection had aggravated the negative effects of globalisation. This fuelled populist and nationalist fires and led to calls to halt globalisation by de-coupling the world economy. For some, 'globalist' became a term of abuse.

The Elephant Curve

Unequal distribution

From 1988 to 2008, income gains were greatest for people around the 50th percentile of the global distribution (point A) and among the richest 1 percent (point C). Gains were lowest among people around the 80th percentile globally (point B), most of whom are in the lower middle class of developed economies.

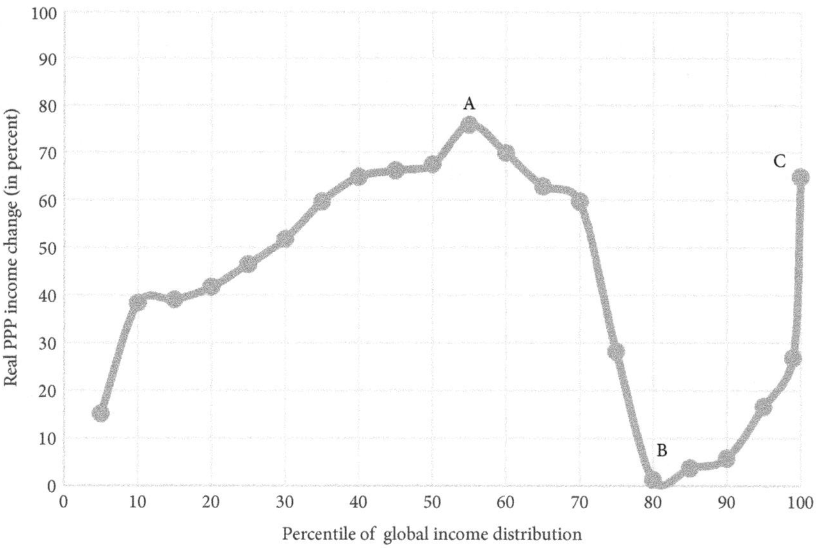

Source: Branko Milanovic.
Note: PPP = Purchasing power parity.

Looking at all this, I found myself once again in a contradiction. I thought that the potential for reducing world poverty through globalisation was far from over. But I could not deny the costs that had occurred through open global markets; the pain that many had experienced; the widening gap between the rich and everyone else especially in the North. I rejected calls to roll back globalisation and de-couple the integrated world economy. I searched for ways to keep globalisation going while ensuring that losses were compensated for and gains more fairly distributed.

I saw a need to sharpen the critique of those legal institutions that had contributed to this situation. Along with Alvaro Santos and Chantal Thomas I brought together a group of international economic law scholars to analyse the distributive effects of world trade and investment law. With the support of the Institute for Global Law and Policy at Harvard, we produced a book of essays entitled *World Trade and Investment Law Reimagined: A Progressive Agenda for an Inclusive Globalization.*[14] The book brought together critiques of IEL with progressive ideas for reform, showing how the negative aspects of globalisation might be limited and losers compensated without the kind of de-coupling that would end prospects for using global markets to further reduce world poverty.

'Inclusive globalization' had a nice sound. But really it just restated the dilemma rather than resolve it. We really do not know the distributional effects of alternative strategies but there are sure to be tradeoffs between protecting workers in the North and expanding production in the South. The effort to find an emancipatory path today runs head-on into the emerging US–China Cold War. Anyone seeking to keep the poverty-reduction engine of globalisation going today will have to take on a powerful anti-globalisation coalition what has crystallised around cutting ties between the US and China.[15] There is no simple solution, no silver bullet that will maintain globalisation while ensuring the welfare of all. And so once again I found myself trying to pursue an emancipatory vison while embracing contradictory ideas and confronting an all-too complex reality. And once again I decided to plough ahead: living in the contradiction, I sought allies and solutions, tried to set new ideas in motion, and helped diffuse a critical discourse on globalisation and its discontents.

[14] A Santos, C Thomas, DM Trubek, *World Trade and Investment Law Reimagined: A Progressive Agenda for an Inclusive Globalization* (London/New York, Anthem Press, 2019).

[15] In a blog post I noted that anti-globalisation forces included groups concerned with the profits of import-competing business, those who were worried about declining workers' wages, those who saw China's rise as threatening US national security, and those who wanted to use trade policy to challenge Chinese violations of human rights. These trade hawks had coalesced around a Cold War approach to trade with China and were a formidable opposition to efforts like those promoted in our book and by Dani Rodrik and people in China who sought a progressive way to handle trade conflicts and achieve globalisation with equity. 'Dani Rodrik and the Hawks: A Field Guide to the China-US Trade War': https://ielp.worldtradelaw.net/2019/11/guest-post-dani-rodrik-and-the-hawks-a-field-guide-to-the-china-us-trade-war.html.

F

Commuting between Academy and Social Movements: Reflections of an Insurgent Feminist

KALPANA KANNABIRAN

My primary effort as an insurgent feminist living and working in south India has been to work at the intersection of social sciences, law, advocacy and public education on rights through social movements. This combination of collaboration in academic work, teaching, and solidarities with collectives/movements on the ground at the international, national and local levels has been instructive in ways that defy description. My own approach has been guided by movement politics imbibed through feminist and civil liberties praxis – small local movements, rather than large mass struggles – over legislative impact. I attempt here to thread together these different strands of my work – hopefully to understand them better myself and of course present a somewhat coherent account. In doing this, I focus on my experience as a rights educator and archivist of movements, rather than my experience with formal teaching in law school. The patterns of collaboration and mutual learning I speak of here straddle my experience in higher education and formal teaching. As an insurgent feminist I have worked with women's movements, Dalit movements, movements for disability rights, Adivasi rights movements, groups engaged in securing minority rights and queer rights collectives. Grappling with interlocking oppressions and forging intersectional solidarities – cross-pollinating learnings between fields was constitutive of my method both in teaching and activism, as were deep conversations around justice, democracy, law, constitution and international human rights standards.

I. Learning about Adivasi Rights

My indecision about where exactly I belong – more in the interstices than within any disciplinary/institutional setting, is reflected directly in my work. An illustration of this is my experience with rights advocacy among Adivasi/indigenous/tribal communities (designated as Scheduled Tribes under the Constitution of India) in the south Indian State of Andhra Pradesh since 1998. By this time, the feminist collective I co-founded, Asmita, had made significant strides in the popularisation of feminist discourse and ideas in the State.

Over two decades, my focus had seen shifts –

(a) as a feminist sociologist interested in the ways in which Adivasi women framed 'the political' in distinct ways, as *Adivasi women*;
(b) as a human rights advocate disseminating and dialoguing constitutionalism among a group of Adivasi community organisers with a rich knowledge of the issues that beset their communities, but little formal education;
(c) as an archivist of an ongoing struggle interested in capturing the moods and resonances of the demand for a separate State of Telangana – finding the distinctive agendas different forest-dwelling Adivasi communities brought to this struggle for statehood;
(d) as a rights educator attempting to provide continuing training and advanced legal education in litigation practices and strategies to lawyers from Adivasi communities;
(e) as a nomadic sociologist travelling around Nallamalla forest trying to grasp the realities of Chenchu life, finding myself working to strengthen community organising around the right to education, building capacity for monitoring student and teacher performance in schools for Chenchu children; and
(f) as an academic administrator and teacher, building a digital resource base on Adivasi Studies to aid researchers working in this area, and working with law students, law graduates and doctoral scholars to sustain a robust conversation around Adivasi rights.

My learnings have been twofold –

(a) the interweaving of the economic and the symbolic – there is a recognition by these communities that the question of equality is tied to economic rights – to land, forest, wages, employment and constitutional protections; and
(b) the realisation that for equality in collaborations to be sustained, self-representation and participation in politics at the local level especially are indispensable.

Law and the Constitution have in my work been the medium of conversations on Adivasi rights and its context. The immersions – mine and the peoples I have worked with – have been in questions of constitutionalism and an understanding of (in)justice predicated on constitutional conversations.

These conversations have simultaneously spoken to several intersecting themes: to name a few, sovereignty and autonomy, self-governance, and particular forms of legal and cultural pluralism that intersect with dispossession, disentitlement, neglect, impunity of state and non-state actors and jurisprudential dissociation.[1]

II. Why Focus on Law?

With formal qualifications in law, I have been a pro bono feminist case counsellor for the past 25 years – never having practised litigation. And although in very recent feminist debates in India, 'due process' is a stern reprimand if not abuse, I have an unshaken faith in the Constitution and in due process as something that must guide not only litigation but also settlements in plural legal spaces, and this is what I have explored and shared in the course of my limited work with Adivasi lawyers and community organisers.

As I look back on this work, it is all part of the same thrust – to build capacity, autonomy, and an understanding of the Constitution and the place of formal courts/legal spaces in the every-day lives of Adivasis within a larger context of inequality and dispossession – the latter especially focusing on [il]legalities and bureaucratic misdemeanours that require a formal counter-engagement within institutional spaces of the law. There have been questions and dilemmas pertaining to the problem of sustainability in rights advocacy: *What happens when the participant rights educator withdraws from the work site? What is the opportune moment for such withdrawal and what ought to be the quality and intensity of continued contact post withdrawal?*

My work has been more in the nature of working with small movements/community-driven networks, attempting to build skills for negotiating with local authorities and courts – support that is mutual, close, immediate and yet distant in that I am a kind of 'absent presence' in the field (if one can call it that). Our work together has been guided by an agreement that the initiative for interventions and documentation must rest with them – the Chenchu of Nallamalla and Koya of Bhadrachalam – and must focus on initiating change – in bureaucratic approaches towards Adivasis, in statutory interpretation, in advocacy, and in (inter- and intra-) community practices that precipitate inequality. In order to share the texture of these engagements, I provide below a brief recapitulation of three such initiatives.

[1] By jurisprudential dissociation, I refer to a set of interpretive practices adopted by courts both in relation to statutory and constitutional claims, that reduce the act of interpretation to a technicality devoid of substantive application of the law. This results in the negation of claims, and most times of justice itself – I have, elsewhere, pointed to a plethora of case-law where jurisprudential dissociation is the judicial strategy to bolster impunity.

A. Adivasi Aikyavedika (United Forum of Adivasis)

During my first interaction with members of the Adivasi Aikyavedika, a loose federation of small community-based groups sprinkled across the State, in 2004, I posed a question: What is law? (*chattam ante emiti*)? The spontaneous and unanimous response was 'Law means 1/70' (*chattam ante* 1/70). It took me a couple of minutes to decode that. Law means Act 1 of 1970, Andhra Pradesh Land Transfer (Regulation) Act, 1970 that prohibits the transfer of land in Schedule 5 areas of the State from scheduled tribe to non-scheduled tribe. I was aware from my earlier work in the Godavari districts in 1998 and 1999, that the one point of focus in struggles for Adivasi autonomy in Andhra Pradesh in recent years has been the demand for stringent enforcement of Act 1/70. However, what I was less prepared for was a response that saw 'the law' and 1/70 as synonymous. Of course, they were aware of various provisions of the Indian Penal Code, and procedure – especially in relation to murder, arrest, bail, and prohibitory orders on assembly – but those were described as murder, cheating, 144, 'bindover', etc., not as '*chattam*' (law). Our conversation meandered along. I asked if they knew of 'fundamental rights' – *praadhamika hakkulu*. They replied that they knew about Schedule 5.[2] When I suggested that fundamental rights figured in the same *chattam* as Schedule 5 – *Raajyaangam*, the Constitution, there was much amusement: 'Is that really what is written? We can't see any of that anywhere around us …'

Importantly, this conversation also helped active interventions at the level of the *gram sabha*,[3] applying constitutional principles of justice, in an autonomous space that was generally governed by local custom, thereby bringing in an intermediation between Constitution and custom – the situation inverted in an important sense. It was no longer a court saying that custom that militated against public law cannot be upheld, but the *gram sabha* saying that the Constitution is a repository of core values that must be respected and affirmed by custom especially because the Constitution recognised autonomy for Adivasis that was their biggest strength in an otherwise 'hostile environment'.

I had the opposite experience of teaching Adivasi rights in a law school, where students knew fundamental rights but were never taught Article 15(1) that prohibits discrimination, Article 17 that proscribes untouchability, Article 19(5) that places restrictions on freedom of movement in Schedule 5 areas, or Schedules 5 and 6 that guarantee autonomy and self-rule in Adivasi homelands. This gap in the teaching of Adivasi rights in law schools is one I will return to briefly in the conclusion.

[2] Schedule 5 of the Indian Constitution, governing administration of Scheduled Areas and Scheduled Tribes.

[3] Village assembly.

B. Koyas of West Godavari

Seven years earlier in 1998–99, I travelled around West Godavari district, preoccupied with understanding the nature and constraints of women's leadership in movements (a long-standing preoccupation), following the land struggles of Koya women around litigation spearheaded by Sakthi, an NGO working in the area.[4] The lands in the 13 villages I visited were declared to be covered by Act 1/70, and returned to the possession of Adivasi families.[5]

My attempt was to explore articulations of governance and citizenship by the Koya women of West Godavari that emerged in the course of the struggle for land rights. In fighting for repossession of Adivasi lands, the State figures as a complex, multi-layered entity, both ally and adversary, central yet marginal, shaping local politics and being shaped by it. References to 'the State' are indispensable to any recounting of the land struggle. As has already been detailed, the struggle began as a demand for the implementation of the Land Transfer (Regulation) Act (Act 1/70) passed by the State legislature. On the ground, therefore, it was a demand for accountability on the part of functionaries of the State. In an important sense, the State, in passing this legislation and others of this kind, makes itself an ally of Adivasis. While making this demand, however, Adivasis become acutely aware of the fact that 'the State' itself is a splintered entity – in fact, perhaps not 'an entity' at all.

When they asked for the implementation of the legislation, Koya women had to negotiate with two sets of functionaries – the officials of the *mandal* revenue department and the police. When they went to the office of the mandal revenue officer (MRO), they found the non-tribal farmers being entertained by the MRO. On seeing the Adivasi women, the MRO's first reaction was, 'Move! Move! Koya Stink! Move!'. The police, who in fact were there to safeguard the rights of the Adivasis through the implementation of constitutional provisions, instead went into one village after another threatening to rape Koya women if they persisted in their demands. When the threats did not dampen their spirit, cases were booked against these women and they were imprisoned for four to six weeks.

Notwithstanding this coercion, in accordance with court orders, non-tribal farmers were not allowed to enter any of these villages, and the Koya cultivated as much land as they could afford, and shared the produce between villages and

[4] The respondents in these petitions were the government of Andhra Pradesh; the district collector, West Godavari; the special deputy collector, tribal welfare; Sakthi (a voluntary organisation impleaded through a government order in 1992); and 122 tribal people who impleaded themselves through a court order in 1997. Of these 122 tribal people, 63 were women between the ages of 18 and 60 years.

[5] Thirteen villages in two *mandals* – Jeelugumilli and Buttayigudem – of the West Godavari district of Andhra Pradesh. The villages are: Panduvarigudem and Patachevulavarigudem, hamlets of Darbhagudem village, Vangavarigudem, Barrenkulapadu colony, Taatiramannagudem, Chandramma colony and Sirivarigudem hamlets of Jeelugumilli village, and Palacherla Rajavaram, in Jeelugumilli mandal; Kangalavarigudem, Kommavarigudem, and Regulagunta hamlets of Lakshmudugudem village, Bhoosarajupalli, and Marlagudem in Buttayigudem mandal.

families. Some villages cultivated jointly, while others divided the land up with each family taking responsibility for what was under its control. All the women interviewed were, however, clear that they did not want joint cultivation to carry on indefinitely, because it was only when individual families had complete control over their land that they would act responsibly towards it.

Having won a major battle, the women and men were unsure of where they should go from here. Speaking of the importance of the *panchayat*,[6] one of the men in Barrenkulapadu colony said,

> Only men can be sarpanches. What do women know? It is because we are hot blooded and prone to rash acts that *we pushed the women forward* in the struggle. That was the only way we could ensure that the struggle was relatively peaceful (emphasis added).

Women in another village, Marlagudem, said in the presence of the men, 'If we had left matters to our men, they would have been bought over by the non-tribal farmers long ago. *It was our obstinacy that sustained our gains* and kept the land with us …' and, 'We have got a handful of earth. We must not let go of it' (emphasis added). Gender lines in Adivasi communities, for me, continue to be the most difficult to speak about even today.

To reach this far, the women in one village kidnapped the MRO, made him walk miles without footwear and gave him gruel to eat when he was so hungry that he begged for food. When he complained that his feet were sore, they reminded him of countless instances when he ordered them to remove their footwear before entering his office; when he asked for food, they asked him how he would eat food given by people who stink. Importantly, the order of the High Court of Andhra Pradesh and the text of Act 1/70 was written on walls of community halls and temples across these villages as a constant reminder to themselves of what they had won. *Are these extralegal routes to legality or is this legal pluralism too?*

Later reports suggested that non-tribal farmers did not need to wait too long to return to the land, regaining control by leasing it from Koya families. Although the observations of the Supreme Court in the *Samatha* judgment,[7] for instance, point directly to the need to pose the Adivasi question in the law differently, this experience points to the fragility of legal victories without a deep and sustained immersion in legal self-representation in a situation of extreme asymmetries of power, managed and sustained by a majoritarian state.

A point to note here is the Adivasi engagement with formal courts and legal procedures. While the processes were formally initiated by non-governmental organisations working with Adivasis in the area, I found that this was strongly backed by village-level mobilisations across the entire area, with Adivasis leading

[6] Governing council of the village.

[7] *Samatha v State of Andhra Pradesh and others*, AIR 1997 SC 3297.

the conversations.[8] The problem, however, still remains that with Adivasi struggles, especially interventions in formal legal processes, there is a continuing absence of indigenous advocates that inhibits the development and sustenance of rights advocacy on the ground. Perhaps as a result of this experience and my experience with Adivasi Aikyavedika, later phases of my work have focused on building litigation skills and knowledge of legal representational practices.

III. Adivasi Lawyers and Self Representation

In this segment I draw on detailed interviews, conversations, and dialogue with a group of 22 lawyers in the first phase; seven lawyers, two community organisers and one school teacher, in the second phase; and four lawyers and two community organisers in the third and current phase. The conversation has meandered and evolved over a period of seven years and began as an attempt to train lawyers from the Scheduled Tribes in litigation and legal practice. The lawyers' programme drew in young male lawyers from Lambada, Yerukula, Koya and Konda Reddy communities. The ones that continued through the second and third phases were the Koya and Konda Reddy, with the Lambada and Yerukula lawyers not opting for a continued engagement. Several of them were already in practice and had connections within the legal fraternity and local politics. This was clearly not the case with the Koya and Konda Reddy at that time in 2012. This disconnect between the experience and access to opportunities of Lambada and Yerukula on the one side and a host of other forest-dwelling tribes on the other has been an extremely contentious one in my daily conversations and work with Adivasis from different communities. The lawyers' group was an all-male group through all three phases. Women rarely got past 12th standard,[9] and when they did, they went towards nursing or skill-building vocational courses, not professional education like law. This appears to be the case across all the tribes in the two States of Telangana and Andhra Pradesh, and for me, poses a major inhibiting factor in rights advocacy.

[8] The struggles for land in Adivasi homelands came to a head in 2019, with the Supreme Court appearing to follow the trail of wildlife conservationists in labelling indigenous forest dwellers 'encroachers' and directing their eviction from forests, rolling the Constitution back through juridical moves. Stopped in its tracks by widespread protests from Adivasi and forest-dwelling communities across the country, the Supreme Court stayed the eviction during the pendency of the hearing (still ongoing). Adivasi leader from Chhattisgarh, the late Abhay Xaxa in a tweet dated 1 March 2019, attributed this juridical volte-face to the fact that 'the supreme court was told that 2 million Adivasis are sharpening their bows and arrows before marching to Delhi … No benevolence.'. With a team of lawyers and NGOs, I coordinated work by the CSD team in putting together detailed evidence from 24 sites spread across 11 States in late 2019, on the problems in implementation of the Forest Rights Act, 2006 – documentation that is aimed at assisting the court in deliberating on the question in an evidence-based manner.

[9] High School graduation level at age 17–18.

But, of all these, the Chenchu of Nallamalla[10] have been marked by disentitlement and dispossession in ways that are far more stark than the others.

There were no Chenchu lawyers in our programme simply because there were very few Chenchu youth who had managed to continue with an education beyond high school. Those that did tended to opt for a diploma in education and become government school teachers in the ashram schools – the only avenue to government employment available to educated Adivasi youth in this area. Our later sustained work on education and schooling in Nallamalla forest showed us that the biggest problem that the Chenchu faced was being able to continue and complete a formal education until high school. There were/still are practically no Chenchu in higher/tertiary education – our interventions in Nallamalla therefore have focused on providing Chenchu teachers with the opportunity to monitor and ensure retention in schools. Interestingly, the opening in Nallamalla was provided by a visit during the height of the movement for a separate Telangana in 2009, when one of them mentioned that his father was Haimendorf's host in Nallamalla,[11] and offered me his non-literate, 95-year-old father's very old and precious copy of Haimendorf's book on the Chenchu – which all of them knew about and had checked to ascertain that their family names had been included.

IV. By Way of Conclusion …

In this note, I have attempted to examine the possibilities of justice that may be realised through radical approaches to understanding, teaching and researching sociology, law, gender studies and Adivasi rights – to evolve a framework for justice that provides the tools to put in place an imagination of what I like to see as the 'Constitution-as-commons.' In attempting this, I have adopted an insurgent feminist approach that is self-reflexive, critical, inclusive and constructive. Basically, this has meant examining the idea of justice in all its complexity – in a holistic sense, not in terms of personal gains and losses, but in terms of societal transformation towards greater equality. And there can be no 'trade-offs' in this. The non-negotiables must be set such that justice is at the centre of social science endeavour, and law a tool that may be used creatively to multiply this larger goal.

I have always hoped for effective intervention and the promise of delivery. The struggle is unceasing as we see with the Supreme Court orders on forest

[10] A forested range of hills spanning the southern districts of the States of Telangana and Andhra Pradesh.

[11] Christoph von Fürer-Haimendorf (1909–95). Austrian ethnologist and professor at the London School for African and Oriental Studies who studied tribal cultures in north east India and The Deccan for 40 years. Haimendorf wrote a monograph titled *The Chenchus: Jungle Folk of the Deccan* in 1946 when he was invited to Hyderabad State by the Nizam of Hyderabad.

rights (2019)[12] and Adivasi teachers (2020).[13] Questions of law, Constitution and justice re-surface around the same concerns, with dominant hegemonic control over institutions of justice tightening their hold. The question of representation on benches and at the bar has never been more urgent, and yet that is where we have made the least progress. In addressing these gaps in pedagogy and practice, I brought law school students together for a national moot court competition on Adivasi rights in 2015 – possibly the only one of its kind both in the thematic focus and in its location outside a law school. We lacked the resources to make this a regular feature.

I have also hoped that my work – even while I enjoyed it immensely and did it for the sheer joy it gave me – would be relevant both to societies like ours and societies unlike ours. I am interested in the flow of ideas and in contributing to an environment that fosters debate and deliberation on the possible contours of Dr Ambedkar's[14] idea of constitutional morality. It is for our generation and the coming ones to develop it in the spirit in which he proposes it. And I am interested in the ideas of insurgency, disobedience, and criticality in fleshing out the field of constitutional morality. I am interested in and committed to exploring intersections – we can scarcely forget that Dr Ambedkar's use of the term constitutional morality lay buried until it was resurrected by the Delhi High Court in 2009 in its upholding of the rights of queer communities in the *Naz Foundation* case and in several cases that followed.[15] We need to be able to make impossible/unimaginable connections in our exploration of justice.

In doing this kind of work, we need spaces that allow for a different kind of thinking and provide platforms for a debate of a different kind. Asmita, the women's collective that I co-founded, has been that space for me. In the days when no university would give me a job, leave alone recognition, I was able to keep working at my ideas because there was a collective that was willing to debate them. My attempt has been to take the spirit of our work in Asmita to the formal spaces I have moved to from time to time and I think it has been a fruitful attempt. In the decade

[12] On 13 February 2019 the Supreme Court ordered all States to evict forest dwellers whose claims under the Forest Rights Act had been rejected. This order, after large-scale protests across the country, was stayed and further information has been sought from the States. *Wildlife First and Others v Ministry of Environment and Forests*, Writ Petition (Civil) 109/2008.

[13] On 22 April 2020, the Supreme Court reversed the government order in the southern State of Andhra Pradesh which mandated that only Adivasi school teachers would be appointed in publicly-funded schools in Adivasi homelands (protected under Schedule 5 of the Constitution). Rolling back special protections, the Court observed that they were put in place for tribes in the first instance because 'their language and *their primitive way of life makes them unfit* to put up with the mainstream and to be governed by the ordinary laws.' (emphasis added): *Chebrolu Leela Prasad Rao and Others v State of Andhra Pradesh and Others*, Civil Appeal 3609 of 2002 decided by a 5-judge bench of the Supreme Court of India on 22 April 2020.

[14] Dr BR Ambedkar (1891–1956), jurist, economist, politician and anti-caste philosopher. Independent India's first Law and Justice Minister, chief architect of the Constitution of India, and author of its Preamble.

[15] *Naz Foundation v Government of NCT of Delhi* case, 2 July 2009, 160 *Delhi Law Times* 277.

that I taught at NALSAR,[16] my attempt was to open out the protocols of sociology and law to students to imagine worlds of difference, and I learnt immensely from them in the process. When I left law school, dissatisfied with the structural limitations it imposed, I returned to Asmita, where I spent a year and a half writing my book on constitutional law and discussing it.[17] When I moved back into formal academia in 2011, to head the Council for Social Development in Hyderabad, it was in a different capacity and in an institutional space that was vastly different. Working with doctoral scholars from vulnerable backgrounds – some of whom had taken long breaks after graduating, all of whom had vast experience working with social movements on questions of marginality and the politics of organising, and were also interested in excavating unwritten histories – my world as a teacher, collaborator, advisor and academic administrator grew boundlessly. I was learning a new lesson every minute – from learning to read data to initiating academic collaborations across extremely uneven capabilities and language competencies. What was important was that we were all in it together, shoring each other up, and putting together collaborations that were extremely unusual.

Doubtless there were moments of doubt, of deep disquiet within me, but is that not what life and work should engender? Every institution I worked with – at the time that I began my work in it – came to be known and recognised in small measure because of our collective effort. And as it stabilised into recognition, I moved on to begin afresh again. I had chosen a different, itinerant path – or had the path chosen me?

[16] NALSAR (National Academy of Legal Studies and Research) University of Law, Hyderabad.

[17] Kalpana Kannabiran, *Tools of Justice: Non-Discrimination and the Indian Constitution* (New Delhi, Routledge, 2012).

G

Ballakrishnen and Dezalay's Feast: Guess Who's Coming to Dinner on the Island of Misfit Toys

DAVID B WILKINS

It began with dinner in Mexico City on the last night of the 2017 Law and Society Association (LSA) annual meeting. Or more accurately, my hope of having dinner with Swethaa and Sara that night as soon as possible.

With all due respect to the panels, plenaries, and parties, I have long viewed the primary purpose of LSA's annual meeting as the opportunity to have dinner with friends who I rarely otherwise get to see anywhere else. And ever since Swethaa left her position as a Research Fellow at Harvard Law School's Center on the Legal Profession, we have made it a point to share our mutual love for fantastic food and wine at the best restaurant in the meeting's host city where I can score a reservation on short notice (not being sufficiently organised to plan ahead). Over the last few years, we have persuaded Sara to join us – being French, it was not hard, especially since the deal is that I pick up the check for anyone who doesn't yet have tenure. I was therefore very much looking forward to having a fabulous meal with Swethaa and Sara in Mexico City, where the food is fantastic, and you are almost obligated to have both Tequila AND wine with dinner.

There was only one problem. When we met that morning in the always bustling lobby of the main conference hotel to make plans, Swethaa and Sara told me that they couldn't eat until 7pm because a panel they were co-chairing was scheduled for the last session of the day from 4:45–6:30pm. While normally this would not have been a big deal, given that I had just flown in from London the night before (where I had been the keynote speaker at another conference), and had to fly back to Boston early the next morning for another commitment (remember when we used to travel like this?), I was really hoping that we would be able to eat early – especially since dinners tend to last a long time. So, partially to ensure that my dinner companions did not linger chatting after their panel, and partially to make sure that there was at least someone in the audience – having learned from long experience that any panel scheduled for the last session of the last day would have grave difficulty meeting the 'Trubek Rule' for a successful LSA panel, to wit having more people in the audience than speakers on the panel – I decided that I would go to Swethaa and Sara's panel to cheer them on, and speed them up. So at 4:30, I gamely fished out the giant conference programme from the 'swag' tote bag that LSA always provides, and looked through the 30 or so panels that had also been assigned to the graveyard slot on the last day until I found Swethaa and Sara's 'Invisible Institutionalisms: What Can We See When We are Looking?'.

The first thing I discovered was that what was not so easy to see when I was looking was where the heck this session was taking place! I assumed that the 'Salon Session: Room Indepencia' listed in the programme would be one of the small seminar rooms on the hotel's second and third floors where I had attended other panels. Instead, it turned out to be located in the bowels of the hotel, accessible only through the book exhibition space, which, not surprisingly, was shut down and empty by the time I finally got to the right floor. As I tried a succession of locked doors at the back of the vacant exhibition space before finding one that finally opened, I remember feeling as though I was leaving the conference altogether and entering a subaltern world. The feeling was only reinforced when I realised that rather than walking into a typical seminar room, I was entering a giant, dimly-lit ballroom with dozens of wooden banquet tables and chairs strewn around haphazardly from whatever function had been in the room the night before. As my eyes adjusted to the light, I could see that located among this dinner detritus were small groups of people huddling together trying to talk quietly enough so as not to disturb the other groups, but loud enough to be heard in spite of the dampening effect created by the cavernous space. And there, clustered in a circle with the table pushed to one side, were Swethaa and Sara, and their merry band of invisible institutionalists.

As I pulled up a chair in the back of the small circle and began to listen, I realised that the form and substance of this 'panel' was as unusual as the setting. Rather than the standard format of 3–5 speakers desperately trying to cram years' worth of careful research into 15 or 20 minutes, followed by comments that too often have more to do with the commentator's ideas than the authors, Swethaa and Sara had structured this session as a real conversation. For 75 minutes, presenters, respondents, and the small but intently focused audience traded riffs in a free-flowing dance that moved seamlessly between substance and method, theory and practice, macro and micro, global and local – and most of all, visible and invisible. Occasionally, Swethaa or Sara would interject to nudge the conversation forward – or backward. But mostly they just let the ideas go where they wanted to go. Gradually, I found myself being carried along by the energy of the group, casting my own small contributions into the river of thought and then marvelling where the others took them. By the end, I was the one who wanted to linger, completely forgetting about the fact that I hadn't eaten in 30 hours, intent on feeding my intellectual curiosity about the bright young scholars around the circle.

Later that evening, over a very long dinner featuring copious amounts of tequila and wine, and an incredible band playing Mexican pop songs that after midnight turned into a raucous sing along with half of the jam-packed restaurant joining in, Swethaa (Sara ended up having other plans) told me the method behind the magic I had witnessed in the session. As Swethaa spoke, I could see just how much it meant to Swethaa and Sara to create a space for a conversation about globalisation that moved beyond the typical hub-and-spoke story in which everything in the Global South is compared – either positively or negatively – to its doppelgänger in the Global North; a conversation in which junior scholars could develop their own voice without comparing or contrasting themselves to the authorial voices of their elders.

The image that Swethaa and Sara now use to capture this idea is The Long Table. And that is exactly what it felt like on that late afternoon in Mexico City. It was like being invited to the Algonquin Round Table,[1] only instead of being skewered by Dorothy Parker's acerbic wit, you were being fed by Swethaa and Sara's generosity of spirit. Indeed, for me the heart of the image is not so much the table as the food – and who Swethaa and Sara have invited to dinner. There was, after all, no table in Mexico City – the battered wooden dinner tables where the other groups clustered around having been pushed to the side in favour of sitting in a circle 'Indian Style', as we used to say in my youth, now strangely appropriate given the number of brilliant Indian scholars in attendance. But while there was no table, there was bountiful nourishing and delicious – indeed thrilling – food for the mind and soul.

Rather than the Long Table, I prefer to think of what Swethaa and Sara have created as their version of *Babette's Feast*. Like the heroine in the 1987 Danish film, Swethaa and Sara have cashed in all of their lottery winnings, in the form of the social capital they have acquired by dint of hard work, luck, and privilege (as both would acknowledge, it always takes all three) to be the kind of young scholars with enough clout to start their own CRN[2] at Law and Society, to prepare a gourmet feast for the most unlikely cast of characters. Just as Babette fed the selfless sisters who had spent their lives toiling in obscurity to render visible the invisible humanity of the villagers in their tiny flock, Swethaa and Sara have prepared a feast for scholars seeking to render visible the invisible sites where globalisation is occurring on its own terms, independently of whatever theories of mimesis or resistance others might chose to use to explain it. And in their ultimate act of generosity, Swethaa and Sara, like Babette, have invited the village elders to sit and eat – whether they appreciate the exquisite quality of the gourmet intellectual cuisine or not.

In their Introduction to this volume, Swethaa and Sara graciously refer to us aging villagers as 'prominent scholars in the field of law and society engaged in law and globalisation' who could foster an 'inter-generational dialogue' with a

[1] A group of New York writers, critics, actors, and wits who met for lunch each day at the Alonquin Hotel from 1919 until roughly 1929, many of whom subsequently collaborated creatively.

[2] Collaborative Research Network.

new generation of scholars focused on the 'frontier zones'. In their gentle but firm way, however, they make clear that they expect us to earn our seats at the table by 'openly, keenly, and expansively' discussing 'What made [us] successful? What risks did [we] take? What opportunities did [we] have, and what limitations did [we] confront?' In other words, to render visible the hard work, luck, and privilege that have allowed us to win the lottery that it takes to become village elders.

To be sure, every successful person has this kind of back story, whether they care to admit it or not. For those of us who labour in the vineyards of law and society, however, exposing these roots is especially important. After all, we routinely write to debunk narratives that posit the status quo as natural and neutral, rendering the structural causes of inequality invisible, particularly to those at the bottom of the hierarchy. It is only fitting that we be asked to turn that critical lens on our own success stories.

But doing so can also be painful. Even scholars who have 'made it' to the top of the law and society hierarchy are acutely aware that they continue to be marginalised in their home disciplines. Sociology has always been at the margins of mainstream legal discourse, just as the sociology of law (let alone of the legal profession) is at the margins of sociology. Even 'prominent scholars' have had to deal with this marginality. As the head of the appointments committee at a top law school once told me over a dinner in which he was trying to persuade me to leave Harvard and join his faculty: 'It was *so* smart of you David to get involved in such a weak field!' – meaning, of course, that if I did contracts or constitutional law like he did, I'd be 'just another putz'. Luckily for me, thanks to Watergate, his law school and every other one in the US is required to have at least one putz around to teach the required course in legal ethics. But as anyone who teaches this course – or otherwise stakes his or her professional reputation on *lawyers* rather than *law* – is painfully aware, putzes like us have never been particularly valued in law schools. Since I joined the Harvard Law School faculty in 1986, the school has hired dozens of tenured and tenure-track faculty members. Not one has a primary scholarly or teaching interest in the legal profession.

To be a socio-legal scholar in a law school is a bit like being Rudolph the Red-Nosed Reindeer in the 1964 'Claymation Christmas Celebration' classic of my youth. You know that your red-nosed interests and commitments make you different, and that in their heart of hearts, your colleagues laugh at your discipline, calling it names like 'merely descriptive', 'unscientific', and 'theoretically uninteresting'. You long to find a place where you could meet other scholars who share your interests, commitments, and methodologies: scholars who will appreciate your difference as strength. And if you are lucky, like Rudolph, one day while wondering in the forest of legal academia, you meet a guide who can take you to an island called LSA off the coast of mainstream legal thought, where everyone is a 'misfit toy' just like you, and where your unique talents can be nurtured and grow.

I know because this is exactly what happened to me. And it changed my life.

As I have said many times, if it weren't for Dave Trubek, I would have been just another boring law professor.[3] Trubek was visiting at Harvard during my first year of teaching, and by total luck of the draw, he was teaching the same courses that I had been assigned – a fall civil procedure class, where (along with Al Sacks) we each were teaching a third of what was then a 145-person first-year section, and a spring course on the legal profession. Sometime in early August, Sacks asked Trubek and me to come to his office so we could discuss ideas about how we could best coordinate our mini-sections of civil procedure to give the students a unified experience. I, of course, had absolutely no idea. Unlike virtually all my peers in the legal academy – then and now – I had never intended or expect to be a law professor. Instead, I got my job through a combination of illegitimate hierarchy (I had been on the *Harvard Law Review* and had a Supreme Court clerkship with Justice Marshall), and affirmative action (Harvard's Dean James Vorenberg specifically and persistently recruited me and several other young black lawyers as junior professors because, to his great credit, he did not want to preside over a law school that had become all-white, shortly after he took office in 1981). I therefore intended to teach exactly as I had been taught as a law student at Harvard in the late 1970s, which was some combination of case exegesis, leavened by arm-chair policy analysis.

Trubek, however, had different plans. After a few pleasantries in our meeting with Sacks, Trubek held up a copy of Peter Schuck's recent book *Agent Orange on Trial*,[4] chronicling the law suit brought by veterans against the chemical companies that manufactured agent orange during the Vietnam war, and declared that he was going to use the book to illustrate how the rules of civil procedure actually work in practice. I remember sitting in stunned silence, wanting to blurt out: 'You can do that?!'. It had never occurred to me that you could teach the curriculum's most rigidly technocratic and formalist course through the prism of the real experience of lawyers and judges. And, to my even greater surprise, Al Sacks, whose bow-tie and stiff demeanour marked him (falsely as I would discover) as one of the most traditional members of Harvard's traditional law faculty said: 'That sounds like a great idea!'.[5] And so we did.

And this was just the beginning. For the next year, Trubek introduced me to a 'who's who' and 'what's what' of law and society. I met the legends of the field – Mark Galanter, Jack Heinz, Rick Abel, Robert Gordon, Carrie Menkel-Meadow, Stuart McCauley, Bryant Garth, Susan Silbey, Sally Merry, Carol Seron – and

[3] David B Wilkins, 'Where the Action Is: Globalization, Law and Development, Sociology of the Legal Profession, and the GLEE-full Career of Dave Trubek' in Grainne de Burca, Joanne Scott and Marsella Eleonora (eds), *Global Governance, Critical Perspectives* (Oxford, Hart Publishing, 2013).

[4] Peter H Shuck, *Agent Orange on Trial: Mass Toxic Disasters in the Courts* (Cambridge MA, Harvard University Press, 1986).

[5] As I came to learn over the next 5 years before his death, Al Sacks was one of the most open-minded and generous people I have ever met. See David B Wilkins, 'In Memoriam: Albert M. Sacks' (1991) 105 *Harvard Law Review* 1, 20.

through them, the rising stars – Bob Nelson, Beth Mertz, Elizabeth Chambliss, Pat Williams, Becky Sandefur, and many more. Over the years, these scholars and many others under the law and society tent have nurtured and supported my work, giving me the courage to speak in my own voice, something I found initially very hard to do. In my first three years as an assistant professor, I published nothing other than a short tribute to Justice Marshall – the thesis of which (that traditional legal scholars wrongly dismissed the Judge's legendary prowess as a story-teller as disconnected from his equally legendary prowess as an advocate and a judge) was itself a metaphor for my own paralysis.[6] It wasn't as though I wasn't writing. During this period, I produced hundreds of pages of drafts of the pair of articles that would eventually become 'Legal Realism for Lawyers'[7] and 'Who Should Regulate Lawyers?'[8] But I was too afraid to publish any of it, convinced that it was either stupid or obvious, or most likely both. Like Sidney Poitier's character in the ground-breaking 1967 comedy of manners *Guess Who's Coming to Dinner*, I felt that everything I did had to be perfect in order to prove that I was worthy of being invited into a place where I was never expected to be, and frankly didn't feel like I belonged.[9]

Which is why LSA has been so important to me, and to so many others. LSA provides a safe space for all of us 'misfit toys' to congregate with like-minded scholars to explore the questions at the intersection of law and society that we care so deeply about. So every year we gleefully come together by the thousands – and thanks to the concerted efforts of the last several presidents – from every corner of the globe, to share ideas and fellowship, and to build a community where the things that make us different from the mainstream of our home disciplines are not only tolerated, but celebrated. I hardly ever go to the annual meeting of the

[6] David B Wilkins, 'Justice as Narrative: Some Personal Reflections on a Master Storyteller', (1989) 6 *Harv BlackLetter J* 68.

[7] David B Wilkins, 'Legal Realism for Lawyers' (1990) 104 *Harvard Law Review* 469.

[8] David B Wilkins, 'Who Should Regulate Lawyers?' (1992) 105 *Harvard Law Review* 801.

[9] As the film's writer and director have acknowledged, they intentionally made Poitier's character perfect – graduate of a top medical school, working for the World Health Organization to develop innovative cures in Africa, even refusing to have premarital sex with his white fiancé, notwithstanding her evident willingness – so that the only conceivable reason for Spencer Tracey and Katherine Hepburn's characters to possibly object to their daughter marrying this paragon of virtue would have to be race. All of which was great for attacking stereotypes in a country where interracial marriage was still illegal in 17 States until the Supreme Court's decision in *Loving v Virginia* 388 US 1 (1967), six months before the film's release. But as every black boy or girl whose parents have drilled into their heads that they must be 'twice as good' as their white peers to get half as far, also knows, this is a heavy burden to bear. Interestingly, while much was made of the racial difference between Poitier and Tracey and Hepburn's daughter, there was no mention of the 14-year age difference between the two. Proof once again, as Ballakrishnen and Dezalay teach us, that even as some things are made visible, others, like the still unexamined assumption that it was perfectly acceptable for a 35-year-old man to date a 21-year-old woman (at least if he marries her), remain hidden from sight. The fact that Hepburn and the much older and married Tracy were carrying on a 25-year secret affair at the time the movie was being made undoubtedly contributed to the invisibility of this element of patriarchy. See Christopher Anderson, *An Affair to Remember: The Remarkable Love Story of Katherine Hepburn and Spencer Tracy* (New York, William Morrow & Co, 1997).

American Association of Law Schools – even though my law school pays all the costs. I hardly ever miss LSA, even though my law school does not.

But like any institution, there is always the danger that this joyful cacophony of marginality will develop an orthodoxy that will paradoxically end up marginalising the very people whose youthful energy and fresh perspectives are essential to preserving and extending LSA's core mission: understanding the ever-shifting relationship of law and society in a world that is at once increasingly global and intensely local. Through the years, critical legal studies, law and literature, feminist theory, critical race theory, queer theory, and post-colonialism, have all raised challenges to core law and society ideas and methods. For the most part, the law and society movement has found ways to engage and incorporate these divergent voices, although not always without tensions or costs.[10] But the older I get, the more conscious I become that I have now moved – as Swethaa and Sara not so subtly remind me – from the 'frontier zone' to the status of 'prominent scholar', whose voice now has the potential to silence others.

This danger has become particularly acute as my own work has turned toward the intersection of law and globalisation. In 2008, with the help of my friend and mentor Dave Trubek, I launched the Project on Globalization, Lawyers, and Emerging Economies – or GLEE as Dave Trubek quickly dubbed our initiative with characteristic aplomb. As the name implies, the project seeks to understand how globalisation is reshaping the market for legal services in important emerging economies in Asia, Latin America, and Africa, and how these changes are in turn reshaping the legal professions and political economy in these rising powers, and the increasingly global market for legal services generally. To accomplish this ambitious goal, we have assembled a multinational, multidisciplinary, and multi-institutional team of researchers to conduct original empirical research on the key changes that globalisation is producing in these increasingly important places in the world. To date, GLEE has produced books on India,[11] Brazil,[12] and China,[13] and we are currently beginning to do work in sub-Saharan Africa and South East Asia.

[10] Dave Trubek has been at the forefront of many of these harmonisation and inclusion efforts. David M Trubeck, 'Where the Action Is: Critical Legal Studies and Empiricism' (1984) 36 *Stanford Law Review* 575 (1984) (discussing the tensions between law and society and critical legal studies); DM Trubek, 'Cracking the "Red, White, and Blue" Ceiling: Toward a New International Role for the Law and Society Association' (2003) 37 *Law & Society Review* 295 (discussing the tensions between law and society's traditional domestic focus and the challenge of globalisation); DM Trubek, 'Back to the Future: The Short, Happy Life of the Law and Society Movement' (1990) 18 *Florida State Law Review* 1 (addressing the tension between the narrative turn in law and literature and critical race theory and the law and society movement).

[11] David B Wilkins, Vikramaditya Khanna and David Trubek (eds), *The Indian Legal Profession in the Age of Globalization: The Rise of the Corporate Legal Sector and its Impact on Lawyers and Society* (Cambridge, Cambridge University Press, 2017).

[12] Luciana Gross Cunha, Daniela Monteiro Gabbay, Jose Garces Ghirardi, David Trubek, and David B Wilkins (eds), *The Brazilian Legal Profession in the Age of Globalization: The Rise of the Corporate Legal Sector and its Impact on Lawyers and Society* (Cambridge, Cambridge University Press 2018).

[13] Sida Liu and David B Wilkins (eds), *The Chinese Legal Profession in the Age of Globalization: The Rise of the Corporate Legal Sector and its Impact on Lawyers and Society* (Cambridge, Cambridge University Press, forthcoming 2021).

In doing this work, it has become abundantly clear that my status as a senior member of the Harvard Law School faculty confers many important advantages. Although I have always tried to be cognisant of what one of the lawyers I interviewed for my black corporate lawyers project many years ago referred to as the 'H-Bomb effect – as he said, even the most racist partner would pause after finding out that he was an HLS graduate, as if to say: 'he can't be completely stupid if he graduated from Harvard!' – I quickly found that this effect is magnified exponentially the farther one travels from Cambridge, Massachusetts. This halo effect has undoubtedly been extremely helpful in gaining access to the resources and networks necessary to make the GLEE project a success. But it can also be a liability, trapping the project in established networks consisting of the kinds of people who have the knowledge, desire, and ability to volunteer for a project led by a Vice Dean from Harvard Law School.

To guard against this insularity, we have worked hard to always include junior scholars in the project, and to give them prominent roles. Swethaa and Sara, for example, were both graduate students when we recruited them to work with us on India and Africa, respectively, and there are many others. But the danger persists, particularly as the junior scholars we recruit become – as we hope they will – senior scholars, often (again, as we hope, if that is what they want) located in prestigious academic institutions in the Global North.

Which brings me back to Ballakrishnen and Dezalay's glorious feast. As I discovered in that dimly-lit ballroom in Mexico City, Swethaa and Sara are ensuring that a new generation of critical voices will have a seat at their Long Table. And, that village elders like me will engage these new voices on their own terms, in part by revealing our own pathways from disciplinary marginality to the relative centre and security of the Island of Misfit Toys that is the Law and Society Association. In so doing these consummate hosts invite both young and old to participate in a conversation that has no end or purpose other than the nourishment of the dialogue itself. As I finished the draft of this refraction in COVID-19 lock down on what would have been my brilliant friend and collaborator Shamnad Basheer's 44th birthday,[14] I can think of few things more important than to continue to strive to make the invisible visible, and to keep the conversation going.

Swethaa and Sara and I did not get to share our decadent dinner at the 2020 LSA Annual Meeting, which was, like everything else, held virtually. But thanks to the conversations memorialised in this seminal book, I and countless others will be able to nourish our minds and our souls until we can eat together again.

[14] Like Swethaa and Sara, I was blessed to work with Shamnad on our GLEE India book. See Shamnad Basheer et al, 'The Making of Legal Elites and the IDIA of Justice' in *The Indian Legal Profession in the Age of Globalization*, above n 10. He was, quite simply, one of the finest human beings I have ever met.

Conclusion

Reading Between the Lines

SARA DEZALAY AND SWETHAA S BALLAKRISHNEN

We close this book at a deeply unsettling juncture. As we write this conclusion the world is newly different and still startlingly more isomorphic than it was when this process started. On the one hand, lives continue to be destroyed in the name of violent identity politics; people continue to feel the bane of everyday poverty; migrants continue to try and escape horrific fates determined solely on what side of the border they happen to be on a given day. Yet, alongside that, the world seems trapped in an eerily all-encompassing pandemic that with seeming equality threatens and leaves in a range of material conditions more people in similar – or at least relatable – kinds of excruciating hell than ever before. Living alongside this palpable contradiction is the very term globalisation: a term that appears at once a dramatically material reality and an elusive concept. Perhaps this has always been the case, but thinking about globalisation in these times offers new kinds of purpose, and embedded in uncertainty, the conversations in this book take on new meaning. If virtual discomfort and meaning-making across new kinds of intimacy is what we inherit from this new normal, how can that shape the usefulness of methods such as this? In these times when actual dinner table conversations can be hard, where, as David Wilkins asks (p 266), do and can we find 'nourishment'?

Despite our call to seek out the invisible, the answer, we suggest ironically, lies in imagery. Were we to ask: '*what about legal globalisation now?*', based on the narratives assembled in this volume, we could find ourselves teetering in front of two opposed images. The first is that of Bruegel the Elder's *The Tower of Babel*:[1] what Usha Natarajan (p 199), responding to Andrés Palacio's empirical chapter, aptly describes as a 'sense of inevitability that accompanies post-colonial legal failure', and the ever-reinvented myth of building (conceptual/political) scaffolding upon scaffolding to push away fatalism and sublimate it. The second is that of Bosch's *Garden of Earthly Delights*:[2] revelling in conversation for no other purpose than

[1] Pietr Bruegel the Elder, *The (Great) Tower of Babel* and *The (Little) Tower of Babel* (Oil on wood panel, c 1563).

[2] Hieronymus Bosch, *The Garden of Earthly Delights* (Oil on wood panel, 1504).

conversation itself, with an illusion of a levelling of the playing-field that would have no end, or building blocks. Between these two images lies an important disjuncture – there is the possibility of radical hope that exists when we undo the concreteness of existing structure. But it can only exist if we make way for it on new terms, allowing for the possibility of new expectations and goals to frame what we see as 'ends' or 'blocks'. Exits, in a sense, are where potential thrives.

It is with these images in mind that we revisit the process that we started this book with, and its renewed meanings of interconnectedness (often by *not* being connected) now that we are at the end of this journey. As we lay out in the Introduction, we invited contributors to this volume to take part, and to offer glimpses of what could be gained from it. Enthralled by her *What Will You Do/Do What You Will* work, which formed the initial building block of her series 'Reading Between the Lines', we asked talented Gail Tarantino, a San Francisco-based artist, to contribute to our volume with her art (on the cover) as *voice*. The published layout of all 448 documents in the *New York Time*'s two-page spread of the Mueller Report[3] was, as Tarantino suggests (p 25) her initial 'launching pad.' Her 'intention', however, 'did not begin as a political overture.' Instead: '(t)he subtly pencilled letters within the monochromatic palette were intended to be read and misread as they recede in and out of a viewer's focal point' (Tarantino p 26). More than the cover of this volume, Tarantino's work provides the *spine* of this book. Much like the unfathomable library of Jean-Paul Sartre's early childhood, whose books were still undecipherable to him while he wished them to be pried open like oysters, its indented marks are an invitation to pause and ponder, supporting a slower pace of interpreting and re-interpreting. Put simply, if you were to ask about this book, this process, this journey, '*What can you see when you look?*' we'd have to say, '*What you will.*'

But despite the poetics of ambiguity, what, then, was this process? As we explain in the Introduction, we invited our contributors to the *Long Table*, to lend themselves to a twofold break. We borrowed the first arm of this strategy from Brecht's *Verfremdung*, or estrangement-effect. Subjecting the theorised framing of a given empirical site to the gaze of someone with a differently-shaped disposition to that setting provided a way to question the natural – what would otherwise appear as objective, because of its hidden, unconscious, unquestioned apparent objectification. Second, we asked each contributor to be *reflexive* about their own (dis)position (in)to the various social spaces about which they wrote and in which they navigated. Borrowing from Galanter's wise reflection in the *Foreword* about his own journey, we perhaps expected this immersion to expose presuppositions and to show us the ways in which the familiar were problematic (Galanter p viii). But this narrative of our process is retrospective. And aligned with his experience, we imagine it was 'celebrated but not painless' for all the actors in question.

[3] Report on the Investigation into Russian Interference in the 2016 (US) Presidential Election.

At the same time, as Wilkins so generously pays witness in his refraction (p 260), we did not nudge too much in a singular direction for these conversations, and when we did, they were meant to be ambi-directional – we moved forward only as much as we paused and pulled backwards. Some of this capacity for staying open to a multitude of directions was because there wasn't a clear vision that this project was working towards or backing into: in learning alongside our collaborators, it necessarily was an a-linear metamorphosis. We built this, too, as a strategy of rupture, which we borrowed from Bourdieu: what we *see* classifies us, and it classifies the classifiers. We thereby asked contributors to reflect on their own position(ality); that is, to confront themselves with their own strengths and limitations in terms of social position, field, and from a scholastic point of view. The process required *trust*: from our contributors towards us, but also among contributors, through the commonality that was built in the collective that we constituted. What our contributors embarked on was *brave* – in ways that we were not fully conscious of from the outset. But hopefully, it was also indulgent in meaningful ways.

We hypothesised – or at least self-soothed in times of doubt about the process – that both arms of this strategy could foster benefits; they also, of course, entailed risks, and costs. But seeped in all of this was a conviction that together they – we – could build collective reflections on legal globalisation. Some of this was, as we offer in the Introduction, method: a trust that repeated returns to places and conversations with new kinds of synergies would produce new kinds of knowledge. As we set up early in this book, this collaborative knowledge production by talking across and between fields and sites and spaces has long been feminist praxis. But in engaging with it in this way, we offer it as important law and society praxis for the global worlds we seek to inhabit, observe, and engage with. That together they – we – could collapse into *The Tower of Babel* – or allow for displacement, even disappointment, by opening a space for *disruptive* alternatives as the *Garden of Earthly Delights*.

I. Building a 'Pure' Gaze on the (In)Visible(S) of Legal Globalisation

The nature of this process requires that we start by examining carefully and unpacking the opportunities it could open, as much as its limitations. What did we mean by *rupture*? Why and how? The conversations were built against – while being determined by – two truisms derived from the seemingly *pure* and *disinterested* nature of the universe of scientific knowledge.

Scientific fields, like any other fields, are social spaces characterised by power relationships, monopolies, conflicts and strategies, interests and profits. Yet, as Bourdieu underscores, 'the scientific field owes its main characteristics to the fact that the producers generally have no other possible clients than their direct competitors'.[4] By this, he pointed to the fact that scientific authority is conditioned by scientific *products* being accepted, that is, valued as legitimate. In other words, the *definition of what is at stake* is part and parcel of the stakes that drive the field. Conversely, the 'disinterestedness' that comes along with science being hailed as 'pure' is itself contaminated by the definition of interests and the stakes they are tied to in other fields. This is something that became central for the purpose of this volume: to trace and unpack the conditions under which dynamics of legal globalisation and institutional change are (in)visibilised.

Politics of (in)visibility in legal globalisation are at once a product of scientific authority and an outcome of policy push and pulls. At the core of this volume is an interrogation raised by most contributors: what to make of Western-driven typologies that push three-quarters of the world outside of mainstream categories of knowledge about legal globalisation – a scientific objectification that is the corollary evidently, though problematically, of successive dynamics of colonial, postcolonial, and hegemonic drivers of legal globalisation. The circulation of knowledge about legal globalisation is therefore *trans*-field – as it is related to the state of the game within national fields of scientific knowledge and (inter) national fields of power. But it is also, simultaneously, conditioned by the (social, political, economic) drivers of production, export and import of scientific products across national fields. Yet, the scientific production of knowledge about law and globalisation also apparently *maps on* fields of power and the ebb and flow of policy pulls on legal globalisation processes – what Steinmetz described as 'imperial entanglements'.[5] Fabio de Sa e Silva, in his response to Goyal, directly points to this by emphasising the close articulation between conceptual flows (and counter-flows) and economic transformations (de Sa e Silva, p 78). Eve Darian-Smith, in her refraction note, also aptly captures this ruse of imperialist reason through her recounting of the journey of the concept of 'globalisation' since the 1990s which closely mapped on her trajectory – as a trailblazer herself – from the edge of mainstream to conventional wisdom requiring, again, subversion (Darian-Smith, pp 235–239).

The 'pure' gaze – that which could question the invisible in the ordinarily visible of legal globalisation – implies a break that has to be at once scholastic and political. Wilkins' description of the LSA as an island of misfit toys (p 262) alludes to the history of groups like this that have tried to make visible connections that were historically less so – and the costs of gaining legitimacy once such vision is obtained. We might be in new places because of such knowledge creation, there might be silos of possibility that these engagements produce, but what we do with that possibility and who we do it on behalf of remain crucial. To confront these concurrent dynamics of knowledge production, legitimation, and circulation

[4] P Bourdieu, 'Le champ scientifique' (1976) 2(2)-(3) *Actes de la recherche en sciences sociales* 88.

[5] G Steinmetz, *Sociology and Empire: The Imperial Entanglements of a Discipline* (Durham NC, Duke University Press, 2013).

qua scientific products, along with their articulation with political processes of hegemony, we invited each contributor, individually – be they authors of empirical chapters, respondents or authors of the refraction notes – to ask themselves *to whom* they were writing, *against what*, and how their narratives *mapped onto* or *diverged* from ordinary globalisation scripts. Our belief in the power of these circulations and this method was intuitively in line with what Kate Bedford offers in another context (p 218). Stories, she reminds us, acquire value as they circulate. And it is the reason we chose these stories, in these voices, to make the rounds that they did both with each other – to create the fractures and ruptures that they did in edits against our gaze – and before you now, in this book.

II. From Subversion to Carving Out a Space for Critique about Legal Globalisation

In enabling this circulation and offering a space for its consumption, we also aimed to push against the limitations induced by a second truism, which, albeit apparently self-evident – was much less easily negotiated and rationalised. Wilkins couldn't be more right when he says we will both be quick to acknowledge the role of privilege in our journeys, alongside our marginality – luck or incidence and hard work only sit if privilege is also at the table. And alongside this individual privilege is the further institutional acknowledgment that scientific knowledge about legal globalisation – as all knowledge (and in some ways, *all* things) – is about power. Yet this is not always a proclaimed power, it is often socially naked, and obtusely capable of holding on to its power exactly because of such nudity. Science implies a denial of the social of the *observer* themselves. Of course, we could not do away with power or position altogether, but we could offer modes within which critique of them was heard. At a first level, we responded to this by inviting our contributors to question their own *positionality* – in relation to how they defined the scientific fields they belonged to, and how they determined the parameters of (and their relation to) their empirical fields of study. In the narratives assembled in this volume, there are self-evidently visible suspects: the dominance of the United States – both the US field of power and US scientific fields – in controlling the layout of the cartography of binary oppositions between *mainstream* and *contender* scientific knowledge; or the statistically visible distribution of hierarchies and legitimate *doxa* of disciplines. In his contribution, Yugank Goyal beautifully encapsulates this: 'Paragraphs on "method" in peer reviewed journals have been assumed to echo academic rigour. This echo is deafening' (Goyal, p 68), while de Sa e Silva responds by wondering if 'in the absence of these extended conversations and efforts to bridge societal contexts and stereotypes, Goyal's chapter would be categorised as an extremely interesting but ultimately irrelevant read – not because of what it shows (which is potentially a lot) but because of what its readers may be un/able to see' (de Sa e Silva, p 77).

Doing this allowed us to acknowledge trajectory for scholars across position and claim, both to situate themselves and the other, as well as to contend with their discontents. It also allowed us to bear witness to this process in subversive ways. Richa Nagar asks what it means to co-produce relevant knowledge and create truly discursive geographies.[6] Looking at those who are less – or differently – adept in the language of globalisation and law, engaged in work that is still essentially what could be seen as legal globalisation, reveals to us the aesthetics of scripts that have defined these fields. Still, our refraction notes from senior scholars remind us that language is cumulative, learnt over time, and often happenstance. Key to this methodology of the – seemingly – invisible, then, is a call to pay attention to actors who might not otherwise have been asked to 'sit at the table' and to critically introspect their invitation and seating. So much of branding someone as 'the other' comes from an entirely secure position of the self as a non-other. Kalpana Kannabiran, for example, is a 'Global South' or 'globalisation' scholar, only when seen from the axis of a certain positional perspective. From her own writing, for her own vision, the cores and peripheries are different, the audiences less linear or straightforward. What is global, then, is constantly flowing but it is also consistently metaphorical.

Deep in this inquiry both about bringing together scholars that might not always speak at and to each other is a question about methodology and what it means to 'know'. Goyal mentions (while talking about the proximity of the field site as actually becoming native to a point of non-remembrance, p 69) that the ability to take something for granted, to not code it in one's conscience as a thing or as a memory of significance, is something to take note of in its own right. Forgetting, he offers, is a kind of memory too (p 69). This idea of negative identity that is accorded to categories without attributes is powerful, especially when one thinks of knowledge production and the ways in which we seek to code its coordinates within disciplinary, movement, and political praxis. Just as memory includes the things forgotten, not knowing is – or can be – a kind of knowledge too. How we code this knowledge, what we expect its coordinates to be, how we allow its texture to parse our analytical categories, are all linear categories of path dependency and production that we need to pay attention to and afford appropriate credit to.

These processes of objectification of the politics of (in)visibility at play in scientific fields are evidenced too in the choices made to enter and navigate these fields. Beckford, in her refraction note, wittingly recounts how her desire as a PhD student to trace the role of multilateral institutions in shaping sexuality was met: 'I was told by a prospective supervisor that he hoped I was independently wealthy because I'd never get a job in a US political science department if I did a dissertation on sexuality. He was, of course, correct: I didn't' (Beckford, p 223). Similarly illustrative is the real-life experience of one of the authors of this conclusion,

[6] R Nagar, *Muddying the waters: Coauthoring Feminisms Across Scholarship and Activism* (Champaign IL, University of Illinois Press, 2014).

venturing to present her work at an International Studies Association annual meeting, confronted by a senior colleague (in this story, yes, a male) exhorting her to justify *her* approach to him – implying obviously that in this setting, mainstream thought which he embodied was *not* interested in international lawyers, nor did it require any explaining. The evident also lies in the apparently open-ended impetus for *inter-disciplinarity* embraced by most, if not all, contributors to this volume as a way to push against the limitations they perceive with their disciplinary alma mater. Yet, inter-disciplinarity can mask as much as it can overplay inter-*national* (mis)translations, by invisibilising dynamics of co-optation of scientific *alternatives* as acceptable, that is, legitimate, or their rejection as illegitimate.

Those issues, among others, inform, more or less consciously, more or less strategically, our positionality *qua* scholars. Only by a careful exploration of scholastic positions *qua* structural positions – in terms of individual positions in fields, the structuration of national fields of knowledge and the social conditions for the import and export of scientific knowledge across national fields – might we be able to grasp what these individual iterations express. Tracing the invisible in the visible would imply, therefore, for each contribution to this volume, a careful unpacking of the processes at play in its production as a knowledge *product* and its articulation with social conditions (that is, power relations) that would undergird its classification as (il)legitimate.

But it would not be sufficient to overcome these initial self-evident dynamics of classification. The self-iterative process of 'uncovering' the invisible in the visible in one's individual work is itself limited by all the partial objectifications which the actors involved in the game perform on each other – but foremost on themselves. What Rachel Brulé (p 34) calls 'vision gaps', for instance, aptly describes what she, as an individual, perceived as the *mismatch* between her own scientific positionality and what she observed empirically. This is not to call into question the *authenticity* of the voice of our contributors. Rather, it is a recognition that our capacity to see is a function of the knowledge, or concepts – that is the words – that are available to us to name (in)visible things, and which are, as it were, what Bourdieu referred to as 'programmes for perception'.[7] By this he meant that what we see is a function of (cultural, social … but also family) competence – that is, of having implemented – consciously or unconsciously – the codes into which concepts are encoded. This is what we aimed at overcoming by suggesting a *relational* break: pairing each empirical chapter with 'responses' from a contributor from an adjacent field was a way to foster *inter-textuality*; that is, to *suspend* the meaning of the empirical chapters *qua* scientific products through their confrontation with another text reflecting the gaze of an individual with a different (dis) position to a given set of conceptual and empirical material.

[7] P Bourdieu, *Distinction: a Social Critique of the Judgement of Taste*, Richard Nice (trans) (Cambridge MA, Harvard University Press, 1984), 12.

III. The Games of Dissonance

The universe of *possible* interpretive alternatives could thereby be seen to derive from what stands out explicitly – belonging (or striving to belong) to academic fields with their distinct rules of the game – and foremost implicitly: those more or less conscious or unconscious biases that inform our vision of the social world, that inhabit our fears to *not* fit in, or that are staked as claims to belong to an elusive mainstream or to represent an invisibilised, oppressed, empirical world. In her contribution, Brulé expresses this as a 'dissonance' (Brulé, p 33), as at once a discomfort and a strength: that of experiencing a gap between her scholastic training and what she observed on the ground, that of being a 'tenure-track mother', a permanent outsider as Jewish, which she saw as capital in itself – namely, of being able to navigate across different social spaces. These characteristics could also become biases: informing her vision of social classifications in India but also reverberating on how her empirical subjects viewed her as a single, white, woman requiring 'protection'. For her part, in her response to Maryam Khan, Prasad describes herself as 'embroiled in an uncomfortable tussle between the roles of researcher, activist, social worker and judge' leading her to question her own legitimacy: 'is there a place,' she asks, 'for strong conviction and simultaneous insecurity of adequacy in these spaces of both intervening and theorising?' (Gitanjali Prasad, p 172). Yet, in their reflections on their trajectories, Kannabiran and David Trubek reflect back on the paths opened by these contradictions: both to straddle contradictory social positions, and to deviate (scholastic) stasis, and political backlash. Describing herself as an 'insurgent, itinerant feminist', Kannabiran (p 258) 'commuted' between social sciences, law, advocacy and public education. Trubek, for his part, retraces a trajectory lived 'in the contradiction' (p 248): that of navigating the social and academic plane from the platform of an 'outsider,' but also that of having to constantly adjust to and fight against the unintended political outcomes of scientific positions.

These tensions also mapped on their narratives about social power being 'intimately political' in ways that begged questioning. Who *gets* to express their inner contradictions, how and with what outcomes? This issue is addressed throughout the volume. In his response to Brulé, Danish Sheikh uses the term 'archival ache' to question the (im)possibility for the LGBTQ community in India to gain 'access to a past that exists as much in the fragments of dust on a page as it does in the written words' (Sheikh, p 52). But he also defines himself as a queer researcher – and therefore activist – actively involved in the game of 'archive fever'. This proximity is also hailed by both Goyal and Christopher Williams in their contributions. Both ask the question of 'authenticity'. Goyal grew up in the Agra slum he describes, as the son of a shoe trader family. This, he explained enabled both affinity with his empirical subjects and access in ways, he implies, that lent legitimacy to his endeavour – at the very least more so, he claims, than a researcher who might conduct fieldwork during their sabbatical in the Agra slum while visiting the Taj Mahal. 'How much native I remained, I am still to learn' (Goya, p 69) and foremost, 'can theory be built without experience?' (Goyal, p 70) he asks, thereby echoing Williams' related (and relatable) fear, as an African-American, that his one experience and perspective will become unfairly generalisable, and be coded in perpetuity as '*the* black perspective' despite any nuance he may provide. (Williams, p 86).

For its part, the self-deprecation that Beckford uses to trace her 'career suicide' strategies maps on closely, delicately, with her bingo-playing subjects. But it contrasts markedly with the *strategic* dissonance described by Yves Dezalay and Bryant Garth. Being 'double agents' themselves, individually and as a tandem, enabled them to study double agents. Their exceptional trajectory as a tandem built precisely out of a strategic knowledge of the opportunities and limits of their respective national academic fields; the ambivalence of the alliance that they constituted as a tandem in turn strategically echoed that of the double agents they were studying.[8]

'Writing from the edge' lends itself thereby to layered, contradictory meanings: for instance, is Bedford's ironic self-deprecation a marker of proximity (defined by social proximity or vindicated, political, proximity) to her empirical subjects? Or does it hail intersectionality as a condition for 'authenticity' – that is, politically meaningful, research? Conversely, Dezalay and Garth's focus on 'elite' lawyers, while playing into their strategically performed proximity also opened a mismatch with the existing legal sociology or law and society approaches to studying the legal profession (Dezalay and Garth, p 212). Similarly, Khan's counter-narrative about the mainstream thesis of 'constitutional theocracy' in Pakistan also begs the question, implicitly, of how she, as a Muslim Pakistani woman, negotiated the tightrope of inhabiting the contradictory position of both combatting, as a woman activist, female-adverse *Shari'a* laws, and contesting narratives about Pakistan as a foil for legal globalisation scripts. All these are not just narratives by and from a specific positions or voices. They also remind us of the wisdom that can be gleaned from the generosity of their reflection. Where we start, how we traverse paths, where they make us end up, and what we do from our new locations, are all crucial.

IV. *De Te Fabula Narratur*

By raising these as questions, we take in this reminder which Bourdieu meant as much for the scholar as for her (scientific) reader. What he called the 'law of mutual lucidity and reflexive blindness' governs this *mutual* performance of objectivity: a scholar of discipline or orientation X cannot grasp the objective reality of a scholar of discipline or orientation Y without abandoning their 'grasp of the true

[8] See D Bigo, A Cohen and J Chatel, 'Investigating the internationalisation of state nobilities: reflective feedback on double-game strategies. An interview with Yves Dezalay' (2020) 1 *Political Anthropological Research on International Social Sciences* 132–45.

nature of their own activity'.[9] At some level we could escape this trope through the *collective* that we represented. As we explain in the Introduction, this volume is the outcome of an iterative process of building a community. While hailing from different scientific traditions and parts of the world, we all shared a common belonging to the field of law and society, and with it, a common repertoire of words and concepts.

This could foster exceptionally rich critical conceptual displacements. Responding to Shamnad Basheer's resounding plea to 'open ourselves to "testimonies" for the informal world' (Basheer, p 123), for example, Jules Naudet questions the conditions for social criticism as resilience by pointing to the fact that the excess of attention to processes of informal resilience can in turn sometimes invisibilise potentialities of emancipation that exist in the formal sphere (Naudet, p 143), while Amy Weissenbach traces the paradoxical codification of 'open testimony' at play in the regulation of innovation in the field of synthetic biology (Weissenbach, p 136). For his part, Suryapratim Roy's response to Rahela Khorakiwala's contribution evaluates the contrasted agentic potential of the visual compared to the discursive (Roy, p 108).

But it also opened a risk: our inability to escape the play of opposing images that we see (even when we aim to dislodge them) as binaries driving the field – the opposition between a nebulous mainstream and critical alternatives, that between word and image, that between core and periphery. That risk is major: it could lead us to confuse critical alternatives hailed as scientific revolutions with those invisible, discrete, mini revolutions. Revolutions by which the continuous struggle between the conservative strategies of (mainstream) dominants and the subversive strategies of contenders could lead to co-optation and with it, the mainstreaming of critical alternatives as naturalised. In her response to Palacios, Natarajan brilliantly encapsulates this pitfall. The only way, she contends, to address the 'inevitability that accompanies post-colonial legal failure' would be a kind of return to fundamentals in a sense. Faced with the impossible task of going back to original encounters, we suggested an alternative entry. We invited accomplished scholars within the field of law and society – those individuals had sometimes been our mentors and those of our contributors – putting them in a position of gatekeepers into the field. Those individuals, due to their position, could also take the *risk* of responding to our carte-blanche invitation as openly, keenly and expansively as they were able and willing to, so as to confront the following puzzle: What made them successful? What risks did they take? What opportunities did they have, and what limitations were they confronted with? Although they are daunting as points of comparison, there is something comforting about seeing these trajectories of 'senior' and 'junior' scholars together: we all start someplace. As Wilkins (p 262) comforts and calls to action: behind every individual's success is a backstory and exposing these roots is crucial to make way for future harvests.

[9] Bourdieu (1984), n 4 above, 12.

'Of you the tale is told.' By this Marx meant that the future of Germany was already visible across the water in England. And so it was. Germany industrialised too, toward the end of the nineteenth century. This collection of contributions, relationally, reminds us, as Stefan Kroll does in his response to Khan, that, foremost, 'legal change is the result of evolution rather than revolution' (Kroll p 178). While pointing to the political entanglement of law, Galanter's journey from India to the US is also about refraction: 'the larger realisation that much of what I once thought peculiar to India turned out to be pertinent when I looked more closely closer to home' (Galanter p x).

Unpacking these dynamics of refraction requires us, relentlessly, to revisit history to question the futures of possible alternatives, while also demanding from us, just as relentlessly, that we question our responsibility. These narratives are about daring. Recall Kannabiran staunchly identifying as an insurgent or Carrie Menkel-Meadow (figuratively) slamming the door as a young researcher against a policy pull which would have co-opted her work on poverty lawyers into conservative politics. Reminiscing on his trajectory, Trubek describes 'living in the contradiction' as a constant, yet necessary, juggling exercise between a 'desire to manage big enterprises and create and reform institutions while at the same time maintaining a critical sensitivity' (p 242). Perhaps, as Kannabiran offers, these paths were chosen only as much as they chose these agents, and in this potential for recursive agency, there is optimism – what can be seen, from many of these notes, as journeys that are well thought out, are journeys only when structured in retrospect and recall. For young scholars in new, other, 'law and society' waiting rooms, there is perhaps this call: capital and networks and associations matter, but so too does conversation, community, and *chance*.

We close this conclusion by taking the cue of Goyal (p 72) by paying 'heed to how the texture of the canvas may affect the kind of painting that emerges over it.' This is what *we* saw and *read* from the process, but we invite you, the reader, to read between the lines. To *See what you Will.*

INDEX

www.ingramcontent.com/pod-product-compliance
Ingram Content Group UK Ltd.
Pitfield, Milton Keynes, MK11 3LW, UK
UKHW020219041026
15470UKWH00012B/662